A
BORDER
OF
BLUE

ALONG THE GULF OF MEXICO FROM THE KEYS TO THE YUCATÁN

HENRY HOLT AND COMPANY
NEW YORK

A
BORDER
OF
BLUE

FREDERICK TURNER

Henry Holt and Company, Inc.
Publishers since 1866
115 West 18th Street
New York, New York 10011
Henry Holt® is a registered
trademark of Henry Holt and Company, Inc.

Published in Canada by Fitzhenry & Whiteside Ltd.,
91 Granton Drive, Richmond Hill, Ontario L4B 2N5.

Library of Congress Cataloging-in-Publication Data
Turner, Frederick.
A border of blue: along the Gulf of Mexico from the Keys to the
Yucatán / Frederick Turner.—1st ed.   p.   cm.
Includes bibliographical references.
1. Gulf Coast (U.S.)—Description and travel.   2. Gulf Coast
(U.S.)—Social life and customs.   3. Mexico, Gulf of—Description
and travel.   4. Mexico, Gulf of—Social life and customs.
I. Title.
F296.T87   1993   92-30283
976.4'1—dc20   CIP

ISBN 0-8050-2072-1

First Edition—1993

Designed by Lucy Albanese
Printed in the United States of America
All first editions are printed on acid-free paper. ∞

1   2   3   4   5   6   7   8   9   10

ONCE AGAIN,
FOR ELISE

ACKNOWLEDGMENTS

IT IS ALWAYS A PLEASURE TO ACKNOWLedge those people who have helped along the way, the more so in the writing of a book that depends so greatly on what assistance native dwellers may choose to give a stranger passing through. To all who gave me advice, encouragement, and some of their time, my sincere thanks. Without them there could be no book. To list their names is not, of course, to make them accomplices.

James Allen; Barry Ancelet; Raymond Authement; Jo Bigelow, Koreshan State Historic Site; James Bond, Marine Coordinator of U.S. Customs, Tampa; Christopher Botsford; Jane Botsford; Raymond Boudwin; George Campbell, Special Agent Group Supervisor, U.S. Customs, Tampa; "Yellowlegs" Campbell; Henry Carley, NAACP, Tampa; John Crewes, Assistant U.S. Attorney, Brownsville; Daryl Davis; Robert Davis; William deBuys; Patricia Franklin, Agent, U.S. Customs, Tampa; Banu Gibson; Bernard Guste; J. Hawkins; Willie Humphrey; William James; Allyson Jones; Robert Jones, Terrebonne Parish Engineer; Robert Kahn, City Editor, Brownsville *Herald*; Blaine Kern; Dorothy Lill;

Winston Lill; Donald Lirette; Melvin Maxwell, Ranger, Laguna Atascosa National Wildlife Refuge; Lisa Merrill; Cindy Moran; Joseph Moran; Mary Anderson Pickard; Murrella Hebert Powell, Biloxi Public Library; Armando Ramirez, Special Agent in Charge, Drug Enforcement Administration, Brownsville; "Red," Superior Seafoods, Tampa; Ron Ridenhour; Anne Rudloe; Jack Rudloe; Elizabeth Silberman; Dolores Davidson Smith; Steve Thompson, Refuge Manager, Laguna Atascosa National Wildlife Refuge; Nicholas Tirone, Agent, U.S. Customs, Tampa; Bonni Tischler, Special Agent in Charge, U.S. Customs, Tampa; Patricia Tolle, Public Affairs Specialist, Everglades National Park; Charles H. Turner, U.S. Attorney, District of Oregon; Thomas Van Cleave; Anthony Zavaleta; Diane Zwicker, District Director of Customs, Tampa.

Christopher Merrill, Eugene Newmann, Charles F. Turner, and Elise R. Turner read all or parts of the manuscript; in revising it I have tried to be equal to the excellence of their suggestions. Alexandra Turner and Jessica Turner were wonderful helpers along the way. My agent Robin Straus cheerfully took on a project that in its inception was not hers and has worked on it with all the diligence and imagination any author could wish for. My association with my editor, William Strachan, goes back more than twelve years—forever by today's publishing standards. I have ever found him to be patiently encouraging, and on this project he was right in character.

SPRING

A LIGHT TAP ON THE TIN ROOF, AN-other, and then a soft flurry against the windows awakened me to a late-afternoon April shower. I'd seen it coming and had hastened back to my room where I'd drifted off over my travel materials—maps, guidebooks, oddments of literature about the Gulf of Mexico. Through bone-gray lattices I could see palm fronds swayed by a breeze and beyond them a sky that matched the lattice wood. I was in Key West at the beginning of a long journey, but I was feeling more as if I were at the end of some-thing: end of the day, end of the continental U.S., too, Mile Zero, as Mr. Flagler's railroad marker had it. Beyond was water, then Cuba (*regio odiosus*). Beyond that and yearning toward Cuba and the Keys, as if it wished to touch them and so make of the Gulf a great inland sea, was the dog's head of the Yucatán Peninsula. Between these points was an immense curve of coast, and the thought that I planned to travel all of it in the coming months did not at this moment inspire me with the professional traveler's bright anticipation. Almost as if it had occurred to another I recalled my own image of the Gulf: the tropical blue of its encircling current, its palms and protecting marshlands, warping fishing villages, gritty oil towns, and at the far end of the coast, the fabulous pyramidal mounds of the Mayas settling slowly into the jungle—the very source and fount of our New World history. The image had inspired an eagerness that had brought me here, but what I felt now was a dull dread. Maybe it was the glass of wine I'd had when I'd come back to the room and settled down with my materials. Maybe, too, it was what I'd experienced of the Keys on my way down here along a tawdry ribbon of road with development crammed from shore to shore. Or perhaps it was simply the pineal gland at work—the third eye or, as some believe, the mind's eye—now feeling its creaturely dread at the dying of the light, the coming of dark's clustering uncertainties.

From the jumble of travel materials I fished out again the map of the Gulf and looked at its representation of more than three and a half thousand miles of coast, not counting bends, bays, and bayous. However you portioned it off into manageable units of travel—Florida's west coast, the panhandle, the slivers of Alabama and Mississippi—it was a hell of a long way around this underbelly of the continent. I dropped the map back onto the pile, leaned into the now-comfortless pillows, and wondered, as often the traveler must, about the sanity of these plans.

I'd begun in the rain, and not a small one like that now glistening on the waving fronds outside the window, but a real, hard-driving rain, hammering its blue notes on the tin roof of a Florida City motel where I sat in front of a flickering TV screen, watching the water roll off the eaves to splash down in heavy counterpoint to the rain on the roof. Beyond in the blackness were the amber lights of the motel's other buildings. At such an hour and in this weather Florida City had seemed sufficiently slatternly, out-of-the-way, even vaguely sinister enough to answer my expectations of the Keys and the Gulf as a whole, bringing back black-and-white images of the Bogart/Bacall/Edward G. Robinson film *Key Largo*. In the movie, Bogart's character, Frank McCloud, is haunted by World War II—the deaths of buddies and of the ideals for which they'd fought (this was 1948 and already postwar realities had killed off a brief euphoria)—and seeks a kind of annihilation himself. And what better place than the Keys, these little islands trailing away from the mainland to end in the Gulf and the stony scatter of the Dry Tortugas? No matter that except for a few shots *Key Largo* was filmed on a Hollywood set: John Huston gave viewers the feel of what the Keys ought to be like, a mysterious, dim sort of place peopled with drifters and fugitives. As a kid I'd seen that film, and that was what I still thought the Keys were like, even though not long after the film I'd seen them with my own eyes, not Huston's.

That must have been 1949. I was twelve. In those years my family was beginning to shoot up the socioeconomic scale, and one of the things you did to prove it was to take a Florida spring vacation. In the company of family friends named Hendriksen, we drove to Key Largo and there chartered a cabin cruiser that took us down the Atlantic side to Key West. We fished, swam, and docked here and there for dinner. The Hendriksens had their surly lout of a son along, and he did not improve in the close acquaintance of shipboard. When we fished, I sat next to my older brother in a swivel chair, a large belt cinched about my meager middle, and hopelessly trolled the roiling wake for tarpon. I caught only small "trash fish" and "trestle fish," our exasperated guide's way of explaining that once again my line had become fouled on the concrete supports of Flagler's bridges. No one did much better, and at length Mr. Hendriksen became utterly bored with our days of sun and empty sea. An avid hunter and fisherman, his blood lust was unslaked, and one day he directed the guide to take the boat through to the Gulf side to anchor off a salt flat. Who knew, he said, what life we might surprise and trap in that shallow spot? At any rate, it would be a change from the brats, the wives, the canasta games. Armed with short gaffs, he led the huntsmen out onto the flat, the water's opalescence churning white around our plodding legs.

Perhaps a half hour later the huntsmen struck their prey, or rather Hendriksen did: he gaffed a small hammerhead shark, plunging his weapon into the creature's back with a glancing blow. The hammerhead veered suddenly and darted between my paralyzed legs, just grazing one of them, with Hendriksen after it in lithe bounds that belied the heavy set of his build, his gaff raised high like a paleolithic savage. But though wounded, the shark was gone, and Hendriksen hurled the gaff after it in disgust. Behind, a small cloud of blood stood in the shallows, then began to break up into waving strings. I stood there, looking at the blood, still feeling the fleet graze of the fish against my skin, then seeing Hendriksen, blond, red-faced in the brilliance of the reflected light, arms still tensed, a stone killer.

But except for the incident of the shark, the Keys had been prosaic and safe enough. I recalled no sinister Edward G. Robinson types sitting in the sterns of canopied cruisers, Panama hats pulled low over their faces and suit coats bulky in the sun. Nor had there been anything sinister about my night in Florida City. In the Capri Restaurant, which even at a late hour had its customers, nobody looked as if they were doing bad deals, and though the calamari felt like toy truck tires between my molars, the bread was pretty fair and the service friendly. When I paid my bill the man at the register asked whether I was coming or going, and though I have never been entirely sure of the answer to this question, in this instance I said, "Going," since Florida City was for me the jumping-off point for the Keys. "The Keys," he said, handing over my change, "you'll find them interesting. Most people do, anyway. They got fishing, if that's what you want. They got women, they got drugs—they got whatever you're looking for. And if you're not looking for anything, they got that, too."

The man's gloss on the Keys was probably better, more poetically comprehensive, than anything I'd read, with the single, brilliant exception of the tongue-in-cheek guidebook Joy Williams wrote some years ago. In his few words I got once again a whiff of that vagrant air that has historically hung over this place ever since old Ponce de León first blundered into it, searching for deliverance.

That had been in spring as well, 1513, and Ponce had cruised south along the shore of what he supposed was an island, the huge, heavy current of the yet unnamed Gulf Stream trying to push him northward and eastward, back toward the ruined Old World he and his kind had so willingly left behind to fashion out of this new, undemarcated one a facsimile. On his slave plantations in the islands, rumor had come to Ponce—an old native woman telling him of Bimini, of a marvelous spring there. His mortal needs glutted, Ponce felt the need for something more, something beyond even this New World that had in so many ways proved disappointing, and so took ship, sailing down an apparently endless coast until at last he had cleared the chain of *cayos* (keys) and then the Tortugas (turtles) and started up the other coast, as far as is known the first European to shadow those waters with his keel, his heavy hopes. And though no one noted it, at that moment the history of the Gulf entered a new phase. The old order of things, which had existed here for thousands of years and which had been so little affected by the arrival of tribal peoples that to the Europeans the Gulf looked like a perfect wilderness, was about to undergo a profound alteration. In that spring of 1513, the *cayos* were still what they had been: sandy bits of coral or limestone, buffered on the Atlantic side by extensive reefs and on the Gulf side by land-building mangrove swamps. Dense hardwood hammocks covered the northerly Keys while to the south the hardwoods mingled with royal palms and gumbo-limbos. Tiny deer that looked as if left over from the age of the *Eohippus* grazed on one of the lower Keys, and in the trees and marshes was an astonishing gathering of bird life—

with satisfaction. Not Flagler. He looked at the Keys and saw a new world to bend to his iron will. Like Cyrus the Great channeling off the force of the River Gyndes because it opposed his will, Flagler saw the Keys as an obstruction to his dream of a railroad that would reach all the way to Key West and give him access to the Cuba–Florida trade. He meditated their conquest, the only question being one of method. Would it be best to run the line southwest from Homestead to Cape Sable, throw a giant bridge across Florida Bay, and then use the available lands of the Keys to reach Key West by means of shorter bridges? Or should he take a more direct line south from Homestead to Key Largo and there begin his assault on the Keys? Whichever way he went the physical composition of the territory was to him no more than a temporary obstacle—a business competitor, say. His original plan was to fill in all of the southeastern portion of the Everglades as well as the channels between the Keys. He was only temporarily disconcerted when it was pointed out that if he did this, he would divert the Gulf Stream, with environmental consequences that might affect all of the Southeast at least. So, the plan was dropped, and Flagler's force of four thousand drove down from Homestead through the Keys, clear-cutting the hardwood hammocks and burning the felled trees, bridging the channels, including a two-mile span between Bahia Honda and Big Pine Key, and arriving at Key West near the end of January 1912. It was in every way a stupendous achievement, in terms of engineering, ecological alteration, and cultural transformation.

The changes Flagler wrought on the Keys were both dramatically immediate and long-lasting, and though I knew it was shallow and snotty of me to do so, I couldn't stop myself from muttering time after time, "Thank you, Mr. Flagler," as I followed one hundred and seven of his mile markers down toward Key West through what has charitably been called Coney Island South. True, not every bit of the Keys had been opened to commercial exploitation. It only looked that way to the traveler. If you knew something about the back country, the Gulf side, or knew someone who did, it was possible to partially avoid what the Keys had become. The backcountry where the much-scarred mangroves continued to hang on was the province of fishermen, marine biologists, and drug runners, while the rest of the islands had been ceded long ago to the hucksters and their human chattel, the tourists. Here and there were nature preserves where tiny specimens of the original environment were suffered to remain, notably at Lignumvitae Key and Indian Key. If you wanted to see the fabulous—and imperiled—coral reefs and the equally fabulous aquatic life that wavered over them in the milky blue water, there were a good number of dive shops that would take you out snorkeling. And then, suspended in the waters of the Straits of Florida, you could feel yourself in touch with something native to this place, as in fact I did one afternoon at Looe Key. But that was just about the only way to get beneath the scabrous surface of contemporary Keys culture. Otherwise, you were condemned to run the gauntlet of Route 1, down through the Matecumbes, Long Key, Vaca, Big Pine, Cudjoe, Boca Chica, the narrow coral spine so screaming with commerce it was dangerous to drive it, there were so many claims on your attention: time shares, dive shops, souvenir shops, boat rentals, tackle shops, drugstores, restaurants, and all of them hollering at you like a "Grogge Shoppe Lounge" that had on its marquee LIQUORS 500 MINIATURES 50 KINDS OF BEER DANCERS WANTED. Along here there was something for everybody. At the Holiday Inn on Key Largo, for instance, there rested the battered little tugboat used in the filming of *The African Queen*. That was for those, like myself, who associated the Keys with Bogart.

The assault continued with a grim determination right to Mile Zero, Key West, its presence announced by a tangle of T-shirt shops, ice cream parlors, bars, and sport-fishing boats bobbing in Garrison Bight. When Flagler's army hammered its way in here the town's population was about seventeen thousand and its fortunes in decline. Its geographical position had made it a natural for whaling and then for salvagers. Depending on your point of view, the salvagers were either a species of pirate or else tough nuts who risked their lives in a dangerous and honorable line of work. Key West was also the nearest American town of any size to Havana, and if you were a Cuban cigar manufacturer and had labor troubles, you might think of a ninety-mile relocation as an efficient solution. Vincente Martinez Ybor brought his cigar operations here in 1869 and for some years prospered. But by 1912 the whaling business had long since gone elsewhere, the salvaging business had been taken over and regulated by insurance companies, and Ybor had decamped yet again, this time to Tampa where he founded the company town that still bears his name. So Key West had slumped. Its residents raised some fruits and vegetables, fished, dived for sponges, and did what salvaging jobs fell to them. Just as its geographical position had once made it a natural for salvaging, so too was it a good place for smuggling, and in slack times some ran contraband.

Then came the railroad, and with it the town's fortunes and population rose again only to fall back once more at the end of World War I. Prohibition made work for those who had a gift for smuggling, but when John Dos Passos came here in 1924, Key West seemed to him a sleepy, slightly seedy place devoted to fishing, shipping, and coaling, and the air

~ 9

smelled of the Gulf Stream. It was linked, he later wrote, "by car ferries with Havana. Cigar factories had attracted a part Cuban, part Spanish population," the rest of the residents being Conchs (English-speaking natives), whites from the Bahamas, retired railroad men, and descendants of New England whalers. Ten years after Dos Passos's visit the town was flat broke, and there was talk of abandoning the place. But then came a godsend, characteristically disguised as a terrible natural disaster, as in the Old Testament: the hurricane of Labor Day 1935 that roared through the middle of the Keys and killed as many as eight hundred people, many of them construction workers on the Overseas Highway that was to supplant Flagler's engineering monument. In the great storm's aftermath the state was able to purchase the now-bankrupt railroad at distress prices and to incorporate its structures into the highway that opened to traffic in 1938. Significantly, one of the few on-location shots that John Huston used in *Key Largo* was an aerial one showing a passenger car overtaking a bus on one of the Keys' bridges, for by the time the film was made the highway had brought all of the Keys and especially Key West back from the dead yet again.

This time the resuscitation was so violently successful it may yet kill off Key West forever. With the coming of the highway and its tourists the population shot up so quickly that both natural resources and human services have become strained to the breaking points. Before adequate zoning regulations could be framed and sewage treatment facilities installed, the town's beaches, coral reefs, and waters became badly polluted and the aquatic life poisoned. These problems have been somewhat ameliorated but hardly alleviated, and unless some permanent check is put on development, Key West, which has shot up and down so frequently it has got the bends, may this time truly expire. In the old days it used to be called Cayo Hueso, Bone Key, because of the many aboriginal skeletal parts found there. The old-time Conchs shrugged off the significance of those artifacts, but they may have been a kind of warning after all.

🌴 THERE came a knock at my door. It was the hotel's manager whom I had earlier advised that the drain of my kitchenette sink was clogged. Could something be done? Now here the young fellow was with an affable smile but innocent either of a plumber's tools or the plumber himself. Instead he handed me a blender, an item he evidently believed more essential to Key West living than a functioning drain. He proved to be right. Before long I began to eye that blender sitting there on the sideboard next to the clogged drain, and it did seem essential that I use it, that I fill it with the ingredients of some tropical drink such as one of Somerset Maugham's dissolute characters, or Conrad's, might indulge in. When the shower ended near sunset and a weak rose color suffused the sky I went out to purchase several fruit juices and a bottle of heavyweight Jamaican rum. Then I poured my liquids into the blender, gave it a whirl, and succumbed to the influence of this place where toasting the daily death of the sun from Mallory Square is a tradition.

As far as I knew there was no corresponding fete to greet the sunrise, but after the sun had been up awhile the next morning I went for a more leisurely stroll through what was called Old Town—to distinguish it from the claptrap that had accumulated here in the fitful years since the coming of the railroad. Walking these narrow streets I was again struck as I had been on the previous afternoon by how well Old Town had in fact weathered the town's great changes. There was an air of negligent, decadent grace that clung to this little portion of Key West. The well-tried look of the buildings, even the lines of their roofs and porches, suggested that nothing short of a total, leveling hurricane—not gentrification, nor its attendant boutiques and b & b's, nor the transient presence of the youths I saw everywhere and who waited on the tourists—would quite be able to efface what Old Town was. It appeared somehow capable of assimilating everything that had thus far come.

At intersections I stepped over the tiny lakes that had formed where the pavement dipped toward municipal drains in poor repair. Locals splashed through them on scooters and tourists on mopeds. In the gutters, in the cracks of the sidewalks, the angles of fences, and on porch steps were scatterings of bougainvillea blossoms like discarded party favors. On Whitehead Street I passed a crowd of tourists at the Hemingway house. In his Key West novel *To Have and Have Not*, Hemingway has his protagonist claim that "What they're trying to do is starve you Conchs out of here so they can burn down the shacks and put up apartments and make this a tourist town. That's what I hear. I hear they're buying up lots, and then after the poor people are starved out and gone somewhere else to starve some more they're going to come in and make it a beauty spot for tourists." This from the mid-1930s when along with the talk of abandonment there had also been talk of clearing off the real residents and making Key West a sort of movie set for tourists. Looking at the crowd on the porch and steps of the house, I knew I didn't want to go in. A large man in shorts and polo shirt and toting a cumbersome camcorder made me recall what Joy Williams had said in her guidebook, that "Hemingway is as dead as a doornail in this place." I turned back into Simonton Street where Hemingway and his second wife, Pauline Pfeiffer, had stayed in an apartment when they'd first come here in 1928. For the moment, anyway, I was done with Hemingway. But, as I was to learn over the next few days, in Key West it's not that easy.

On the same street was the Simonton Court, which might have been the archetypal Old Town lodging experience. It presented a blank, beaten face to the street and was flanked by an establishment whose awning read simply PSYCHIC and by a shop selling exotic birds. On the telephone pole outside the hotel entrance a notice from Island Wellness advertised classes in Aerobics, Zen Meditation, Breathing Gymnastics, Fasting and Food Combining, Crystals and Healing, and A New Way of Living. An upcoming special event was a slide show on UFOs. Inside its walls the Simonton Court was a pleasant warren of courtyards, cottages, and bathtub-sized pools bowered by bougainvillea and palms. In the mornings, sipping Cuban coffee in my sun-barred room, I heard the strange cries of those next-door birds come sailing over the board fence. Or I took a book down to the rearward pool that was frequented by two large raccoons; they didn't mind my presence as long as I kept to my end.

Through this quiet, well-kept preserve the young managers went about their chores in a languid way, barefoot and clad in shorts. In the mornings one of them had coffee and joints with friends who dropped in to get their own days in gear. In the afternoons a speaker system shared recordings of Paul Simon and Arlo Guthrie. There was no real way to avoid this amenity, and after a couple of days I found myself sort of settling for it. It seemed part of the general, loose seductiveness of the town.

On his Key West vacations of forty years ago, Harry Truman's smiling face, florid shirts, and straw fedoras had often graced the front pages of the newspapers, and these photos never failed to enrage my father, a committed Dewey man. Truman was still well remembered here, though in view of the state of the town's waters it was a question as to whether today he would be permitted to take his daily swim. The town also remembered Tennessee Williams, for years a resident here. But better than either of these, Key West remembered Ernest Hemingway, who was shamelessly merchandized in fulfillment of his worst fears about the fate of the town and of himself as an artist compelled to go *mano a mano* with celebrity. I had been easily able to resist a visit to Hem's old home, but on my last night in Key West I paid a visit to his bar, Sloppy Joe's at Greene and Duval.

At the end of the Twenties when the town was still as his friend Dos Passos had described it, Hemingway found it a fortunate isle. He liked its local characters—the dockhands, fishermen, and the tough, salty little bartender, Joe Russell, who ran Sloppy Joe's and who served Hemingway as a model for the protagonist of *To Have and Have Not*. When in residence here, Hemingway made Sloppy Joe's his clubhouse. Once he told his friend A. E. Hotchner that he'd been a silent partner in the place. But he did more than carouse in Sloppy Joe's and fish the Straits and the Gulf, and for all its selling of Papa, Key West in fact had some legitimate claim to being an important Hemingway site. Here he worked on the revisions of *A Farewell to Arms*, worked on his bullfighting book, *Death in the Afternoon*, wrote *To Have and Have Not*, and in the house on Whitehead wrote "The Snows of Kilimanjaro," which, he told Hotchner, "was as good as I've any right to be." This by a long shot was more work than he ever turned out in Paris. But by the time Hotchner visited him here in 1955 the Whitehead Street house had become a mausoleum of bad memories, and he had used up Key West. Now he thought of Bimini as the fortunate isle, an escape from what Key West had become and from what he had made of it. He would rather "eat monkey manure" than die here, he claimed. After he had used up Idaho, too, and killed himself in Ketchum, his widow, Mary, had come back to Sloppy Joe's to retrieve a trunkful of manuscripts that had been silently moldering in a back room.

Now Sloppy Joe's was an undergraduate's dream and a middle-aged man's nightmare, a urine-stinking hangar with numerous images of Hemingway, including some curling photos tacked to a dim back wall and showing the writer posed beside huge dead fishes and drinking at Sloppy Joe's bar. A large painting of Hemingway, scrupulously copied from the Karsh photograph, served as the backdrop of a bandstand just then mercifully empty. But though there was no band, sound was not lacking here, both from the youthful clientele and from the sound system that dispensed heavy metal at a high level. Even the staff contributed to the merriment. One of the bartenders was at odd moments given to making a running leap at a cowbell suspended from the ceiling by a long leather strap. Grabbing the bell, he would fling it up against the ceiling where it struck with a clank, then came clanking down in its arc, then back up again, until its momentum was at last exhausted. At which point he would leap at it again. He appeared to me as demented as one of those caged big cats you see in zoos, but then I was sober.

So were some other staff members, the beefy bouncers who surely would be needed here, to judge from the feel of the place. They moonlighted from the local naval installation, as I learned from talking with one of them under the dripping awning while I waited for a cab to pass. Another late-afternoon shower pelted the streets and the pedestrians, some of whom simply accepted the rain and sauntered along in it, their T-shirts soaked and clinging. The bouncer was a squat, immensely powerful-looking man in his late twenties, his torso squeezed into a Sloppy Joe's T-shirt over which he wore broad suspenders. I asked if things often got rough in Sloppy Joe's.

"Oh, yeah," he said, not taking his gaze from the street. "We get trouble in here just about every night in some form or other. But at the first sign, they're gone." His delivery suggested he was perfectly at ease with the demands of his nighttime job with its rank bouquet of urine, stale beer, and spilled tropical drinks and the unpredictable behavior of the customers. I asked him whether this was the wind-down of the high season (it was mid-April).

"Well," he said, still watching the street, "we got a week or so more of these spring breaks, then things'll get pretty quiet. In the summer, this place *dies*. That's when they lay off a lot of us. Here's your cab—" He whistled shrilly and stepped into the street with arm extended.

The cabbie was a lank-haired woman in her mid-forties who made a defiant gesture toward fashion with some carelessly applied eyeliner. "Oh, God," she said when I'd slammed the door on the rain, "I know how you must hate this! But for us, well, this has been a very strange winter. A few sprinkles here and there is all. And my lawn! It's history! Today, we get this forecast, and you know what I did? I just went out and spread that fertilizer I'd been saving all over my lawn. And then what? Nothing. Same thing all spring. Now we get this, and to be honest with you, I hope it goes on all night." She tossed her hair off her shoulder as we splashed the back streets toward Dickie's, a well-recommended restaurant. She said she was a native of Orlando, "but I didn't get here from there.

"Back then I was traveling . . ." Her voice trailed away for a moment, as though she were quickly reliving some part of the winding road that had put her behind the wheel of a cab on a rainy evening at Mile Zero. "That was eighteen years ago," she resumed, "and I've been here ever since. Oh, it's too easy here, I know that. I came down here eighteen years ago for a *weekend*!" She waved a thin hand in my direction. "Now I have a house, a lawn, plants—

"It's too easy here, the life. I went through my period of hating it, and there's a lot of people here like me. Most of the people I know here are like me: came down for a weekend from somewhere else, and they're still here. I've *gone* through the Caribbean. I've had that. Now I'm just stuck here, and I guess I love it. I guess I'll have to admit that." She laughed. "Whatever . . ."

I IN order to reach the Gulf coast from the Keys I had to retrace Flagler's route to Homestead, then cut up on 997 to the Tamiami Trail that runs west through the Big Cypress National Preserve, skirts the northern edge of Everglades National Park, and delivers you on the coast at the fishing village of Everglades City. Because the Tamiami Trail was one of only two east-west roads below Lake Okeechobee, the farther out on it I got, the more I was at the mercy of the few merchants strung out along its lonesome, animal-smeared stretches. Especially those offering airboat rides "through the Everglades." Some years ago in another access to the Everglades I had actually gone with some family members on such a ride through a small section of the park, and afterward—blown, dirty, and deafened—all we'd been good for the rest of that day had been to holler at each other and abuse strangers. I couldn't imagine a worse way to see so splendid a work of nature. Here even the advertising was bum: the airboats didn't really take you into the Everglades but instead roared a distance along the Tamiami Canal and then brought you back—deafened and defrauded into the bargain. I learned this by stopping at a couple of these outfits and inquiring about the route, and after the second stop I felt that merely making the inquiry was itself likely to be the most exciting part of the adventure. You got out of your car in the muddy clearing that passed for a parking lot and walked resolutely toward the porchful of beer-drinking loungers and their pack of curs. You managed to nod at them when you'd come within the danger zone, stepped over the lead dog, and paused at the bottom step. There you noticed that there were signs all about—on the walls of the shop, the bumpers of the spattered pickups, the panels of the loungers' caps—saying equivocal things like THE SUPREME COURT SUCKS and BURN OUR FLAG AND YOUR ASS IS MINE! and EAT SHIT AND DIE. Then you inquired about the airboat rides.

At my third stop my mind had been made up for me that I had to have the ride, fraudulent though I was sure it would be. That is the cumulative power of repetitive roadside advertising: by the time you've read enough Burma Shave jingles, signs telling you how far it is now to Wall Drugs in South Dakota and what you could buy when you got there, or action-packed billboards for South of the Border in northernmost South

Carolina, you've been softened up for the knockout, and so it was with the airboat outfits along the Tamiami Trail. No doubt the thing worked in both directions, those motorists driving toward Miami succumbing at last to the ads of the more eastwardly outfits just as I had now to a westerly one.

My guide into the jungly mysteries of the 'Glades was an Indian, a nice touch, I thought. Wayne had long black hair and was appropriately silent and stone-faced as we walked from the shop across the highway and then down through the tall grass to the landing on the canal where the boat was tethered. The only information I could get out of his broad back was his name and that he was a Seminole. Maybe he was, though I suspected he might have invoked that tribal name because it was the only one the white man would recognize; if he'd said "Calusa" or "Miccosukee" he would have been greeted with blank incomprehension and then contempt. Perversely Wayne opened up only after he'd cranked the huge engine and zipped away from the canal banks into the smooth brown water, and then almost all his talk was of gators, how there were so many of them now, and how they had to hunt them in the spring to thin their numbers. To our right and in plain view the big rigs barreled along the Tamiami Trail, making for the coasts. When Wayne spotted a gator, he would cut the engine and drift past it, pointing at its partly submerged form without saying anything, as if the gator made its own dangerous statement.

But if Wayne's voice-over was almost cartoonlike in its emphasis on man-versus-beast-in-the-jungle, it, too, was probably a response to commercial realities he had come to know too well. And there were several points at which I was glad that he did confine himself to the gators—as when we roared past a bedraggled Indian village, its plastic refuse and junked cars sliding down behind it into the canal. And I was glad also when he turned the boat around and we went wordlessly back toward the landing. When he returned me from the wilderness, unchanged, he marched stolidly up the bank toward the shop, and I was left to ponder the future of this giant natural phenomenon I had just brushed, one sliced up and hemmed in by this canal and the Tamiami Trail itself.

And the Everglades were so giant and so inaccessible that even today with airplanes and airboats it was difficult to get a good sense either of their tangled extensiveness or their inherent qualities. Lacking the time, money, or opportunity to hire a guide and a boat, what most visitors saw was really not much more than I had seen on this "tour." The rest was mystery, and in characteristic national fashion most Americans evidently continued to assume that the Everglades remained as they had always been, a kind of marshy and inviolate Mt. Rushmore, that reports of their demise were greatly exaggerated by the bunny-hugger lobby. But when you looked at a Landsat photo of southeastern Florida, *then* you got a sudden, shocking glimpse of the realities, and you saw how carved up the Everglades had become. You saw how on the north the farmlands of the Everglades Agricultural District were critically interposed between the 'Glades and the life-giving Big Water, Lake Okeechobee; how urban sprawl and agricultural advance had encroached from the east and southeast; how the Tamiami Trail and Canal, Alligator Alley, and the Miami Canal sliced through the heart of the 'Glades, opening the state to that east-west commerce that had been a dream almost since the Spaniards had coasted around the peninsula and wondered how to open up its interior. The Landsat couldn't show fouled waters, but if it could, it would have revealed nutrient overloading in Lake Okeechobee and the disastrous die-off of turtle grasses in Florida Bay. On every side but due west the Everglades were endangered—and perhaps the biggest danger had been from that direction with the currently dormant proposal for a jetport just inland from Chokoloskee Bay.

The Spaniards had lacked the technology and administrative apparatus to open up the Everglades. But that couldn't be said of their American successors, and since 1881 when they first began to plan to drain and destroy them more than a million acres of the Everglades have disappeared, replaced by pasturelands, farmlands, towns, and condominiums. Hamilton Disston, Napoleon Bonaparte Broward, Albert Gilchrist, Flagler, the developers of the jetport proposal—all have had their pet schemes to destroy the 'Glades in order to save them for civilization, and if none had succeeded on the grand scale of his dreams, all had played their parts in bringing the Everglades to their current imperiled position.

As Pat Tolle, Public Affairs Specialist at Everglades National Park, explained it to me at park headquarters, the basic issue in the Everglades was and always had been water. The original Everglades ecosystem was two hundred miles long, running from the Kissemmee Lakes near present-day Orlando down to Florida Bay. South of Lake Okeechobee was a "river of grass," as Marjory Stoneman Douglas beautifully put it in her book on the Everglades, a sheet of water fifty miles wide and scant inches deep, flowing through an almost level landscape of sawgrass down to the bay. But what might seem to some of us now an extraordinary natural phenomenon was to Hamilton Disston and kindred visionaries merely an extraordinary problem, for to such men the unregulated sprawl of all that water prevented the exploitation of the rich land that lay just beneath it. All the schemes hatched since Disston tried to drain the 'Glades in 1881 had this one object in common: to get rid of the great river of grass, whether by lowering the level of Lake Okeechobee; by draining the Everglades through a grid of ditches and canals; or simply by planting dynamite in the 'Glades' limestone base and blasting it open—a scheme of Broward's he was convinced would take care of the water problem.

As far as agriculture was concerned the ongoing, massive tinkering with the original ecosystem had proven successful. There were cows pastured now where water once rolled over the sawgrass, and south of the Big Water they now grew sugarcane and celery on the muck laid down by centuries of sawgrass growth and decay. As far as the ecosystem itself was concerned, though, the schemes had been an almost unmitigated disaster, and no part of the system had been more adversely affected by the tinkering than Everglades National Park. Now, Pat Tolle said, park management found itself in the situation of having to try to maintain an ecosystem that relied on the water that came to it from lands over which park management had no control. Some of the water the park got, she said, had already been used for agricultural purposes and was full of those nutrients that had produced the algal blooms in Lake Okeechobee. Sometimes the park got too much water, and sometimes it got too little. And there were still other occasions when it got water at the wrong time for wading birds and edge-of-the-marsh species, both now drastically reduced in numbers.

But Tolle wanted to put the issue of water in what she considered its correct context, and that was population growth in southeastern Florida, which had been massive since the Sixties. The state as a whole took in a staggering 386,000 new residents in the peak year of 1987, and though the numbers had declined every year since, through the end of that decade Florida was still annually absorbing more than 300,000 new-comers, many of them migrating down to the southeast. This, she said, had a ripple effect, for as the population grew denser in the areas immediately adjacent to the Atlantic Coast, feelers of suburban develop-ment went westward into what had been an exclusively agricultural area. Eventually the farmers and ranchers had to move west toward the Everglades, bringing with them their water-intensive, chemical-intensive practices that had a powerful impact on the lands within the park boundaries. "Nature," Pat Tolle said patiently, "is no respecter of boundaries. What happens outside the park affects what happens inside it. Until very recently the farmers adjacent to the park denied that what they did with their water affected what happened in here. Well, we conclusively proved to them that it did.

"In the past we always took what I'd call a reactive stance to whatever developments came along. But now, because of population growth in the area, we find we must change our tactics if we're to fulfill our responsibilities. We have to take a more active stance. We have to try to anticipate developments, and we have to become advocates for the park. If we don't, well—" she paused and lifted her long slender hands slightly from the desktop, "—we're looking at the death of the park—or at least at the death of the park as we know it. I know that must sound drastic, but it could well happen. Before you leave, let me give you what I call my 'Doomsday Packet.'"

ON my large-scale map of Florida's Gulf coast the designation read simply, cryptically, KORESHAN. I wondered what that could possibly mean and was in the mood to find out since I was still smarting a little from my utter failure to raise a single worthwhile conversation back in Everglades City where I'd stopped after my talk with Pat Tolle. "You ought to stop there," Pat Tolle had said. "It's a real, old-time Everglades community, just a really interesting place of the kind you don't find much anymore." I'd have to take her word on that, for after I'd had a plump half-dozen oysters at a dockside restaurant there, I'd wandered, shunned like a vagrant, through the town's few crushed-shell streets, trying to find someone who'd talk to me. At Johnson Seafoods I'd futilely followed Speedy, the owner, about the yard, the warehouse, and the office, asking him dumb questions about the stone crab business, which he'd grudgingly confided was his main line of work. He had shown me how a crab box worked, but that was all, and when he'd spotted a car pulling into his lot, he'd said, "I gotta talk to this guy," and had left, almost at a trot. Back on the road, I wondered whether my nose had been clogged and checked it in the rearview mirror. No. Visions of months of travel around this coast—friendless, shunned, notebook empty—suddenly stretched before me, the beguiling blue Gulf of my imagination now turned black with my failure.

Above Naples I stopped for gas, and there the attendant was so friendly I had to remark that it was quite a change from back down the road. "Oh," he said with a smile, "they probably wondered who you were, a stranger, you know, and asking questions. But they're good folks.

Had a big DEA bust down there—oh, must be six, seven years ago, anyway. DEA came in there, cordoned off the road. Only way you could get out was by boat. Made a bunch of arrests. Thing is, those folks were run out of the [Everglades National] park when they closed it off to commercial fishing, and so some of 'em—just *some*, now—turned to running drugs. Understand, I'm not *approving* here. I'm just telling you what they say happened down there. Say, you going to Tampa, you be sure to see Busch Gardens."

Later I ran across Peter Matthiessen's description of the people of that region in his novel *Killing Mister Watson*: "thin piney-woods crackers with them knife-mouthed women, hollow-eyed under bent hats, lank black hair like horses, touchy, on the run." A "region of desperadoes and bad actors," another of Matthiessen's characters calls it, "hiding out down here in our trackless swamps like dregs in the bottom of a jug of moonshine." That made Everglades City interesting all right, but that was later, and for the moment, as I say, I was in the mood for a more rewarding kind of encounter, and so I now took the turn for Koreshan.

At Estero there was a sign on a side road off Route 41 that read HISTORICAL SITE, and then at the end of a tree-bordered parking lot there sat an oddly shaped slab-sided building. Inside, it appeared to be a combination library and museum containing, in addition to some fat, murky-looking tomes, material artifacts of pioneer Florida life—agricultural implements, desk, chairs, an antique hide-a-bed. In the years of my American travels I had been into so many county and town museums and looked at so many two-headed calves, stuffed or afloat in vats of ancient formaldehyde, so many 1919 Underwood typewriters, rotting galoshes, and faded, captionless photographs of dead home-steaders that I thought I probably didn't need the Koreshan variety, whatever it was. I was just on the point of leaving before anyone had seen me when a late-middle-aged woman materialized out of the gloom, and I learned I had blundered into a site of quite a different sort. I had, in fact, just now come in touch with the concave wall of Truth.

I couldn't tell whether Mrs. Jo Bigelow was simply tired in the afternoon of a long day or whether living amid all those artifacts, breathing their dead sighs, and having patiently to explain their significance to casual strangers had gotten to her over the years. The mere thought of her work here in the gloom of the museum on a side road in Estero was enough to put me into a nod; maybe I could crash for a few hours on the ancient hide-a-bed? Whatever it was, Mrs. Bigelow's opening delivery was not inspired, and it wasn't until she had made it clear to me that I was presently in the midst of the surviving relics of a sure-enough utopian community that she caught my interest and jerked me from a weary politeness into full attention. She caught the change, too, and responded to it with an enthusiasm that had about it a good deal more than a docent's obligatory instructiveness.

The books on the shelves, she explained, were mostly the collection of Dr. Cyrus Teed, the Koresh of Koreshan. Similarly, many of the artifacts had belonged to the community's founder and presiding spirit. "*Koresh* is Hebrew for Cyrus," Mrs. Bigelow said, "which was his given name. He was born in 1839 in Teedsville, New York. That's up near Moravia, which is fairly close to Syracuse, I think. Yes, the town must have been named for his family, which was quite prominent, having a number of ordained Baptist ministers in it. Dr. Teed was destined, so his family thought, to become a Baptist clergyman himself: he was a wonderful orator and very devout. But that wasn't the way it turned out.

"His father was an inventor and a successful country doctor, and early on Dr. Teed was interested in the study of medicine. Eventually he went into the practice of it with his uncle in Utica. Then along came the Civil War, and Dr. Teed served in it along with his brothers and uncle. As a result of that experience he was appalled at how really little human medicine could do to alleviate human suffering. He came back from the war deeply disillusioned about traditional medicine and also about orthodox Christianity, which he had come to believe had been perverted by human misunderstanding and misinterpretation. It was at this time that he had his divine illumination, which revealed to him the secrets of the cosmos."

At the time of the illumination Teed was back in Utica practicing herbal medicine—what Mrs. Bigelow said some disparaged as "old wives' tales"—and conducting what Teed later described as "alchemical experiments." Then on an autumn night in 1869, as he worked in his laboratory, a figure appeared to him. It was a woman, subsequently interpreted by Teed to symbolize the androgynous nature of the deity. The revelation the figure communicated to Teed was that all life was cellular, that the universe itself was cellular in structure. In fact, the universe was none other than the earth itself on whose interior and concave wall we live. In the center of this blastula were the sun and planets in a gaseous cell eight thousand miles thick. Teed understood that he was to share this revelation with humanity by founding a religious community. Its organizing principle, Mrs. Bigelow said, was the practice of the Golden Rule. Another practice was celibacy, the model here being Jesus: the regeneration of the human race, Teed had been given to understand, could not begin until the practice of generation was discontinued.

But Teed's efforts to found such a community in upstate New York were unsuccessful. His theory of a concave earth was laughed at, his rule of celibacy unpopular, and his alleged claims to being a messiah scorned by local newspapers. "But he never claimed to be *the* messiah," Mrs. Bigelow said. "At least we can't find anywhere in the records where he made such a claim. What he did say was that the Bible was written in symbols and that every age had its teacher who would come along and interpret those symbols. That was what a 'messiah' meant to him, 'wise teacher.' He was the wise teacher of his age."

In 1886 Teed was invited to address a Chicago convention of what were then called mental scientists. The fit between audience and speaker was perfect, for at least since his Civil War experiences Teed had been thinking along the general lines of the mental scientists, particularly in their conviction that illness and disease were mental and spiritual in nature and that true healing came through faith, not through standard medical practices like surgery. He was a sensation at Chicago, subsequently set himself up there as a faith healer, and began to draw true believers. Within the city, Teed and his adherents established a microcosmic community, complete with restaurant, lace-making operation, and broom factory. Branches were also established in San Francisco and Lynne, Massachusetts. But like Joseph Smith (who also had received illumination in upstate New York), Teed was still searching for the right spot to found his New Jerusalem, and despite his successes in Chicago, he knew that city wasn't it. Then he made a scouting excursion to Florida's lower Gulf coast.

"There was an old German immigrant living down here," Mrs. Bigelow told me. "His name was Gustav Damkohler, and he had a fair amount of property he'd been homesteading on. Damkohler had been many places, he'd been a gold miner, lived in Missouri, and so on. When he met Dr. Teed, he told him, 'I've been about to leave this place and go somewhere else. But something told me not to leave yet, that *a man would be coming*. I think you may be that man.' He talked with Dr. Teed and became convinced he was the man he'd been told to wait for, and he donated his land to the community and joined them." On the last day of 1893, Teed moved the Chicago Koreshans to Estero to found a community he envisioned as eventually numbering ten million souls. "There was nothing small about the man except his stature," Mrs. Bigelow said.

Then began the labor of building the New Jerusalem on Gustav Damkohler's unimproved lands. "Dr. Teed's ideas of how the community should function were based on his understanding of primitive Christianity," Mrs. Bigelow explained. "It was a kind of communism, though not in the Russian way. You brought your family and everything you had. You had to stay a minimum of six months. His ultimate goal was to establish a fully self-sustaining community, and in fact after several years he had done just that. They had their own farms and gardens, their own general store where they sold items they'd made, their own publishing house, even their own newspaper." I followed her now across the room to a stack of back issues of *The American Eagle*, and Mrs. Bigelow said that eventually the community's paper had become an important horticultural review, based in part on the many successful experiments carried out by community horticulturists. In brief then, Teed had himself been a remarkable physical and metaphysical horticulturist, transplanting his Chicago community to the Gulf coast and tending it as it began to bloom. If at its height, what Mrs. Bigelow termed its "golden years," it numbered only 250 members, still in this part of the state the Koreshans were an active, enterprising, successful community that was the envy of their neighbors.

And that was the trouble: they were becoming too successful to suit some of those neighbors. It wasn't so much Koresh's singular view of the cosmos that caused local friction, Mrs. Bigelow thought, though this must have played a part. Much more controversial was the celibacy rule. "Can you imagine," she asked rhetorically, "what people here thought of celibacy in those days? I'll tell you: they thought it was a laugh, that's what." But there wasn't anything funny to the neighbors about the Koreshans' growing economic and political importance in this still sparsely populated area. The Fort Myers "rawbones," as Mrs. Bigelow called the natives of the nearby town, "were used to running things around here. They just weren't about to hand over leadership to these strangers. So, even though the Koreshans were always mannerly and well dressed, they were told they weren't welcome anymore over at Fort Myers. Then one day in 1906 Dr. Teed was over there, and he got into a discussion with a not-very-intelligent individual. I think they were discussing celibacy. Anyway, a crowd gathered, and one thing led to another, and then for some reason the deputy sheriff, who had been standing by and watching all this develop, hit Dr. Teed over the head. And that was the cause of his death two years later. I don't think after that blow he was really ever able again to function as the leader of the community." She gave a shallow sigh, maybe because she was finished with the story or maybe because the story of the Koreshans was finished with the death of Koresh. As is so often the case with cults, the death of

the messiah was the death of the community, though here not immediately. Mrs. Bigelow said that after a time efforts had been made to
reestablish the community at Sanford, Florida, at St. Petersburg, even at
Fort Myers. All had failed. Meanwhile here at Estero the rule of celibacy
continued to militate against the perpetuation of the original community. No new members were coming in and younger members were
leaving. The successful horticultural activities dwindled and withered.
Eventually only a handful of retirees remained, and in 1952 the Koreshans began to cast about for some means of preserving, if not the
living fact of the great experiment, at least the artifacts of it. In 1961 their
efforts were crowned with the incorporation of the community grounds
and remaining structures into Florida's state park system. Mrs. Bigelow
urged me now to walk across the road and stroll the grounds; she was
sure I would find them interesting. She didn't have to urge me. Her
story had gripped me in a way I hadn't bargained for, and I looked with
new eyes at the desk, bed, and library of the messiah, the heretofore
undistinguished artifacts sitting stolidly there in the gloom but now
pulsing with a strange sort of life. As we said good-bye at the main
entrance, I asked Mrs. Bigelow if she believed Cyrus Teed had been the
messiah. "I think he was a wise man," she said finally, "and a good one.
He never said he would return from the dead, though some expected
him to. But he did rise from the grave: he was buried over there at Fort
Myers, and afterward a hurricane hit there and washed him out to sea."

In the museum I had seen a layout of Dr. Teed's plans for the grounds
of the community. As nearly as I could recall, the design had called for
roads and walkways in the shape of two diamonds, one set within the
other, and a large circular road cutting through the edges of the larger
diamond. On the grounds I tried tracing out this pattern but soon gave it
over to an inspection of the few remaining buildings, especially the art
hall and the founder's house. The former was by all odds the best
preserved, a spacious frame building resembling an old-time railroad
depot with a triangular roof that sat atop it like a lid. Inside, it was
dominated by a podium and a stage on which sat a concert grand piano,
two trombones (one the valve variety), a set of drums, a cello, mandolin, and a tarnished tuba. The faded, blurred inscription on the bass
drum read KORESHAN UNITY ORCHESTRA ESTERO FLORIDA. The effect was
ghostly, not generally the strong suit of those who set up museum exhibits, and I wondered who had contrived to make it look as if the players
had so recently departed that their last note yet hovered in the still and
musty air. When I first spied the piano I had been taken with the desire
to sit down at it and riffle its keys. Now it seemed blasphemous to

do so; the last note sounded in here, I thought, should remain that struck by the players who had ventured so much of themselves in building the New Jerusalem in this "green and pleasant land."

To the podium's right stood a boldly lettered board set on legs:

KORESHAN PREMISE

A STRAIGHT LINE EXTENDED AT RIGHT ANGLES FROM A PERPENDICULAR POST WILL MEET THE SURFACE OF THE EARTH AT A DISTANCE PROPORTIONATE TO THE HEIGHT OF THE PERPENDICULAR

And to the right of that in a kind of tabernacle was a model of the earth as Koresh had been given it in his Utica illumination, the model opened to display the globe's concavity and the ball of celestial bodies that formed its core. Farther along the same wall was a diagram of "The Language of the Physical Cosmos Scientifically Translated Into the Domain of Human Affairs and Reduced to Diagram." Here again were the circles I'd noted in the layout of the grounds, only more of them, many of their lines crossing one another in the diagram's center in what I found a bewildering profusion. Atop the reductive schema a caption read KORESHANITY IS THE IMPERIAL SYSTEM OF THEOCRACY OF THE GOLDEN AGE. No doubt from behind the draped podium Koresh had explained all this in his compelling style.

But whatever you thought about Teed's cosmology—and there have been others who have shared his belief in a hollow earth (including Edmond Halley, the famed British astronomer of Halley's Comet, and possibly Adolf Hitler, as well)—Cyrus Teed was in important respects securely in the American grain in his search for a more noble kingdom than earth had yet disclosed. His ancestry went back to the Puritans in Massachusetts who had founded a theocracy there and whose spiritual descendant Emerson had been so powerful a liberating intellectual influence in the pre–Civil War days. Emerson had been an inspiration for the utopian experiment at Brook Farm, and there is no doubt that the Swedenborgian strand in his thought played a significant part in the work of Phineas Quimby, the major figure of the New Thought movement of which Cyrus Teed had been a part.

Poking about the outside of the sagging, barnlike structure that had been Koresh's house, I looked into a rear window that was black against the light and saw only a spider's web that glowed silver, as if lit from within by some strayed spark of the messiah's fire. Florida's coasts were peppered with latter-day utopias, the very latest ones advertising their earthly virtues from a hundred billboards, all of which seemed to feature a male golfer swinging his club head into an eternal sunset. Compared to these leisure communities the Koreshan Unity looked sane and moral, a worthy experiment in New World living, and walking its pathways back to the parking lot and the present, I was bound to give it my respect.

LIKE many another American place Tampa's origins are "shrouded in mystery," the common euphemism shrouding the fact that the conquering whites so quickly routed and exterminated the local aborigines that almost no record of prewhite history survived. "Tanpa" was supposed to be a Calusa word, meaning "unknown" but designating the location of that tribe's northernmost village. The same tribe is supposed to be the one that gave old Ponce his fatal leg wound when he returned to Florida's Gulf coast in 1521, but much of the bay area appears to have been the territory of the rival Tocobaga. When Pedro Menéndez de Avilés dropped anchor at present-day Safety Harbor in the spring of 1567, the Calusa tried to set the Spaniards on the Tocobaga, but without notable success. Menéndez was fresh from the massacre of some four hundred French colonists over on the east coast and may have had bigger things in view than settling intertribal rivalries. When he sailed back to Havana he left behind only a small garrison, one that proved inadequate to asserting Spanish dominion in the bay area, and the next year when supplies and reinforcements arrived, the Spaniards found the garrison wiped out to the last man. Thereafter and for almost two hundred years Tampa was bereft of white civilization.

When the whites did return it was the Spaniards again, looking this time not for gold or aboriginal empires to sack, nor for fountains of youth. By 1756 Spanish expectations had been so reduced by New World realities that they looked only for the more homely treasure of timber for their ships. Now, though, they didn't have to worry about the Calusa or the Tocobaga, either. British raids from the north, the consequent dislocation and southerly migration of northern tribes, and communicable diseases—civilization's advance agents—had done in the Tampa tribes: an eighteenth-century British map of the area includes the bleak designation: "Tocobaga Indians, Destroyed 1709." Possibly by this time the Calusa had merged with the Seminole. If they had, then they had not escaped the future, for now the Seminole were seen as the "problem," and plans were already afoot to drive them deep into the Everglades—and probably into Florida Bay, for that matter. In the bay area the site of what would one day be known as Tampa was in 1824 a Seminole-fighting military installation called Fort Brooke, a name it retained for ten years before a corruption of the old Calusa word came back into use. So, "Tampa" it has been to this day. The name does have a certain historical legitimacy, and who knows? In the linguistic muck of conquest, maybe that Calusa word was really "Tampa" to begin with. In any case, "Tampa" is certainly to be preferred to "Fort Brooke" if for no other reason than that pronounced in the soft surrounding company of a Southern drawl, it can become the engine of certain japeries: e.g., the girl who reproaches her boyfriend for lying to her. "You tole me," she says, "that when I turned eighteen you was gonna take me to Florida." "No, babe, what I said was that when you turned eighteen, I was gonna tampuh with yuh."

I did not learn whether Tampans found such word plays on their city's name amusing. But I had long ago learned that it was risky to blow into a new town as a stranger and crack jokes of any sort before the natives. It is a curious thing but confirmed by a traveler's bitter experience that before you can find anything funny in a new place you must first take everything seriously. Only after you've established your general sobriety do you earn the right to laugh and make others laugh, as well. Like too many others, this is clearly a backward custom: it ought to be the other way around.

For instance, I thought there was something pretty funny about Tampa's winter carnival, the Gasparilla festival, especially its piratical motif, which featured a crew of well-heeled white guys rigged out as pirates and lurching about the city with bandanas, eye patches, and cutlasses. Each year since 1904 this had gone on, founded on no more substantial authority than the stories told by a salty old windbag named Juan Gomez who lived on Panther Key in the Ten Thousand Islands and who in his declining years was amused to load up the credulous with plagiarized reminiscences of pirates he had known. Some of his stories concerned a highborn man turned pirate he named José Gaspar (same initials as the teller), a.k.a. Gasparilla, the Terror of the Gulf, who had made Charlotte Harbor above Fort Myers his retreat and stronghold. After Gomez died his tales were pirated by Tampa, where they served as the basis of the festival that now drew many thousands to the city in a kind of cut-down version of New Orleans's Mardi Gras.

Some in Tampa, though, didn't find certain aspects of the festival funny at all. Henry Carley, president of the local chapter of the NAACP, pointed out to me that the highly prestigious club that put on the festival parade, Ye Mystic Krewe of Gasparilla, was traditionally all white and all male. When the National Football League awarded the city the 1991 Super Bowl, protests were lodged. "It made a difference," Carley said, "to have this thing given national exposure, and it was an opportune time to point up the fact that it was an all-white affair. The club sponsors the parade, but the city pays for security and sanitation." As a consequence of the protests, in which Carley and the NAACP were prominent, the Krewe canceled the parade that was to have taken place on the day before the Super Bowl. The parade itself, Carley said, had for some years been integrated, and now "the club is too. They took in four black members, but the initiation fee is pretty steep. I understand it's something like five or six thousand dollars. I don't think you're going to see a lot of blacks going in there at those prices." In any case, he said, black membership in Ye Mystic Krewe of Gasparilla wasn't by itself the point. "The point was—and is—that in some unfortunate ways the club and the parade are symbolic of the way things are here and have always been. The occasion of the Super Bowl was an opportunity to point that out, and I don't apologize for that a bit." Had I seen Busch Gardens? Well, when I went, I would see something of what he was referring to.

"It's a theme park," he said, "the 'Dark Continent.' But when you go there, you see very, very few black people. My wife used to work there, and the only time I'd go in would be when I dropped her off and picked her up. Just about the only blacks you see in the 'Dark Continent' are the players in that trumpet and drum troupe—and they're entertainers. You certainly don't see many blacks in the crowds."

Busch Gardens was the sort of attraction Florida specialized in: outdoors, extravagant, allegedly educational, relentlessly commercial. Like its inland relative, Disney World, it had that fascist order and antiseptic air about it, which, to a cast of mind like my own, was vaguely threatening in precise measure to the clean friendliness of its surface. The assault began at the main entrance where a loud, disembodied voice, which seemed to have been tracking your movements, announced with great patience that the full fare for adults would be twenty dollars. Twenty dollars lighter and wondering whether I ought to have tried for a press pass, I pushed through the turnstiles and was on my way to "Morocco." In Morocco there was an ice cream stand, two theaters, and the Zagora Café in the shade of which people sipped soft drinks and ate sandwiches while in the sunny plaza the strolling trumpet and drum troupe Carley had mentioned belted out "In the Mood," "Baby Face," and other oldies, their faces smiling and shining in the afternoon sun. They were dressed in smart colonial uniforms and berets, and they were good. Maybe they were a trifle too good: there was some real heat coming from them, and I thought their audience was more polite than enthusiastic.

After they had finished their routine in Morocco they marched away to the beat of the drums, and I followed the signs directing me to CROSS THE BRIDGE TO NAIROBI. Here huge alligators snoozed on sandy spits while fifty feet away a belly dancer gotten up like silent screen star Theda Bara swayed to recorded music with a serpent draped over her shoulders. A Moroccan palace abutted a jungle of caged primates. There was a lot to take in here, and this, as I was learning, was the park's master plan. At Nairobi Junction a stack of old-time trunks and valises, all bearing stickers and the stenciled NAIROBI JUNCTION on their sides, lay waiting on the little platform. Across the tracks on the Serengeti Plain, camels, zebras, and giraffes browsed or stalked stiffly about while over their heads gondola lifts carried passengers to Timbuktu to see the dolphin show.

Timbuktu, once a synonym for nowhere, proved to be the busiest place yet. Here there was an arcade of electronic games, market shops offering a vast assortment of "Crafts to Amuse and Purchase," and kiddie rides called the "Scorpion," the "Phoenix," the "Sandstorm," and the "Crazy Camel," all of them whizzing through the air to the screams of the kids and the swirling minor sounds of African reed music. A number of visitors reacted to all this as I did: we stood in the shade of the market, simply stunned by the tableau and its choices.

On one side of Timbuktu stood the cavernous Festhaus, a beer hall with a central circular stage on which a band performed Bavarian dances for the customers munching huge corned beef sandwiches and other generic delicacies. Here in the heart of the Dark Continent was an evident concession to the ethnic background of Budweiser's Busch family. Sitting in the coolness at a long table I was startled to hear once again the opening strains of "In the Mood": the strolling troupe I'd encountered at Morocco had caught up with me in Timbuktu's Festhaus. Their deft licks quickly drowned out the elephantine oompahs of the Bavarian band, and when they swung into "April in Paris" the globe had been imaginatively encircled. I laughed aloud at this innocent gallimaufry being thrust upon us and remarked on it to my near neighbor, a man up to his eyebrows in a piece of cake. He raised up long enough from his confectionary delight to say "That's the way it goes sometimes." That deepened the mysteries among which I moved, and I had to wonder as I wandered away from the Festhaus what places his life had taken him to induce so blasé a reaction.

Everywhere I went in the park I found that little was left to chance and still less to the imagination, so that my spirits began to sag away from the high and managed hilarity that was all about me. In those few places where the walker was between diversions, speakers concealed in the shrubbery dispensed the pedestrian equivalent of elevator music to smooth over the silence. Particularly lively spots were pointed out by signs reading PICTURE TAKING SPOT. KODAK. BECAUSE TIME PASSES. And everywhere there were things to buy—caps, T-shirts, brass and copper ware, safari clothing, wood carvings, and African curios—and places where you could get your photo taken in the appropriate costumery there provided. After a while it seemed to me that every child in the place was carrying a newly purchased stuffed animal whose goofy, Disneyfied face leered back at me over the child's small shoulder.

My final stop—and this might have been the park's design—was a tour of the gleaming Anheuser-Busch brewery. If you wanted to find out how Germans had learned to make beer taste like soap, you were out of luck here; if, though, you wanted to learn something about effective packaging and merchandising, this was your place. As you were whisked through the plant you heard piped-in Bud commercials, the Bud theme song, and saw everywhere giant company logos. When you were turned out at last, a bit breathless from all that energetic sparkle, you were a strong-willed traveler indeed if you could choose then to go on to Stanleyville and the Congo instead of to the next-door Anheuser-Busch Hospitality House where the beer was free, three cups to the customer.

Afterward and driving west to Tarpon Springs where I now decided to spend the night, I felt the whole thing had been rather like television where, with only the slightest effort, the world was dropped into your lap, attractively packaged, sanitized, and sponsored. Busch Gardens was cleverly designed, superbly managed—and devoid of spirit. Not a whisper anywhere of what the "Dark Continent" once had meant. Not a shadow of that heart of darkness of which Joseph Conrad had so indelibly written. On a map displayed within the park there had been no designations of those European-built slave castles that disfigured the Dark Continent's west coast, points of final departure for the ancestors of the American blacks so conspicuously absent from the park. In a sense, to be sure, Busch Gardens was every bit as real as those gaunt, brooding slave castles—Cormantine, Fort Metal Cross, Christianborg—but in many other ways it was a ghastly hoax, and leaving it behind the only reality I remembered seeing within its confines was a pile of elephant turds freshly smoking in the setting sun.

I COULD, of course, have stayed in downtown Tampa since I had business there the next morning, but after Busch Gardens I was hungry for some sort of authenticity and thought I might find it at Tarpon Springs. At one time Tarpon Springs had been a wintering spot for well-to-do northerners, but what drew me there now was its history as an enclave of Greek sponge fishermen. After dropping my bags in my room at the Scottish Inn (these random ethnic stews were not, after all, confined to Busch Gardens), I took a few minutes to page through the phone book and came across a goodly number of recognizable Hellenic names. But the Greek presence in Tarpon Springs, whatever it may once have been, had seemingly shrunk to include only two streets and a church. St. Nicholas Orthodox Cathedral gave me something of the feel of Athens in its high roominess, but Dodecanese Boulevard and Athens Street had more the feel of a museum than of a real, vibrant community. I had been steered to Louis Pappas' restaurant on the docks, but one look inside this vast place told me too plainly that it was indeed more museum than restaurant, and so I wandered farther along the dock until I came to a small, homey place from whose open door came the welcoming wailing sounds of recorded bouzouki music. Standing outside, a young man was patiently explaining to his father that, no, this wasn't another American restaurant but a real Greek one. "Look, Pop," he said, then read out the list of house specialties—avgolemono, moussaka, souvlakia, diples. The old man scratched his close-cropped white hair and looked dubious. Over the old man's shoulder his son looked at me, smiled, and shrugged. I went in before them, but soon I saw them take a table.

The dining room was packed with couples and their children, and much of the talk I heard was Greek. Since the tables were right up against the open kitchen it was hot, with the range and the grill showering their heat over everything, but with the Greek-flavored talk and the strong, honest smells of the cooking there was a good feeling in here. After a couple of glasses of cold retsina I invited my waiter to join me in one. He couldn't sit down, he said, but if I didn't mind his comings and goings, he would enjoy a glass. I poured it, he smiled and sipped, and since I had already pleased him by mustering a "thanks" in Greek, he responded in kind and moved off.

On his visits to my table I learned that most of the Greeks who had originally come here had been islanders and seafarers who had taken naturally to the sponging business that had boomed here around the turn of the present century. But a blight had destroyed the industry, and many had moved away. "Most of the Greeks here were born here," he said. "I was, and so was my brother and sisters. And now, of course, there's been a lot of intermarrying—Greeks marrying English, Italians, what-have-you—so the community isn't as tight. It's more spread out. But as you see, there are still some real Greeks here." He laughed. "You can still see the old guys with their worry beads and their coffee and their cigarettes."

After my coffee I walked the rest of the way down the now dark and mostly deserted dock, past souvenir and pastry shops. Only one place was still lighted, a restaurant, now empty and its boy hosing down the walkway in front. Inside a middle-aged man moved behind the counter, cleaning and stacking. I asked him about the sponging business, for I'd seen some sponges displayed in the darkened windows of a couple of the shops. What, I asked, had been the cause of the blight? He didn't know.

He had, though, dived himself as a kid. "But around the time of the [Second World] war, that's when you had the blight, and then everything just quit. A lot of people moved away. The guys who went into the service, a lot of them never came back here. But," he went on, "the industry is coming back—or would be if you could get the guys to do the work.

"But there are damn few who want to do it. Damn few. To get guys who really want to do it, who know how, you practically have to get 'em from Greece. And there you've got immigration problems and so forth. The guys who were born here, hell, they don't want to do the things you got to do if you want to make it work. There is work in sponging now. The sponges here are back, and those in the Mediterranean, there's a blight there now, so they say. But these young guys!" He sniffed and wiped his nose with his apron tip. "We'd stay out two months sometimes. Now you can't get a guy to stay out ten days. Me? Hell, I'm too old." He took a theatrical glance at the stacked dishes and the empty tables, as if to say, Look what kind of work age has brought me to.

MY business in Tampa the next morning was with U.S. Customs, whose operations I was interested in learning about, especially drug interdiction. This put me in the temporary custody of Bonni Tischler, Special Agent in Charge, a sharp, articulate woman who might have been in her late thirties. She was businesslike almost to a fault, speaking so directly to the issue and with such a comprehensive grasp of it that it was hard for me to keep up. Though I was to meet this day with two other women in this line of work, men must predominate, and this might have been why Tischler salted her talk with colorful profanities that she seemed more at ease with than did her male assistants.

"Our problem," she said for openers, "is obvious if you've driven along any sizable portion of the Gulf coast. I mean along [Route] 41, not 75. You get what I mean? It's a fantastically intricate coastline. Half the time you don't know whether you're on a bay, a peninsula, a swamp, an estuary, whatever. And there are twenty-six hundred miles of navigable water from Naples to Mobile: *that's* our problem. We can't begin to cover it all. No way. The west coast of this state is just wide open. It's like a door they forgot to close.

"You were asking me about Everglades City? Well, Everglades City is an example of what we have to deal with here. Whoever told you those people got into drug-running because they were locked out of the park doesn't know what they're talking about. That's just wolfshit. Those people have been into homemade illegal activities for generations. They ran slaves after it was illegal. They ran rum during Prohibition. They poach. They run drugs, what-have-you. And they're very inbred." She laughed shortly. "A lot of them have gaps in their teeth and look kind of funny. But you get to look that way if you stay in a small place and intermarry: the gene pool gets pretty small. But they're tough people, you'd better believe that, and shrewd. For you, it would be a difficult situation, coming in like that. I mean, the information you're gonna get is gonna be pretty minimal. These are *natives* I'm talking about here, not newcomers. Crackers. They don't take too kindly to outsiders—which means most of the rest of the world. That's why that guy you mentioned at the fish house wasn't so friendly. That and the fact that those people the DEA busted back in 1983 are getting ready to get out. I'm actually surprised he'd talk to you at all. Fish houses are great cover for smuggling—always have been.

"I don't know how much you know about drug trafficking and seizure other than 'Miami Vice.' But our problem is different from theirs over there [on Florida's Atlantic coast]. There it's a go-fast situation where the dopers use those high-speed Cigarette-type boats. Here it's a go-slow situation. The carriers here use sailboats, yachts, shrimp boats, pleasure cruise ships. And then there's the stuff that comes in in cargo containers: one of our biggest busts here was a cocaine shipment concealed inside pieces of lumber. Later I think you should go over and talk with Diane Zwicker, the district director [of Customs in Tampa]. She can fill you in on that. But we're trying all sorts of programs to spread as wide a net as possible along the Gulf coast, and still we can't begin to cover the whole thing effectively."

Tischler herself was a Florida native, I learned, though from the Atlantic side. "When I was a kid in Miami," she said, "we hardly ever heard of the west coast. People from the east coast just didn't tend to go over there. The retirement places—St. Pete, Sarasota—were there, all right, but basically Florida was a north/south state. Then they put through [Route] 4 [from Daytona Beach to Tampa Bay], and that opened up the upper part of the west coast a bit. But the real change here has been with the completion of 75. Since then the west coast has been discovered pretty fast—by all sorts of people—and the whole of it is going to see big changes, I think. The days of the sleepy, undiscovered west coast are numbered, probably were doomed by Disney World. This area [Tampa Bay] used to be mañanaland. It had that laid-back Hispanic character with lots of Cubans and Puerto Ricans. Well, that's changed." She appeared to think better of this and rose from her desk chair. "But even today with all the changes, it's still not what you imagine when you think of a Florida city—all that glitter and fast pace. Come over here." She led me to a picture window that overlooked the downtown. "See? That's all there is to it, really. It's still pretty much a small-sized city. But, like I say, I have this feeling that all this is going to change pretty rapidly in the next few years."

Tischler sent me on to George Campbell, Special Agent Group Supervisor, who, she said, could give me an idea of some of the specifics of drug interdiction; she herself had a date in court. Campbell was a native of Tampa who appeared to have soaked up something of that laid-back character Tischler said Hispanics had given the city. If he wasn't thrilled with his assignment to the visiting writer, he was certainly accommodating, and on the way over to Clearwater to show me Customs' surveillance and intercept boats he outlined the present state of operations.

The department, he told me, currently had four boats in operation, one a platform-type boat used for surveillance and three go-fast boats. Based on intelligence reports a specific area of the Gulf waters was identified as what he termed "potentially active," and the four-boat convoy was dispatched to it. The platform boat was equipped with highly sophisticated electronic equipment and served as a spotter for the go-fasts. After a target boat had been identified, a go-fast was sent to inspect it. How, I wondered, was a boat targeted for inspection?

"Well," said Campbell, pausing as he searched for a way to break all this down for the layman, "let's see if I can give you an easy example. Suppose you see a coastal freighter in close to shore. You ask yourself, 'What's he doing in so close? Where could he be heading in here? If he's making for New Orleans, he ought to be well out to sea.' Something like that might give you a clue. Of course, you might not be right at all, but that's what the go-fast boat's supposed to find out."

Once in range, the inspector in the go-fast identified himself and requested permission to come aboard for a documents check. "While he's on board," Campbell said, "looking through the papers, he's also looking for signs the boat might be from a foreign port—say, Mexico or Colombia. What's the ethnic composition of the crew? What's the captain's nationality? Does this add up? What brand names can he see on cans of food, liquor bottles, and so forth? Then he's also looking at the physical makeup of the vessel. Has something been moved in the galley, for instance? Are there scratch marks on the planks? Are some of the planks newer than others? Are there new screws in old cabinets? If he sees something that doesn't look right, he requests permission to search the vessel. Usually the captain grants this. You see, these people aren't the producers or the dealers. They're simply delivering, and they can always claim they didn't know the stuff was on board. Anyway, regardless of whether or not permission is granted, the search is made. But, as I say, it's unusual to have a captain refuse. But at this stage diplomacy and tact are essential; there's no point in trying to bully people around, and there's a certain amount of what I guess you'd have to call 'understanding' between men out on the water together."

By this point we had crossed the bay to its Gulf side and had arrived again at water ourselves. Campbell checked in briefly at his dockside office, then led me along the docks to have a look at a platform boat and two go-fasts that bobbed in the light chop, their huge engines gleaming under a hazy sun and looking more as though they belonged on a plane than a boat. Two agents stood in the stern of the platform boat. One will here be called Jeff, though that wasn't his name; the other said I could call him "Van Ness." Why Van Ness? "Well, I happened once to be in San Francisco and saw that name on a street sign, and I thought, 'That would be a good name for an alias.'" He smiled, and I stepped aboard. Campbell shook my hand in farewell and headed back up the dock.

Jeff and Van Ness were just back from a five-day, around-the-clock operation in the Gulf, and they looked weary, their voices sounding flat and heavy. Yet they were trying to give me a sense of their work as they showed me through the big vessel. It was designed, they now pointed out, to be self-sustaining during these operations and was equipped with a desalinization device for drinking water and a galley, of course, as well as a TV and VCR. Its centerpiece was a gleaming complex of electronics, the individual functions of which I was told and promptly forgot. The boat, Jeff said, could ship eight though its normal crew was six. Top speed was twenty knots (about eighteen miles per hour), pretty impressive, so I was told, for a boat of this size, though, to be sure, it would be no match for the go-fasts. When we had finished the tour we sat in the cabin with its window blinds down, talking of the hazards of the work. Van Ness sipped coffee, trying to stay awake.

Both men had been in Customs work more than twenty years, and they agreed that things weren't getting any easier. The advances in technology, they said, were available both to law enforcement and outlaws, and there seemed to be more and more of the latter, so that Customs men found themselves slipping farther and farther astern of their targets. I asked about the dangers of getting shot or knifed or bludgeoned, imagining the risks must be significant in the interception and inspection of suspected vessels. There was real risk here, Van Ness said, especially when the Customs go-fast came alongside the suspect craft.

"First of all," he said, rubbing his sparse gray beard, "it's not exactly easy to tie up to another ship in a high sea, and you might get men hurt here in any case, even without the other guy doing a thing. Then, your attention's on getting tied up securely, and maybe you're getting bounced around by the swells, so you aren't watching what the other guy's doing—or you aren't giving him your full attention, let's say. But this is the point, if there's going to be any shooting, it'll most likely come here." The Customs people, he said, carried sidearms—usually .357 Magnums, though now 9 mm automatic pistols were becoming popular. They also carried what he called an "aug rifle," a shotgun capable of firing three-round bursts.

Jeff explained the inspection procedure from a boatside view. "When we come up on a likely target, the first thing we try to establish is the locations of the people on it and how many of them there are. Can we see them or some of them? Then we do a check through our computer to see if any information is available on this boat. Has it ever been seized or suspected? Then, when we get on the boat, we're looking to see if it's in disarray. If it's supposed to be a pleasure boat or an American boat in our waters, then what's it doing with all that salt all over it? Does it have a lot of rain gear lying around, suggesting it was really crossing from a foreign port? You know, the car that's been driven from Alaska will look a lot different from the one that's just been driven down from the northern part of the state.

"Then you look for other discrepancies, like whether they're carrying water cans but there's no water. Or maybe they show a hot water heater, but when you turn on the tap there's no hot water. You name it, they've thought of it: double-hulled boats, ones with false water lines, hollowed mastheads. . . ." Van Ness reminded him of the infamous instance in which they had intercepted a boat but couldn't find the dope they *knew* was hidden somewhere on it.

"It was like that scene in *The French Connection*," he said, "where the police haul this Lincoln in and take it apart, and they still can't find the stuff they know is there. Drives you nuts. In this business you're allowed to make mistakes, but only a certain number of them will be tolerated. And here we had this boat we'd intercepted and ordered to follow us back to port. It sat so funny in the water, way down low in the bow. And there were just a lot of other things that didn't add up. The crew, for instance, was two Canadians and two Marielitos. Now what the hell did that mean? Anyway, we spent three days going over that boat and couldn't find the stuff. Couldn't find anything. We sawed the damn thing almost in half and *still* couldn't find anything. One day we had the diver down there again looking at the hull because it sat so funny, and he just sort of pushed in a certain place, and the part gave way, and there were the compartments: seven hundred and fifty pounds of coke."

Later the agents took me out for a spin in Tampa Bay and beyond into the Gulf; they thought I ought to get a feel for what a go-fast could do. Once we'd cleared the NO WAKE sign, Jeff opened the boat up, and it indeed went fast, the hull slap-slapping the water in great, convulsive leaps, my knees jolting up toward my chin with each slap, and the tears streaming across my cheeks toward my ears. Jeff smiled at my obvious discomfort and told me over the roar of the engine that this was after all a mild day. "You should feel this when you're running in rough seas," he hollered. "After a few hours of this, you're ready to give your legs a rest." After little more than an hour of it, I was certainly ready for port and was glad to wobble up the dock for my return to Tampa with Jim Bond, Marine Coordinator of Customs, yet another of the relay team of informants Bonni Tischler had arranged for me.

Bond used the drive back to itemize a few dozen of the things he and his colleagues took for granted in this business but that I had never thought of. For instance, he said, some of the items and affairs of everyday life had significations that were hidden from ordinary citizens but to the dopers and their pursuers were commonly understood. Like what? I wondered. Like Lysol and trash compactors and pleasure cruises, just for starters. Lysol, he said, was regularly used by dopers carrying shiploads of marijuana to disguise the smell. "You can smell the bales [of marijuana] a mile off," Bond said, "so these guys'll just douse everything on board with Lysol. But, of course, that, too, has its problems, because when you get a whiff of that, you're immediately suspicious." And trash compactors? The majority of Sears's South American sales of trash compactors went to those who used them to compact marijuana into tight, easily concealed bales. "It's called the 'square grouper' here," Bond said, "because it comes in on fishing vessels. People say, 'He's going after the square grouper,' which means a guy is running marijuana. Marijuana is making a comeback around here after a few years where we saw a lot more coke than grass; there seem to be more guys going after the square grouper than ever before."

And what of those innocuous-seeming pleasure cruises he'd mentioned, the ones so heavily advertised on TV and in the newspapers? Those, Bond told me, were prime locations for dope sales. The crews of the pleasure cruisers were not well paid, he said, and some crew members supplemented their income by bringing dope on board and selling to the mostly young, upscale passengers.

Like Jeff and Van Ness, Bond felt things weren't getting easier in the drug interdiction profession. He cited the rise of synthetic drugs as a new and troubling development and the recent influx of amateurs, Marielitos, and Jamaicans into the American drug trade. It was a lot easier, he thought, to deal with professional drug traffickers than with amateurs because "you never can predict what an amateur will do. Sure, he's probably easier to catch than your pro, but it's after you catch him that's the problem. Say a guy's doing this to pay his way through college—don't laugh: we see it a lot. Or say he only runs drugs once in a while. He's the guy who might just start shooting if he gets in a tight place, whereas your professional will calculate the situation and take what comes. He knows what his chances of going to jail are, and he knows how much time he'll have to serve. He won't make things worse by resorting to violence. Now, the Jamaicans are the most unpredictable. The most. They're worse than the Marielitos. They're just *crazy*. You never know what they're likely to do in a given situation. Even the other dopers steer clear of them."

DIANE ZWICKER, District Director of Customs, did indeed show me the lumber that had been hollowed to conceal cocaine—or rather the photos of it that ran along her office wall. But rather than talking about the drug problem in the bay area, she thought it would be more instructive for me to have a tour of the docks and see for myself what was involved in cargo inspection. For this my guide was Pat Franklin, a blond woman in her early forties who wore her hair pulled back in a shining ponytail and carried a pistol at her hip. She'd been with Customs thirteen years, she told me, and on our drive to the docks she gave me a bit of general information about the port of Tampa, which, she said, was somewhat unlike other ports in that the kinds of cargo coming into it were relatively restricted. "Mostly what comes in here," she said, "is lumber, steel, bananas, orange juice concentrate, and phosphate-related chemicals. There are other items, too, of course, but this is mostly what we get."

Down on the docks the heat and glare were ferocious, but Pat Franklin seemed as cool and composed as when we'd been in her office or the air-conditioned car. As for me, I felt pounded by the heat and dwarfed by the size of everything—the cranes, the cargo containers, and mostly the huge hulls of the vessels. They towered over everything, stretching in rusty immensity toward a white and blinding sky. The hulls, the cargo containers, the bales of wire, forklifts, trucks—everything down here caught the sunlight and threw it back metallically raised to an even higher power. In the near foreground a tanker was disgorging its cargo of salt, the dust from which rose stinging to meet the sun. I kept watching Franklin out of the corner of my eye to see some least bit of shine to her face, some crinkling of her eyes, some reaction to what felt to me like an assault, but I saw nothing. She went on with her calm explanations as though she were showing me through a garden.

Near the unloading tanker a gang of khaki-clad men was sweating under the direction of a uniformed Customs officer. Pat Franklin explained that this was part of a cooperative effort in which National Guardsmen assisted Customs in the inspection of cargo. Most of the men were inside a long metal cargo container, and when I joined them in there I found it was as hot and black as boiling pitch, the container's sun-beaten surfaces radiating heat like a convection device. The men's uniforms were stuck to their frames as they went slowly about the business of inspecting a shipment of Guatemalan coffee, poking each of the burlap sacks with metal rods that resembled the skewers used for shish kebab.

Officer Nick Tirone explained the logistical impossibility of actually opening even that 20 percent of the cargo they were able to inspect, and hence this measure, which he said was probably the best that could be employed. When the men had finished with this container and had moved on to another Tirone told me something of that visual inventory he kept in his head, explaining that it wasn't simply the contents of the containers that needed inspecting; it was the containers themselves, as well.

"I look for any signs that something's been changed," he said. "Like is there fresh paint somewhere around the ends?" He ran his stubby fingers over a portion of the broiling edge of the container, illustrating his inspection. "Is there a weld seam here? What's it doing here? Shouldn't be here. There's no reason for it, see? Is the paint burned anywhere? That might mean they'd welded something inside. Same thing with any burned planking inside. Sometimes they'll take the top off up here." He ran his hand along the metal strip above the container's entrance. "They'll conceal the stuff in there, then weld this strip back on."

We moved on to rejoin the guardsmen in their slow-motion probings, and after I'd said that this truly looked like the needle-in-the-haystack game, Pat Franklin nodded but said nothing and we departed for a look at a tanker unloading OJ concentrate.

In the morning I was back at the docks. Nick Tirone and his crew were at work on a container of pickles, untying the wire strands at the necks of the large plastic jugs, then gingerly sending their probes down into the pickles floating in brine. The already serious heat magnified the smell in the container into a smarting intensity I found almost intolerable, but Tirone seemed cheerful enough and willing to talk further about the tedious problems of his work. But this morning my attention wasn't on drugs but on a man I'd chanced across the day before when I'd been down here with Pat Franklin, a tall, rangy fellow, a broad-brimmed straw hat shielding his freckled face from the sun as he hosed down the docks behind Superior Seafoods. I'd stopped then and exchanged a few words with him, though aware that Franklin was waiting for me. He'd kept his eyes on his work but had responded out of the corner of his mouth. I'd asked about shrimping, and that had set him off on the manifold problems shrimpers faced these days, what with the interference of the government, scientists, and environmental activists. "This," he said soberly, the spray from his hose sending shrimp scraps shooting off into the port waters, "is a dyin' industry they don't quit foolin' with it." I'd asked him if I might come back the next day and talk with him some more, and for the first time he turned to glance at me and shrug. I took that for a yes, and so here I was.

He didn't want to give his name. I might call him Red if I liked. We sat in the long corrugated shed of Superior Seafoods, where it was cool, with the shed open at both ends and a mild breeze wafting through. Before us a long string of shrimp boats bobbed at anchor—*Peggy-Anne, Little Rae, Nuthin' Fancy*—white-hulled with vertical rust stains that ran down into the water, their outriggers folded up like wings. Though initially reticent, Red proved to be a talker once started, shaping and framing his verbal conceptions with large and curiously expressive hands. He'd been born and raised, he told me, in the West Virginia mountains where his father had been a coal miner. Recently Red had moved his father down to Tampa, though at eighty-seven the old man was "sorely afflicted" with black lung. For a while Red himself had thought his destiny was to be a miner, and he had been one as a kid. "That's the hardest work any man ever has to do," he said, shaking his head at those memories. Then followed stints in a steel mill and a glass factory. At twenty-five he followed his younger brother Virgil south to St. Marys, Georgia, just up from the Florida line on the coast, and from there down to Key West. "I was lookin' for work on the shrimp boats," he said. "This was 1949, and they'd found new shrimp beds off Key West, and so pretty soon everybody was down there lookin' for work same as me. All the captains asked if I had experience, and I said no, and so did they. I musta asked five hundred captains. Well, then I come back up to St. Marys. People were walkin' around in jackets, shirts—cold, y'know. And there I was with my shirt off, lyin' on this pavilion they had over the water, sunnin' myself. And this guy comes along and says, 'Say, mister, you mind if I ask you a question?' 'No,' I say. 'What is it?' 'Are you from *Alaska*?' He couldn't believe I'd be lyin' there with my shirt off. Well, we talked, and I told him I was lookin' for work on a shrimp boat, and he told me his daddy had just bought a boat and was lookin' for men. 'I'll tell him you're the third hand,' he says, and that turned out to be my first trip. His daddy fell overboard and drowned. We looked and looked for him, but it was night and we couldn't find him. Never did. But, I'll say this: shrimping's one hell of a lot easier work than mining. It's like the farm boy who said he liked the navy because he didn't have to get up until six o'clock."

Still, it had been hard work with a dash of real danger to it, shrimping from the Tampa area around the curve of the coast with the progress of the seasons, coming back to Tampa in late December. In the early Sixties, Red and the others had begun shrimping off Campeche and Guyana, Suriname, and French Guiana. "In the old days," he said, "why, you could fish three, nine, twelve miles off Mexico and Honduras. But then the New England cod fishermen got the government to protect 'em from the Russians by claiming a two-hundred-mile limit, so's to protect their beds, and then all the other countries jumped on our ass and claimed the same thing. So that restricts us now to the Gulf from here around to Texas. Some of the boys goes around now to the east coast for rock shrimp, but me and my brother never did. We sold our boats years ago in French Guiana and come back here to start this business. We sell strictly to processors, not to restaurants. They keep too many books." He winked at me. "They skim. I don't like to deal with 'em."

There were many reasons Red and his brother had sold their boats and gone from shrimping to selling shrimp, but the two main ones he cited were the growth of the sport-fishing lobby and the combined attack on shrimpers by government scientists and environmental activists. These were the forces, he predicted, that if unchecked would kill the industry. The sport fishermen, he claimed, were out to stop all trawling in the Gulf. "They claim trawlin's tearin' up all the breeding beds," Red said. "You watch and see: they aim to stop it all. They don't tell you that, but it's true all the same." But by far his harshest words were reserved for the government scientists and the "do-gooders," the environmentalists.

Trawlers in general and shrimpers in particular have long had their critics among marine scientists and environmentalists because trawling is by its nature an inherently wasteful and extractive way to fish. It is the maritime equivalent of mining and logging. In shrimping, the waste—that is, the random harvest of unwanted marine life—is called "by-catch," and it is dumped overboard dead. For every pound of shrimp caught in the Gulf, something like ten pounds of fish are also caught and discarded. In some areas of the Gulf the ratio is much higher, as much as twenty to one. Over a year's time, this translates into a wasting of something like two and a half billion pounds of fish. Not all of it, of course, would have been valuable to commercial fishermen or sportsmen, but about 70 percent of it would be. Thus the finger-pointing, which comes not only from the enemies Red cited but also from fellow fishermen.

The most visible casualty of the shrimpers' nets is the sea turtle, particularly the loggerhead and Kemp's ridley, and it was the drowning of great numbers of these creatures in 1988 that prompted a reluctant federal government to require the use in Gulf waters of what are called turtle excluder devices (TEDs), which are supposed to—and in fact do—allow sea turtles to escape drowning in the nets while other, smaller organisms travel on to the end of the trawl bag and are snared there.

Some environmentalists claim that the loss of shrimp through the TEDs' escape hatch is negligible, a claim hotly, often profanely, disputed by the shrimpers. Indeed it appears now that something between 15 and 20 percent of the shrimp are lost through the use of TEDs, a significant loss to men who work close to the margin of economic failure. And there is, too, the fact that the threat of extinction that now hangs over the sea turtle is hardly the fault of shrimpers exclusively. Centuries of human activity, of gluttonous turtle harvesting, of fouled marine waters and developed beaches have brought these grand, mysterious creatures to their precarious place in the chain of being. Shrimpers may now be the single biggest preventable cause of turtle mortality, but this, too, they hotly dispute.

Red thought the whole controversy a "bunch of crap," a plot to put American shrimpers out of business. "They say as much as fifty percent of the shrimp escape out of that thing [the TED]," he snorted. "Shrimp're dumb, I agree, but they ain't that dumb. What the turtle can do, the shrimp can. There was a guy got a great big grant to study turtles and he come up with a figure of the daily turtle catch, and based on that they say the turtle's gonna be distinct [*sic*]. Hell, there're more turtles in the Gulf than there ever were. You just ask any shrimper: he'll tell you. But now, like I say, they got to tow those rings on the nets. Well, I'll tell you what's gonna be distinct [*sic*], and that's the shrimper, that's what!" He slapped his knee with the flat of his hand.

As we walked back through the shed and into the warehouse so that Red could show me the operation, he said there was no future in shrimping and maybe not in this end of the business, either. The more he talked about it, the more dire his predictions and the more doleful he became. When we came upon Red's son, John, horsing around in the warehouse with two workers, Red glanced at him out of the corner of his eye but said nothing. Then we were out in the hot sun of the parking lot, and Red stood, hands on hips, looking back into the shadows at his son and his playmates.

"He *barely* got outta high school," Red said with a weary asperity. "Barely. He don't see no future in this, that's for certain. Way back in first grade we knew we had a problem there. He got bad marks, but when we tested him, why, the principal of the Catholic school said, 'I don't understand this. Your boy isn't doing well, but look here at these tests: he's *smart*!' And that's the way it's been. He told me once, 'Daddy, if it wasn't for football, I wouldn't stay in school another day.' Red looked at me in wonderment, almost as if asking for help. "I told him, 'You gotta have that piece of paper. You can't do nothing without it.' Day he got outta school, he said he didn't want to go on to college. So I said, 'Then your ass is down here. You ain't gonna lay around.'

"Well, you see 'im. He's here. But he don't like it. Don't want to be here. He's twenty-three and don't know what the fuck he wants to do. I don't either."

THE multicolored sign outside the Tropical Sandwich Shop on the Tampa docks depicted a lavishly stuffed sandwich and bore a legend that read HOME OF THE CUBAN SANDWICH. Inside at five minutes after noon a hard-pressed staff of five tried to keep pace with the demands of the horde of dockhands who stood in ragged lines before the counter, hollering out their orders. The shop's specialty was a legacy from the days when Tampa was the major cigar-producing city in America. Vincente Ybor and Ignacio Haya had been lured here in 1884 from Key West and labor troubles and had founded the company town, Ybor City, that served as a mecca for Cubans for half a century. In the old, long, high-ceilinged factories of Ybor City the Cuban immigrants had laboriously assembled the famous cigars while from his throne in the front of the room *el lector* (the designated reader) had instructed and diverted them, reading aloud from Spanish newspapers and the classics like *Don Quixote*. In those days the cigar-shaped Cuban loaf was a staple of the local diet, and the bread man, delivering it fresh in the mornings, would simply jam a loaf to the nail on the door of each customer on his route. The factories and the bread nailed to the doors were memories now, but *pan Cubano* was still here, brought over daily to the Tropical Sandwich Shop from a bakery next door.

The Cuban sandwich was filled with ham, cheese, chopped lettuce, and mayo and was clearly a popular item. So, too, were the deviled crab rolls, batter-fried, about the size of a softball, and a bargain at seventy cents. Fried chicken wings and legs went four for a dollar. *Boliche* was slices of beef cooked with onions and peppers. Stuffed potatoes were filled with ground beef, olives, and garlic. There were also the usual American sandwiches like hamburgers, Sloppy Joes, and tuna, but among this crowd there were few calls for these. Inside a bank of glass-doored refrigerators along one wall were supplemental items like flan, rice pudding, juices, soft drinks, and more than a dozen brands of beer.

The dockhands were absolutely black with dirt, many of them bare to the waist, flashlights, pliers, screwdrivers, and knives hanging from their belts. With their often elaborate tattoos and swarthy beards they looked like a crew of pirates from central casting. "Large Cuban, all the way!" the shout rang out. "Gimme six wings!" Though there were five booths along one wall, almost all the hands took their lunches out to their cars, which sat in the blazing lot overlooking the water. By twelve-fifteen the rush was over, and the staff of the shop looked a little like blown runners on the other side of the tape, hands on hips, eyes bulging, trying to regain wind. They only had a few minutes, for now came a second, different shift: the deliverymen, each in his identifying uniform and cap, bunches of keys at their belts instead of heavy-duty tools. They were mostly Anglos, more leisurely in their movements, and spread out in their arrivals. None I saw ordered beer with their food, whereas the hands had done so almost to a man, and some had left with quarts.

At quarter to one there began an assorted shift—a few women, a few elderly men, kids in muscle shirts. By twenty after the place was quiet, and the staff was beginning to straighten up. "We've had shops in three other locations in this area," Carlos Carrillo told me. "Plus another at Plant City that did real good." He said he'd come from Cuba at the age of six. "This is a good spot for us, too. A working man, he can't go over to the Sea Breeze [a dockside restaurant for business types]. He's got to come to us. And we fix him up good. Good food. Good prices. Then at six, the shifts change. We get the beer guys on their way home. We get the guys coming on for dinner. By seven I'm gone."

ON my last morning in Tampa I decided I needed exercise. The night before I'd gone over to Ybor City to see what was left of it and had dinner there, an affair that was still heavily with me. Ybor City had been a disappointment, a mostly deserted husk of a place. At seven in the evening almost all the shops, bars, and restaurants along Seventh Avenue, its heart, had been shuttered. Outside the famed Columbia Restaurant, a black valet gently reproached me for parking for free down the block. "Bad place, my man," he said. "Security there is not good." When I'd asked my waiter why all the shops had been closed at so early an hour, he had said, "Neighborhood youths. It is a great mistake." Whether this last referred to the depredations of the youths or the timidity of the local merchants I never learned. José went silently about the fairly lugubrious business of serving me my meal—tepid black bean soup, assorted fish in tasteless tomato sauce garnished with retired sprigs of parsley—and then presented the bill. So, for company and recreation I had turned to a nearby table of Anglo tourists and after dinner joined them for rounds of drinks nobody really needed and jokes that ran to those featuring three men who go up to heaven and are questioned there by St. Peter.

That was why this morning I was on foot accompanying the commuter traffic along the stately six and a half miles of Bayshore Boulevard where the city's social heavyweights had once lived. At this hour a city parks crew was out in a truck, tooling slowly along the boulevard and stopping to turn on the sprinklers embedded in the wide grassy median. Farther up, where the sprinklers had been on awhile, the traffic swished through the lavish overflow, and the drivers had to turn on their wipers. The traffic was steady but not stagnant this morning, and there was, too, a steady flow of pedestrian traffic along the sidewalks on either side of the boulevard. Elderly women and men walked small dogs, younger women did the Jane Fonda strenuous walk, their arms pumping like pistons. Watching them, I momentarily thought better of my own slovenly slouch, straightened up, and squared my shoulders, reminding myself thus of my childhood years in a reform school disguised as a military academy. It was a good thing I did this, for not long after I saw a platoon of marines jogging toward me in khaki T-shirts and red shorts, dog tags bouncing against their heaving chests. At their head was the drill instructor, and as he approached, up from my military academy days came a foul old cadence count, and I found myself saying to the DI, "Every swinging dick." He didn't miss a beat, only smiled slightly and snapped off a short salute, and then they were past, going eastward toward the high-rises that now were catching the lifting light.

On the boulevard's landward side a phalanx of old homes presided in a faded seignorial way over changing patterns of city life, many showing FOR SALE signs in the Bermuda grass lawns that defended them from the street. There were gaps in their ranks where houses had been razed, and in other places clubs and civic organizations had taken over the residences of families that had gone elsewhere or died out. Soon I overtook a young mailman in shorts, sunglasses, and pith helmet, his Walkman unit turned up so loud I could hear the thumping roar filling his head. When I spoke to him, he obligingly turned it off long enough to tell me that the Bayshore homes were "almost always in transition now, it seems like. Just in this area here there's been almost twenty families moved or moving since I got this route four months ago. I don't know what it is. This"—gesturing to a fine old place at Bayshore and Edison—"is Mr. McKay's home. Beautiful, isn't it? But he says he's going to move, too. He says he doesn't need this big a place anymore with all his children grown up and gone. It used to be, when you thought of Tampa, you thought of Bayshore, just like Fifth Avenue in New York or Worth

Avenue in Palm Beach. Class, you know? And it's still class, but it's changing and fast."

🌴 FROM my waterfront motel room at Cedar Key I could watch brown pelicans slide slowly past my salt-flecked picture window. Every once in a while a cormorant would change the pace, zipping past the stately pelicans. And every once in a while, taking this in, my feet propped on the window ledge, I let out a sigh of relief at being in this small town that had so far escaped the fate of too much of the coast between Tampa Bay and Crystal River. Beyond the window and the gliding birds lay the low humps of the Cedar Keys, so that my room gave me the feeling of being aboard a ship and one that wasn't going anywhere in a hurry. Nothing seemed hurried here, in fact, and at high noon the town's main intersection had been all but deserted, only a few customers at the two food stores and a pickup or two rolling down toward the motels on the edge of town. On the main wharf a score of fishermen sat on chairs or leaned on the railings, poles outstretched, their bodies etched darkly against the water's glitter. For the moment at least Cedar Key permitted me to imagine that this was the way things once had been all along what Bonni Tischler had styled the "sleepy, undiscovered west coast," that coast whose older style and pace had been "doomed" by the construction of roads linking it to Orlando and the east coast.

Certainly I wasn't the one to argue with Tischler's use of the word "doomed." Somewhere in America there might be a longer, uglier strip than Route 19 between Tampa Bay and Crystal River, but I don't know where. There for miles and miles in numbing succession were gas stations, auto supply stores, tire stores, fast food restaurants, RV parks, motels, malls, furniture outlets, liquor stores, and marine-supply outfits. Every few miles the traveler was subjected to a reprise of what he had just apparently cleared when he passed by another Chili's (a Mexican restaurant chain), an Olive Garden (an Italian one), a McDonald's, and a Texaco station. Was he in fact getting anywhere, or was this another Florida outdoor attraction, a Rod Serling World in which your odometer's forward roll was belied by the stationary quality of the landscape? Or maybe it was a kind of in-your-face Zen *koan*, designed by some enlightened master planner to force upon you the realization that all progress was an illusion? Whatever, it was psychologically taxing enough that when at Crystal River I saw a diamond-shaped sign advising that the next five miles was a favored bear crossing point, I wasn't sure this wasn't part of the same trompe l'oeil effect. It appeared not to be, for the landscape was suddenly bereft of shops and billboards, and 19 ran through a solemn pine woods where I met no other cars.

I was suddenly seized with the conviction that if I turned off along here I might get a glimpse of the Gulf itself, unadorned with improvements, and I did this at Inglis. Inglis hugged the main artery and so was disappointing with its Circle K, gas station, and church, but farther along the short, west-running spur I was rewarded when it brought me to the edge of a salt marsh. Before me were mangroves, palmettos, and a flat stretch of those saline-tolerant grasses that buffer the land and provide critical nutrients for the aquatic life that nestles here. Standing at the marsh's edge, I could see the dark, tannin-filtered water stirred by unseen creatures, and as my eye roved farther out there was more and more water, the marsh dispersing into isolated hammocks on which stood a few last palms. And then, under a white sky, there was the great Gulf. To pause here, even for a few minutes, was to be taken into a deep, warm embrace, as though even this part of a much-abused coast could forgive us and our ceaseless meddlings. Here was the look and the feel of that Gulf coast into which Ponce and his flotilla had sailed centuries ago and whose historical tides they had so profoundly altered.

Cedar Key wasn't the natural coast, but it had a broad margin of marsh behind it and the Gulf in front, and except for a small sector of bars and souvenir shops at the end of the town wharf it looked wonderfully sane. The qualities I liked in it had, I was to learn, come only after it and the surrounding area had been pillaged and reduced to what I now found so restful. Its sleepy, slightly slatternly appearance was, in other words, a kind of historical booby prize for a place that at one time fancied itself becoming another Mobile or New Orleans. After the local aborigines had been greatly thinned out, the Cedar Keys were the haunts of smugglers and pirates: the ubiquitous Lafitte and Kidd were said to have used the islands I could see from my motel window. Later the town site of Cedar Key had been a military depot during the Second Seminole War. Permanent white settlement began in 1843 with the building of a resort for wealthy planters, but Cedar Key's grand aspirations, like those of Key West, took wing with the coming of the railroad in 1860.

That project was the handiwork of David Levy, a.k.a. David Levy-Yulee, as improbable a character as can be found in Florida's annals: a Jewish/Arabic, Indian-hating slaveholder, born in the Virgin Islands, who helped write the state's constitution and served two terms in the U.S. Senate. As senator Levy-Yulee used his position to further his grand personal scheme, which was to run a rail line from Fernandina on the east coast over to Cedar Key, a place he felt was destined for commercial greatness. But as happened in so many other places in the haphazardly building nation, Fortune smiled elsewhere, and Cedar Key never really took off as its boomers had hoped. It does, though, sit on the westernmost border of Levy County—if that is any consolation to Levy-Yulee's ambitious soul.

One who did prosper here was Eberhard Faber, a name familiar to any American school kid who ever stared idly at the barrel of a pencil in the days before the triumph of the ballpoint pen. The Pencil King was born in Bavaria into a family long in that line of work. When he came to America in 1848, joining the great wave of immigration that rolled unchecked to the Civil War, it was to sell pencils. By the time of the war Faber had bought up large timber tracts in the Cedar Keys area and was milling cedar at Cedar Key. Other pencil makers followed after the war, and in January 1890 the Cedar Key town council was able to brag in an advertisement in the *Florida Times Union* that enough pencils were produced locally to go around the earth forty-eight times. But ten years later the cedar forests were gone—and so were the mills. So, too, was most of the population, driven away by the exhaustion of the timber resources and by a devastating hurricane in 1896. Even the local waters were fished out, the turtles and stone crabs and oysters once so abundant now almost vestigial. By 1900 Cedar Key's grand metropolitan dreams were over, and it was free to drift into its somnolent present. If you wanted to go to seed quietly on Florida's Gulf coast, this was your spot.

When I asked the management at the Beach Front Motel where to go for a quiet dinner, I was told the Other Place. Like almost everything else here it sat on the water, and a stiff onshore breeze brought a sedgy, salty smell in through the open windows. A deck raised above the water allowed customers to sit out there in fair weather and watch the sun drown itself in ruddy glory while dining on mullet, oysters, and shrimp: after some years the fish had come back here. Even the sea turtle had returned, but the fabulously abundant mullet was the local delicacy. I had the fried mullet plate and read the local paper's latest edition.

When I went to pay my bill I mentioned to the man at the cash register that the restaurant was in the news. "Let me see that," he said sharply, holding out his hand for the paper. I gave it to him, and he scanned it quickly. The item in question reported on a city council meeting at which zoning ordinances were the subject of some debate. The owners of an RV park were found to have been illegally encroaching on city property and were ordered to quit this. Then an unnamed member of the audience pointed out that there were a number of other zoning violations the council ought to look into. For instance, the owner of the Other Place was using his place of business as a domicile in violation of City Ordinance Whatever.

"Oh, *that*," said the man at the register, handing me back the paper as if it were a soiled diaper. "That's Salty. He owns this rag, and he's been out to hang something on me ever since he came here." James Allen was a tall, leathery fellow with a bad eye that glittered and jumped about when he talked. He poked his finger at the paper. "You didn't get that in here," he said flatly. "Notice I don't allow it sold in here. It's just a rag is all it is. That 'Salty Sez' column is written by him, and it's just a way of trying to get stuff out he thinks is important. Nobody who's from here pays any attention to him or what he says. It's like at the city council meetings: those of us who're from here elect those council members to do the work, and then we leave 'em alone to do it. When they need our help, they'll ask us, and we'll give it. Did you see the rest of that item there?" He poked toward the paper again. "See, here: they went and passed a new ordinance that allows me to live upstairs.

"Reason he's mad at me is we took this place when it wasn't nothing but a dive, and we've made it into the best place in town. They sent you over from the Beach Front, right? They send all the tourists here because it's the best, and the reason it's the best is we serve good food, and we serve it the right way. You won't find any profanity or drunkenness in here. This is a family place, and we intend to keep it that way. You start in using cuss words, I'll give you one warning, and that's all you'll get. Next time you're gone, and it don't make a difference to me if it's horizontal or vertical. I wouldn't even sell liquor in here at all if I could help it, but if you're in the restaurant business, I guess you got to have it.

"And as you see, it's not only tourists who come in here: we get the native people, too, because they know we're clean, we're reliable, and we run a good place. And we know how everybody here likes their food done. We see Shorty over there come in, we know to just burn it up. Another fella'll like his just barely warmed over. And we cook to order for 'em without their having to say a word. That's what you call service.

"Now, before, this was a dive, like I said. And who do you think was running this before? Salty himself, that's who. He had this little band come in here weekends, and they had dancing, and I don't know what all. But nobody from here ever came over because it was just a dive. Nobody knows where he gets his money, where he got the money to buy this place and the newspaper. But there're suspicions. You know, when we moved in here we found he had this whole place wired? Every window, every step. Now, what kind of fella is it that'll go to that kind of trouble? A fella that's got something to hide is what. And after we bought this from him, he came snooping around one night, and I took a shot in his direction. I coulda hit him if I'd wanted, but I'd rather he just got the idea. Saves trouble that way. He hasn't tried that again, I'll tell you. Am I handy with a gun? You betcha. I'll shoot your eye out in a heartbeat.

"No, Salty is just typical of the few outsiders we get here. They come in here and see it's a nice place, and the *first* thing—the very *first* thing—they want to do is change it over so's it'll look just like where they came from! Ain't that something! But like we tell 'em when they start trying to mess with us: 'The same road that took you in here will take you out, and if you start in trying to mess with us, you'd better take it, too.' We're, oh, kinda . . . clannish, I guess you might say. We like it the way it's always been, and we don't take to outsiders, especially those that come in here and think they can change things. We take care of each other. We might fuss, I might hate somebody's guts for something he did, but a week later it's behind us. And don't *you* start in on the fella I'm having trouble with. If you do, I'll take care of you right quick. We like to run our own lives in our own way and without you interfering. That's why Cedar Key has stayed pretty much the same. Oh, you see those new motels over there, but I'll guarantee you, that's all there'll ever be. We won't have no condos, and Cedar Key won't be no fancy resort, either.

"See these election ads in here?" He pointed them out in Salty's paper. "I can sit here and tell you exactly who's gonna win every one of these races. Know why? Because I know who's from here and who isn't, and we *are not about* to elect anybody from outside to run us. Would you let some stranger come into your kitchen and start ordering you around? You wouldn't. You'd get your gun first. Well, that's the way we are. No different.

"No, we like things the way they are. We keep the developers outta here, and we keep the drug people away, and we have a nice, quiet, orderly place. Your wife could get outta her bed at three in the morning and walk around town in her nightgown and wouldn't a single thing happen to her. Oh, some old drunk might say 'Hey, baby.' But he wouldn't do nothing. That's the way it is here, and there's very few places left in the United States where that could be." He nodded a curt affirmation of the claim and turned to the woman who had now joined him at the register.

Anne O'Steen looked fifteen years Allen's junior with lively dark eyes, and it was immediately obvious she was the other person who made up the "we" in Allen's account of the fortunes of the Other Place. Like him, she was a Cedar Key native who liked things the way they were. "This is just a real close community," she told me, where in times of need people helped each other out in big ways and small. "Like tonight, there was this play over at the school? You should've seen the number of cars they had there, and many of those people don't even have kids in the play. They just went because they want to show support. Last month there was a family the husband died of cancer, and you wouldn't believe the amount of food and clothing and even cash that mother got for her kids. That's Cedar Key for you.

"It's true the younger people tend to leave after they graduate [from high school]. There's not that much for them here. But they all come back. I did. They come back because this is a good way to live. We're poor, sure, but there's a *slowness* to life here that's wonderful. There's a serenity on the water you can't find anywhere else. A man that works on the water, he'll hate to tie up to the dock because that's where reality begins; the wife's down there to meet him: 'The kid's sick, we haven't made our car payment, and the washer's broke.' It's enough to make him want to cut 'er loose and go back on out. That's what causes many a fisherman to become an alcoholic. My husband died of that. He just *loved* the water. He wasn't ever really happy on shore. Then his back went out and he started drinking to ease his back, you know, and one thing led to another. But he was a workaholic before he was an alcoholic, and he kept that boat so spotless you could have performed surgery right there on the deck. And even after he was in the treatment center, he could see out to the water, and one day he raised up and hollered, 'Goddamn! Look at all them mullet!' They practically had to strap him down. My son's the same. The water's in him for good. One day he says to me, 'Momma, Daddy caught a net of trout, and they was so *beautiful!*' Right then I knew I'd lost him, too."

She said she'd once taken a ceramics class over in Gainesville. "It was fun and all, and then one day the teacher, she said if we were going to make anything, it ought to be something that really meant something to us. Know what I made? I made a ceramic white boot, the kind you see watermen wearing all the time here. That meant something. That's where we come from. That's the thing we all identify with."

James Allen agreed, and in talking of the water, he lost that confrontational edge he'd displayed earlier. "The water gets into you and you can't get it out," he said. "You can't leave it. I'm off it now, running this place, but I'm still on it, ain't I?" He glanced out toward the now darkened bayou. "When I was working on the water I just sang all day long, lifting my traps, sun broiling down. It's a hard life, but it's a good one. I got sun spots all over my face, my hands, my arms." He paused and rubbed his lean, sinewy arms, speckled with precancerous spots. "Ought to have 'em scraped off, I suppose." He raised his head and looked away a moment. "But I wouldn't take anything for those years. I didn't get rich, but I raised all my kids, gave 'em all what they needed to get started."

Leaving the Other Place, I walked the dark and deserted road back over the bayou and into town, pausing at the little waterfront park where a plaque told me that this had been the terminus of David Levy-Yulee's railroad. Then I walked out onto the wharf that circled in a horseshoe out from the shore, its far end sparkling with the lights from the bars. The Cedars Lounge had all the trade this evening, and indeed it was a tight little community in there: every man jack I saw looked stewed to the gills. At the bar a man was holding onto it with one hand and swinging a half-filled glass of ouzo back and forth, the liquid slopping over his hand and sleeve. He was telling a younger companion that Cedar Key had the "gentlest dogs you ever seen." His own lay patiently and warily at the man's feet, ready to move if its master should stumble over it.

"Well," said the younger man, his eyes half shuttered, "that one seems gentle enough, anyway." Two other men now joined the talk, and presently all four were down on the floor, fondling the dog, which in response rolled on its back and spread its hind legs in an orgy of enjoyment. The men rolled it about, rubbed its belly, rumpled its ears.

"I ain't been to college," its owner slurred happily, "but I taught this 'ere dog to lie down." He wagged his head in a loose affirmation.

"All right, children, you'll have to excuse me." It was the brassy voice of a hard-featured woman who'd been over at the pool table and now was cruising back to the bar for another Coke and something. "Well," she said, standing over the doggy heap on the floor, "are we playing Old MacDonald or what?"

MULLET is not everyone's dish: it's a bit more like mackerel in taste and texture than some like, distinctly fishy. But in Cedar Key it was apparently everyone's dish and at every meal, too. At Rain's Restaurant on the bayou the breakfast special was fried mullet with grits and toast for four and a quarter, and it was so popular this morning the waitress told me I'd have to wait a few minutes if I wanted it. "People have really been going for this today," she said, "and we have to send over to the fish house for more mullet." The fish house was twenty feet away across the road, and I didn't mind the wait. I had plenty of visual stimulation in here, watching the tables full of good old boys, watermen all, who wore their identifying uniforms of faded ball caps and white rubber boots, their whiskered faces down at plate level, silently shoveling in great forkfuls of the morning special, then raising up to have a drink of coffee or beer. When they had finished, they would lean back, wipe their mouths with their hands, and look out the window. Then low conversations might begin. I saw none of them bothering with a morning newspaper.

When I had finished the special and leaned back in my chair awhile, I went out in search of Yellowlegs Campbell, who James Allen said had been on the water here "as long as anybody. If you want to hear about the water, you could talk to Yellowlegs." Campbell had been born just up the coast a few miles on an island at the mouth of the Suwannee River. "I was six years old before I ever saw any other folks besides my kinfolks," Campbell claimed. "My grandaddy was on the water, and his daddy, and mine, too, and now me. But I ain't good for anything anymore. Too old. After fifty they ought to call 'em all in and knock 'em in the head and finish 'em off—make room for these folks that're comin' along, Cubans, Vietnamese. . . ." His voice trailed away, and he looked about the cellar where he and Mac Bishop were putting together wooden boxes to store fish and supplies on Yellowlegs's boat. When he found the tool he'd been looking for, Campbell explained that the boxes were necessary now for commercial fishing. "They make you ice 'em down, if you want to sell 'em. If you don't and you get caught, it's trouble for you. That's one of these new laws they got that seem to cover just about everything these days."

All of this was delivered with a perfectly straight face, one as folded, seamed, and brown as a piece of ancient oilskin. But set into that face were eyes as blue as Winslow Homer's paintings of the Gulf waters, and after I had become accustomed to the cellar's half-light I could see the twinkle in them.

"We come over here when I was six. We went to school, me and my brothers, and I ran errands for a fisherman here in town. My mother used to cut off my britches here [just below the knee], and I was out so much, running around, you know, that my legs got all tanned. So that fella called me 'Yellowlegs,' and it stuck. I still get mail to 'Yellowlegs.' My brothers were called 'Wheezy,' 'Gator,' and 'Mr. Grits.' Now Wheezy's got so fat they call him 'Greasy.'

"I stayed in school until I was sixteen, but I never got past the sixth grade. In them days, if you didn't get it, they didn't pass you on: you stayed there until you got it. Nowadays, why, they pass you on whether you got it or not. I might get me a college degree if I was going to school nowadays, don't you think? Anyway, I stayed back three years in fourth grade and then three more in fifth, but, by God, by the time I got out [of fifth], I had it *good*! I could see I wasn't gettin' anywhere, so I quit and went to work on the water. That was in, oh, thirty-eight or nine. Times were tough then.

"And they're rough now, too. Between the environmentalists and the sport fishermen, commercial fishin's about dead here. Now, some of these new laws is good, I don't deny that. You got to have 'em. But there's just way too many now. Can't fish redfish no more: they're all for the sport fishermen. Can't catch turtles: they're gonna be extinct. Got all kind of regulation on grouper that don't make any sense. There're 200,000 sport fishermen on this coast and maybe 25,000 commercial fishermen. I don't have nothin' against the sport fishermen, but leave somethin' for the fella's got to make a livin' with his boat. Sport fisherman, he don't have to fish; he does it 'cause it's fun. But why make all the laws for the benefit of the fellas with the big boats?

"Now they claim they got to protect the turtles, those big ole loggerheads? Got to have a hole in your net to let the turtles out. Don't you think the shrimp're gonna get out same's the turtle? I do. Then what? I'll tell you what, we got to stick around just to find out what's gonna happen here. You can't make a livin' here commercial fishin' no more. So what we gonna do?" He spread his arms wide and bunched his shoulders. Mac Bishop went on hammering the heavy boxes together. "Fishin' is all I know, all I ever done, just fish. All I know how to do. Got no education. And there's lots and lots of fellas just like me all along this coast. What're they gonna do with 'em all? I'll tell you what: they'll have to feed 'em is what. I never took food stamps, not because I have anything against them, but because till now I haven't had to. Besides, I don't qualify: I don't have no Cadillac to go pick 'em up in."

IN Tampa I had chanced upon a good bookstore snugged in behind the grand homes of Bayshore Boulevard and had spent too much of my afternoon in it; I'd meant to devote that afternoon to the Salvador Dali museum over in St. Petersburg, but after I'd cleared the bookstore there was time to give Dali less attention than he probably deserved— and certainly less than in his lifetime he demanded. Then, in Chiefland where I'd stopped for a haircut (i.e., to eavesdrop at the town's sole barbershop), I'd dipped into one of the books I'd bought in Tampa and learned with a start that the author of *The Wilderness Coast* lived only about an hour north in the very curve of the panhandle. When I got out of the barbershop my head and especially my neck felt cool: that was the way the boys liked their hair done in Chiefland, I guessed. But I had become so intrigued with the writing of Jack Rudloe that I called him in Panacea and asked if I might stop by for a visit, warning that he was not to mistake me for an escaped felon with my shaved head.

A short, compact man with powerful sloping shoulders and great ham-sized hands showed up at my motel room that afternoon. Jack Rudloe at first glance appeared harried and disheveled, his T-shirt flopping over his stained khaki pants and his close-set eyes darting about as if he wanted to assess this situation but hardly had the time. Behind him his two small sons boiled out of his battered car and immediately took over the motel room, turning on the TV, jumping up on the king-sized bed, and reveling in the air-conditioned coolness. Sky and Cypress, Rudloe explained superfluously, just loved motels. From the way he said it and the glance he gave the boys, it was clear that love constituted a small rebellion against paternal values. And indeed it did prove difficult to get those two boys to give up their borrowed comforts and go home with us.

Home was in a grove of trees and set on high stilts so that the Rudloes could look out on Apalachee Bay. A sizable dock ran from the house out into those waters that were the essential workplace of Jack and his wife Anne who now greeted me in a frank, offhand way. She was busy just then with the boys' dinner, but when she had time to join us over drinks it was evident that she was a full partner in their work in marine biology, conservation, and the collecting of aquatic specimens for sale to medical schools, labs, and hospitals. While the boys bickered over dinner and a large part-Airedale wandered through the rooms dripping sandy water, Jack and Anne talked about their lives here and their work, and I wasn't long in discovering that they were far more interested in talking about the latter: the life of the sea and its marshy margins, they told me, was infinitely more absorbing than their own lives could ever be. I found this refreshing. As we talked, darkness came down on the bay. It wasn't like dusk, which is an accumulated thing that you can see in process. Here darkness happened with a heavy breathlessness as if the day had been snuffed, and at the moment when the light winked out a bird with a call like a chiding squirrel announced the diurnal change.

Later, the boys deposited for a few hours at a neighbor's, the three of us went down the road to a restaurant. The Oaks, I saw, had Jack's books prominently displayed at the cash register, and he was treated with the slightly exaggerated friendliness befitting the village's sole living author.

Anne said there was a Greek somewhere along the line of the family that owned the Oaks, and that maybe that accounted for their respect for literature. She was a lot more certain, though, that any menu item with the word "Greek" in it was a safe bet, and so it proved with my Greek grouper. I doubted, however, that either of the Rudloes was that much interested in cuisine. Earlier, when we'd left the motel with the boys in tow, Jack had stopped to deliver some bonnethead shark to a friend who'd once spent a year in Japan. Jack was interested to learn whether the bonnethead was sushi grade, but I felt his interest was much more speculative and intellectual than gustatory. Now the Rudloes ate their dinners, but it seemed to a confirmed gourmand that the meal was insignificant to them, was, in fact, only an occasion to talk about things that really counted. And what counted tonight was what counted every night and day—that marine world they spent their days and nights exploring. It was so various, so complex, so little understood that up against things like meals—or the synthetic comforts of motel rooms, for that matter—the latter were pitifully ephemeral.

Take the horseshoe crab, for instance, which the Rudloes had been studying for some years. Here was a creature that was a veteran of the earth when dinosaurs were tyros, that had existed when the earth as we now know it had been re-forming itself, the continents breaking apart and shifting into their present positions. And yet much about the horseshoe crab remained a mystery to human beings. No one, Anne Rudloe said, really knew one of the essential facts here, and that was how the horseshoe crab hatchlings emerged from their deep sandy nest and found the release of the sea. And what of the strange life of the toadfish, whose melodious whistles, seven to a minute, made up what to Jack Rudloe was a real song? These songs intensified from seven whistles to the minute to ten and then to twenty-five when an eligible female swam into proximity. Was this not a marvel, and was not the adaptability of the toadfish in itself another marvel? Here, Jack said, was a creature that could tolerate oxygen-depleted water to a degree almost unmatched and that was so tough it could be hooked, landed, and baked on a dock all day and still be alive at sundown. Down in Suriname, he told me, he had seen giant toadfish, fearsome of aspect and more than three feet in length. The Rudloes had also been studying electric ray fish and collecting them to send to laboratories where it is thought their electrical properties might eventually help in understanding the etiology of human brain disorders. What strange design of nature endowed the rays in the depths of the sea with the same energy that flashed in stormy skies was for them a source of daily wonder.

For Jack Rudloe there was above all the sea turtle, a creature of such mystery and power that when he talked about it I was reminded—and not for the last time during my visit—of Melville and his worshipful fascination with the whale. Jack appeared to regard the sea turtle as nothing less than a being the Life Force had put into the waters of the planet as a sign, as if that force were saying through the turtle "This is my mark. Heed it." "There is something about the sea turtle," Jack was saying with slow emphasis, "that I can't pin down. . . . Maybe I don't really want to. But I know it's there." He said he'd gotten interested in sea turtles through the work and encouraging enthusiasm of the late zoologist and teacher Archie Carr, who had studied sea turtles all over the world for many years. Carr, too, Jack claimed, had been convinced that there was a great deal more to sea turtles than met the Baconian, dissecting intelligence of scientists. How, for instance, did the gravid females determine the right beaches to nest on? No one really knew, despite years of study. Where did these females go in the twelve-day intervals between their nestings at these special beaches, and what was the biological significance of the hundred eggs the mothers deposited in each nest? Did the males travel to these beaches in company with the females to mate with them there, or did they arrive at the appointed places by another route? And why did the females arrive at these beaches in such terrific numbers—40,000 (!) ridley turtles once observed on a beach north of Tampico?

The turtle hatchlings represented further mysteries. Emerging from their subterranean nest and never having seen anything of the world, they went for the water with astonishingly little trial and error. Those that made it disappeared for a year. Where did they go? How could it be that there had never from anywhere in the globe been reports of turtle hatchlings at sea during what Jack described as their "missing year"?

And perhaps most intriguing of all was the matter of the sea turtle's long-distance navigational skills. How could these creatures, which even Jack admitted were rather simpleminded, find their ways across vast tracts of featureless sea to fetch up on favored beaches sometimes more than a thousand miles from the point of departure? For years, Jack told me, scientists had been tagging and releasing turtles and offering rewards to fishermen who would return the tags to the study centers. These experiments had established beyond cavil that the turtles could find their goals, no matter how tiny the beach or island or how far they had to swim to get there. "This has to be more than mere compass sense or imprinting," Jack said. Archie Carr wondered if there was some smell the creatures followed to their sacred rendezvous. Jack thought it might turn out that they aligned themselves with the earth's magnetic field. In recent years, he said, scientists had made the startling discovery that a number of aquatic animals did so. Analysis of some of these animals' brains revealed the presence of magnetic particles. Perhaps, Jack suggested, it was true what some had said, that the sea turtle had a "magnetic bone" in its head. But for him, this mystery led into the deeper waters of world mythology, and he for one wasn't at all afraid to take that plunge. Of course, some of the greatest scientists had learned from mythology—as Freud once observed to Einstein—but unless you were working at the very top of your profession, to talk seriously about mythological insights was to court the scorn of your colleagues. Jack said that wasn't a concern of his, that his concern lay with the mysteries of the sea turtle, not with the approbation of the contemporary scientific community. He had learned, he said, that the turtle, like the bear and the horse, was a major symbol in world mythology, that many peoples in various places spoke of a magic turtle rock that brought the turtles home. The rock was located on Florida's Atlantic coast; or it was on Mexico's Pacific coast; or at Tortuguero in Costa Rica, where with Jack's prodding Archie Carr had climbed Turtle Mountain in search of the magnetic, turtle-shaped monolith that not only oriented the incoming green turtles but the great globe itself. So the old people had said.

"The fishermen of Nicaragua," Jack said, "swore for years that they knew where the great Turtle Rock was on this island off Nicaragua. It was supposed to be a black magnetic rock. And yet when Archie Carr set foot on that island to find it, the rock disappeared forever. That's the disappearance of myth in the presence of science." He looked at me across the messy interval of our empty plates and glasses, the salt and pepper shakers—the solid, quotidian realities of this life—to ask with his eyes whether I believed such a disappearance actual or only apparent. And it was clear to me that for him Archie Carr's failure to find that Nicaraguan Turtle Rock said nothing about the validity of either myth or science.

What was not in doubt about sea turtles was the threat of extinction that hung over all seven genera. Jack, as I was to learn, was now deeply embroiled in the TED controversy, and this had made life very complicated for the Rudloes in this village where they had for years relied on the fishermen as informants and as helpers in the collection of marine specimens. The fishermen and especially the shrimpers were enraged by the TED regulations, and their fingers pointed at Jack and Anne as the nearest and most obvious examples of meddling environmentalists.

For years before the enforcement of the TED regulations Jack had tried to get the shrimpers and crabbers to release the turtles they'd inadvertently caught, and while these efforts had earned him a sufficient amount of redneck contempt, it was nothing compared to what he faced now.

Once, down at the Panacea docks, Jack had helplessly watched while the men had butchered a 780-pound leatherback, utterly oblivious to the mysterious dimensions it had for the small man watching who was still and forever an outsider to them, though he had lived among them more than thirty years. For the men the giant creature was just so many steaks, and when the butchering was finished one of them had contemptuously tossed Jack the turtle's penis, saying maybe Jack should take it home and find out with one of his experiments how it worked. But what Jack had remembered most about the incident was the way that leatherback had looked to him as it lay there awaiting its fate at the hands of humans. And sometime later, in a triumph of art over death, he had written these words in memory of the leatherback:

> Those seven longitudinal ridges that ran down the entire length of its carapace made it look even more streamlined and in a way, beautiful. Many call *Dermochelys* the lute turtle, because the raised ridges suggest the strings of a musical stringed instrument. It is said that the Greek gods of ancient times used the leatherback to make heavenly music. Hermes molded the lute after the shell of one he found on the banks of the Nile. And on Mount Parthenon the gods killed the venerated trunkback only when pressed by the need for a new instrument.
>
> No doubt as long as man has been on this planet he has made turtle music. Deep, mystical, and resonant sounds come from string instruments built out of tortoise shells. In Tangiers, beautiful mandolins are still fashioned out of tortoise shells by attaching the carapace to a long stem and stretching strings. Rattles, drums, lyres, and lutes, the turtle is a creature of music. During the green corn ceremony, Creek Indians dance around the town square making the shape of a giant turtle to bring rain for their crops. The Creek women wear box turtle shells filled with pebbles and rhythmically shake them with their quick steps to alert the great turtle spirit. And no doubt coastal people have sat on twilight beaches beating on the carapace of a big sea turtle that gave them nourishment to call up the spirits.
>
> Was this the great leathery lute that the gods strummed to make the most heavenly of music? Seeing it lying limply on the bottom of the boat in a pool of its own blood, I found it hard to believe. Yet perhaps when it was alive, swimming far, far out in that endless ocean, hundreds of miles from the nearest land, perhaps traveling up from the

Guianas or Trinidad, then perhaps it did produce music. The music of life, the open sea, and freedom.

When dinner and its talk were over at last and we'd picked up the boys and dropped them off at home where Anne would put them to bed, Jack drove me the short distance from the house to the Rudloes' Gulf Specimen company. We walked through the darkened offices to the collecting rooms where Jack snapped on the lights revealing the large vats and tanks in which various organisms sat, swam, and scuttled. Here were common bay scallops, blue crabs, arrow crabs, dwarf hermit crabs, sea urchins, northern sea horses, tropical plumed anemones, many of them ticketed for places like the Rochester Institute of Technology, a medical school in New Jersey, a college in Maryland, and Miami University at Coral Gables. Jack showed me through with a brisk casualness I took to be a defense protecting his consuming interest in all this life. We paused before one vat, and Jack reached in to pull out a whelk. "Here's something you might find curious," he said, turning the creature over in his hands. "The whelks found on this coast have a left-handed spiral, whereas the ones you find on the east coast have a right-handed one." He said he regarded the spiral as the fundamental signature of all life, remarking that it was found in shell forms, in DNA, in human fingerprints, in the patterns some aquatic organisms made in the water and on the beach. A few minutes later beside another vat he held a box crab at surface level, and I watched it pump its stream of water out into ever-widening whorls.

THE next morning in a hazy sun I was down at the docks to accompany the Rudloes on one of their collecting excursions into the Gulf. Aboard the cruiser were eight others, but they were different from the guest who did nothing but stand around and watch. These were students, volunteer students, all of them long out of undergraduate school, who went out on weekends with the Rudloes simply to observe the strange and marvelous specimens dredged up from the Gulf. The rest of the time they were investment brokers, educational administrators, housewives and mothers, real estate agents, and lawyers. During that long day every one of them, I found, exhibited a keen and unwavering interest in the process of collecting as well as in the specific identities of the specimens hauled in; even on the return to port, the specimens collected or discarded, and the Rudloes forward talking with the pilot, I saw some of these people back at the collecting vats, handling the specimens with a real reverence and talking to each other about them. Having at an earlier age done time as a teacher, I found this display of genuine intellectual curiosity remarkable.

The pilot was Steve Wilson, a mountain of a man who strained the capacities of the heavyweight swivel chair in which he rode. Affable and easy, with one of those clear tenor voices that always surprises you when it proceeds from such massiveness, he was good to talk with, having a ready flow of nautical discourse, rich with anecdote. While he took the cruiser out into deeper waters where Anne Rudloe thought the collecting might be fruitful, she gathered the students on the rear deck and talked with them in an informal but informed way about what she hoped to collect this day with net, scoop, and shovel. When at last Steve Wilson had gotten the cruiser out far enough and the net went over the side with a light splash, the students stood around the stern expectantly and Jack joined the group, amplifying what Anne had said about their goals for the day. Twenty minutes later the net was hauled up, choked with algae but filled also with all manner of sponges, sea horses, crabstar fish, and other organisms I heard identified but didn't note. The Rudloes picked through this first harvest, tossing usable specimens in the saltwater-filled vats and throwing the rest overboard. Then Anne patiently explained what each organism was, its salient characteristics, why there was a market for it with labs and med schools, and how the organism interacted with competing organisms. Always, I noted, she was careful to leave an ample margin for doubt, for surmise and mystery. There is much, her delivery told her students, that we simply don't know, but here's what we currently surmise.

The farther out we went into the Gulf, the farther down the collecting devices had to go and the more exotic the catches became in form and color, so that at last it was as if we were not on some stretch of our own globe but adrift in another sphere. We had for some time been well out of sight of land and there were now no other ships visible, though earlier we'd been in the company of shrimpers. The sky and sea out here were welded together in a monochromatic slate blue, and on the rear deck lay these gatherings of utterly unfamiliar organisms with all sorts of odd shapes, some of them inky black, others a brilliant red. The uninitiated landsman could have no idea where to begin to examine them or how to begin to guess at their anatomies and functions. Where were their mouths, where were their eyes? Did they even have them? Out here it was hard not to seriously entertain the commonplace conviction that *here* was the source and proper place of our wonder and our scientific investigations, the great seas of the globe, rather than those distant skies we are currently littering with astro-garbage and commercial vehicles, and glittering weaponry.

When we had gone out as far as a day's work could safely take us and port was a good three hours astern, Anne told Steve Wilson to take the cruiser in. Both Rudloes professed themselves satisfied with their catch, and it was obvious their students were. Jack and Anne went forward to talk with Wilson, and the students gathered around the vats to look, to handle, and to discuss. As for myself, I sat on a cooler in the shade of the cabin's overhang, thinking I might jot down as best I could some notes and impressions of the day. But with the slowly sinking sun and the steady undulation of the cruiser's homeward coursing I became captive of a private narcoleptic shroud. I wasn't asleep—my eyes were open—but I wasn't awake, either. What thoughts I had were mostly vague and unformed, embryos from the deep, but I remember feeling the thinness of the hull separating us from all that life rushing unseen beneath us, down there in those black and unsourced depths from which the strange specimens had earlier been gathered. Life on deck is what we are pleased to call "life on earth." Out here that seemed a terrifically shallow conception. I remember thinking, too, of my heroes Melville and Conrad and of the moody, introspective traits bequeathed them both by their years on the sea; of Conrad laboriously teaching himself to think and to write in English on those long, often harrowing voyages that took him from Venezuela to Sumatra; and of Melville's sense, recurrently expressed in *Moby Dick*, that our life on deck is a metaphor for our mortal existence and that though "in many of its aspects this visible world seems formed in love, the invisible spheres were formed in fright"; and of his character, black Pip, who fell overboard, "carried down alive to wondrous depths, where strange shapes of the unwarped primal world glided to and fro . . . and the miser-merman, Wisdom, revealed his horded heaps." I couldn't really tell about Anne Rudloe—she met the world in so practical and level a way—but I thought it little wonder that Jack was not only a marine biologist but also a mystic.

I HAD coffee with Jack the next morning in Sopchoppy, a neighboring village where he had an errand to run. He said that in the coming fall Cypress would be entering school here and that it was a rite of passage his father dreaded. "I hated school myself," Jack said, sipping his coffee and looking away, "so putting him in there is kind of like putting myself back in there." He told me he'd never done more than three months of college in two tries at it and that he remained unconvinced he'd really missed anything by being so completely self-taught—though he had also come to know that there were continuing professional penalties for his academic outlawry. He was, he said, threatening to many of those within the academy. "They can't figure out where I'm coming from," he said. "I don't have the pedigree, and yet there I am, so that bothers them a lot. And then I guess I'll have to admit I'm sort of a gadfly: I like to upset things somehow." In illustration, he used the issue of taxonomy. He could not, he claimed, see that a great deal had been accomplished by assigning names to things, though he knew that to do so was to establish a kind of control—as it was for Adam in the Garden. "Sometimes," he said, "when I do presentations at schools I don't let the kids identify anything. I put the specimens out there"—plunking his great hands, fingers spread, on the table—"and I tell them *not* to try to label but to *look*. There's a difference, though I don't seem able to make that point to the academics."

As for Anne, Jack said she got some of the same flak he caught, though this was mostly because her name was linked to his; she had her Ph.D. "But so many times," he went on, looking into his empty cup, "I'll find that her application for this grant or that one has failed because they can't label her, either. She isn't attached to a university, she isn't in there teaching regularly, and they resent that. Recently she applied for a study grant, and we heard from the inside that initially it had been turned down because her name was Rudloe. Then, at the second session of the tribunal, it came up again. 'We're not going to fund this thing: Rudloe's a loudmouth and a troublemaker.' 'But wait a minute,' someone else said. 'This doesn't have *Jack* Rudloe's name on it, it has *Anne's*.' This time at least, she got the grant—which she deserved all along."

From the Black Water Diner in Sopchoppy we drove out to the home of a couple Jack knew, where he was to pick something up. As we curled back along a deeply rutted sandy road to the house, Jack said he'd attended the couple's wedding out here some years ago. "A wood sprite was also in attendance," he said matter-of-factly. "During the ceremony, in back of the group that was standing there in the glade was this apparition of a young woman with long brown hair holding a bouquet of wildflowers. Someone took a picture of it, and I saw that photo with my own eyes. It was kind of hard to see, especially when they blew the shot up to get a better look, but it was there, all right. The bride told us she'd seen this same woman several times when she'd been out walking in the woods. The spirit seemed to want to keep her company, but whenever she'd look at it, it would disappear. But then, if she just looked out of the corner of her eye, she could see the spirit, or the sprite. Nowadays, in our ridiculous culture 'sprite' is the name of a soft drink and nothing more. The soft drink is the 'real thing.' "

The couple wasn't at home, so Jack asked if I'd like to take a short hike out into the hammock that lay behind the house, and we did that, walking single file into the tall grass. "This path is like my current involvement with fingerprints," Jack said over his shoulder, "except that in this case I know where the path leads. There, I don't. It seems I'm always getting into these investigations that don't necessarily lead anywhere—anywhere practical, that is. And after all, as Anne reminds me, I do have the responsibility to put food on the table. The sea turtle is one thing, and now there's this fingerprint business. I can't get it out of my mind that the spiral—and that's really what fingerprints are made up of—is the basic signature of life. There's something about all the whorls and spirals I see everyday, and then there's this whole business of DNA, that just grabs me in a way I can't really define. It's like I *have* to investigate these things. So I find myself up there at Tallahassee spending hours going through the literature on fingerprints and just getting myself in deeper and deeper."

We were now ourselves getting pretty deep into the hammock. To our left a small pond stood black and shining under the mounting sun. "What's going to come of all this, I don't know," Jack said, turning to face me. "Maybe nothing." He spread his hands wide, holding them out a little from his sides. "Years ago I saw this tape of Joseph Campbell, and he was telling Bill Moyers that now that he was an old man and at the end of his path of life he could look back and see that everything he'd done— every choice, every decision about which path to take—had been the right one for him. And that was because when he'd come to those decisions, those turnings, he'd always 'followed his bliss.' That was his advice: Follow your bliss. I suppose that's what I'm doing with this fingerprints thing, with the turtles, and really with everything else. I wish, though, I could see a practical end, not that I want to be Campbell at the end of my path. But I hope that when I do get there I'll be able to see that all my choices have been the right ones for me."

JACK thought I ought to hear for myself what the local shrimpers had to say about turtles and TEDs, so that afternoon we went down to the docks at Carrabelle. Outside Millender and Sons Seafood we stood chatting with a couple of shrimpers, surrounded by rusty fishing equipment, nets, oyster shells, rope, and the hot spring sun drenching everything. Things were more orderly and a good deal cooler up in the tiny office perched above the docks. There we had the company of James Sparks, a shrimper; Edward, another shrimper who had long assisted the Rudloes in their work; and Vance, the Millender company accountant. A hawk-faced female secretary typed and talked on the intercom while the air conditioner hummed and sweated and the talk swirled about her black beehive hairdo.

And the talk was of TEDs, most of it between Jack and Sparks (Sparky to everybody). The latter was a weathered, red-faced man in his forties, his teeth ground down to yellowed stubs, wearing rubber boots and a battered cap with the Millender logo on its front panel. He was clearly intelligent and witty, too, and he was just as clearly profoundly angry about the law requiring him to tow a device that he claimed would soon enough put him and the other commercial shrimpers out of business. Jack said he had to agree that contrary to government blandishments, the TEDs, whatever model was being used, did in fact cost the shrimpers a substantial portion of their catch.

"You're damned right it does," Sparky said with controlled heat, "and we aren't even the ones that're killing the turtles." Jack said he wasn't so sure about that, though now he added over the loud objections of Sparky and Vance that he himself had come to be less sure than he once had been that the shrimpers were chiefly responsible for the turtle kills that had mounted so alarmingly in recent years. "But," Jack said, "what we do know is that the turtles are found where shrimping's being conducted and that that's where a lot of the kills have been."

"Of *course* they're found there!" Sparky said scornfully. "That's where the food is, for Christ's sake!"

Jack said the turtles couldn't catch shrimp, especially ridley turtles, which had suffered the greatest mortality. Sparky said they could. "You environmental types yourselves have said they have that short burst of speed," he said, pointing his cigarette in Jack's face. "They can accelerate to thirty miles an hour, right? Well, that's fast enough to catch shrimp." Jack said he wasn't sure that was fast enough, thought it probably wasn't.

"And another thing," Sparky said, "when the shrimp get in that sea grass to hide, they can't maneuver in there, and the turtles can get 'em in there." Jack said nothing to this, only glanced over at me. I surely wasn't going to add anything.

"Well," Jack said after a tense pause, "I'll agree with you this far: that provision that says you have to drag TEDs in the bay but not outside it doesn't make any sense at all to me, because it's been in the deeper waters that most of the kills have been made, and that's where the majority of the turtles are normally found."

Sparky remained hotly adamant that the shrimpers weren't the primary killers of the turtles, that turtle kills in any case weren't significantly up, and that the whole issue had been created by the state's enormously powerful sport-fishing lobby. Echoing Yellowlegs Campbell, Sparky said there were "thousands more sport fishermen down here than there are commercial fishermen," looking my way to be sure I was getting the point. "And do you think they're making themselves heard up there?" gesturing with his head in the direction of the state capital at Tallahassee. "You know damn well they are! They have more money and are better organized than the commercial fishermen'll ever be, and their plan is simple: it's to put the commercial guys outta business. And they're gonna do it, you mark my words." He drew glumly on his cigarette, his blue eyes squinting in the flare of the coal and looking out the window toward the Gulf.

"See," he said to me in a slightly softened tone, "we're marginal already. Seventy percent of the shrimp sold in America is foreign— Japan, Peru—and now they're beginning to farm shrimp, so they won't ever miss our thirty percent." Jack cut in to say that commercial shrimp farming wasn't yet economically viable. "It will be," Sparky said, "it will be. This is the same deal as the redfish. Then it was, 'Oh! the commercial fishermen are fishing the redfish out! *Save* the redfish!' Save the redfish for the sport fishermen. So now you can't fish for redfish, and there're more redfish than ever. And they're farmin' redfish now, so they won't miss our catch there, either. The plan is to turn this whole state into a total tourist state. That's a fact! Then the real people that live here and have to work here'll have to move somewheres else or go on welfare. I said the same thing the other night on TV when they did that interview on my boat." He interrupted himself to ask if we would like to see a tape of that segment, and we said we would.

Sparky got on the phone to his wife. "Darling," he said into the mouthpiece but playing broadly to the tiny roomful, "I have some 'high officials' here who want to come over to the house to see that TV interview. Actually, they're both ERs, but can you stand 'em? Good. We'll be over then in a few minutes, and if you'll get that thing ready, why, we'll look at 'er." There was a pause while Mrs. Sparks said something. Then Sparky responded: "You know what? You're a pretty good ol' gal. I don't care what your boyfriend says." He winked at us and hung up.

Just at this point Farris Millender entered his office and took the seat his secretary had vacated. His shirt was open exposing a sizable paunch that ballooned above his pewter belt buckle with its Marlboro logo. His thick black hair was combed straight back and, like his deeply tanned face, it was shining with sweat. He settled himself in the chair, pulled a cigarette from his shirt pocket, lit up, and puffed. Jack and Sparky went back to talking turtles, and Millender listened a few minutes in silence, puffing on his cigarette and looking from one man to the other. Edward sat silent in a corner of the room, right under the laboring air conditioner, his jaws working steadily on his gum. Vance had dropped out of the contest, leaving the field to Jack and Sparky, but now Millender weighed in, picking up Sparky's diatribe against the federal government.

"We've seen the good times in this country," he intoned heavily from behind a small cloud of smoke, "and now we're going to see the bad ones. Here you've got a government that has the biggest part of its payroll going to pay its own workers. What does that tell you?" He was looking at me with a hard, inquisitive stare. "And here you've got a government that spends its time harassing honest men trying to make a living when it ought to be out there going after all those dopers. Don't you think they could stop this dope thing if they really put their energy into it?" He scoffed at his own question. "Of course they could! But they spend their time and resources and *our* dollars doing damn fool things like this turtle thing!

"You know what America originally was?" He was looking my way again, and there was nowhere to hide. I tried to look steadily back as best I could and shook my head in the negative. "America was escape from taxes. That's why they came here in the first place: to escape taxes. Now what we got? Where's the *Mayflower*?" he asked, turning suddenly a bit playful. "Where's the *Mayflower* now that we really need her? Get me on the *Mayflower*! I want to go to Jay-pan!" His smile was a very small one.

With all the state and federal regulations and the normal, everyday overhead, shrimping, he said, wasn't going to pay. "And don't you think that's an accident. They don't *want* it to pay. They know that between imports and [shrimp] farming they can make up any shortfall in the catch. They want this state turned over to tourists, to the sport fishermen: that's where the money is, and that's where they're going to put their money." Millender took another deep drag and snubbed out the butt, glancing out as he did so over the roofs of his sheds and warehouse. "I'm looking here at a debt of over a million dollars I got tied up in this business," he said, turning back and looking again at me, "with very little chance of ever paying it off." Then he swung abruptly in Jack's direction.

"All this fuss about turtles!" He snorted. "Did you ever think you might be better off without the turtles?" He drew another cigarette and lit it. "What if the dinosaurs were back? Do you think you'd be here? You wouldn't. The earth is a better place without the dinosaurs."

"Oh," Jack said quickly, "it isn't at all the same thing. But this earth wouldn't be the same without the turtles. Maybe it wouldn't even be the earth without the turtles. Did you ever hear that some people believe that the earth is supported on the back of a turtle?" There was a slight shifting of bodies in the office, a turning of heads as the men looked at one another, as if they were silently asking, "What are we gonna do with this crazy fucker?" But what Jack had done was to move the talk onto another plane, one where he, for a moment, anyway, had the higher ground. What interested me was that he'd had the brass to say such things to these hard-handed men in a highly charged setting; that and the fact that the men respected Jack enough to let him say them without booting him out of the office and off the premises. They simply looked at him in silence while trying to come at his last remarks.

Sparky broke the silence to say that his wife would be waiting for us, and that ended this session of the debate. Millender led the way out of the office and down the long narrow flight of stairs, still saying, over his shoulder now, "Yes, we've seen the good days, and we should be grateful we had 'em, too. We did have 'em, God knows. So now, let's see what the bad days look like."

Sparky lived only two minutes from the docks, and his wife was waiting for us at the front door. "He hasn't fixed my porch," she called out cheerfully enough, "so you got to watch where you step. Don't step there! Don't step there, either!" She laughed as Jack and I tried to dodge the porch's mine field of weak spots. Inside the shadowy, cluttered living room she had the TV and VCR ready to go, and as soon as we were seated she snapped on the power and we watched the tape made the previous day by a Tallahassee TV crew that had gone out with Sparky on his boat and had spent the night filming the trawling process. Sparky had done a very creditable job on camera, appearing direct, candid, intelligent— and angry about the TEDs; in short, he was a worthy representative of his craft. He showed the TV crew the harvest of shrimp he was able to make dragging the TED and then showed them his more ample catch when he wasn't required to drag it. "This thing is going to put a lot of smalltime shrimpers like me out of business," he claimed, staring into the camera's eye. "Some of us will try to get by, doing our own little thing, for as long as we can. Others of us, the ones that can, will go into something else. But the ones that can't, they'll go on welfare, and they'll be paid for by the people who pass these fool laws." At the end of the five-minute segment, Sparky was shown speaking to the off-camera reporter: " 'Endangered species,' " he intoned rhetorically. "You got your camera on him right now." Mrs. Sparks ran the tape back, and we watched it a second time. Then Sparky accompanied us back to the docks where we'd parked. Taking leave of his wife, he hollered over his shoulder, "Don't wait up for the shrimp boats, honey, I'm comin' home with the crabs."

On the way back to Panacea, Jack was having further dialogue on turtles and TEDs, this time with himself. He was becoming convinced, he said, that the federally approved TEDs did cut down significantly on the catch, and at the same time he had growing doubts that the shrimpers bore primary responsibility for turtle kills. Clearly they bore *some*, but whether it was a high enough percentage to require the use of the TEDs—this he was beginning to wonder about. Maybe the initial correlations between shrimping activities and turtle kills had not been as conclusive as he and other turtle protectors had thought. "These kinds of questions," he said at last with a kind of resignation, "will make me an outcast when I voice them, and it won't make any difference to the environmental community that I've fought so many bloody battles for them. All they'll see is that I've become a traitor. And some of them are going to say it's because I use shrimpers to help me in my work. So, now I guess I'll be a traitor to both groups." He shrugged his heavy shoulders. "I guess that's just the way it'll have to be. How can I say I believe wholeheartedly in the TED business when I'm coming to have these questions about it?"

I had a question of my own, niggling though it was. "Jack," I asked, "when Sparky told his wife we were coming over, he said we were a couple of 'ERs.' What's an ER?"

"Educated Rectum," Jack said.

THAT night I had dinner again with the Rudloes, this time at their place, and afterward Jack took me out to the end of his dock. Cypress came along, holding on to his father's hand, and the dog, too, panting in the warm, close darkness. Nighttime, Jack explained to me, was the time of awakening for the creatures of the sea, which now came out of their burrows to dance in the water—brittle stars and pink shrimp and mullet and plankton that made the water glow when the mullet swam through. In the ensuing silence I could hear the hissing and beeping of invisible life all around us. It was a great, brothy sort of sound, rich, mixed, and deep. Only a fool, I thought, could fail to recognize that here was authentic contact with the primal stew. I wondered aloud whether the small boy standing quietly next to his father and holding his hand could sense something of the mystery so obvious here, so visible in the phosphorescence of the wavelets in which the thousands of creatures danced.

"Oh, I think he does sense something of it," Jack said with what I found a surprising softness. "I don't think he could live out here the way we live without sensing something of it. What he can't really do yet is verbalize it. But then we don't do very well at that ourselves." Maybe, at this moment at least, there wasn't any need.

The next day as I took leave of the Rudloes I remembered that when I'd first set eyes on Jack at the motel I'd thought there was something odd about his appearance, something unkempt and even asymmetrical. When I said good-bye to him in the grove in front of his house, I thought him one of the handsomest men I'd ever met.

SUMMER

ONE WAY TO DRIVE THE COAST ROADS of Florida's panhandle from Panama City to the state line is to buy a few beers and then pick up a sack of fresh-fried chicken gizzards. Even if it's deep summer, as now it was, you must also open your car windows to get the heat's full blast and the powerhouse aromas that arise, commingling, from petroleum plants, petrochemical producers, and wood-processing installations. If you were to drive this in air-conditioned comfort with Diet Coke and a package of trail mix, you might as well be anywhere else. So my first stop after clearing the Panama City airport was a tiny Mom & Pop beachside package store.

It was the end of August. Mom and Pop were sitting on the shallow gallery, partly protected from the sinking sun but not at all from the noisome blasts of the hurrying cars on Route 98. They could have saved themselves from this continuous assault by going inside the store and closing its door: I could see the sizable air-conditioning unit that hung at one side of the gallery. But no. One look at their faces told you they would rather suffer the heat and the carbon monoxide than the shuttered silence of each other's company inside. This, the grim set of their faces said, is our life, *and we like it just this way.*

You couldn't, I learned, buy anything less than a twelve-pack from Mom and Pop. Not four cans, nor even the conventional six-pack. I could understand—sort of—their not wanting to break a six-pack: it was becoming standard practice over much of the U.S. But the sanctity of the twelve seemed excessive, and I said so. Mom flared, the thin gray flanges of her nostrils dilating while her lips receded until they looked like an old wound across her face. If I didn't like company policy, I could just take my bidness on down the road. At which point I should have done so, except that, unbidden, up from the murky recesses of my neural garbage heap, came images of preschool, kindergarten, and grade-school marms: those prim, bespectacled, black-clad ladies with stout laced shoes whose idea of education was Order and who, God knew, had done their best with the froward brat I was. I knew whom I was speaking to here, however different her line of work now was, and so I foolishly persisted. Surely the sale of a six-pack beat no sale at all? Not a bit. Mom arose to her full, diminutive height, and I stood below her in the parking lot, thus uncannily reproducing the same physical relationship of teacher and little student. My neck was beginning to glow, even though I knew this was ludicrous. Yet I felt in the grip of a tide that was pulling me out into the deeps of the past when all I wanted at the moment was a few cans of beer. And maybe Mom herself was similarly gripped; maybe she was remembering my archetype even as I recognized hers.

Pop saved the situation, arising without a word to enter the store and ring up the sale of a six-pack. I gratefully took it, reaching over the counter filled with the usual offerings of such places—pickled eggs, beef jerky, small cellophane bags of peanuts, jars of sausage suspended in liquid like lab specimens in formaldehyde. Our eyes met briefly in the gloom, but I couldn't read what his were saying, and maybe I wasn't meant to.

Twenty minutes later I had a sack of hot fried gizzards in my lap next to the beer, the grease spots already beginning to show gray against the bag's crisp white, and was on my way out of Panama City, Mom already forgotten, and my mind instead on an anecdote of a friend who had once endured a summer working in a Panama City oil storage terminal. The only thing in town that smelled worse than the terminal, he said, was the paper mill. "I lived in a really cheap hotel that backed on a bayou," he recalled, "and when I'd get in my room at night, first thing I'd do is spray bug killer all around the walls about a foot below the ceiling. Then I'd hit the lights, jump into bed, and listen to the roaches begin to lose it on the wall and drop off onto the floor. They'd spin and flutter there, making a noise like a tambourine until they died. It was my lullaby that summer. But later, in the middle of the night, if you had to go to the can— barefoot, of course—you encountered the roaches again. My job was cleaning out the insides of the storage tanks, and I thought the air in there was probably lethal. When I look back on it, though, I guess the bug spray was worse. Week nights I'd be way too tired to do anything except eat and go to bed in the roach warren. Weekends I'd go to the movies. I'd go to the same show until they changed it. That summer *The Graduate* came out, but then *The Green Berets* with John Wayne came to town and by popular demand stayed a month."

I and my movable feast quickly left Panama City behind and headed for the new hamlet of Seaside, about halfway between Panama City and Fort Walton Beach. Looking out on the miles of haphazard development that lay between Panama City and the turn for Seaside, sipping beer that quickly lost its cool, and steadily dipping into my sack of gizzards, I successfully blotted out the depressingly undistinguished landscape that looked as if it might vanish in a stiff blow or else fall down of its own weak accord and mused instead on the state of mind of the old conquistadores who had coasted blindly along this very stretch in 1528, expecting at any moment to see signs announcing their entrance into the harbor at Pánuco and the safety of Christian civilization. This was the Narvaéz expedition that had departed from Cuba in the spring of 1527 and that by the fall of the year following had degenerated into a gang that no longer looked for gold and glory but only deliverance. But Pánuco was in reality a long way off—about 1,800 miles along this curving coast at what is now Tampico, Mexico—and each day as the half-naked men bobbed along here in their improvised open barges, their feet cut to shreds by shells, their armor cast aside as a terrible mockery of their needs, their spirits sank lower and lower until around Choctawhatchee Bay they must have been right at water level. Near present-day Pensacola a hurricane blew in, hurling the flimsy barges away from the coast and into the raging Gulf. "None of us doubted," wrote Cabeza de Vaca in his official chronicle of the expedition, "that his death would come at any minute."

Somehow they survived and drifted back toward the Mississippi coast, battered, terrified, and now bereft of all hope. Some historians think one or another of the barges may have fetched up on one of the barrier islands in the Mississippi Sound—Horn Island is mentioned as a possibility—before they came to a deltaic promontory "on the other side of which flowed a vast river," as Cabeza recalled this sighting of the Mississippi. And here the expedition came completely asunder, the governor and his barge being separated from the others, the chain of command severed, and a bitter wind raking the huddled survivors. Out of a land force of around three hundred men there were left at last but four who went ashore near what is now Galveston to melt there into the coastal tribes, into the land they had thought to subdue. In all the literature of bad trips in the New World there are very few to rival that of the Narvaéz expedition. It made even the thought of a summer in Panama City seem rather idyllic in comparison.

When I arrived at Seaside it was late afternoon. The sun was partly obscured by huge heavy clouds it had colored rose and mauve and jasmine. The Gulf seemed supine under the clouds and the heat, and indeed everything else seemed stilled as if awaiting the great gradual change of season, summer having done all it could and come now to a last, heavy ripeness before decay. The hamlet of Seaside itself fully partook of this end-of-the-season air. A suite of pastel wooden houses with deep shady galleries and glinting tin roofs adorned with widow's walks, it looked almost deserted with but a few vehicles in the office parking lot and none visible on the wide brick streets.

Seaside was the creation of an Alabama-born businessman named Robert Davis who, like old Ponce, Cyrus Teed at Estero, and uncounted others, found the unpopulated reaches of Florida's Gulf coast filled with Utopian promise. This night I was to be Davis's guest in a charming robin's-egg-blue house I had all to myself and, later, at his home for dinner. After strolling about the dead-quiet streets, watching the evening news on my TV, and testing out the solitary pleasures of my front porch, I arrived at the Davis home, a long, high structure that arose with an understated majesty from among the shining newness of its neighbors.

I might have been a trifle early since for a few minutes my only welcome was the piercing, incessant barking of Bud, the family dachshund, whom I could see bouncing up and down just inside the door. At last Mrs. Davis appeared, clad in white short shorts that set off her tan trim legs. She smiled brilliantly and led me into the kitchen where something temptingly Italian simmered on the commercial-quality range. Bud followed on his stubby legs, his tail switching like an electric wand, but for the moment my lavish love of dogs was taking a backseat as Daryl Davis poured some chardonnay and commenced a conversation that steered a beguiling course from the witty to the friendly to the disarmingly candid. I was here to talk with Robert Davis about his version of Utopia, but this was a more earthly kind of paradise, and, charmed by Mrs. Davis's beauty and presence, I took great, unseemly gulps of my wine. It was momentarily disappointing when Robert Davis finally appeared, but maybe he was used to being something of a letdown when preceded by his wife.

Though a native of Birmingham, Davis had been schooled—and radicalized, it turned out—at Antioch and Harvard, and when he inherited eighty acres of scrub, dunes, sea oats, and sand from his grandfather in 1979, he yearned to make something more of his bequest than simply a buck. What exactly, he was telling me now, he didn't know. He felt some obligation to seize upon his opportunity here, to "improve" his bit of coastline. But at the same time he felt an obligation to be true to his own experience, as a student, as an American with emotional as well as intellectual ties to his culture's republican traditions. He had seen the newer developments along Florida's west coast and panhandle, felt their heartless vacuities, and as a counterweight he had felt the communal solidness of the older, relatively undisturbed small towns of Florida, Alabama, and Georgia where life and work remained in intimate proximity and where the residents interacted daily. These places had heart, and Davis became determined that he would create such a place, a place that would, he said, "sort of stand suburbia on its head. Suburbia as we've known it is obsolete and probably has been for some time. We just don't recognize that yet, and so we go on building them." For while the suburbs provided the illusion of community over against the anonymity of the metropolis, in reality, Davis claimed, they were little more than atomized aggregates of bedrooms, and this to the precise degree that they were separated from shops, marketplaces, workplaces, and schools. The typical suburbanite, he said, was compelled to spend increasing amounts of time in the car, driving to work, driving to shops, chauffeuring the kids. And the greater the amount of that car time, the greater the felt need for rest, for privacy at home, until the suburb had become a place where little was shared except carefully segmented space.

Together with a husband-and-wife team of architects Davis planned a fundamentally different kind of community, one whose layout and building code fostered ("forced" was a word that came to mind that night and subsequently, though I remain uncertain of its appropriateness) a sense of sharing a good deal more than physical space. Here shops carry staples as well as delicacies so that driving to stores becomes an option, not a necessity. Here, too, are community rooms for meetings and entertainment, a long, beautiful community beach, a community restaurant, a P.O., even a community newspaper, *The Seaside Times*, that prints "All the News That Washes Up on the Beach." Each of the more than three hundred homes of Seaside must have a porch that measures at least half the length of the structure's front. No ornamental gimcrack here, either: these porches are meant to be functional, commodious affairs that people really use. They must be at least eight feet deep to allow for sitting and visiting and for the sheer visibility of the house's occupants. Such porches, Davis believes, are an essential part of neighborliness. So, too, is the intimacy of porch to obligatory picket fence that fronts the street: no more than sixteen feet of space so that porch sitters and passersby may easily converse.

Though the Davises' house and those surrounding it were certainly sumptuous in an arty sort of way and even the narrow guest house I was staying in was beautifully and expensively appointed, the beginnings here had been modest. As a kid, Davis had seen the area and its characteristic crackerbox houses: "a porch, kitchen, and dormitory space with cloth dividers," as he described them. Davis moved a couple of these to his property and built another one. "But then," he said, leaning back from his plate, "people wanted things more elaborate." Among the elaborations he mentioned were television sets and air-conditioning. The sizes of the houses and the refinement of their interiors had also taken great leaps. At first Davis had envisioned a TV-less community where "people could learn to relax and genuinely be together instead of existing around the enforced intimacy of the TV set. But we learned there are just some things people think they can't live without, and TV and air-conditioning are some of them." Soon to come in as well were solid brick streets to replace the vernacular dirt roads with oyster-shell borders.

Davis's original building code remains in force, but there was little he could do, he said, to oppose the increasingly lavish styles of the houses being built. And in any case, he claimed, he was not unduly upset about this. The original concept, he said, remained intact. Many of the newer houses, though, have back porches as well as the obligatory front ones, and so even here suburban-style privacy begins to intrude on the concept of neighborliness. Nor was this all. Except for the Davises and their employees, the residents of Seaside were even more distanced from their places of work than ever. Davis said Seaside drew the bulk of its residents from people living within a nine-hour driving radius—"from Memphis into Texas." The work was in all those far-flung places. Here there was only play beside the quiet Gulf, so that maybe all Robert Davis had really done was to create a retreat where you didn't have to drive anywhere if you didn't want to but could instead relax in a handsome, intelligently planned resort.

As a dream, Seaside was by no means ignoble, and it certainly was infinitely better than the prosaic and often meretricious visions manifest in the developments found all over the state, where the imaginative apex was reached in the design of the golf course and the comprehensiveness of the security system. But as I gazed up from the Davises' dinner table into the broad, open second story and the row of pith helmets than ran along one wall, I couldn't escape the feeling that Seaside in all its newness, its intelligent sensitivity to human patterns, was kin to that quiet, steadily decaying husk of Utopia at Estero and that like it the reality of the hope already lay in the past. "We started out small, too," Robert Davis was saying, raising one hand in a gesture toward the house's spacious interior, "but here we are with a big house just like everybody else."

IN the nacreous morning Seaside wore the same hushed, end-of-the-season air it had at evening. The Bermuda grass lawns sparkled under the new sun and the sprinklers. The Modica Market wasn't open yet, but the papers from Panama City and Montgomery were racked up inside vending machines. A small Japanese-made maintenance truck rolled quietly down Seaside Avenue, two bronzed young men in ball caps in its cab, their well-muscled arms hanging out the windows. I strolled down toward the water, passing the outdoor marketplace Daryl Davis managed much of the year. At the East Ruskin Beach Pavilion there were showers with alabaster and nickel handles and a long, grace-ful ramp of weathered wood sloping down to the beach, whose sand this morning was a blinding, virginal white. Already at this early hour wood-and-canvas chairs had been placed under sea-blue umbrellas, awaiting the pleasure of what few Seasiders had yet to depart for the real world of traffic, commerce, and irreversible anomie. The Gulf rolled in as or-dered in small, perfectly marcelled wavelets in which the musing bather could spy schools of minnows. If you waded out a bit farther and then submerged looking eastward into the light, the view through the salty flux was marvelous.

A tempting surrender, this. Visions of a quiet leisure almost Euro-pean in feel stole over me, and I saw myself ensconced here for the fall with a bag of books, newspapers, writing materials; clad in voluminous creamy flannels with big trouser cuffs, a jacket, maybe even a foulard. I wished suddenly for a volume of Thomas Mann but settled instead for a bookless, aimless stroll westward along the beach.

Several hundred yards on I came upon a woman whom I shall call

Nancy, though this was not the name she gave. Since she never stood up during our chance encounter it was hard to estimate her height, but she must have gone a good five ten, and as they used to say in the old gumshoe scripts, "she was definitely easy on the eyes"—deep tan, long, sun-bleached hair, everything. But after this unlooked-for gift from the sea what caught my eye were two volumes of Martin Heidegger that lay among the cigarettes, sun cream, lighter, and pocketbook next to the beach towel on which she lay. I tried quickly to summon up a ghost of a memory from an undergraduate philosophy course of what Heidegger had been about, but all that would come was an image of myself falling into the little nothingness of sleep over the impenetrable pages of a paperback having something to do with Being.

"Heidegger was a Nazi," I said.

"So what?" she came back, glancing up from the blue page of a letter she was writing. "So was Nietzsche, and probably we should throw in Wagner. How much of the last century and a half do you want to throw out to scrub it up?"

I took this as a kind of invitation to sit down; I was already beginning to feel awkward standing over her. "Oh," I said then, "I don't mean proto-Nazi. I mean a real, honest-to-God Nazi who made speeches for Hitler."

"He made a couple, that's all," Nancy said, laying her ballpoint on her interrupted correspondence and shifting sideways onto one elbow to face me from behind her modish shades. "And anyway, there are plenty of other icons who were about as much into that as he was, and not just in Germany: Konrad Lorenz, the kindly lover of dogs and geese, Maurice Chevalier, Lindbergh, Jung maybe. Lotsa blame to go around. Lots." I was afraid she was going to ask what my point was because I really had none other than to have some sort of a conversation with so striking a woman who carried her Heidegger with her to the beach. But she must have known that and so forbore the question. Reaching for her cigarettes, she asked if I minded if she smoked, but the question was clearly rhetorical, and I said I didn't.

"I have cigarettes, and I have funny cigarettes," she said now, rummaging in a flip-top box. "Want one?" I thought of appropriating the line of a friend to whom I had once put a similar question and who had declined, saying he had no intention of ever putting anything in his mouth that was on fire. But all I said was, "Neither, thanks." She shrugged and lit up a funny cigarette, sank onto her back, and blew a breath of grass toward the sky.

Nancy was from Montgomery, she told me, and was down here

staying at the home of a relative. She had been here since April, which accounted, I supposed, for the deep evenness of her tan and also that air she gave of owning this particular spot of beach.

"Wasn't Zelda Fitzgerald from Montgomery?" I asked, trotting out another of my stable of hackneyed conversation starters.

"A Sayre," she said, giving the family name after the custom of the region where such things are still important. "Zelda was a twit." She took another hit and balanced one long, lovely leg atop the crooked knee of the other.

"That's surprising to hear," I said. "I mean, hardly a day goes by without some new publication coming out about her. I thought we'd just about arrived at the point where it had been decided that Fitzgerald cannibalized her and her imagination, that if it hadn't been for her, he wouldn't have had anything at all to say. And if it hadn't been for him, *she* would have been the Fitzgerald we knew and admired." I mentioned the parallel phenomena of Frida Kahlo/Diego Rivera and Camille Claudel/ Auguste Rodin.

"Except they were different," she claimed, "because when it came to the truly deep shit they had substance. Zelda didn't. She got in way over her head, and when she realized that, her response was to decide she'd always wanted to be a ballerina!" She snorted in contempt and blew the thin smoke out with her next words. "That would be sorta like you at your age"—she gave me a quick once-over from behind her shades, and I inwardly winced, imagining the consequence of her appraisal— "deciding you really wanted to be a trapeze artist. Pretty silly, huh?" I had to agree. But she had only a slightly better opinion of Fitzgerald and his work. Nor did she care for fiction in general, observing that "to the extent that they ask to be taken seriously most novels are very disappointing. And if they aren't supposed to be serious, why are you readin' 'em?" Her thing was philosophy, which until last year she had been studying in graduate school. She looked slightly older than the grad students I remembered. I judged her to be within three years of thirty on either side, and I was wondering whether, Zelda-like, she, too, had been consumed by a tardy enthusiasm. "But then," she was telling me now, "I seemed to be getting into some pretty deep shit myself, so I dropped out.

"This is about as good a place to be a dropout as I know of, don't you think? Fact is, nobody knows what to do with me, so I'm kinda stashed here for a while while everybody tries to figure out what next. It's quiet, clean, everything's taken care of, nobody hassles you. And speaking of Nazis, how about these folks?!" She laughed a short, harsh two-note laugh, "Ha-*hah!*" and sat up to take another shallow hit. "This must be the way Hitler and what's-his-name . . . Speer! imagined their future Nazi paradise: everything planned, right down to the exact dimensions of the house you live in. That's the kind of freedom they're selling, right? I mean, the anxiety of options is removed for you, so you're free to think about the things that really matter." She laughed her short laugh again and snuffed the stub of the joint in the sand, observing then that she wasn't sure that sort of freedom had been productive of any particularly original thoughts among the Nazis—or even if thinking about things that really mattered was itself such a good idea.

In her own case, she wondered whether thinking about existential matters had been good for her. Heidegger began to come back just a little for me now, and I asked whether that hadn't been a concern of his. But it turned out that what she had in mind was the unanswerable question the philosopher had raised: that since Nothingness would seem to be a more logical state than Being, why is there Anything at all? I said I could see, sort of, how such a question might prove troubling to a graduate student for whom there were enough profoundly puzzling matters such as the Byzantine designs of academic programs and the inscrutable cruelty of those who administered them. Maybe then thinking such thoughts led you finally to achieve a kind of academic Nothingness by dropping out?

She laughed again, shook her shining hair, and flipped over onto her stomach. "Heidegger," she said over her shoulder, "also said that in the face of such matters it's characteristic of us to talk bullshit. It isn't much of a defense against existential terror, but I guess it's better than nothing."

GULF SHORES, Alabama, has for some years enjoyed its reputation as the Capital of the Redneck Riviera, and certainly the four-lane stretch of Route 59 that leads you there from Foley is tacky enough to answer to anybody's idea of what such a region should look like. It would give any portion of Highway 1 in the Keys a good run for its money, for here was another bristling jungle of billboards crying the seaside pleasures just ahead and an uninterrupted string of businesses selling everything from margaritas to life rafts.

But the town of Gulf Shores itself was quiet now, Labor Day being just past and the weekend revelers gone back to get ready for college or for another type of seasonal work. The stores still emptily advertised their fun wear. The Margaritaville Bar announced the finals of the "Miss Sol Bikini Contest," but the place looked so shuttered I guessed they hadn't bothered to change the marquee from some time ago. At a neighboring watering hole the sign said a group called Split Decision was appearing nightly, but inside its Egyptian blackness it didn't look as if anything would ever happen in here again. A bartender and his single customer watched a Cubs-Phillies game and muttered about the Cubs' chances in the National League East.

From an upper-story room of the Quality Inn on the beach I watched sunset on the Gulf, the combers turning from blue-green to gray and the last of the mostly middle-aged bathers trooping in with beach towels wrapped about their middles. Below me at poolside the Miller Lite sign began to take on a pronounced glow. When it was true dusk I went out for a drive about town.

As the Capital of the Redneck Riviera, Gulf Shores was said to be an occasionally violent place, and cruising the beachfront and then the backcountry marinas like Bear Point where I stopped for a beer that might momentarily disguise my stranger's curiosity, I felt there was substance to this rumor. The bar at Bear Point was crowded—mostly men with a few women who appeared to be wives—as were the dinner tables. And though everyone I noticed was friendly if a trifle loud, it felt to me as if it wouldn't take too much to whip this bunch into a slugging, bottle-slinging temper. Maybe I was being misled by the plethora of bull necks and bare, bunchy arms in evidence or the narrow flatness of eyes that looked as if they were saying, "Whatever it takes." But when I considered the volatile mix of sun, sea, booze, and exposed young flesh endemic to Gulf Shores, I thought it likely that things here might have a way of getting out of hand, that trifling differences would be taken outside and quickly settled.

At Cotton's, a restaurant where I scribbled in my notebook and had some indifferently prepared seafood, I asked my waitperson about the town's unofficial name.

"Yes, it's called that," said Allyson Jones. She was from nearby Foley and off and on attended Faulkner Junior College. "But a few years ago they stopped calling it the 'Redneck Riviera,' and started calling it the 'American Riviera.' I guess they didn't want to scare people off." I thought I ought to go slow here and not raise a wake. You could easily enough go up on Boston's Beacon Hill, ask someone there if that wasn't the Capital of Waspdom, and get a proud affirmative, like as not. It was another thing, though, to ask someone if they lived in redneck heaven. So I decided to go the longer way around and asked Allyson Jones to take me through the seasons of Gulf Shores.

"Beginning in the winter, we get the snowbirds. They come down from, oh, Michigan—up north there. At that time of year it only averages about sixty degrees here, and it's too windy for them to sit on the beach, but still it's cheaper and probably more comfortable for them to come down here and put on their sweatpants and fish than it is to pay their fuel bills up north. They come in here and take up tables and read their newspapers and drink coffee. Then when their bill comes and it's three-fifty, they complain because they didn't realize they've drunk up three pots of coffee or whatever.

"Along about late March things start to pick up. Spring breaks begin, and they keep on going, oh, about three, four weeks. The schools get out at different times, and, well, it just keeps going. Mostly it's kids from Alabama schools—Auburn, Alabama, Southern Alabama—but the last two years we've gotten more, it seems like, from the north. Maybe they heard what you heard." She laughed lightly. "Anyway, it's crazy here then. They hire extra help everywhere—extra waiters, extra bartenders, extra police, extra everything. If you want to know why this is called the Capital of the Redneck Riviera, the place you want to see is the Flora-Bama Bar in spring. It's just down the road here about two miles, just a hole in the wall. But you can get anyone in there from Ronald Reagan to Kenny Stabler to, you know, bikers. They have the Mullet Toss Contest in March where they see how far they can throw a mullet. They'll have five, six hundred people [a night] there on the big weekends. They'll have two, three hundred people there just on the back deck that hangs out over the water. I don't work there because it's too rough. Too many things happen over there.

"Well, along into May things are good here. May, we do three-fifty, three seventy-five dinners a night, but then it begins to slack off some. Most of the business gets to be weekends, and they're mostly Alabama people. They tend to be pretty conscientious about keeping their money in state. We get a few from Louisiana when the beaches are muddy. Some from Georgia. Not many from Florida—they tend to go to Fort Walton. Things are really flat then from after Labor Day through the middle of December. Then we close down for two weeks. There's just nothing happening. But then we start getting the snowbirds again, and so it goes." She smiled.

In this recitation I hadn't heard any mention of the rednecks who were said to make Gulf Shores their capital, and this seemed as good a time as any to ask who they were. Allyson Jones paused briefly and glanced about the dining room with its mostly empty tables and flickering oil lamps, as if she wanted to exercise some care here.

"There are people here," she said at last, "natives, that you could call 'rednecks.' But they aren't the ones who had the ambition to develop the area—put up the hotels and the condos, rent the beach chairs, and so forth. They just kind of *live* here, you know? Things change, but they're—I don't know—just the same, like. If you want to see redneck fun, you want to go to the Flora-Bama."

I did. And Allyson Jones was right: the action in Gulf Shores this night was at this roadhouse straddling the state line where things were already in full swing, as Fats Waller once put it, the place jammed with drinkers, dancers, and pool players. They stood three deep at the bar, drinking from the plastic cups management preferred to glassware, doubtless on good experience. At the pool tables young men in muscle shirts and ball caps showed their dates how it was done. The most conspicuous segment of the crowd was a group of marine flight cadets over from Pensacola: big, burly, crew-cut white guys in T-shirts, making time with the local girls and crammed right up against the bandstand from which J. Hawkins and Alan Rhody sang blues, country-western, honky-tonk, and an occasional Dylan number.

Hawkins was a deep-voiced, hard-driving entertainer who kept his unruly audience rocking with a succession of good-time songs, some of which, as I later learned, he had written himself. Rhody was no less a musician, but he couldn't ride the tiger as well. His "Lay Lady Lay" did little for the crowd. Ditto "The City of New Orleans." He did better with the Jimmy Buffet favorite "Wastin' Away in Margaritaville." Even the hardworking waitresses, dodging the cadets' high-fives and flying beer cans, stepped lively to this one. Better still was "Rocky Top, Tennessee," which brought all up on their feet and clapping time. I thought this had to be bedlam itself, but I was wrong. On came J. Hawkins again with a song whose refrain was "Pissed me off, fuckin' jerk." They were delighted with the candor of that one. Hawkins followed with a song about a man who tells his honey to read his message "loud and clear / Get your head out of yer ass / And yer ass on outta here!"

But when Hawkins went into the Hank Williams song "If Heaven Ain't a Lot Like Dixie," that took it. The girls forgot about the attentions of the flight cadets and leaped atop the tables where they clapped accompaniment, their eyes shut tight in orgasms of regional patriotism. And Hawkins kept them up there in that unbearable state with "Take It Easy." On this number a comely blond woman took center stage, lip-synching the lyrics and performing violent pelvic thrusts that were intended to leave nothing misunderstood. A young cadet with a vicious crew cut and a Milton Caniff square jaw screamed into my ear that Blondie was married to a navy pilot and was pregnant. She didn't look either one to me. Brian, the cadet, wanted me to understand that flight training was a tough and serious business, not at all like this every night. "The program's *intense!* But when you look at your flight schedule and you see you're not up tomorrow, then you can kinda cut 'er loose! We come over here a lot! This guy [Hawkins] is a legend!"

Hawkins was now into another regional stem-winder, and the girls who had climbed down from the tables mounted them again, cavorting wildly while the marines below them urged them to greater excesses. Through this cauldron of noise Dan, a marine from Wauwatosa, Wisconsin, said to me that sometimes he found all this frenzy about the South rather puzzling. "They brag about it so much," he screamed, "it makes you wonder. What do you think it is, sir?" I shrugged.

"It's like they have to talk about it all the time, and if you don't join in, they look at you like you're some kinda weirdo or something. I had a girl in here tell me last week, after she'd heard me talk, 'Oh, I see: you're from up north somewhere. Probably Memphis or someplace.'" He rolled his eyes.

Brian couldn't hear Dan but punched him affectionately on the shoulder and told me the occasion for this outing was that Walt, one of their own, was getting married in two days, and all of them were going up to Quantico for the ceremony on military flights. By now our three heads were almost touching in the center of the table as we attempted to hold a conversation, but at the mention of the Quantico ceremony Dan and Brian jumped up and did a high-five above me. "So," Brian hollered happily when he landed, "we got to get old Walt laid tonight!" They jumped up again for another high-five. They pointed out Walt across the tables where he sat in what looked like intimate conversation with an attractive brunette in pink.

"See that T-shirt he's wearing beneath his shirt?" Brian asked. "It says 'Have a Nice Day,' but down where you can't see, it says 'Bitch.' I think it's working, don't you, Dan? Hey, Walt!! Is it working?" Walt smiled loosely and held one thumb up. Brian and Dan doubled over in guffaws at this comic irony. Walt continued to look across at them, and you had to wonder from the vacancy of his gaze whether he would later on be capable of anticipating his nuptial bliss. Then, touchingly, I thought, Dan put his lips into my ear and asked, "What do you think, sir? Is it better to get laid before you get married?"

"I think it's better to get laid while you're married," I said.

Now Terry, another husky out of the same mold, leaned his heavy shoulders over toward Brian to report on his progress with the girl next to him. "Ten bucks I either get a hummer or I eat box!" he shouted. Brian looked at the girl and shook his head, evidently declining the bet. Another exchange then, lost to me in Hawkins's hammering beat and the crowd's response. Then Terry again: "I'll fuck 'er in the ass. She can't get pregnant there!"

Up on the besieged platform J. Hawkins was concluding his second set with a number called "The Square Grouper": "Now once in a while I'll take a hit / But I'm tellin' you man, this was some righteous shit." And that was the note on which I took leave of the Flora-Bama for the night, feeling that I had indeed seen a species of fun—maybe as much of it as I was meant safely to get.

I WAS back the next afternoon to talk with J. Hawkins. The day was another scorcher, and the Flora-Bama's sandy parking lot gave off a glare that made me squint even behind my mirror shades. Inside, though, all was a coolish gloom pervaded by the sweet, ineradicable bouquet of spilled beer, stale urine, and rest-room deodorant soap. In the long, low rumpus room of the night before only a single elderly man without a shirt sat sipping a mixed drink and brooding on injustice. His white paunch, dotted by hemangiomas and warts, flopped into the crotch of his green Bermuda shorts, and his 'Bama ball cap was set at an angle more slovenly than rakish. J. Hawkins stood chatting easily with the barmaid who was clearly pleased to have an alternative to the complaints of her customer. A long, lean fellow, Hawkins wore the same shirt and Flora-Bama cap in which he'd performed the night before.

Hawkins had been born on a Glasgow, Kentucky, tobacco farm and had early on expressed a serious interest in music: at age twelve he had sold his prize heifer and bought a guitar with the proceeds. "This was the late Sixties," he said, "and so naturally I bought a Dylan songbook and learned everything in it." He was also listening to a lot of Southern blues, country music, and the Allman Brothers. From this program of study he learned that he had what he considers a "natural country voice." I asked what that was.

"Well, it's deep and kind of nasal, and you've got to have that whine in it somewhere," though he said he didn't consider himself a real, pure country singer. "I guess I'm more of what you'd call a 'honky-tonker.' I like to play music that has that good, hard beat to it, music that, I'd guess you'd say, makes people get up and dance and enjoy themselves—good-time music. Of course, sometimes that can become a problem for you, as you saw in here last night. That was about standard for this place at this time of year." Sometimes, he went on, the good-time music got the crowd so worked up it was dangerous to go on performing.

"You saw how crowded it was in here last night. That's nothing to what it's like when the college kids come down here for their breaks. Then it'd take you half an hour just to wade from one end of this bar to the other, and out there"—gesturing toward the rearward two-story deck—"we have 'em stacked up, waiting to get in. Sometimes they'll try to tear this place to pieces. The management tends to be pretty permissive, so sometimes that'll give you a real problem if you're up there trying to play. If things get too rough, I'll just fold 'er up after a set. Or I might say something. One night we had a bunch of strippers in here from Mobile on their night off, and they were really getting into it. We were getting concerned about what they might do and what might happen when they did it. So, I thought I might try to cool things off just a bit by playing something a little less up-tempo. I played 'Your Cheating Heart,' and that did it: they jumped up on the tables and stripped to that." He smiled thinly at the memory and wagged his head slightly, the hard light from the east-facing window coming in on his sharp, sallow features and making gray the smoke that curled up from his cigarette.

In 1970 Hawkins was arrested on a charge of possession of marijuana. "I was riding in a car with two black guys and a Chicano," he recalled, "when we got pulled over. We went to the station, and one of the cops who'd made the arrest put his cap top-down on the desk, and one of the black guys threw up in it. That made me laugh—which turned out to be a mistake: they let the Chicano guy go and kept us." Later, released on bail, Hawkins went up to Nashville to get money for a lawyer and was arrested there for selling speed. He did two years in the state penitentiary at Nashville.

"Looking back," he said evenly, "that was the best thing that could've happened to me. I'd likely be dead by now if I hadn't been arrested and served time. That life-style will eventually just eat you up. But in the pen I *had* to see that I'd come to the end of that life-style: there wasn't any place left for me to go."

In the pen he continued his singing and guitar playing. "A bunch of us would take our guitars and go up on the hill and jam. The warden was a fiddler, and he encouraged us to keep on playing. Then one time my counselor slapped five of us together for a job outside. I doubt we were very good, but it was an eye-opener. I was learning to be a welder in there, but I knew I still wanted to be a musician.

"At that time I thought I wanted to play rock-'n-roll, but I really didn't have the voice for it. Like I said, I knew I had a voice better suited for country. But still that music didn't quite satisfy me. I wanted more of—I don't know—a beat, I guess: that surfboard beat, you know, or maybe more like western swing. So I tried to incorporate those things into my repertoire, but I wasn't all that good: I'd sing out of tune, miss changes, that sort of thing. But one thing I learned about myself early on, and that was that I could get people caught up in my music, even with all the things that were wrong with it. I had that energy, you know, I could get 'em caught up and take 'em along."

At the end of the 1970s Hawkins's musical travels brought him to Florida's panhandle and the Flora-Bama, whose owner immediately sensed what a good fit this singer would be in his brand-new bar. Though he has played other places and this night would work in Mobile, the Flora-Bama has been home base for Hawkins ever since. He said he had friends in Nashville who would be glad to help him break in there if he wanted to try for the big time, but he wondered if he did. It was a matter of fame versus contentment, "and feeling the way I do, I don't know if I'm really suited for fame. There's a lot of pressure there and a lot of time you have to spend on the road. I love it down here. I really do. My wife and I both love to fish. That's a real relaxing thing. We'll just get in our boat and go out. . . ." His voice trailed away and he raised his hands, then let them fall back into his lap. "It's a good way to spend your time off. If I should hit it big—and I'm not saying I know I could—I wonder if I could live as easy as I do now." The money here wasn't great, he said, a hundred a night for three sets, three nights a week. Once in a while he might make a bit more when he played in Mobile or down in Key West. But the life here suited him.

I asked him to look ten years down the road. Would he be content if he should find himself still at the Flora-Bama?

"Well, it isn't so much the Flora-Bama versus someplace else," he said slowly, pausing to light another cigarette. "It's the life. I don't know how long a guy can keep it up. Everything in your life is kinda upside down. Your days are when you sleep, and your nights are when you work. It makes things kinda strange, year after year. Nowadays I get in bed about three [A.M.], and even if I'm not working, I'll stay up till about then because I can't sleep any other way. Generally, I get up around noon or a little after. That's just the way I'm set up now, and it's hard for me to get on another kind of schedule. Well, after a certain amount of time at this you can tell it's wearing on you. Plus, there're the things you have to work with all the time. There's the alcohol, for one: you're around it all the time. Everybody's getting juiced every night, and so naturally you're going to have a couple, and you know that's not good for you, night after night, year after year. Then, your lungs are filled with smoke, and that's not good, either. The crowds're generally rowdy, and that's a strain on a performer, trying to be heard, trying to concentrate on what you're doing. Respect is very important to me. Recently I was voted the Number One Male Vocalist in northwest Florida, and that was important to me, I can tell you. I was very surprised, and I was very pleased people thought that highly of me."

Hawkins had a date to make in Mobile, and we went out through the shabby, empty scene of his nightly triumphs and into the smaller bar-room beyond it where they also sold package goods, and then on into the front room where there was a lively concessions area: Flora-Bama T-shirts in various styles, and another one that showed a shrimper harvesting the "square grouper" by the light of the moon, the legend below this reading SAVE THE BALES. Also caps, shorts, mugs, pennants, and so forth. There were several copies of Ken Stabler's autobiography, *Snake*, which prompted me to ask the man behind the counter whether it had been in here that Stabler had bitten a man's finger off in a celebrated barroom brawl. "It wasn't in here, though Kenny comes in a good bit when he's around," the man said levelly. "And anyway, it wasn't him. It was Billy Walker." He told then how during the subsequent trial the judge had asked Walker's wife, a witness, whether she had in fact seen her husband bite off the digit. And Mrs. Walker had said no, "I only saw him spit it out."

IF some residents of Alabama's Gulf coast seem to be backing away just a bit from the name the Redneck Riviera, people along the Mississippi coast would never think of courting such a term, whether for fun or profit. To them, "rednecks" lived elsewhere. They lived on the Gulf, and their history and culture had been shaped by it. When I asked a young Mississippian about the northernmost limit of his state's Gulf coast culture, he laughed a bit scornfully and replied, "I-10," referring to the east-west highway that in some places runs so close to the Gulf that you can see the water. This was something of an exaggeration, apparently, since he went on to say that, as in other places along the Gulf, "the culture seems to follow the watercourses inland a ways." But the exaggeration had its point, and this was that the life of Biloxi or Pass Christian had as little to do with Hattiesburg as Hattiesburg had to do with

Indianapolis. In the days I spent along the Mississippi coast I came to believe this.

I remembered vividly the Sixties when to much of the country the name "Mississippi" had been like a fire bell in the night; remembered the incredulity of outsiders when the state's racial codes came under the media's scrutiny then: "*This* is America?" I remembered how Dr. King had seemed to single out Mississippi in his Lincoln Memorial address, calling it a "desert state sweltering with the heat of injustice and oppression." And I remembered Nina Simone singing that though Alabama had her so upset and Tennessee made her lose her rest, everybody knew about Mississippi, "God-damn!" Remembered, too, my own excursion into the northern portion of the state, how it felt even to an insulated motorist hell-bent for New Orleans but bearing a Massachusetts plate: "God, don't let me have a breakdown in this dark and dangerous place." Even into the late 1980s the Delta Country—Marks, Clarksdale, Swan Lake—had felt alien to me: heavy, somber, terrifically impoverished, the faces of the black populace bearing the aspect as of some profound and unrelieved sorrow.

But on the coast I felt none of that. Partly it was the presence of the water, which always offers at least the illusion of freedom or escape. With the wind blowing in off a wide, watery expanse whose horizon is apparently limitless, it is possible to believe that fate may be avoided and that if need be you can change your circumstances. A long row in a soybean field with a stand of woods at the end is not similarly encouraging. And though I had already learned enough about the hard realities of commercial fishing to look anew at the boats snugged up in the Biloxi marina, I remembered as well the words of that couple at the Other Place in Cedar Key, with what feeling they had spoken of the freedoms of those days on the waters of the Gulf, the sun broiling, the work tremendously taxing, and its financial rewards so marginal. Or old Yellowlegs Campbell there who, with all his confessed limitations, retained a certain lightness of spirit I had trouble imagining might be possessed by an inlander similarly circumscribed.

Partly what I was responding to on Mississippi's coast were the faces and bearing of the people. They had known hardship and tragedy, and you couldn't get ten minutes into a conversation with anybody over the age of thirty without hearing about Camille that leveled this coast in August 1969, with winds in excess of 230 miles per hour. (The precise upper limit remains forever unknowable since at 230 mph the gauges disintegrated.) Yet there was something about these folks that said they liked life where they were, would willingly bear its vicissitudes. They were here, they seemed to be saying, because they chose to be here, not because they had been trapped. There was the elderly woman I saw in an Ocean Springs convenience store wearing a T-shirt that celebrated the joys of eating crawfish (locally "mud bugs"): PINCH MY TAIL / SUCK MY HEAD / EAT ME. Or the sandy-haired man in a Biloxi oyster bar where I sat eating a half dozen. When I had forked up my last oyster he said, "They're supposed to be good for your sex life." I said I'd heard that. "Don't believe it," he came back. "I was in here last night, had a dozen, and only seven of 'em worked." Up in Bay St. Louis as I walked the beachfront thoroughfare of the little, low-cut town that for so many years had served as a getaway for New Orleanians I saw a mailman in shorts and white rubber waders. This, I told him, was the first time I'd ever seen that particular Postal Service attire. He laughed, his round reddened face shining in the sun. "Oh, we been havin' so much rain, y'know. These yards don't have no drains, some of 'em, and it just come up over my knees sometimes. So I put on my boots and tell folks, 'I'm goin' soft crabbin'."

Partly it was the fact that the Mississippi Gulf coast derives its distinguishing spirit from its proximity to New Orleans with its tolerant Latin-flavored culture. Here they still celebrate Iberville and Bienville's 1699 landfall at Ocean Springs, an event that inaugurated six decades of French colonial control and sets the cultural tone to this day. Even the brief rule of the British served only to reinforce the emotional allegiance of the coast-dwellers to New Orleans. And New Orleans returned the sentiment: by 1810 city residents were beginning to come down to the Mississippi coast to spend the summer months as yellow fever scourged the city. Of course, yellow jack was present on the coast, as well— though this was consistently denied—but not nearly so virulently, and some New Orleans hoteliers leased grand coastal properties, closed down in the city by the end of May, and moved their entire staffs to Mississippi, not to return until the first cold announced the end of the pestilential season. At the Pass Christian Hotel, popularly known as "Montgomery's" after its manager, there was, said an 1840s account, "eating and drinking; bowling and flirting; billiards and snoozing; gossip and toilette; driving and novel readings; sailing and yawning; bathing and mosquito scratching; dancing and music . . . boat excursions, lovely storms, snow-capped billows, boats capsized, bold swimming, sharks pursuing." From time to time through the nineteenth century there was even talk along the coast of seceding from Mississippi and joining Louisiana, but nothing came of it.

These days the New Orleans influence is as strong as it ever was, in commerce, in cuisine, in attitudes. New Orleanians still flock here to the beaches and to charter fishing boats. Newsstands carry the New Orleans *Times-Picayune* and TV stations the New Orleans channels. At Mary Mahoney's Old French House restaurant in Biloxi you can get café au lait and beignets, those staples of New Orleans morning life. And even if the former is spelled "cafe-o-lay" and the latter are industrial weight, it is still New Orleans you feel, not Hattiesburg or Jackson or Mobile.

This is not to say that there aren't vestiges of the plumb deep South and its history here or that the rest of the state is of no consequence. A terrible lynching at Poplarville in 1959 ushered in a period of racial tension along the coast whose handsome beaches old-time segregationists were (vainly) determined would remain as white as their sands. And on Beach Boulevard in Biloxi there is one of the essential shrines of the Lost Cause, Beauvoir, last home of Jefferson Davis. A graven inscription at the central gate reads STRANGER, TREAD LIGHTLY HERE, FOR THIS SPOT IS HOLY GROUND.

On a Saturday afternoon across from Holy Ground seven shirtless and muscular young black men gestured, laughed, and hollered at passing cars and at other bathers. They were clearly oblivious to the inscription and the formal entrance, oblivious to the big house itself, the way the hedge-bordered walk enslaved the eye and led it inescapably to the out-curving balustrades of the front steps and the long gallery atop. Maybe the irony of this tableau was too simple and too obvious, but I couldn't resist it, and so instead of entering Beauvoir as I had been about to do, I crossed the boulevard to join the young men juking about on the seawall. They saw me coming, watched warily from behind their shades as I dodged through four lanes of steady traffic.

Did they know whose house that was over the way?

"Yeah, man, we know."

"He was president," another added. "They had us study 'bout him and the Confederacy." Now that it appeared that The Man was harmless they gathered about in a loose knot, holding beers wrapped in foam coasters. "But they didn't get the whole story, man. They didn't tell 'bout what the black soldier went through, what he can do."

"Do you mean," I wondered, "the black soldiers who had to serve the Confederacy or those who fought for the North?"

"The North, man, the North! You seen that movie *Glory*? Man, I *love* that movie." Assenting murmurings here. "The black G.I.! No matter what come down, he hold his own, *he hold his own!*" Now there were high-fives, and some took sips from their beers.

Had they ever been to Beauvoir? I asked.

"No, man," one came back. "Been here all my life and never been in there yet." He gave it a quick glance. "And to-dayyyy . . . is . . . not . . . the day!" They all laughed and I joined in. But then I invited them to be my guests for a tour of the house and grounds. I would pay for their tickets, I told them. Of course, I had no idea what might happen if they took me up on this, but I felt sure it would be interesting. Instead, they looked quickly at one another and moved about slightly on the wall.

"No, man, we got to stick here," one said then. "See, we been *deported* from the beach."

"Yeah, we been *sold down the beach*. Said we was troublemakers. We weren't causin' no trouble. Just salutin' the women, y'know." Two hundred yards away two women in bikinis picked their way up from the lapping brown waves.

"Hey, baby!" one of the group shouted. "You in the pink!" The shouter thrust himself into the sun. *"Bam! Bam! Bam!"* Then he collapsed in silent laughter on the hood of their car. This was a lot more fun any day than a history lesson with a white stranger, and I left them to it, recrossing the boulevard to enter another zone, the past, where any impulse to laughter was stilled, not only by the graven inscription at the gate but by the somber tone of the exhibits in the Jefferson Davis museum you had to pass through in order to get to the house itself.

There was the catafalque, for instance, that had borne Davis through the streets of Montgomery during the long ceremony of his reinterment in 1893, and the photo of his coffin resting in the chambers of the Alabama Supreme Court, above it a banner reading HE SUFFERED FOR US. An inscription ran in large letters along one wall, quoting the martyr: "Should I die, tell the world I only loved America and that in following my state I was only carrying out doctrine received from reverenced lips in my early youth and adopted by my judgement [sic] as the conviction of riper years." And in all the rooms under the funereal lighting there were photographs of Davis and his tragically brooding eyes. The older he got, the more Lincolnesque he looked, life's last cruel joke on one who wouldn't get it.

The house itself, its outbuildings, and grounds were a relief from the Tomb-of-the-Holy-Sepulcher approach of the museum. The house had been framed of cypress by slave hands long before Davis had come to live it in. A handsome, high-ceilinged affair, it was bisected by a formal hall leading back to a broad rearward porch and sleeping quarters beyond. In the garden behind the house were a large cypress cistern, a replica of the tiny separated kitchen once used to prepare meals, and another replica of the barracks that housed Confederate veterans and their dependents.

Beyond all this lay the cemetery of Confederate dead, their white slabs sunk into the luxuriant turf like worn teeth. I missed any marker that might have designated the site of the house's original slave quarters and so asked the obliging young guide about this. She explained that the slaves who had built the house had come from a neighboring plantation to work on the construction and had then "gone back home. And when Mr. Davis lived here, it was long after the war, and so of course they didn't have slaves then. But the kitchen replica you saw, the servants lived in it."

On my way out and vaguely dreading the return through the museum, I stopped to peer in the windows of the Library Cottage and found it fitted out like a captain's cabin—shelving, compact escritoire, round table. And maybe that really was the idea: that this was to be home port after the long storm—war, defeat, ignominious flight, and even more ignominious imprisonment. And then at last Beauvoir and the Library Cottage where he wrote *The Rise and Fall of the Confederate Government* with the sound in plain view and the waves coming in just the way they went out.

MISSISSIPPI has contributed its full share and then some of writers and artists and musicians. In this century alone it has given the world William Faulkner, Eudora Welty, and Tennessee Williams—more than enough literary talent for an entire region, let alone for a single state isolated from the alleged nurturing centers of New England, New York, or California. The odds then that it would contribute in addition two of the authentic geniuses of American art must be very high indeed. And yet Biloxi was home to George E. Ohr (1857–1918), perhaps the greatest master of the potter's wheel this country has yet produced, while a scant two miles away in Ocean Springs Walter Inglis Anderson (1903–1965), working in hermetical obscurity, created a huge and magnificent collection of watercolors in celebration of the natural life of the Mississippi Gulf coast.

If Walt Whitman had been a potter instead of a poet, he might have produced work as profuse, as wildly unconventional, and as wonderful as George Ohr's. As with Whitman's poetry, there was nothing like Ohr's work in America before him, and there has been nothing like it since. Experts in the history of ceramics have detected the influence of ancient Chinese techniques and shapes in the work of Ohr's mature years; also the influence of the ancient Greeks, of the sixteenth-century French master Bernard Palissy, and of the nineteenth-century Scots designer

Christopher Dresser. But as Robert A. Ellison, Jr., remarks in his definitive monograph on Ohr, "only a few fugitive references to historical forms appear in Ohr's work," and one is left to suspect "that he appropriated more than is readily apparent, but that his idiosyncratic interpretation so thoroughly transformed the original source that it became unrecognizable."

Of his training, Ohr himself said little. After serving apprenticeships to a file cutter, a tinker, his blacksmith father, a ship chandler, and a sea captain, Ohr said he finally served a potter and "learned to boss a little piece of clay into a gallon jug." His master was the well-known New Orleans potter Joseph Meyer, and after learning his craft, Ohr left for a two-year tour of sixteen states that took him, he later said, as far as "Dubuque, Milwaukee, Albany, down the Hudson, & zigzag back home." Nor were these mere *Wanderjahrs*; rather they were a purposeful, if highly personal, idiosyncratic tour of inspection in which the fledgling potter discovered what the current competition was and evidently satisfied himself that he could do as well or better. "I sized up every potter and pottery," he recalled, "and never missed a show window, illustration or literary dab on ceramics since that time."

Such, evidently, was his training in pottery. It hardly seems adequate to account for what he was subsequently to produce, but there it triumphantly is. Pots of every conceivable shape and a good many that would seem inconceivable. Pots with sinuous shapes and even more sinuous handles and spouts, reminding you vaguely of Hector Guimard and French Art Nouveau, except for their almost fierce, defiant democratic individualism. Pots shaped like natural objects—seashells, snakes, birds' wings. Pots crinkled and folded like frozen flowers. Ornate, monumental vases over five feet high that might serve as sentries at some formal entrance. Tiny, fabulously colored footed vases that might grace a coffee table in a drawing room. Sensually curved bowls that powerfully evoke the feminine principle and pay tribute to it. Frankly vaginal-shaped pieces serving no discernible function other than to provoke a smoking-parlor guffaw. Trick teapots. Puzzle cups. Whistling jugs. Pitchers that look as if they were in the act of pouring. Lyrical, achingly beautiful, funny, vulgar, they poured in an almost hysterical profusion from the brain and down the hugely muscled arms to the slightly squarish hands of this singular man who went resolutely his own way, secure in his belief that he was the supreme art potter of his time. Responding to the United States Potters' Association request for representative samples of his work, Ohr sent four pieces and a note advising the association that it would be "as easy to pass judgment on my productions from four pieces as it would be to take four lines from Shakespeare and guess the rest."

His son Oto remembered his father's unshakable confidence in the merit of the body of work he was creating. " 'There's ten thousand pieces here, and no two pieces alike,' " Oto recalled him saying as he worked at his wheel surrounded by the chaos of his artistic fecundity. Oto recalled, too, his father's solitary trips into Biloxi's Back Bay and elsewhere, searching for the perfect clays. "My father," he concluded, "was a pretty wise man" even when many Biloxians thought he was mad because of his many eccentricities. "He was a wise man the good Lord sent down here to make stuff and show the world."

Show the world he would, not only with his art but also with his ceaseless and often inventive self-promotions. Wherever he went on his travels or to fairs and expositions he carried along large signs screaming his talent: THIS WORLD IS MINE (along a sign's top border); MY NAME IS MUD and WE ARE FROM CLAY (along its sides); GET ON TO MY EARTHENWARE (at its bottom); DEEDS ARE FRUITS, WORDS ARE LEAVES / VISIT POTTERY AND VIEW OHR'S DEEDS IN CLAY; AMERICA HOLDS THE GREATEST VARIETY POTTER IN THE WORLD (these last in the sign's center along with a drawing of a globe). He wrote up uncounted handbills: "American born, free and patriotic, blowing my own bugle, and will tackle the greatest of all the great potters in the world, creating shapes on ceramic wheel." He cultivated a bizarrely arresting appearance that masked his natural good looks, wearing a long beard and an even longer mustache the ends of which he tied behind his head while at work. He wrote endlessly to the newspapers, blowing his own bugle in letters and poems. His surviving literary effects reveal a rough, untutored verbal inventiveness of a man in love with the sound of words and the magical properties of language, hopelessly addicted to all forms of wordplay—puns, rhymes, antonyms, phonetic and orthographical coincidences. Fascinated to discover that his initials also formed the abbreviation of his first name, he fashioned for his children names that would perform a similar magic: Oto, Clo, Ojo, Flo, Geo, Leo, and Lio. Much of his surviving poetry runs close to the doggerel, but there is more heart than forced meter and end rhyme in "The Potter and the Pot," a poem Ohr contributed to the *New York Sun* in 1902 and that was subsequently reprinted in the *New Orleans Times-Democrat*. In a footnote to it Ohr instructed the reader to pay special attention to the fifth verse and its third line. Here in a single line, Ohr said, was "a whole history":

Sometimes his strange brain working, which his fingers quick
    obey,
He fashions birds and animals, or lizards from the clay.
If we could fully understand him—but most of us do not—
How we would heap with honor this potter and his pot.

Another newspaper contribution reads:

I KNOW

I'm quaint & very queer.
So is my work, so I appear;
    As I write I likewise talk & work—
& otherwise I could not B—
I am no poet, but just mud—
And term myself

POT-OHR-E.

    Also yours most mysteriously,
a mistake, mysfit, & some sort of
myssing lynx, who is the "IT" and
"Hymself that AM."

Probably he was both misfit and missing lynx, and surely much of the
history of the Mad Potter of Biloxi was expressed in that third line of the
Sun poem. In part victim of his own inexhaustible inventiveness—what
one contemporary called his "fatal facility on the wheel"—in part victim
of his protean self-promotions that cumulatively portrayed him more as
freak than genius, George Ohr died without the honor so obviously due
him. By that time it had been at least a decade since he had worked at his
art, and his hopes of selling a large collection of his most ambitious pieces
to the Smithsonian had not been realized. Rightly, as it now appears, he
regarded his work as a national treasure that ought to be kept together,
but the institution's curators did not. The fabulous Pot-Ohr-E on what is
now Biloxi's Howard Avenue had been whittled down by his sons into
the prosaic Ohr Boys Auto Repairing Shop. And when he died, rather
than using that verse from "The Potter and the Pot" with a whole history
in its third line—or any other of his lines, for that matter—his family
chose to have his tombstone inscribed simply "At Rest," as if the "Rest"
referred to was really theirs, not his. They haphazardly stashed his collection of pieces, what he termed his "Mud Babies," in attic crates, and

Leo, a disaffected son, burned most of his papers. The Mad Potter at last seemed only that, a gifted, wayward wacko the memory of whom faded in his hometown until he was remembered there as a man who in his final years had become a minor public nuisance.

But this was only the history of George Ohr in his time, not in ours. In 1972, due to the detective work of a New Jersey antiques dealer, George Ohr reemerged onto the American scene, and before the end of the decade he had become a cult figure in American art circles, his work prized by ceramics collectors, antiques dealers, and avant-garde artists. The dealer, on the track of antique automobiles, had visited the Ohr brothers' shop in Biloxi and had been shown not vintage Cadillacs, but over seven thousand of Ohr's pieces, which the family had by that time providentially removed from the attic to the more durable cinderblock shed of their used-parts lot. Eventually the entire collection was sold for $50,000 so that today little more than a handful of Ohr's best work remains in Biloxi, a situation that recapitulates that of so many artists whose best work is not to be found in the place they called home: northward in Mississippi at Oxford, for instance, where the university holds but a few, marginal Faulkner papers.

The Biloxi Museum of Art, which may be reached on a one-block back street recently rechristened to honor Ohr, has three small pieces on display, two of them stunning. At the Biloxi Public Library, which adjoins the museum, I talked with Murella Hebert Powell who runs the library's genealogy section. She took me into a cluttered room of files, and there on a topmost shelf were eight dingy, unglazed pieces of earthenware that might have been turned out by any undistinguished artisan. Not much of a show for Ohr in his hometown, I said. "No, it isn't," Ms. Powell said. "As you must know, most of his best things are now in New York. These are just things he did to make a living, and even these we acquired mostly by accident: they were discovered underneath some floorboards. There's a message on one of them in his handwriting."

I stood on one of Ms. Powell's chairs and gingerly took down the pots, one after another, searching for the message. They felt grimy and heavy in hand, and I could neither see nor feel the touch of genius in any of them. But at last I got to the message pot, its fading inscription in Ohr's florid hand having something to do with "going fishing." Perhaps if I could have deciphered all of it, I might have gotten at least some stray spark of his antic muse. As it was, I had to settle for the heavy pots as they were, evidence of the workaday reality of a life, and also the few fugitive scraps of Ohriana the library had been able to gather, such as newspaper notices and an itemized bill for his funeral: silk-lined coffin, two sedans, two small cars. Leo Ohr had signed for it. "One hundred and forty-one dollars doesn't sound like a great deal today," Ms. Powell said in comment on the bill, "but actually, by the standards of that time it bought you a pretty nice funeral."

She took me down a narrow hall lined on one side by microfilm machines to the room at the end where there hung an 1889 painting showing Ohr at the wheel of the New Orleans Art Pottery, his hat on, his hands shaping a large vase. Despite the scores of photographs taken of Ohr during his mature years (he was fascinated with the medium's tricky possibilities), the painting struck me as far more remarkable, an intimate glimpse into the life of the then-unknown artist, before the full flowering of his genius and before the commencement of his ceaseless promotional campaign. I wondered what had inspired the painter to make the assistant and not the master the subject of the work, for there in the background is Joseph Meyer, who had taught Ohr the wheel.

Following tips from Murella Powell, I stopped that day at Moran's Art Studio in Biloxi and the day following paid a call on Dolores (Bobbie) Davidson Smith across the Biloxi Bay Bridge in Ocean Springs.

The Moran of Moran's Art Studio was Joe Moran, son of Ohr's daughter Clo who had recently died and whose unexamined house was believed possibly to contain some of Ohr's papers that had escaped Leo's incendiary hand. Moran's daughter Cindy, bright, blond, and obliging, seemed to be in charge here and took me into a room of the gallery where a small glass case dimly displayed a few of Ohr's earlier pieces but none that looked to be from his great period, c. 1895–1905/6. Next to the case was one of Ohr's boastful signs: WARES CANNOT BE CATALOGUED; DUPLICATES CANNOT BE MADE; IF SO OHR'S POTTERY SHAPES ARE UNRIVALLED AND HAVE VALUE. Cindy Moran was inclined to apologize for this faded relic of her great-grandfather's braggadocio, but I told her of the remark attributed to baseball great Dizzy Dean: "It ain't bragging if you can do it." She laughed. "Well, I guess not. He always said, 'In fifty years I'll be famous for these,' and he was right, though it's too bad he couldn't have lived to enjoy it. I remember when I was quite young seeing the whole collection together, and it really was something." No, Joe Moran wasn't around, and in any case he could add little to what I already knew. As we stood there chatting in front of the case an elderly man groped by on his cane and disappeared into a rearward room. Cindy Moran watched him a moment, then asked if I would like to see one of the very few official commendations Ohr had received in his lifetime. She took me back into a storage room where there hung a framed certificate awarding Ohr a silver medal at the 1904 St. Louis Louisiana Purchase Exposition. While I inspected its busy contents the elderly man materialized out of the gloom and extended his hand in silent greeting. It was Joe Moran. Cindy had been protecting his privacy.

Great black tufts of hair sprouted from Moran's ears and nose, and in the wan lighting silver stubble sparkled on his waxen cheeks. Here clearly was one of the few people left alive with vivid memories of George Ohr, but he looked too ill to ask anything of, and so for a few moments the three of us simply stood there before the framed certificate, Joe Moran still holding my hand in greeting. Then Cindy broke the little spell by observing, "Joe, we think, inherited his [George Ohr's] artistic abilities," nodding toward a couple of seascapes propped against a wall.

"These aren't very good," Joe Moran mumbled.

"*We* think they are," Cindy loyally rejoined. Then Joe Moran excused himself, and I asked his daughter if there was left any vestige of the wonderful Pot-Ohr-E where Ohr had created his wonderful works. No, nothing was left of even the garage that had been made out of it.

"After Camille," she explained, "they made a whole lot of changes here, and that was one of them. In a way, it's too bad. It might have been nice to save it. But right there in the big curve on Howard where it was the city's going to put up a plaque."

AS for living memorials, George Ohr could not do better than Bobbie Davidson Smith of Ocean Springs. No sooner had we seated ourselves with cups of coffee just inside the front door of her great, peeling home than she exclaimed, "If you've come to me to hear about George Ohr, you've come to the right person. And don't you be concerned that it's an inconvenience. It's no trouble to me at all. I sing the song of George Ohr! He affects me to my very soul! Sometimes it feels to me as if I'm in love with a dead man."

She wanted to set me straight right away, in case I had heard any stories that might have given me the wrong impression of Ohr. He was not a madman, whatever I might have heard or read, all his zany behavior being simply the only means he had of attracting attention to his work. A good family man, too: "His family adored him." Really? I thought. Leo, too? "His wife looked like Ingrid Bergman, and you can't beat that for beauty. If he did anything over at Newcomb [the New

Orleans women's college where Ohr had briefly taught in the 1880s], it couldn't have been much more than to pinch a bustle, and what would that get you?" She laughed briefly.

"Now, I grant you," she continued, "some of his pieces are in questionable taste, but you have to understand that this was a very sensuous man we're talking about. A very sensuous man. Every one of his fine pieces—I don't mean the early things or the things he had to do to make a living—were *all* sensuous things. He was a man making love to the wheel and the clay!" She arose, went into another room, and returned with a tall plastic bucket from which she pulled an object wrapped in newspaper.

"People ask me why I keep these things this way," she said, smiling at me with what I was beginning to understand was a spirit of mischievous fun. "Just a bucket and newspapers. And these are things that are now worth a great deal of money." Recently, she said, holding me in suspense and the object still swathed in its pedestrian, journalistic wrapper, she had sold an Ohr piece for $60,000. That was something of a fluke, she claimed, since it "had to do with a rivalry between two collectors. I was the beneficiary." She chuckled, and her coffee cup jiggled in its saucer.

"But the reason I keep them this way is that this is the way they were when I first saw them. After 1910, Ohr went back to blacksmithing and didn't do anything with his pots, wouldn't sell them. If a customer came to the garage and saw them, he knew he'd have to have a pretty fast horse to get home with one, because if George sold him a piece, right away he'd change his mind. He'd go after the customer on his bicycle or his motorcycle and chase the man down to buy back his 'Mud Baby.' Well, that meant when he died he had a great many, oh, a very great many unsold pieces there, and the family just sort of threw them in crates with some newspaper wrapped around them. And that's where they still were when I saw them back in the Fifties: just up there in the attic of that old place with the wind blowing and that old building just rocking back and forth."

As a reward for having brought Ohr back to public attention with the first article written about him in many years, Bobbie Davidson was given a number of his pieces by the family. "He had been a legend in his time," she said, "and then forgotten." Now at last she unwrapped the object to reveal a small black pitcher with exquisitely thin, fluted walls and set it on her desk. We both looked at it in silence as it made its statement, and then she pulled up another from the bucket and removed its brittle wrapping to reveal a miniature chamber pot with a feces snaking up toward its rim like a python. She set this next to the black beauty, leaned back in her chair, pulled a cigarette from her pack, and lit it. Behind the little haze of her first puff she said, "As I say, some of his pieces are in questionable taste. I gave my daughter in Memphis the infamous vagina piece. He once gave my father, who thought highly of him, an erectile penis piece, complete with balls. It really was quite funny, but my mother made him give it away.

"My mother was a Victorian. Of the first water. She had five daughters and did everything she could to prevent us from discovering the difference between girls and boys. Later on, this came as quite a surprise to us, I assure you. Anyway, as I say, Mother made Father give the penis piece away, to the doctor, who would appreciate its spirit. The doctor had a reputation—deserved—for being somewhat lascivious. He used to feel the breasts of the girls he examined, and so we wouldn't go to him except en masse, you know. Mother once said to him, 'Doctor, the girls complain that when they go to visit you, you feel 'em up.' He said, 'Now, that may be so, but the reason I do is, if their nipples rise, they aren't virgins.' Clever old devil." She shook with a silent chuckle. Then, picking up the chamber pot, she turned it around in her hands.

"Just the other day I had this over at the Biloxi Yacht Club where I gave a talk on Ohr, and one of the women picked this up and looked inside it. 'Oooooh,' she said, 'what's this?!' 'Oooooh,' I said, 'doo-doo!' In his day people thought George Ohr was peculiar, but I'm here to tell you that in their reactions to him people were a lot funnier than he ever was—and he was doing a lot of that on purpose. People still don't know how to react to him, but when you're in the presence of these things"— she gestured to the pots on her desk—"you're in the presence of genius, and there's nothing funny about that."

Standing on the steps of Bobbie Davidson Smith's house and saying my good-bye and thank-you for a morning of entertaining and instructive talk, I asked her about Walter Anderson, the great watercolor artist of Ocean Springs and Horn Island. "I once asked him if he recalled Ohr's work," she answered. "He said, 'Don't mention that name to me. I hate his guts!' Why? *Why?* Because George could do this." She held up the black vase, and I felt very much as if this were Ohr's triumph and vindication she was celebrating now, that she in no way had confused it as her own. "Everything they do," she said then in reference to the Anderson family pottery located but a few block distant, "is this thick," holding her thumb and forefinger more than an inch apart.

"Now, the Andersons are all weird. They live over there in that compound. . . ." Her voice trailed off as she glanced across the high, weedy lawn of her old home surrounded by big live oaks and also by the later, spurious growths of a Hardees and a branch of the Magnolia Federal Bank. "You can get very ingrown," she said at last. But then, brightening, called back into the present, she said, "But that bright, cute little Mary Anderson, she's the brains behind everything that's going on with the family now. She's the one who has always had the best sense of the outer world. If she'll talk to you, that would be your best source on Walter Anderson."

MARY ANDERSON PICKARD would talk to me, would in fact give me all of her Sunday, though her mother was critically ill and she herself was busy with the details of the Walter Anderson Museum that would soon open to the public. In the meantime, I could go back over the published portions of Anderson's Horn Island logs, and I spent an afternoon doing so under a Biloxi beach umbrella, surrounded by college kids and Keesler AFB personnel. Turning the pages of the logs and glancing up now and again to look across the glittering sound toward Horn Island more than nine miles distant, I found it perfectly easy to blot out the youthful merriment surrounding me, the shouts, laughter, car stereos, and portable blasters, and to muse on the intense engagement Anderson had enacted with the island and with the whole of the Gulf world he knew.

The intensity of that engagement is manifest in the thousands of watercolors Anderson left behind, in his wood carvings, linoleum blocks, public murals, oil paintings, and in the more than ninety logs he kept of his solitary expeditions to Horn Island from 1944 until the year of his death, 1965. It was at the same time an intensity that had to be baffling to the members of his community who observed him from the outer edge of that distance his intensity created and that he took pains to preserve. Perched in tree crotches with sketch pads or the sheaves of the typing paper he preferred for his watercolors; bicycling the local roads or the highway to New Orleans; walking the railroad tracks or cutting across fields—sockless, bedraggled of dress, his fierce, gaunt features daring so much as a salute; or bound out for the island, a bundle of supplies rolled into a tarp, his skiff's sail the size of a child's nightgown and the wind in his teeth: Walter Anderson achieved in Ocean Springs and Biloxi the kind of negative mana that accrued to Thoreau in Concord. Upland, in less tolerant reaches of Mississippi, he might have been beaten to death on one of his wild, dark rambles. Here, though, they put up with him, if they didn't like him, and if on one of his voyages to Horn Island he was seen to be in trouble, he was assisted. Otherwise, he was given the wide berth he wanted. At the Biloxi Public Library, Murella Powell remembered Anderson as "very unfriendly." "He'd come in," she said, "drop his books on the counter, get some others, and leave. Not a word to anyone."

But if the members of the community could shrug off Anderson's behavior and go on with their own lives, it was not that easy for those of his family to avoid him when his mood turned dangerous, especially in the years before his self-imposed exile from daily family intercourse. In 1933, he married Agnes "Sissy" Grinstead, and there commenced a relationship as tempestuous as a Gulf hurricane. Even then he was erratic and given to occasional bursts of violence. But some four years into the marriage Anderson began to exhibit signs of severe mental illness. A suicide attempt precipitated a long period (1937–46) of institutionalization, electroshock therapy, escapes, prolonged disappearances, and agonizing efforts the artist made to reenter the everyday world. Finally toward the end of 1946, both the artist and his wife came to the recognition that for them and the children they now had there could be no "everyday world," that for better or worse Walter Anderson was bound to the intertwined worlds of nature and the imagination. As Sissy Anderson describes it in her memoir of life with Walter Anderson, he came to her at their Oldfields home, a few miles east of Ocean Springs, and asked her blessing to live a life apart. "I am like Jacob," she remembers him crying out to her, "and you are my angel." She gave her blessing, and he moved back to the Anderson family compound at Ocean Springs. The family soon followed, but for the rest of his life Anderson lived apart from them in a hermit's cottage. "He was a painter always," Sissy wrote, "a lover at times, a husband and father never."

For a time after his removal to the cottage Anderson tried to maintain some contact with the world of men by producing art for public consumption. Like Whitman before him and like many artists and writers of the American 1930s, Anderson believed the artist owed his native culture good, inexpensive, available art such as would enhance the everyday lives of ordinary people. So he turned out comic clay figures and decorated pots that were sold through the family's Shearwater Pottery; also linoleum blocks, woodcuts, and two public murals in Ocean Springs. It was the last of these, a gloriously colored narrative of Ocean Springs life from its natural history through the aboriginal period, the coming of the Europeans, and into the present day, that occasioned his final and complete withdrawal. Working at the Community Center, the reclusive man bore as well as he was able the stares, the misapprehension, and the disapproval of casual observers. Still harder to bear was the reaction of some when he had finished his work in 1951: they wanted the mural effaced with a clean coat of whitewash. Fortunately for the community this was not done, and the mural remains as a glowing gift the artist made his home place.

It was the last he made in his lifetime. Thereafter Anderson devoted himself to the Matter of Horn Island as well as to other equally private projects that would not be discovered until after his death. With increasing frequency he made excursions across the sound to the island, camping there for weeks at a time, sleeping beneath his upturned skiff, spending his days sketching and painting the island's animal and plant life, and writing up his experiences in his logbooks. "I made a drawing of the bittern's nest while the flies stung," he wrote in one of his logs; "later a watercolor under my boat while the rain poured. Such is the life of an artist who prefers nature to art. He really should cultivate art more but feels that his love of art will take care of itself if it has things to feed upon." Of one of his excursions—often begun before dawn and in the course of which he might have to row and even push the skiff if the wind was wrong—he wrote of leaving behind the certain comforts of the mainland for the island:

> The lighthouse and the strong and friendly faces, land upon which to walk and infinite refreshment.
>
> But I was indifferent to that place and left it in the night to go to my island. I was accompanied by the stars and that star of morning. I moved with the strength of my hands over the velvet water of the night. The moon lent me her company, distant and poised. I moved respectfully beneath the moon. And when the moon left me her place was taken by the star of morning. I, in my boat, she, treading on the velvet water.
>
> I came to the island in the night, rowing slowly. The island was a long black line in the moonlight. In the magic of the moonlight, ghosts of houses were seen. They dissolved before my eyes. My eyes closed in slumber and I slept, falling from the rower's bench from weariness.

"Those," he laconically noted in another entry, "who have identified themselves with nature must take the consequence."

Anderson was willing. Willing, too, to suffer not only the physical trials but the psychological ones as the island outcast, and not even so that he might, as Faulkner once put it, say "Kilroy Was Here," scratching his puny graffito on Eternity's stony surface: he made almost no effort to promote his achievement. Rather, he lived and suffered solely to see that art and nature really were one thing and that he, Walter Anderson, was privileged to make that great secret manifest.

"A few days after he died, Mother went into the cottage with her sister," Mary Anderson Pickard was telling me. It was a Sunday morning and we were standing in the screened-in observatory of her house in the family compound. Through her binoculars I had been looking at the gray-blue hulk of Horn Island. "Daddy hadn't allowed anyone in there in months. Well, it was a sight. The plumbing was out, all the screens were out. In the bathroom the roof had been partly crushed by the fall of a chinaberry tree. There was water damage everywhere, roaches and rats all over the place, bottles and cigarette butts. . . ." She turned to look toward the island, her small hands held lightly together. "But that wasn't all." Adrift among the wreckage of mortality was Walter Anderson's perhaps unacknowledged bid for something beyond that: thousands of drawings and watercolors. They floated on the littered planks of the floor, swam out of drawers, boxes, a battered chest, swelled in great billows in corners, on shelves: more than two thousand of them that were salvageable and uncounted others that weren't. Nor was this all. For in a rearward room that had for years worn a padlock on its door Anderson had created a breathtakingly beautiful mural on the walls, ceiling, and chimney, depicting the progress of the sun's hours through the Gulf coast world. In a roseate aurora deer fed in the meadows, moving toward the rising light, and great sandhill cranes took wing from the marshes; at midday on a sea bluff all objects were evenly, brilliantly gilded by the petaled sun painted in the center of the ceiling, a naked light bulb at its heart; at sunset rising ranks of gulls were tipped by the lowering rays, and an evening cat brushed through the tall, darkened grass; on the chimney, a young girl, the spirit of the Mississippi River, stood rooted in lilies, rabbits, and deer.

"It was such an affirmation," Mary Pickard said, raising her hands shoulder high and looking upward as she did. "Mother said, 'This man was no failure.'" I asked her what her own reaction to the room had been. "I cried," she said simply, and in reliving that moment of discovery, it looked to me as if she could again. It was, she continued, clearly a hymn of praise, and no one was surprised when later in sifting through Anderson's papers Sissy Anderson had found a carefully copied out Psalm 104: "O Lord, how manifold are thy works!"

"Before he finished the mural at the Community Center," Mary

Pickard said, "he had put the lock on the door. Actually, there were two locks, the other one inside so he wouldn't be disturbed at work. So he must have started it then [c. 1951]. Then he did a watercolor of the room showing the door ajar with the colors emanating outward, and you could just see part of the pattern."

She asked if I'd like to have a look at the cottage, "much cleaned up, of course," and on our way out of her house we passed one of Anderson's few extant oils, a Horn Island landscape accentuating the sinuous forms of the island's pines. I saw in it something of the mature Van Gogh after he'd chucked his Antwerp academic training and had attacked his subjects, apparently naked of technique. I said something about this to Mary Pickard and recalled a passage her father had written about technique being the "demon" the artist had to learn to move beyond. She nodded but said nothing as we went down the curving gravel road with a scattering of leaves underfoot.

"Yes," she said at last, "but I just hate it when art historians write that Daddy 'elected' to work in a 'primitive' style. He didn't *elect* to work in that way: that was the relationship he had to the place. For himself, he rejected studio art. He wanted a different sort of engagement that could only be gotten by being out in the midst of nature." It was that intensity, she felt, amounting to a real merging of the observer and the observed, the painter and his subject, that was so often mistaken for Anderson's alleged primitivism. If this was a comment on my Van Gogh analogy, and I suspected it was, I found it both polite and instructive.

In the clearing before the cottage an old boat lay canted on its side, its gunwales warping away from its frame, its paint mostly chipped off, one of the thwarts loose. It was her father's old skiff, his daughter casually remarked in passing it. I couldn't help stopping to regard it with something like awe; the next day, on my way to Horn Island safely inside a thirty-five-foot motorized launch, I would think back on this craft as I had seen it here and feel suddenly and strongly how dwarfed it was by this expanse of water, how frail a thing it truly was. Now, though, there was the cottage before me, and I had to pull myself away from the skiff to keep up with my guide.

Though much cleaned up, its screens replaced, floors swept, and that huge harvest of drawings and paintings removed and safely stored elsewhere, there was still something in here, some whisper or shadow of old struggle, Jacob wrestling through the long night of his life for absolution and vindication. It was there in the bookshelves on which Anderson's well-thumbed copies of the Modern Library Classics moldered and sagged. There in the skeletal bicycle rusting away on the front porch.

There in the blackened, weather-roughened figure of a giant swimmer Anderson had carved, the hand reaching out to plow through the Gulf waves, a symbol of aspiration. In a corner of the porch a wooden deer stood gazing through the screen at the canted skiff: this was the sole survivor of what had been a magnificent sculptural group Anderson had carved in a nearby grove, representations of the spirit of his chosen place and presided over by a tall god, the great river itself. The other figures, Mary Pickard said, had all rotted to pieces.

In the bathroom the damaged roof had been repaired, but there was again the unmistakable presence. Painted cows grazed on the green planks above the pitted tub. A couple of Anderson's hats, stained and shrunken so they wouldn't fit a child, still lay on a shelf as if just cast there. Another tall shelf was his "treasure chest," containing mostly shells, including the skull of a sea turtle, and I was startled to see how hauntingly humanoid it looked.

But if the soul of the cottage was still here, something vital—its heart?—had been taken. The secret room in which Anderson had created his hymn of the sun's hours had been taken plank by plank to the new museum, and though it was surely right that it be preserved there so that the public could participate in the affirmation it made, I could see the sense of loss on Mary Pickard's face as she stood in the empty replica of the room with its barren new walls. The replica restored the cottage to its original dimensions, but that was about all. Later, as we stood in the transported room with its shaded windows and atmospheric control device, I saw that lost look on Mary Pickard's face again, as if none who would enter here could ever feel more strange, seeing this most inward act of the fierce god, her father, translated into a public spectacle.

Late that afternoon, seated at her kitchen table while the Sabbath light lowered, branch by branch, through the trees, Mary Pickard was still musing on the family history she had so obligingly rehearsed for a stranger. It was as if having been asked about it, it was not so easy for her to drop it again. "I really lived with my father only from 1940 to 1947," she said in a soft voice, as though she were talking to herself but was willing to be overheard. "He left us at Oldfields to move back here. Then I only went to the cottage when I had a specific errand to take me there—if I had a message or something he wanted delivered. You didn't feel free to just drop in. In his earlier years, when we lived at Oldfields, he liked children. But later, if he saw us or if we happened to come across him at work somewhere, he'd say, 'Go away.' He said he never wanted children. People shouldn't have children, he said, to bring into this world the way it was. When I was born he said I couldn't be his child; he said he didn't know where I came from." She stopped, and in the shadowed, sunset room I could suddenly hear the tick of time.

"Sometimes, I wonder what it would be like to have all of W.I.A. cleared out of my head. I wonder what would be left."

APPROACHING Horn Island in a chartered boat, I tried to see it as Anderson might have; or as the doomed men of the Narvaéz expedition might have before him. But the passage was too smooth, and we neared the island too swiftly. Only in those minutes when we had been out of sight of both mainland and island had I been able to capture imaginatively a sense of frailty and aspiration, of humans abroad on the deeps of the waters and dependent on the land no matter how slim a margin there was of it. Gliding toward the shore as I now was and seeing the snaky forms of the pines suddenly stand up out of the horizon, I couldn't get that sense of grateful embrace that had been the artist's. A single shrimp boat, its night's toil over, its nets up, and its crew asleep on the gentle swells, stood three hundred yards offshore. As we passed it I asked the charter boat's captain if the shrimper was carrying his TED. He looked at the silent craft as we passed it, then said, "If he's got one, I'll eat it."

Then I was ashore on the inland side of the island and walking its narrow beach eastward under the shelving cliffs and salt-strangled pines with their exposed root systems, feeling a bit like Crusoe now with the charter boat gone for the day. There were coon tracks, purposeful and firmly incised in the damp sand, but no Friday's step, and so for the moment, anyway, I had something of Anderson's sense of being the lord of my domain. This day there was enough of a breeze on this side of the island to keep the gnats and blackflies from settling, but I knew from Anderson's logs that the Gulf side was always breezier and the place to be if you wanted to sit in some comfort.

Cutting inward, I had to skirt a salt pond and its guardian marsh and in doing so I saw a big gator in its midst, a suspended series of bumps ending at the snout. At my feet fiddler crabs worked the margin of the pond, raising tiny clouds of mud in their slow, steady progress. Then, coming over the low dunes with their waving vegetation of sea oats and panic grass, there was the great Gulf again under a high sky and a stiff breeze. Never yet on my travels had its immensity seemed so real to me as in those first few minutes when I simply stood there gazing at it without a single distraction. Then details began to come into the picture and that particular spell was broken: a flight of cormorants, dense brown against the light, their wing beats slow, strong, steady; the shadow of a gull flashing over the low surf; sandpipers skittering along the rollers' edges; a ghost crab teetering along the slanting sand like a miniature dune buggy. Here was the Great Mystery so clearly on display that only the very dullest could fail to be touched by it: how it all works, severally and together. Once on the beach little Mary Anderson had watched while her father had stiffly stood, waving his arms and conducting the symphony of wind and water. "Listen," he had commanded her with characteristic imperiousness. This was the music he was all his life trying to catch, and standing on the sand of his island I could believe that in death he had caught it at last and become a part of it.

FALL

THE FIRST TIME I SAW NEW ORLEANS I was a young man. This was thirty years ago. After a week there I boarded a train back to Philadelphia and stood on the platform as we jerked slowly out of Union Station on South Rampart, watching the city begin to flit into the past, the train going quicker now and more smoothly, and I remember thinking, Well, I'll probably never get back here, but at least I've had this. Since that time I have visited the city probably twenty times, and though I have never again taken the train out, I've always had that same sense: This is my last time here.

I think this recurrent sense about New Orleans must have something to do with the pervasiveness of the past here. In no other American city is the past so constant a companion: not in Boston with its colonial monuments and sites, its old burial grounds; nor Philadelphia; nor that sliver of old Manhattan that lies below the present-day financial district. But this wet, oozing swampland atop which the French ditched, diked, and laid out the first streets and squares is like the hand of the past, reaching up to pull you back. The force of gravity is no greater here than elsewhere; it just feels that way, and you think that if you were to jab a stick into the earth anywhere in the city, you would strike this ancient ooze—and maybe uncover a skeletal hand, a rusty sword hilt, or a fragment of an old cypress drainpipe. The present floats lightly on this past, fleeting, evanescent, insubstantial. You are in the existential sense Just Passing Through.

Thirty years ago the past was an even more visible presence than it is now. The Uptown and Downtown areas were wholly intact, the riverfront was a blackened, rusty warren of old warehouses and sheds that looked substantially unchanged since at least Reconstruction, and Decatur Street along the river in the Vieux Carré was still redolent of spoiled produce, chicory, and the bouquet of aromas from a dozen small restaurants serving boiled rice and red beans. Trolleys still clicked along Canal, St. Charles, and other streets, and if a white person gave a cabbie a destination for a black part of town, the driver would point out that surely this was a mistake. A phone call still cost a nickel, and if you happened to consult an older directory, it told you in its multiple listings under "Jones" or "Robinson" who of that name was "colored."

All this has changed. Uptown and Downtown as distinct and recognizable districts are fast disappearing. As a consequence of the World's Fair of 1984 the riverfront from around the old Poland Street Wharf to the bridge across to Algiers has been weeded and spiffed up. And Decatur Street has become a Disneyland set of cute restaurants, ice cream parlors, and T-shirt shops in which the French Market has been suffered to remain for the air of authenticity it may impart. The fragrant old Jax Brewery has become a giant arcade. You might still get a funny look from a cabbie if you are white and give a destination for a black part of the city, though now the reason would be different: some areas have become very dangerous for anybody. During the ten November days I was here on what I yet believe will prove my last visit I read of three murders sufficiently arresting to make the forward pages of the papers. In one, a teenaged boy was ordered by a cruising gang to hand over his new gym shoes, refused, and so was shot. In another, a toddler in one of the projects strayed into the midst of a druggers' gun battle and was hit in the head. In the third, a tourist foolishly resisted a daylight robber in the French Quarter and had been stabbed. When I recalled the many nights on past visits when I had rolled back to my motel in the early morning, happily loaded after a night of great food and music, I read these items with a mortal chill.

But New Orleans has always had a reputation as a violent place, from its earliest days when it was garrisoned by French conscripts described either as prison dregs or malignant midgets; to the days of the keelboaters who periodically terrorized the town like that marauding motorcycle gang in the Brando film *The Wild One*; and on into our own century when the local branch of the Mafia was alleged to call most of the significant municipal shots. In fact, it had been the stain of old violence that had brought me here for my first visit. At work on a doctoral dissertation in folklore, I had picked up the trail of a legendary black outlaw, Aaron Harris, who had once been celebrated in song and story in New Orleans in the early years of this century. Jelly Roll Morton had sung of Aaron Harris, "a ready Killer . . . that had very little to say," he told folklorist Alan Lomax. Harris was so tough, Jelly went on, that he could chew up pig iron and spit it out razor blades. And, Jelly added, he wouldn't be talking about Harris even now (this was 1938) had not one Boar Hog caught the outlaw in an unguarded moment and "blotted out his name." A dissertation in folklore required fieldwork by the student, and the obscure, undocumented legend of Aaron Harris seemed a likely opportunity to fulfill that part of the onerous obligation.

The place to begin hunting for Aaron Harris was clearly in the city's jazz subculture. It had been, after all, a jazz musician who had remembered the essence of the Aaron Harris legend, and there was a somber kind of justice in this, for among the first fans of the new music not yet called jazz were the town's marginal citizens: gamblers, hustlers, pimps and their human chattel, and outlaws. Among whom was Aaron Harris, a broad, burly sometime cooper who made a living knocking over gambling games in the black neighborhoods and terrorizing the riverfront. Legend credited him with at least eleven killings, and the police were said to have steered clear. At Preservation Hall on St. Peter I asked clarinetist Willie Humphrey (then in his sixties) if he remembered anything about Aaron Harris. It was at the end of Willie's long night, and he had had enough—music, the adoring crowd, the old, airless hall hung with smoke. He was carefully disassembling his instrument, putting it into its neat, battered case, pulling on his coat. Then he faced me in the wan wattage of the naked overheads. The hat went on four-square over his strong, graying hair. "Aaron Harris. . . . Oh, I don't mess with any of that. You want to talk about that kind of stuff, you want to see Beansie. He talks about that kinda stuff." And he turned away.

Beansie was Ernest Fauria, long proprietor of the Astoria Hotel and Ball Room on South Rampart. The place had been built by Tom Anderson, legendary vice lord and unofficial mayor of Storyville, and since its inception it had been home to every form of the city's remarkably variegated nightlife. Jelly Roll had shot pool in there, and he and Aaron

Harris had played cards there. In the 1930s trumpet star Lee Collins had led the Astoria Hot Eight from its bandstand. When I went into the place off the sunny streets the contrasting light within was momentarily blinding, but soon enough my eyes adjusted, and when they did I said to myself, "Oh, *shit*! This is a *rough* place." It was the sort of place where you step manfully to the bar, place your order, and when it is brought, you stare at your drink and *only* at your drink until you've gulped it down.

Looking back now, it seems obvious to me that Beansie was what used to be called a "police character," that is, someone whose shadowy line of work brings him daily into contact with law enforcement and who can call the officers by their first names without being their friend. He was a person surely who had heard just about everything, and yet here was a new one: a fresh-faced kid with a portable tape recorder standing at his bar and asking about a grisly old ghost. But he quickly masked what surprise he felt and directed me to a rearward booth where he might assess this phenomenon more easily. Perhaps of all the scams he'd heard of, this Ph.D. business was the most murky, and where was the payoff? Finally, though he wasn't at all satisfied with the genuineness of my research, he said he would make a couple of phone calls and then left me there in the scarred, sticky booth, returning a few minutes later to tell me that after all he couldn't help. He paused and then added, as if in afterthought, that I might try walking from the Astoria down Rampart. Somebody along there might be able to help.

What could I do but follow his suggestion, fuzzy and nugatory as it seemed? And near the intersection of Rampart and Clio a black cabbie cruised alongside, slowed, and told me that if I asked at the grocery on Melpomene for "Fatty Moore," I might get some further assistance. What Beansie had done, I now saw, was to set up a relay system of informants, no one of whom knew more than he had to, and when at last I found Fatty Moore, an old man taking the morning sun in a back-porch rocker of his house on Melpomene, I had found my source on Aaron Harris.

"That was a trigger man," Fatty Moore had begun slowly, "that used to deal cards at the Astoria. Boar Hog shot him right over here on South Liberty." Jelly sang it this way:

> Aaron pawned his pistol one night to play in a gambling game
> He pawned his pistol one night to play in a gambling game,
> Then old Boar Hog shot him and blotted out his name.

"YOU know," I said to Willie Humphrey as we sat in the darkened living room of his house on Cadiz, "we've known each other for about thirty years, and a hell of a lot has changed in that time. Allan [Jaffe] is dead. Billie and De De [Pierce], Cié [Frazier], Jim [Robinson]. The hall is different. But, by God, Willie, you're still the same, and you *sound* the same." Willie smiled. It was a Sunday afternoon, and when I'd knocked at the door of his neat bungalow he hadn't heard me over the roar of the Saints game he'd been watching. But now he obligingly pressed the "Off" button on his remote control and swiveled around in his reclining lounge chair to face his visitor. His shoes and socks were off and so was his shirt, leaving only a ribbed sleeveless undershirt stretched over his ample torso. His teeth were out, and the skin under his eyes was dark and gathered. For the first time since I'd known him he looked old and used by life, and despite what I'd just said to him, I found myself thinking that by human standards this man was ancient and mortal after all. In a few weeks he would be eighty-nine.

As if he were reading my thoughts, Willie shook his head once. "No, I'm not the same, either, but I'm doin' pretty good. Pretty good for an old man. You still a young man, though." We laughed together at this matter of relativity, and I asked him how he accounted for the fact that he had lasted so long in a profession that had as many hazards as work in high steel.

"I don't drink like I used to," he said, nodding at the fifth of high-grade tequila I'd brought him as a present, "and I've cut out poker and the horses. Play a little monte now and then." He glanced briefly toward the kitchen where his wife was busy with Sunday dinner. "I've lasted as long as I have because of my wife and the Lord. And I've made a lot of friends along the way. Been to their homes, and so forth. I was to your home once. And that keeps you goin'.

"People always come up to me and say, 'I never could play like you.' I tell 'em, 'Well, you probably didn't stick with it.'" He smiled at me just as he had at his happy fans at Preservation Hall for the past three decades. "Makes you feel good when people come up and tell you how much they've enjoyed you. Yeah, the hall's different." Allan Jaffe's widow, Sandy, was running things now, and, well, she had "her own way." She had been offered a lot of money for it, Willie said, but she had wanted to keep the business going until her two sons finished college.

Talk seemed to want to continue on the subject of Allan, and I admitted to Willie that on that first visit to New Orleans when I'd seen Jaffe at the hall, playing tuba some nights and hawking the band's albums between sets, I'd been immediately suspicious. I knew the sorry, sordid history of the music's white 10 percenters who had so often preyed on the black jazz artists who had no other choice than to trust them. Only very gradually over the intervening years had I come to know Allan Jaffe's profound commitment to the music and his equally profound personal commitment to the elderly black artists he had rescued from years of neglect. In 1960 when he and Sandy had first come to New Orleans, there wasn't a single spot in the entire city where you could regularly hear traditional New Orleans jazz played by those who had been a part of its creation. Once in a while you might come across one of the old-timers at a black club—out at the Bucktown Tavern maybe, or Luthjen's, or playing a dance date up at Tulane. But that was all. Willie Humphrey, whose grandfather had taught some of the first names in the new music and whose father had been a member of the famous Crescent Orchestra in 1913, was living in obscurity, his sound unknown to most in the city and entirely unknown to the world beyond it. But, he said, even then he was "doin' all right. I was satisfied with the money. I taught music, you understand. And I played colored dances, parades, funerals. Up at Tulane I played at the fraternity houses, and I played yacht club dates. So, I was doin' all right. Then Allan come along."

He came along into a virtual vacuum. A bumbling organization calling itself the New Orleans Society for the Preservation of Traditional Jazz had a lease on an old hall that once had been a Spanish tavern and had been holding occasional "kitty sessions" there at which traditional musicians had played and the hat was passed. But even this terribly modest venture was about to end in acrimonious wrangling, insolvency, and local indifference. The Jaffes agreed to take over management of the hall, meanwhile holding down daytime jobs. The admission would be by donation, and on nights when the kitty proved too small the Jaffes made up the difference. Meanwhile, Allan was being tutored in music by old-time brass band musicians Punch Miller and Wilbert Tilman; in New Orleans musical history and culture by William Russell, who had tried in the 1940s to spark a revival of interest in New Orleans jazz; and in local business opportunities by Larry Borenstein, a gallery owner who had first leased the old hall on St. Peter.

"It was rough," said Willie. "Hard work. He [Allan] had some little job over there on Canal or somewhere, and at night he'd come on over to the hall, y'know. Then they raised the [admission] fee to a dollar, but that still didn't ease things up too much. So, after a while he come to me and said, 'I'm gonna have to raise the price of admission some more or else cut down on the number of your nights.' So he raised it to two-fifty, but he was very reluctant. That's the way he was. But you notice even now, the admission is lower there than anywhere else in the Quarter, and they sell those albums there for five dollars. In other places, I don't know what they cost now.

"Then, after a while, things commenced to get a little better, and he realized the music could be a good thing for him. He took advantage of the situation—but not of the people. There's a difference." He paused and looked down toward his bare feet hanging over the edge of the lounge chair. "He was one of the finest people I've ever known, and not only to me but to everybody. Never took advantage of anybody. And he would do the little things, y'know. One time I'd been feelin' kinda poorly, and so Jaffe had these little red buttons made up, y'know, the kind you bend and wear in your lapel? And he give 'em to me to hand out. They said, 'I Danced with Willie Humphrey.' And you know, they made me feel a whole lot better.

"Anyway, Borenstein gave him the idea to sell the band out [to try to get the band out-of-town dates]. He had an agent come down here to hear the band, and he got us some dates." This was in 1966, but before the agent booked the band on a tour of small colleges in the Midwest and Texas, Allan Jaffe had spent several years trying to get an agent to take him on. "I used to spend whole days sometimes," Jaffe once told me, "just sitting in the outer offices of booking agents in New York, trying to get in to talk with them. Nobody wanted to take a chance on us. They were all worried that the guys would die off before the dates. They'd say to me, 'Look, we book a year in advance. How can you guarantee me a band then?'" But that spring of '66 the band did go out in a nine-passenger station wagon with a U-Haul behind it filled with luggage and instruments.

"It was Billie and De De," Willie recalled, "Big Jim [Robinson], [Cié] Frazier, me, and Allan. That was the band that blazed the trail. I'm the only one left now."

Years after that first tour and after I had at last penetrated Allan Jaffe's thick wall of reserve I asked him about it. This was on a sunny day in early spring, and Jaffe was in an accessible mood. The night before his accountant had succeeded in balancing Jaffe's books—no inconsiderable feat, the man had told me as he lurched out of the offices, adding that he could not balance Jaffe himself. Chris and Jane Botsford, Jaffe's managers in an increasingly large and complex operation, had just cleaned up some piece of particularly vexing business, and now they joined us on the shrubberied patio behind the hall. Jaffe got beers from the office refrigerator and sent out for muffalettas (the New Orleans version of the Italian hero). Waiting for them, the four of us sat in the mild sun, sipping. "Near the Indiana/Ohio border," Jaffe said abruptly, "we ran into a hell of a snowstorm. It got awfully quiet in that wagon. But nobody said 'Turn back,' and we crawled along secondary roads and made it. We've had concerts canceled on us, but we've never missed one."

The band that blazed the trail was an instant hit: elderly black men in white shirts and ties, one of them blind; a woman pianist and blues shouter; and all of them able to play with a facility and vigor and joy that was astonishing to their mostly northern audiences. What talent! What energy! From what unsuspected well had this come? How long could it possibly last? For those early audiences there was, along with their pure enjoyment of the music, a sense of urgency, for here, miraculously preserved, was a bit of Americana that was fated soon to vanish forever. Jaffe skillfully traded on this without seeming to; that was what Willie Humphrey had meant in saying that Jaffe had taken advantage of the situation.

And in fact the audiences were right to feel that urgency: the players were all elderly survivors, and their art was authentic and traditional with its roots in the music's formative years. When the last of them died, New Orleans jazz would still go on, but a chapter would be closed. It was true also that by his efforts Jaffe had saved something that might very well have been lost. America and the world would have been the poorer had he not successfully merchandized the phenomenon of Preservation Hall.

The players would have been poorer, too, and while none of them became wealthy through Preservation Hall, Jaffe was able to make good money for all of them. Willie Humphrey and his brother Percy (trumpet) were among the very few who were "doing all right" before the Jaffes had taken charge. Jaffe told me once that he took a certain satisfaction in listening to the players complain about how much money they now had to pay the IRS. I had no way of knowing what the change in Willie Humphrey's fortunes had been as a result of his long association with Preservation Hall, but he told me he owned the house we were talking in and the one next to it as well. They would not, he said, have to hold any benefit concert for him.

If Allan Jaffe had a long-range plan for Preservation Hall—and he was initially as surprised by success as were the players themselves—it was probably simply to keep the operation going only as long as its authenticity could be maintained. As the oldest players died—Billie and De De, Big Jim, Ernest Cagnolatti, Sweet Emma Barrett—Jaffe carefully wove in younger ones who played in the traditional style. And he could have kept things going on such a basis until every member of the original talent pool had taken a turn at the hall. But the losses were intensely personal for him, every one of them a blow to the soul, and he couldn't bear to speak of the departed ones or even to listen to recordings of them. It wasn't clear to me or to those closest to him, Chris and Jane Botsford, how much more of this steady inevitability he could take. Jim Robinson's death hit him particularly hard, Chris Botsford had told me. "Something went out of it for him after that." Then Botsford had grinned as a memory had bubbled to the surface. "Remember that preacher at Jim's funeral, the one who gave that terrible oration over the body—all about sin and damnation and Jim's shortcomings? Well, afterward, when Jaffe filed by the casket, he slipped a fifth of I.W. Harper in there with Jim, so that's the way he went to the cemetery."

Then, surprisingly, it was Allan's turn. "We were vacationing down in Mexico," Botsford recalled. "Jaffe had his shirt off, and I'm looking at this *angry* mole on his belly. 'Jaffe,' I said to him, 'get your ass to a doctor right away and have him look at that.' He didn't. He never took care of himself, and it was probably too late by then anyway." It was a melanoma, and by the time Jaffe did get into treatment it had metastasized into his liver and stomach. In 1987 he was dead at age fifty-one.

I said to Willie that it still amazed me that Allan had died. But at his age Willie had seen so many come and go that nothing really surprised him any longer except the longevity of the Preservation Hall phenomenon and his own ability to stay with it. "In my lifetime," he said, "I've seen that nothin' lasts more than ten years. Nothin'. Now we've been goin' pretty near thirty years. That's very unusual. And it'll last a long time further, way after I'm dead and buried, as long as Sandy wants it to.

"It's been hard, but I've enjoyed it. I tell 'em I won't go on some of the trips. My wife, she likes to go, see all those things, y'know. But now her arthritis is so bad. She goes twice a week over to the Baptist Hospital to have exercise. So, I'm not going on any more of those real long trips, like overseas and such.

"Sometimes I don't even want to go down to the hall at night, like when I'm sitting here like this. I think I don't want to go. But I'm obligated, so I get up, and I go, and after a while, when I'm there and the people are enjoying what you're doing, I feel better than when I was here." He tapped the armrest of his chair with his forefinger. "But you know what? This whole thing, it never would have happened with the local people. You just can't count on the local people. They don't come out. If it was strictly up to them, it never would've lasted this way. We get people from everywhere else. We get people from South America. We get people from Australia. Some of 'em can hardly talk English. But they're all glad to see you." He smiled deeply.

ON my last few visits to New Orleans I hadn't been able to bring myself to go to Preservation Hall. For me the place was now so crowded with ghosts that it felt like I wouldn't be able to squeeze in myself. Once I went by and saw the usual crowd waiting on the sidewalk between Pat O'Briens and the hall, telltale "Hurricane" glasses from O'Briens in their hands. On this night I walked quickly past the gate with Lisa Merrill, a violinist from Santa Fe just in town to play with the New Orleans Symphony, who had some interest in jazz. I wanted to show her at least the location of the place, but our destination that evening lay around the corner on Bourbon where Banu Gibson was appearing at Mahogany Hall with her New Orleans Hot Jazz Orchestra.

Bourbon Street is devoted to trash—food, merchandise, enter-tainment—but Banu Gibson was the real thing. She was a worthy successor to the hundreds of fine performers who have preceded her in this city and against whose pervasive and lingering influence she has had to make her way: a youngish white woman who vamps the blues, does red-hot-mama numbers and novelty tunes from the Twenties and Thirties, and who also plays banjo in her septet when they do classic New Orleans pieces. On this night before a steadily building house she opened with "Wang Wang Blues" and did the vocal. From where we were sitting Lisa Merrill and I could see that a good portion of the audience was wearing name tags identifying them as members of a tour, and Gibson had clearly also spotted this since at the conclusion of "Wang Wang Blues" she immediately began to establish a rapport with them. Singling out a table of male tour members seated closest to the stage, she said, "Boy, you guys are gonna bear the brunt of all this, aren't ya? Have notes all over ya before ya leave. Yeahhh!" Her pretty face broke into a dimpled grin and she laughed infectiously, the ringside men joining in heartily. Then came "Love Me or Leave Me" and "I Would Do Anything for You." Introducing the standard "Tin Roof Blues," Gibson did a bit of stage business, then said, "Over there where City Hall is now they had jazz bands and *nasty* women. Hey! [to a thickset, balding tour member] I got your attention with that, didn't I? Well, you're way too late. It's all gone now. But the song remains." And she turned toward her group and counted off. Charlie Fardella, a very good cornetist with something of the natural comic about him, followed Gibson with a vocal on "Dinah."

Into the second set two men arrived at ringside, and Gibson stopped the show, à la Victor Borge, to tell them they were late. "And you better have a note 'cause we had to wait for you all this time, and these folks have just been sitting here, waiting for us to start!" The crowd, which had been doing anything but that, roared with laughter.

"And, hey! I almost forgot! It's Elizabeth's birthday tonight—and she's buying everyone in the club drinks! Let's have a song for Elizabeth." The spotlight swung toward a corner table and the band played "Happy Birthday" with comic embellishments. When they had finished Gibson said, "We know what we'll be doing now on the break, don't we, fellas? Over there at Elizabeth's table—spanking her!" The set continued with the first notes of Fats Waller's "Willow Tree" mingling with the last of the laughter. Gibson followed with two of the novelty tunes she does so well, "Was There Anything Wrong in That?" and "I Got What It Takes But It Breaks My Heart to Give It Away." Then she announced that the set's closing number would be a "very short one: Charlie's got to go to the bathroom."

At the break Gibson, Charlie Fardella, and trombonist Dave Sagar joined our table, Gibson just long enough for me to invite her to lunch the next day. When she had left, talk turned to the relentless physical grind it was for the professional musician, whether classical or jazz, and Lisa Merrill discussed with the bandsmen certain yogalike techniques designed to relieve the strain that playing an instrument entails. There were, she said, wonderfully restorative exercises one could do to relax the fingers. "It's not my fingers," Charlie Fardella said softly, "it's the chops. Yesterday I played twelve hours."

More than an hour later the New Orleans Hot Jazz Orchestra was still hard at work, but Lisa Merrill had to be going: she, too, had to play tomorrow. Saying our goodnights outside the club where the sounds of the band mingled with the incessant come-on of Bourbon Street, Merrill sighed and glanced back through the open doors of Mahogany Hall to where Banu Gibson was singing and strumming, her face radiating good cheer. "Imagine," Merrill said in real wonderment, "having to manufacture all that gaiety, all night long, and night after night."

Ten hours later I was looking at Banu Gibson again, this time at Arnaud's restaurant, just around the corner from Mahogany Hall. The propinquities of time and place said things to me, not just about the jazz life in general, but about the jazz life in this strange city where in so many instances apparent polarities—night and day, naked hucksterism and old elegance, Bourbon Street and Arnaud's—rub up against each other in a historic embrace. In the restaurant waiters in black tie glided through the white-tiled rooms that were garlanded with flowers and palms; a hundred yards away on Bourbon they had not yet gathered up last night's harvest of plastic cups and vomit.

Gibson breezed in as if she owned the restaurant, just as hours earlier she had owned the adjacent club. She hadn't worn makeup and so inevitably looked different than she had on stage under the lights, but not older, her face expressing an attractive vigor that lit up our corner of the big room. She was stylishly turned out, though not extravagantly so, and wore her outfit with what seemed to me an appropriate nonchalance, as if she were saying, "Hey, I didn't have time to spend my morning on this, but I think I look pretty good. What do you think?" And you would have had to respond, "Banu, you look pretty good." After she'd ordered iced tea and shrimp étouffée I asked her about the incredible strain it must be to manufacture with apparent effortlessness that relentless gaiety, night after night.

"That's the work," she said simply, then added, "I can never tell 'em—in any way—anything negative about what I do. They aren't down here to hear about the sleazos in the business or that you're tired or that you're not feeling well, whatever. I have to project a totally happy, energetic image. Some of that stuff you see up there [the stage business] is to make 'em really *see* that. I might do even more of it, but it's a problem to constantly shift back and forth from that stuff to being as serious and focused as you have to be when you're gonna play. Steve Yocum [the band's former trombonist] was terrific at that. He was really funny, and he enjoyed doing it. We played off each other. Charlie [Fardella] is basically a pretty serious guy, but he can be awfully funny when he feels like it. He'll do a certain amount of clowning around, but for him to take the initiative *everybody* in the band has to be in a really foul mood. When he sees everybody else down, he'll pick 'em up. Dave

Boeddinghaus *hates* any of that stuff. He's the one who calls us back to business when he thinks we're getting carried away. Did you know he's classically trained? Remember that business we went into last night where I say, 'Dave's either gonna play excerpts from *Petrouchka* or else "Do You Know What It Means to Miss New Orleans" '? And then he went into that little bit of *Petrouchka*? Well, we did that bit when we had our night with the New Orleans Symphony, only we did it in rehearsal. Dave played that part from *Petrouchka*—*da-da-DAH, da-da-DAH, da-da-DI, da-da-DAH, dadda-dadda, dadda-dadda....* I wanted 'em to know what kind of a guy they had up there on that bench, ya know?" Then, without a distinct pause she asked, "How much do you actually know about me?"

"Very little," I said, reminding her that on a couple of previous occasions when I'd seen the band perform we had chatted during breaks. She asked if I'd like a thumbnail sketch. "Would a wolf like a lamb chop?" I came back.

Gibson was just getting under way when the waiter arrived with our plates. She nudged hers aside and said, "I was born in Dayton, Ohio. I always tell people that as soon as I found out where I was, I moved. My mother was one of eight kids and my dad was one of thirteen, but I'm an only child. I got my name from an uncle who once had a date with a model who'd been named after an Indian princess.

"My mother liked show business, and I always knew I was gonna be in the arts some way. I began dancing when I was about three. Then we moved to Hollywood, Florida. When I was eight I was in this talent show, and the result was that I went from that into a dance studio until I was nineteen. I probably would've turned out to be a professional dancer except in high school you had to make a choice in electives between music or art; there wasn't any dance. So I chose music." She took a sip from her iced tea and glanced across the room that was beginning to fill with luncheon customers, smartly turned-out couples who for the most part appeared to be locals. "If I had become a dancer," she said, "I'd be retired by now. Anyway, I went on to junior college in Fort Lauderdale where I had a triple major in theater, music, and dance. I wasn't great there, but I learned a lot, which was the point. I never got the lead in any of the shows: I was always the kooky sidekick.

"I started dancing professionally nights in Fort Lauderdale as a go-go dancer, and if you print that, I'll kill you." She laughed quickly. "Then I got in a Miami Beach review—you know, with the feathers and all?" Her hands flew up behind her ears and fluttered in simulation of hoochie-coochie dancers with boas. Which would explain, I cut in, why the New Orleans Hot Jazz Orchestra occasionally gives the impression of being part review, part band. She nodded quickly but evidently felt she'd already covered that subject. She wanted to get on with her narrative.

She then joined another Miami Beach review that ran for fifteen months. "One night Woody Allen was in the audience because he was appearing in the same place, and I did his routine on stage. Afterward I met him, and he said, 'Maybe you'd like to do my second show?'" She laughed, rolled her eyes, and took a distracted bite of her congealing entree. "I was more ballsy then," she added. When the review finally closed she went up to New York where she reencountered a banjo player who had appeared briefly with the review in Miami Beach. Buzzy Podewell would eventually become her husband and the father of her two children. But before that there was a complicated six-year interlude of courtship and long-distance commuting between Gibson's gig at Disneyland in California and New Orleans, where Buzzy Podewell had taken a job in Tulane's theater department.

For any musician, I ventured, the prospect of moving to New Orleans must be both exhilarating and daunting. "You bet," she shot back. "Playing here gives us a certain sort of authority—to others. If you say you're from New Orleans and play jazz, people tend to automatically think, Hey, they must be really great. Which, of course, is bullshit, since where you happen to play out of has nothing whatever to do with your talent. But it can sometimes work to your advantage, and there *is* something special about this place, something I don't think exists anywhere else in the country, or anywhere else in the world, for all I know. This place is really *devoted*—that's the word—to having a good time. People expect it here; it's just the way things have always been. And it's not just the tourists, though they for sure have that expectation. It's the natives, too. They say if you have four people standing in a line, you're liable to have a party.

"Then the other thing, as far as being a musician here, is all that history. I mean, I remember playing on the *President* [the old steamboat that cruises the New Orleans riverfront] and thinking, '*Wow!* Louie played on this boat, and here I am, too!' But at the same time—a lot of the time for me, really—all that history can make you feel . . . distanced, you know? I mean, I didn't know any of those old guys. They didn't have anything to do with me. And here, you're always around somebody who's talking about all that history: 'I knew so-and-so.' She rolled her eyes again, this time in a slightly different way, giving the impression of one struggling under Clio's heavy burden. "Sometimes," she concluded, "I feel so outside all that it's like I dropped in here from Mars instead of Disneyland."

"You must also," I ventured, since she had opened up the subject of the past, "have to deal with the musical expectations of people who come down here looking for a certain sort of jazz."

"You bet I do," she came back, not, I thought, with any bitterness, but with the ready response of someone who has had to give the matter considerable thought. "One time in a radio interview here I said something like 'People think that in order to play jazz here you have to be old, fat, and black.'" She paused, looked down a moment, then went on. "I don't think that's a racist remark. I know I didn't mean it to be. I have as much respect for what those old guys accomplished as anyone, I don't care who it is. But I wanted to say what I thought was really true, and afterward I got calls from people who said they were glad somebody finally had the guts to say that. And then, since my house wasn't fire-bombed or anything, I guess it went down okay. No, I don't resent Preservation Hall or the players over there, not a bit. But if you're asking me whether the expectation they created over there has a tendency to impinge on what we're trying to do, I'll have to answer, 'Yes, it has.' No getting around it.

"And the fact of the matter is that there are a hell of a lot of really fine musicians in this town—black and white—who just don't get the ink, you know? I'm not taking anything away from those old guys at Preservation Hall. They may have been great once, for all I know. In fact, they probably were great. I remember once hearing that famous old trombone player over there—what's his name? Yeah, Jim Robinson. Anyway, on this particular night he took a solo, hit a few notes, and then he kinda clowned around a little. And I thought, listening to the few notes he did play, 'Gee, what a great solo that old guy is playing in his head! It must be terrific!' But that's what I mean: a lot of what goes on over there really refers to the past, not what's happening right now. I think they probably play more for the special sort of trade they get there, and that's fine with me. Allan Jaffe never knocked us, as far as I know. He actually had a few good things to say about us, but whenever I'd say to him, 'Hey, how about promoting us a bit, helping us out?' he'd never answer back. It just ended there." She shrugged.

I asked if this large context was a factor in the band's choice of repertoire, for the fact is that despite its name, the band is not in any sense a traditional New Orleans group. They have, however, retained the traditional instrumentation (cornet, clarinet, trombone, banjo, piano, bass, drums) and when so minded are a tight, hot group that can really swing the local standards. "When we play the usual New Orleans stuff we're good," Gibson said. "We can do that, and when we do you know that people who know what they're listening to are saying, 'Hey, this band is tits! This band cooks!' But people don't listen, most of 'em, with their ears. That's one thing I learned along the way. They listen with their eyes, which in our case gives us something we have to deal with if we want to play in this town. Anyway, to answer your question, no, I don't think what we do is out of any conscious choice not to try to be a traditional New Orleans band. We're all just eclectic. We do what we think will work, what fits our total personality. That's really the determining factor. I can sing in a number of different styles. I started out doing Nancy Wilson and Barbra Streisand imitations. Now I do Bessie [Smith], Ethel Waters, and Lee Wylie."

"Anyway, where was I?" Coming down to New Orleans to join her husband-to-be, I prompted. "Oh, yeah. Well, Buzzy had a gig at Houlihan's [a club on Bourbon that had once been a Chinese laundry], and then he quit, and they needed a banjo player. So he said, 'You're always saying you want to play, so here's your chance.' I said, 'No, no.' But he coaxed me, and I did it. I must have been *terrible*, made so many mistakes. When I think back on how really sweet the banjo players were in this town, I'm just amazed! They were so kind, so willing to offer advice. Boy! When I think of how lousy I was. . . .

"Anyway, then I ran into this guy named Jack London and the Bayou Boys, and that was the first time I really got into singing jazz. I got some exposure with Jack. One year we went to Newport [the jazz festival]. Then in 1981, I began to head a group at Bayard's Jazz Alley on Bourbon at St. Peter. Things really took off then, but the owner lost the club when he was stiffed by some sleazos. Welcome to the business!" She gave a short, cynical laugh, shrugged again, and took a sip of tea.

Currently the New Orleans Hot Jazz Orchestra played six nights a week at the Hilton and the seventh at Mahogany Hall. They also did occasional "run-outs," the musicians' current term for brief out-of-town tours: St. Louis, Kansas City, Wisconsin, Montana, California, Las Vegas at Christmas. These tours were obligatory in the business, Gibson told me, but distressing for her because they took her away from her young children. But when she was playing in town, "you'd be surprised at how normal our home life really is. I'm home in the mornings when the kids get up for school, and I'm there in the evenings to fix them dinner. By the time they're ready to go to bed, I'm getting ready to go out. They just think, 'There's Mommy, putting on her makeup.' "

I told her I'd once known a woman who had sung with some of the big bands of the 1940s and who had related to me some pretty hair-raising incidents of life as the "chick singer"—and some hilarious ones, as well.

"Yeah," she said slowly with a wry smile, "there's always something you have to handle, and I don't care who it is or how long you've been at this. There's *always* that Chiquita Banana image you bring on with you when you get in front of any all-male band—which is almost all of the time. So, you have to win 'em over every time. Sometimes you can tell a dirty joke to break the ice, sort of to tell 'em, 'Hey, I'm just as regular as you are.' But in every new situation it's always my talent versus that situation. When I'm gonna sing with a new group I always ask someone, 'Okay, who's the main guy I have to win over?' Then I concentrate on him." Sitting close to her at our small table and feeling the charm of her candid gray eyes, I had little difficulty imagining her powers of concentration or the eventual success of her efforts. "I remember one time there was this guy who was giving me a real hard time, and when I was trying to tell him how I was going to do a certain number, I said, 'Then I'll be in such-and-such a key, and here's the change: you'll hear it.' That's a joke among musicians, like, you know, 'The check's in the mail,' and that other one. So he looks at the rest of the guys and says, real sarcastic, 'Yeah, the chick says I'll hear it.' Then he says to me, 'I've got this mike stand here. What do you want me to do with it?' And I just turned around so they all could see me and gave him the biggest, sunniest smile I could. They all broke up over that, and I didn't have any more trouble with him.

"But the flip side of winnin' 'em over is the sexual thing, and so then you've got to make your situation clear right at the outset. You've gotta make it clear to them that you're just one of the guys, that you can tell a dirty joke and listen to one, and so forth. But that's as far as it's gonna go. You aren't going to have a sexual relationship with any of them. We can be pals and partners, but it's business. Once you get that over, it's usually okay."

She never did eat her shrimp étouffée, and when it became evident that she wasn't going to and that I had taken as much of her day as I could politely ask for, I wondered whether she'd mind driving me down to the foot of Canal where I was to meet a friend for the ferry across to Algiers. On our way there I asked her a question prompted by Willie Humphrey's remarks about the nightly effort it took to get yourself up to entertain another smoky roomful of strangers.

There were always nights, she said, "when you're in a really pissy mood, or the band is real down, and nobody really wants to do this routine again. But then you look out into the faces—and there's somebody's aunt from Kenosha, and you realize, Hey! You're supposed to make people happy! You better get your butt up there." She looked over from her driving and smiled that brilliant stage smile, and I felt that I was in the presence of an artist who had found her calling and knew it. Right place, too.

HALFWAY across the river to Algiers I went up to the top deck of the ferry to look back through Plexiglas windows studded with raindrops at the slowly receding skyline of the Big Easy. To my left towered the recent works that had transformed the city into a modern mecca for tourists and conventions—the Hilton, the International Trade Mart, Riverwalk and its mall, the Marriott, the Sheraton. Behind these and blocked from view was the grotesque, squat Superdome. Then I let my gaze rove to the right and took in the more human-scale structures of the city's oldest quarter, the spires of St. Louis Cathedral just peeping above the crowns of the trees and bits of the Cabildo and the Presbytère also showing. Everything under the rain was a monochromatic dingy gray.

My companion of the afternoon was Winston Lill, a retired public relations director, and we were on our way to meet with Blaine Kern, the man who had copyrighted for his own use the title "Mr. Mardi Gras." I had met Lill in 1984 when I was covering the World's Fair for an airlines magazine. Then and ever since he had proved to be what every traveling writer dreams of finding: an unfailingly obliging native guide with wide contacts and an informed, imaginative sense of what a writer should see and whom he should meet. If you wanted to go somewhere in the greater New Orleans area or meet someone interesting or important, Winston Lill was your man. If you wanted to go it alone, you never heard a word from him. Lill thought I ought to meet Blaine Kern and see his Algiers operation.

"Most outsiders misunderstand both Carnival and Mardi Gras," he said to me as the ferry nudged into the Algiers Point landing. "Carnival really refers to the whole season that runs from Twelfth Night to Mardi Gras. But Mardi Gras really is only Fat Tuesday." But now, he went on, the whole celebration had become so inflated and publicized that it was probably impossible to insist on original distinctions. More than any single individual, Lill thought, Blaine Kern had been responsible for the growth and change of Mardi Gras in the years following World War II. "It used to be a fairly small affair, really. It was mostly private, except for some things the city provided—police and sanitation, and so forth. Now, though, the city puts in so much money, and it's all been opened up to public participation so that it's really a community affair; I guess that's all to the good."

We were out now in what had become a slow drizzle and walking a high, grassy levee the half mile from the landing to Blaine Kern's offices and warehouses, which, I was to learn, were called "dens." Lill was explaining that in its original form Mardi Gras had been strictly an affair of the city's elite into which newcomers could hope to gain entrance only through the deaths of insiders. Kern's father had begun the business of making floats for the rich and highborn, a business, Lill said, that Blaine Kern and his sons had enormously expanded. But the real change in the character of the celebration had come at the end of the 1960s when Blaine Kern had associated himself with an upstart krewe (the local spelling) that wanted to crash the party with a parade of its own. Kern had built the float for the Bacchus Krewe and against the enraged opposition of the insiders had joined in the festivities. The example proved contagious, and Mardi Gras was changed forever. Kern had gone on to make a fortune building floats for anyone who wanted to participate, though there remained a solid substratum of opinion that regarded him as the vulgar destroyer of what had once been an elegant family affair. Now, of course, the parades were giant affairs that included floats representing such diverse community elements as blacks, senior citizens, sailors, longshoremen, and homosexuals, and new laws passed in 1992 prohibit any sort of discrimination by parading krewes. Nor was this the extent of the Blaine Kern influence. His Blaine Kern Artists, Inc., also created papier-mâché and fiberglass figures for all manner of business promotions; provided props, lighting, and floats for private parties, public concerts, and conventions; and sold a wide variety of celebratory specialty items—coins, medallions, plaques, and so forth. If you lived in New Orleans and didn't care for Blaine Kern, it could be rough on you.

Kern's secretary told us he would be tied up with phone calls for a bit, but while we waited, why didn't we take a walk through the dens? She was certain they would prove interesting to us.

For more than twenty years now the fun house has served as popular culture's metaphor for the insanity of contemporary civilization, and so in walking through the dens it was hard for me to see them as warehouses in which a thriving business stored its inventory and refitted some of it for ever-newer purposes. Instead, I kept seeing myself as lost in some hideous nightmare, compelled to cower beneath the huge icons of a violent and deranged century. In the long, high-roofed buildings you were by turns amused, awed, dwarfed, and repelled by colossal figures, heads, busts, disembodied arms and legs, dry-docked ships, castles and cabins, and silent, raging wildlife. Here Ronald Reagan snuggled up to Howdy Doody while mermaids shook hands with fire gods. On a single shelf I noted the ranked busts of a pirate, an American Indian, Charles de Gaulle, and a Viking girl, one horn of her steel-gray helmet fetchingly crumpled. A huge (the adjective must hereafter be assumed) Poseidon with trident held in his blue arms a clownish fisherman in rubber boots, a juxtaposition I had to believe was a matter of temporary convenience since it was demeaning to both of the personages. In another area a Liz Taylorish mermaid with starfishes concealing the nipples of her lovingly sculpted breasts stood next to a rampant polar bear. Peter Pan's Tinker Bell pirouetted beneath Disney's Dumbo. Here and there, snugged in between these prodigies, were small, real-life tractors, which I imagined were used to haul the figures to strategic locations. Here also were real men, hammering, sawing, painting, on what lavish projects I couldn't imagine, though it was certainly not too early for their work to be Carnival-related.

On our way back to Kern's office we passed across a yard in which were parked tractors and forklifts snarlingly guarded by the standard junkyard dog, and there in one corner was the canted, demasted head and torso of the Poseidon that had so regally presided over a central display of the '84 World's Fair. His hand, which once held either scepter or trident, now gestured emptily at the levee bank and the gray sky beyond, and I thought Winston Lill looked momentarily melancholy as he regarded this relic of an event on which he had spent so many hours of his life. Probably, though, Poseidon had served in some previous capacity before appearing at the fair, and doubtless now he awaited still another transmogrification.

We found Blaine Kern still wasn't ready for us, and so I had the opportunity to inspect the busy walls of his waiting room with its many photos of Kern and his sons, its framed congratulatory messages, its awards, citations, and assorted carnival memorabilia. One wall was completely taken up by a bulletin board listing the float projects on which the company was currently at work, and beneath the headings were lists of the personnel assigned to each. The headings ran: We the People, Americans, Coonass, Oriental, English, Spanish, Italian, Yugoslavian, French, Irish, Oilfield Class, Black, Dutch, Indian, Jewish, German, Polish, Alligator. At last we were summoned.

Blaine Kern was one of those individuals you occasionally run across who almost immediately strike you as quintessentially American and possessed of all the vivid, technicolor excellences and defects of the national character. Bull-shouldered, barrel-chested, with a somewhat closed face that frowned when you asked a question, he was clearly a hard-driving businessman who intended to make a buck and who devoted a ferocious energy to that cause. If this made him somewhat resemble the gross caricatures he created, there was also something of the romantic and the artist in his makeup, and he was unabashedly in love with the idea of America and Mardi Gras. He was shamelessly commercial, it was true, but he had also a feel for color, costumery, pageantry, and history that I found unusual. At first, it was hard to get a conversation started: his secretary kept calling on the intercom to advise him of still another call, and no sooner had we begun talking than he would say, "Excuse me" and turn to more urgent business. I listened overtly to one of these calls, which Kern took in his swivel chair, leaning back in it, his red suspenders in gaudy contrast to his immaculate white shirt and figured tie. While he talked his dark eyes roved restlessly around the Spartan interior of his office, as if even here he were seeking some new opportunity or advantage.

"Jack! Thanks for calling back. Now, I'll tell you what I had in mind. You see how it sounds to you. I've got this float—ab-so-lute-ly *beautiful*! Fan-tastic! It's a Nativity I made for Sidney [Barthelemy, New Orleans's mayor]. Now he tells me he can't use it down at City Hall. He's got reelection problems and thinks the religious thing is gonna hit some people wrong. Yeah, well, that's the way it is. Now understand, this is just a beautiful thing I'm talkin' about here, but what am I gonna do with it?" And then for the next ten minutes he told Jack what to do with it. When he had hung up I could hardly imagine that Jack wasn't completely sold. Then we began again, and this time when he had assured himself that he not only had my deep attention but my admiration as well, he called his secretary and told her to hold all his calls "until I'm done here." Then began a rapid-fire monologue about Carnival, Mardi Gras, and his beginnings in the business. In the course of it his energy and enthusiasm often propelled him out of his chair and caused him to pace the office like a lion. Other times he flung himself back into his chair and, bridging his strong hands beneath his chin, talked with deliberate emphasis. When illustration or documentation was called for, he rummaged through filing cabinets for newspaper articles or strode into his secretary's space to ask for brochures, studies of the economic impact of Carnival on the local economy, advertising materials, posters, Mardi Gras souvenirs. Taking notes as best I could amid all this, I found my lap, the chair next to me, and then the floor at my feet covered with a blizzard of Kerniana. If, fleetingly, in the dens I had entertained the ignorant image of Blaine Kern as a showman/humbug like the movie version of the Wizard of Oz, this had long since been dispelled in the spectacle of his presence.

His father, he said, had been a sign painter, "but actually, he was an artist. But you couldn't make any money as an artist—this is back in the depression years I'm talking about—and he had a family to feed. So, he painted signs. Roy Kern and Son was the name of the firm. He built his first float for Dr. La Rocca back in 1930, and his first Mardi Gras floats were six converted trash wagons he decorated for the Choctaw Krewe." Blaine Kern had served an apprenticeship to his father after what he described as a hard and unsatisfactory period of formal schooling. "I was always in trouble in school," he said with a small, grim smile. "I was always in trouble because all I ever did, all I ever wanted to do, was draw pictures and read books. I was glad to leave school and get into the business with my father."

He built his first float in 1947 and got his first break through the kindness and generosity of a prominent New Orleans businessman, Darwin Fenner of what was then Merrill, Lynch, Pierce, Fenner, and Bean. "Darwin Fenner *loved* New Orleans. He loved Tulane. He loved Mardi Gras. He was a great man, and you can write that down. A great man. He was instrumental in opening up Mardi Gras, and he was instrumental in my career. And now I've helped open up Mardi Gras even more—to blacks, to Jews—not because I'm a liberal, because I'm not. But because fair is fair.

"Anyway, he allowed me to put my floats in the Rex Krewe den, which gave me a place to work on them, and after that all along the way he helped me, he encouraged me. He'd chew me out for spending too much money on this item or that, and then he'd turn right around and write me a check. One time I was all set to go to Hollywood and work for Mr. Disney—the greatest American of the twentieth century—but Darwin Fenner encouraged me to stay in New Orleans and grow with Mardi Gras." He spread wide his arms in an expansive gesture, and I took the opening to ask why Mr. Disney was the greatest American of the century.

"He was the first environmentalist," Kern shot back. "And he was the first internationalist. Who else before him was interested in the wild animals, in the desert, and so forth? He was there before Cousteau and all those others. Who else showed us the life of other countries and built bridges of understanding between peoples? He did a lot of good, he was a true artist, and [smiling now] he was one hell of a merchandiser."

Back to Darwin Fenner. "In 1954 he sent me to Europe to study. He wanted me to see how they put on carnivals over there. So, I went to Austria to study how they made crowns; also for the tiaras and scepters. I went to Pforzheim, Germany, to study the medals and ducal chains, which they know how to do so beautifully. I went to Italy, to Viareggio, to study their huge, animated figures. I went to Spain for the sculpture at Valencia. I went to France to study the carnival at Nice. And now I have four kids who're following right after me. There's Barry, Thais, Brian, and Blaine Junior. He's the one doing the lights and sound for the Rolling Stones' concert tonight, and that's fine with me, that's his side of things, and he's very good at it. Me, why would I want to be associated with those people, with all their drugs and nakedness, and so forth? And we have twenty-eight dens in various parts of the U.S. and overseas. Barry handles most of the overseas business. He's fluent in several languages. We do a number of other festivals besides Mardi Gras. We do the Dallas Cotton Bowl parade, we do Macy's Atlanta Christmas parade, we do the Mummers' Parade in Philadelphia, and the Bastille Day parade in Cannes, France.

"And I've trained not only my own kids but dozens of other kids up into the business. When you were out in the dens, did you notice that black fella working on the float that's just below this office? Well, that's Alvin Darcey. He's been with me forty-one years since at age nine he sneaked under the door of a den to see what was going on. I gave him a roast beef sandwich—that was his pay—and a broom, and he's been with me ever since, except when he went to Vietnam.

"Now, where else but in this country could I have done all this? And where else in America but New Orleans? Nowhere else, that's where! And Mardi Gras has grown so, just like Darwin Fenner predicted! I'm just glad to be a part of it." But now, he said, arising from his chair and putting on his suit coat, he really did have to be going: there were appointments he had to keep across the river. But he would walk us to the parking lot, which now he did. On our way he took us through a den that was devoted to a family enterprise called "Mardi Gras World." "My sister manages this," he said, not breaking stride, "and they sell all kinds of souvenirs, as you see. And they show movies of Carnival and give tours of the dens. It's quite educational."

Then we were out in the parking lot, I with my arms full of the gifts he'd showered on me. Sometime during our interview the drizzle had let up, but the sky was a solid leaden mass that looked as if it had a lot more rain in it. Kern shook hands with us, then turned abruptly toward Algiers Point and its low, huddled buildings. "I was born just a few blocks from here," he said after a brief silence. "We call ourselves Algierines because really we're separate from New Orleans. Take a good look around you on your way back to the landing. You'll see every kind of architecture here: Steamboat Gothic, Greek Revival, plantation raised cottages. It's a real interesting community—just a great place to live!" With those words still hanging in the heavy air he jumped into his car and swung it sharply around to the exit.

Walking the levee back toward the landing, Lill and I felt the beginnings of the new rain and snugged down into our collars against it. "Sometimes I wonder," Lill said in his soft voice, "where he finds all the bushels to hide his lights under." He laughed gently, and it was clear he hadn't meant the remark meanly. "But you see that sometimes in people here: a fierce local pride and a love of community."

YEARS ago there was a TV serial about life in the city that used for its closing lines ones that ran something like "There are a million stories in the city. This has been one of them." A city kid myself, I recall being struck by the astonishing, vaguely appalling implications of those lines: that a city was a vast multitude of unvoiced narratives, any one of which, if you chanced to hear it, would prove remarkable. But, the lines implied, only a few stories would ever be heard; the rest would go to the grave unvoiced. In New Orleans with its slowly settling layers of history, who could say how many lost stories there were down there in the marl and the black river water? And how many more were walking about in the light of the present day, awaiting the chance to be told? What were your chances of being there at the right moment to hear one of the stories that are always life-and-death matters? If, for instance, I hadn't idly thumbed through a magazine of popular history in the Dallas airport on my way to New Orleans this fall, I might not have heard the story of Ron Ridenhour, and it is virtually certain I would never have met him.

Ridenhour was an investigative reporter for the New Orleans periodical *City Business* and had won a coveted George Polk Award for local reporting. But distinguished as his journalistic career evidently was, this wasn't why *Memories* magazine had mentioned him. No, Ridenhour was in there because he was the man most responsible for the uncovering of the massacre at My Lai during the Vietnam War.

I decided to call him from Dallas, not, I told myself, because of the My Lai thing but because he looked like a man who could tell me a lot about how New Orleans really worked—or didn't. I knew his involvement in the My Lai massacre could never be put entirely out of mind. If I talked with him, it would be there, lurking in the background like the unquiet ghost it was. But I decided I would never bring it up, and we might be able then to discuss the inner workings of the city as he had come to know them. As it happened, when I reached him through Information his first question was how I had learned of him, and so there it was, right at the outset, and I had to tell him. He listened, there was a slight pause on the line, and then he said he wasn't with *City Business* any longer. He was now, he told me cordially enough, in the early stages of planning a book proposal and so had to guard his time. But maybe an hour or so might not be too much of an intrusion, and he said to meet him for breakfast at the Blue Bird Grill a couple of days hence.

More than a year after some four hundred Vietnamese villagers had been rounded up and murdered in a hamlet American soldiers knew as Pinkville, an unknown ex-G.I. living in Phoenix wrote a startling five-page letter to President Nixon, the secretaries of state, defense, and the army, the chairman of the Joint Chiefs of Staff, and twenty-three members of Congress. The letter detailed the events of that March 1968 day as Ron Ridenhour had pieced them together from interviews he had conducted among his service buddies in the weeks following. In March 1969 the wheels of U.S. military justice began ponderously to move, and an investigation of Ridenhour's charges was ordered. But the war was still very much on, and no one in the government or the military was especially keen on discovering the truth of an affair that might further sully the image of an adventure already badly tarnished in the public eye. Still, an investigator with the inspector general's office in Washington was put on the case with orders to discover discreetly what basis in fact, if any, Ridenhour's charges might have. "In the best of all worlds," that investigator recalling thinking, "Ridenhour would turn out to be crazy, but the tone of the letter—eloquent, thorough, absolutely convincing—didn't leave much hope of that." At the end of his investigation the same man said, "I had prayed to God that this thing was fiction, and now I knew it was fact." The fact was the murder, maiming, sodomizing, and rape of unresisting civilians carried out —and subsequently covered up—by members of the U.S. armed forces.

By October 1969 small snakes of rumors had begun to crawl about. It was being said that the army was going to secretly court-martial an officer for his involvement in the Pinkville affair. And it was in tracing this particular rumor that reporter Seymour Hersh came across the name Ron Ridenhour. Subsequently he flew to California, talked with Ridenhour, and then broke the story of My Lai, an event, he has said, that changed his life in ways he could not have then foreseen.

Nor was Hersh's the only life forever altered by the telling of that story, as I was about to learn, waiting over coffee and the morning paper at the Blue Bird. I had gotten there early, but none of the chattering crowd matched up with the magazine photo I'd seen of Ridenhour. Then I saw him through the window, a big man with long, powerful hands and flat stomach, putting coins in the meter and turning resolutely toward the restaurant.

I don't know whether it was that he didn't believe that I wanted to talk with him about city politics, whether he was simply impelled to discuss Vietnam that morning, or whether there was some other motive at work. Whatever the case, he began on Vietnam almost as soon as we'd made our introductions and placed a breakfast order, saying that he had come back from the war "like a lot of others, pissed off. Really *pissed*. I'm still pissed. And I *will . . . always . . . be . . . pissed*." He hunched his heavy shoulders forward over the table and cradled his mug in his hands. Above a close-cropped salt-and-pepper beard his dark eyes blazed. "If that makes me bitter, well, okay, I'm bitter. But it's not just about myself. It's about the thousands and thousands of young guys—nineteen, twenty, twenty-one—having to make decisions of a terribly critical nature at that age. One of the things I promised myself when I got out was that those motherfuckers were never going to get a kid of mine and put him in the situation we'd all been put in over there. I said I'd never have kids, and I never have.

"I was drafted out of college. I guess I was about as intellectually immature as most undergraduates then. I spent a lot of time on the courses I liked and neglected the others. I was spending a hell of a lot of time on a writing course, and then I dropped a couple of other courses, so my load got down to eleven hours. That's when they dropped the nickel on me. I went to Fort Bliss, Ord, and then to Benning for jump school. Then to Hawaii. If you went to Hawaii, you knew you were going to Vietnam.

"While I was in Hawaii and when I'd be on weekend passes I tried to find out a little something about this thing I knew I was going to be involved in. Well, there wasn't very much available, but I did finally get hold of a couple of things by Bernard Fall [the French war correspondent whose reportage was highly critical of the war], and I took these with me on the troop ship over. There were five thousand troops on that ship, and I'm sitting up there on the deck reading these things by Fall and thinking, 'Oh, shit! Oh, *shit!*' There was this asshole sergeant who got it in for me right off—I don't know if it was the reading—but anyway, every one of the thirteen days over he had me on KP. But I'd just go up on deck and hide out and read this stuff and wonder what the hell I was getting into. He never caught me."

Ridenhour glossed his Vietnam tour, which included duty as a helicopter door gunner and long-range reconnaissance patrol, by saying that he had returned to the States with what he characterized as a "deep and unappeasable anger." "I was forced," he said, "—we all were—to act out the contrast between our professed values and what we were actually doing over there. And at that tender age! How in the hell are you going to sort all that stuff out?"

The question seemed almost an agonized challenge, and I felt called upon to say something. "Everybody," I said, "likes to imagine that, faced with the kinds of choices you had over there, they'd inevitably make the right ones. But now I wonder about that. I can remember too clearly a certain self-righteousness in the protesters over here; I know I felt some of that, especially when we all got together in these monster rallies. But now, all these years later, I wonder if any of us can really say what we'd have done over there—"

"But if not there, where?" he asked, his hands tensed, fingers spread wide as if to suggest the issue of moral choices. His voice had risen a trifle, though he was a long way from shouting, and it was clear to me that he had little interest in whether or not a neighboring diner might overhear him. "Where could you possibly hope to have a more obvious choice between good and evil, right and wrong, than at My Lai or My Khe—another hamlet next to it where that same day they killed another hundred and twenty-three or maybe it was one twenty-nine, I don't have the figures here. And it wasn't just those incidents: it was the whole conduct of the war." I said I'd read Neil Sheehan's *A Bright and Shining Lie*, and that if half of what he claimed was true about the conduct of the war from its very earliest days, then it was morally and politically bankrupt before Lyndon Johnson ever took office. But Ridenhour didn't want to talk now about books. He wanted to bear witness to what he'd seen with his own eyes.

Like the way villagers were routinely questioned. "If they made any kind of resistance to the questioning, they were in danger of being killed. It happened *all . . . the . . . time*. People here were shocked when that photo appeared of the South Vietnamese officer shooting a suspect in the head on the street in Saigon. That stuff went on all the time out in the field. It was routine. Under the rules of engagement, they were all V.C. when they were dead."

I asked if he had actually seen the massacre at My Lai. There was a pause here, a little longer than that which had ensued when the subject had first come up over the telephone. "We flew over something," he said at last. "We were flying light air cover for infantry, which means you're dipping up and down pretty close in. It's great fun if you're not being shot at." He suddenly spread his arms and uttered a harsh burst of laughter. "Look, no holes. There was a lot of smoke down there, and there seemed to be a lot of confusion. Everyone in the copter was asking each other what the hell was going on down there. Then some officer got on the radio and told us everything was under control and to clear out. A few days later when we were back in the area we saw a woman's body some ways out from the hamlet. It had been left right there on the path. It had an army shoulder patch placed between her legs.

"Then some weeks later I run into this guy I'd trained with in Hawaii who says to me, after we'd talked a bit about what had been happening to us and so forth, 'Hey, man, did you hear what we did in Pinkville?' That's what the hamlet was called by the Americans, partly because it was a suspected center of V.C. activity. He says, 'We went in there and just killed everybody.' I was thunderstruck. How could this be? And so I began on what I now recognize was my first investigative story. I began to pursue this. I talked with everybody I could about it, and finally I satisfied myself that *it was true!* and that nothing had been done about it. By the time I got out I was obsessed by it.

"I went back to Phoenix, and I was sickened. *Sickened*. The first night back I sat down with my parents and told them this long, weepy story. They had expected to get back a war hero, macho, and all that, and what they had instead was a kid with a long story about something they didn't want to hear. And it was all I wanted to talk about. Finally my dad said to me, 'Look, if you ever tell this to anyone, your life will never be the same. They'll fuck with you, and they'll come after me and fuck with me.'

It turned out he was right, but at the time, how could I know that? I just had this terrible thing I was carrying around with me, and I was trying to find a way of getting rid of it. But most of the people I talked with didn't want to hear about it either and advised me to forget about it. There was such *rage* there, such denial. I was astonished by that, too.

"I went around for a hundred and twenty days, searching out those people who had sort of set my moral compass—my dad, my Boy Scout leader—before I got to a former English teacher who told me, 'You have to write a letter, and if you want help on it, I'll help you.' He was the first one who really said what I'd been feeling, which was that if I didn't do something about this, I would become a part of it." He looked at me over his partly raised mug, but I'm not sure he saw me. Later, I would think of Coleridge's Ancient Mariner who was endlessly compelled to tell his story of crime, but now I was feeling almost singed by the blast furnace of the man's outrage. "So, I wrote the letter, and he helped me with it, and I sent it to thirty of them—Laird, Nixon, the Pentagon, my congressman, and so forth." I asked if he had a copy of the letter, and he said he didn't, that over the intervening years so many people had asked for copies that at last the author himself no longer had any. Copies were available elsewhere, he said.

He continued, "Anyway, there was the letter, and things began to slowly bump along. I thought I was a pretty tough kid and could take whatever the consequences were from this thing. I *was* a pretty tough kid. I went to work at fourteen doing a man's work, and I mean a *hard* man's work. I felt I was prepared, and I think I was prepared—for almost anything. But who could have been prepared for what happened? I mean, page one for a year? Well, after I sent off the letters at first nothing happened, and I kept calling the Pentagon every week from Phoenix. At first they would accept my calls, then after a while they wouldn't anymore. I'd say to them, 'I know you motherfuckers are going to try to cover this up, and if you do, I'll burn your asses!' Who was this crazy kid out there in Phoenix? I was powerless, and they knew that. But after a while they must have gotten at least slightly worried because the Plumbers sent out Ulascewitz to shadow me." He shook his head and added with a sardonic weariness, "I made them right away in their black suits. One day I'm in the truck on the way back from the ice cream plant, and I see these guys trailing me. Oh, I made 'em all right. At the time I was working at the plant and waiting to go back to school and trying to deal with what I now realize was big-time stress.

"Anyway, you know the rest. Hersh got hold of the trail of Calley's court-martial, and that's how he heard about this kid out in California who'd amassed all this information on the massacre—and I had it, too: I'd collected a lot of evidence. So, he calls me and asks, 'Are you the Ron Ridenhour who keeps calling the Pentagon about an alleged massacre?' I said I was. He said, 'I'll be out to see you tomorrow,' and he was. We talked, and I showed him what I had. He said, 'Give me three days with this. Don't talk to anybody else. If you give me three days, then you can talk to whoever you like.' He told me I'd have lots of people to talk with after that, and he was right because by then he'd broken the story, and the next morning there were reporters all over my doorstep." He shrugged slightly and took a sip of coffee. In the silence it seemed as if for now he'd said all he wanted to about this terrible thing he had carried home from the war, had gotten rid of, but hadn't.

I waited a bit and then said, "You know, you're a hero. A real one." He looked away toward the street, shook his head very slightly, and I thought I saw his lips move as if he were saying something to himself. I scratched at my plate of pancakes, wondering what I should say next. So I asked him what he had done in the aftermath of the story.

"Hersh helped me get a couple of small grants because I'd told him I wanted to go back to Vietnam as a civilian and report on the war. Well, the grants came to about three thousand dollars, which we figured was enough for one round-trip ticket to Saigon and a few months in the country. So I bought a one-way ticket in the summer of 1970.

"I knew almost nothing about writing, but I just went out into the country and started hittin' it, talking to whoever I could find. I knew so little about how to put a story together that I actually would write out each sentence on a three-by-five card and then try to assemble them into something coherent. Can you picture that?! I did a year of this, and that was enough. I'd done as much as I was going to do. I wanted to come home and marry my high school sweetheart. So, I came home"—he shifted his gaze from the blank middle distance to look directly at me— "but it just didn't work out."

Since that significantly apposite ending to his Vietnam experiences Ridenhour had fashioned a career for himself as an investigative reporter in the States. For the past eight years, he said, he had worked for "about every hippie rag in this city. Most of it's been reporting on governmental corruption, business corruption. I guess I'm not very bright after all, because it's taken me all this time to realize and to understand how fundamentally and basically corrupt—*fundamentally*—our society really is. And now I begin to see that this is the nature of all human societies. And if you think for a minute that in reporting corruption you're doing anything more than providing career opportunities for the next generation of crooks, you're crazier than I am. What your work really does is to teach the coming generation how not to get caught. Your work points out, 'These people got caught this way. If you make the same mistake, you're gonna get caught, too.'

"Be that as it may, I've worked my butt off on these papers. I was in such a sustained rage about Vietnam that I used to work night and day covering this scandal, that one. *Night and fucking day!* If there was a new scandal brewing, the others on the staff would say, 'Send it to Ridenhour.' If there was a guy waiting in the hall to see me, they'd call him the 'Scandal du Jour.' But nobody can keep that pace up. Nobody. It'll eat you alive. So, I left *City Business* a couple of weeks ago. Now I'm fiddling around with the idea of a book on black army units in World War I, what they went through, what happened to them. My agent seems to think it's potentially a good idea. We'll see."

We paid our bill and rose to leave, Ridenhour stopping to chat with a friend on the way out. On the street the sun had climbed toward noon, and we stood there, our hands in our pockets. "My dad was right," he said then. "The intelligence community fucked with me. My life hasn't been the same. They watched me all through the Seventies. Oh, I don't mean every day. They can't. There aren't enough of them to go around. But it was there. It *was* there. Oh, yeah." He paused and looked at me. "I have proof of that."

He said he would walk me to my car, but there was no car to walk to: anxious about my meeting with him, I'd neglected to read the fine print of the sign I'd parked under. Now it was plainly telling me that today was street-cleaning day. The car, Ridenhour explained, would be waiting for me at the city pound. He said he'd drive me there.

In the shadow of the Claiborne Street overpass there was the pound, complete with high chain-metal fence, guard dog, and bored, surly attendant at its entrance. Across from it a gaggle of exasperated motorists waited at an office window to pay their fines. Ridenhour swung his truck around under the overpass, braked, and extended his hand. He wore a small, tight smile. "Welcome to the city," he said.

🌴 NEW ORLEANS is often said to be the only place in America that bears comparison to France in its delight in and devotion to food. In fact, though, the whole of the Louisiana coast and the immediately adjacent portions of Mississippi and Texas not only recognize authentically good cooking but demand it, even in the most humble establishments (fast food outlets excepted). This is an area where, as in France, diners may be overheard knowingly discussing the merits of the meal of the moment and contemplating the savory possibilities of others to come; dinner is quite an acceptable topic of the lunch table. To some culturally disadvantaged folk—New Englanders, perhaps, where gustatory abstemiousness is a necessary virtue—this might seem evidence of gluttony. It is instead a frank acknowledgment that since eating is one of human life's chief pleasures, the food ought to be as skillfully and imaginatively prepared as possible. And this has nothing to do with cost. All these traits reach their plentitude in New Orleans, where good food can be had in a remarkable number and variety of restaurants, from neighborhood no-frills soul food places to elegant establishments like Brennans, Galatoire's, and, of course, Antoine's.

For me, the best of the soul food places was a modest, noisy one called Buster's that stood at the corner of Burgundy and Orleans. Allan Jaffe steered me there, telling me to be sure to order an oyster loaf. One lunchtime I did that. The place was jammed (as it was every time I ever went there). Laborers, coatless businessmen in white shirts and ties, musicians, off-duty waiters, and neighborhood shopkeepers stood in line or sat at the Formica-topped tables. All of the help, including Buster Holmes himself, were black, but they didn't seem to mind that the majority of their customers weren't.

Buster was behind one wing of the long counter, his face shining with heat, effort, and good humor. He was a country man, raised downriver near the old Magnolia plantation, and had brought his rural recipes and know-how up to the big city where he had prospered in an unostentatious, down-home manner. When I told him what I wanted, his mouth spread wide in a gold-capped grin. "Boy," he squeaked, "you don't want no oyster loaf."

"But I do," I protested, surprised. Was there some kind of code here that Jaffe hadn't told me about? "Allan Jaffe sent me here, and that's what he told me to order."

"Boy," he repeated, still grinning, "an oyster loaf is *this* long," holding his hands two feet apart. "What you want"—he looked appraisingly at me, taking the measure of my capacities—"is a quarter oyster loaf." And without further fuss he hollered that order over his shoulder, then heaped my plate with slaw, red beans, and rice. When I sat down at a crowded table with my plate and a sweating can of Jax beer and reached for the Louisiana hot sauce, I knew the kind of contentment that is peculiar to that part of the world.

Buster's is gone. But Antoine's remains, and it is hard to imagine that the city would ever permit this civic treasure and landmark—a century and a half old now—to disappear. In its way it is as vital to the city's image as traditional jazz and Mardi Gras. One afternoon I went in to talk with Bernard Guste, who managed the restaurant for his family and was now the fifth generation since Antoine Alciatore founded the restaurant in 1840 as a part of his hotel. Guste was still at lunch with a table of businessmen, talking intently through the cigar and cigarette smoke, the table cluttered with bottles of mineral water, coffee cups, and ashtrays. It was well after three, and I was reminded of the traditional four-hour businessmen's lunches I had often observed in Paris. When he saw me he came over to say he would be a few minutes yet, then directed a waiter to "give Mr. Turner whatever he wants." I thus had the leisure to simply sit there in the mellow light of the main room, sipping the faintly sweet coffee-and-chicory, and watching the transition take place between lunch and dinner. The black-tie waiters were clearing and the busboys setting up, and with the long pleated drapes shielding you from the contemporary realities of St. Louis Street it might have been an older, more gracious time—a century ago, maybe. Everything in here looked graceful, from the cut of the waiters' uniforms to the shapes of the newly placed napkins to the pattern of the heavy table service to the curve of my coffeepot's spout. I could happily have sat there for hours, I was thinking, and was almost sorry when Bernard Guste came over.

He didn't miss a beat, he was that smooth, and our conversation commenced as if it had been the other table that had interrupted us. Only now he was telling me about the history of the restaurant and pointing out the surviving relics of the old hotel of which this had served as the lobby. He would be glad to take me on a quick tour of some of the restaurant's sixteen rooms, though, regrettably, he was just very busy this afternoon and didn't have as much time to spend with me as he would like. Another day, perhaps? As we were about to pass out of the main dining room to go upstairs an elderly couple, last of the luncheon crowd, hesitantly approached him, and Guste turned toward them, smiling to ease their way. The wife wanted Guste to know that her husband had been here during World War II "and he always said he wanted to take me here." She giggled, then added self-consciously, "So here we are."

"I haven't been back since," the husband chimed in, "but I'll never forget my time here. I've been talking about it all these years." He smiled at his wife. "And now she's seen it, too."

"I don't know why I was looking at you folks," Guste said wonderingly, a quizzical smile on his handsome face, " 'cause I know I couldn't know you: I wasn't born until 1949, but you look . . . *familiar* somehow." He asked if they wouldn't wait a moment, and he went to the front desk, returning with a souvenir menu from the restaurant's centennial celebration. He chatted with them a minute or so, and the couple left happy.

Then we toured the bewildering warren of the restaurant that more and more came to seem like a metaphor for the city as a whole. It was a fantastic congeries of odd corners, blind corridors, roofed patios, walled gardens, portions of city streets now cut off and enclosed within the restaurant's walls, even some small, narrow rooms that once had been slave quarters and now served as private dining rooms. Tucked away on the second floor was a recognizable remnant of the original hotel—the Jackson Square of this elaboration—that had been here even before Antoine Alciatore. There were a couple of antique coat racks in its corridor, a glass-doored bookcase, black with age, that might once have served the literary needs of guests, and heavy brass numbers on the doors. Guste said the rooms were now used for storage. I swung open the glass doors of the bookcase and gingerly lifted out a copy of Soard's *New Orleans Directory* for 1805. Here on the musty, brittle pages were names and addresses behind which I could almost catch the faint and confused murmur of some of the city's lost narratives. Guste stood patiently and at a polite distance while I mused over this artifact that doubtless he himself had long taken for granted.

In all of the public dining rooms and most of the private ones as well the walls were covered with framed photographs, telegrams, congratulatory messages, news clippings, old menus, and printed guest lists from fetes of long ago. When Bernard Guste said he really must break away I asked if I might wander back through the rooms to inspect some of these documents. "Take all the time you want." He smiled. "And stay on for dinner as my guest. I'll have a table reserved in your name."

So I wandered through the empty rooms and back into the past. Here was a much-faded telegram from Walter Winchell, 1934; an autographed photo of "Oscar of the Waldorf"; photos tarnished sepia-and-cream of forgotten celebrities; and group shots of stiffly posed men and women at formal tables. In one photo British royalty, the Duke and Duchess of Windsor, were shown bowing to the local and temporal royalty of the Rex Krewe. The duke wore a bemused smile. In the former slave quarters there were framed autographs of Mary Pickford, Errol Flynn, Jack Dempsey, Harry Blackstone, Mildred Kingsbury (Miss Louisiana, 1931), Thomas E. Dewey, Ethel Barrymore, and some of the New York baseball Giants of the 1930s, including local hero Mel Ott.

That evening I took Bernard Guste up on his invitation and dined at Antoine's, accompanied only by the copy of Frances Parkington Keyes's once-famous novel *Dinner at Antoine's* that Guste had given me. "Maybe you'll even finish this," he had said, "which is more than I can claim." Now I skimmed through it while joyfully consuming my crevettes remoulade, poulet au vin rouge, and too many glasses of an excellent white Bordeaux. Like Bernard Guste, however, I found the literary dinner at Antoine's less satisfying by half than the real thing and at length laid the book aside and surrendered to the spectacle before me. This included a group of heart surgeons in town for a convention and their stylishly turned-out wives. My waiter, Val, whose father and uncle had been waiters here before him, joked that tonight Antoine's might be the best place in town if you were planning to have a heart attack. Watching the way the doctors comported themselves, I wasn't so sure.

There were also the usual tourist couples, many of them looking just a trifle unsure of themselves in this proud, old place. The women were invariably dressed far more presentably than their often coatless consorts who favored open-necked sport shirts. When these men entered and the staff had sized up their attire, they were politely advised of the restaurant's long-established dress code and then escorted to the cloakroom to be fitted there with one of the house's blue blazers. After I had seen this routine repeated a good number of times I asked Val just how many such coats Antoine's had in stock.

"Oh, I wouldn't know, sir," he said softly. "Must be thirty anyway."

I HAD always wanted to see the mouth of the Mississippi where it sent its rich, brown, silt-laden load pulsing into the blue of the Gulf. Francis Parkman had engendered this desire in me years ago with his description of La Salle's party coming down to the river's end in the spring of 1682, feeling the breeze freshen with the "salt breath of the sea," and then at last on April 9, seeing before them the "great Gulf . . . tossing its restless billows, limitless, voiceless, lonely as when born of chaos, without a sail, without a sign of life." On that day, Parkman writes, France received a "stupendous accession," of whose nature it was wholly ignorant: "The fertile plains of Texas; the vast basin of the Mississippi, from its frozen northern springs to the sultry borders of the Gulf; from the woody ridges of the Alleghanies to the bare peaks of the Rocky Mountains—a region of savannahs and forests, sun-cracked deserts, and grassy prairies, watered by a thousand rivers, ranged by a thousand warlike tribes. . . ." And all this now became France's "by virtue of a feeble human voice [La Salle's, taking possession], inaudible at half a mile." Who, attending to the grand music of this passage, could resist the urge to stand where La Salle had and contemplate the conclusion of his heroic quest?

Yet La Salle himself never stood there again, though it was his aim to build a fort on the site. In the winter of 1685, sailing into the Gulf and heading for the river, he overshot it by some four hundred miles to fetch up in Matagorda Bay. There at his pitiful Fort St. Louis his company quickly wasted away to dysentery, rattlesnake bites, malnutrition, and desertion while the leader himself made three desperate attempts to get back to that "fatal river," as his faithful lieutenant, Joutel, referred to it. On the third of these he was assassinated by members of his party and his corpse dumped in some bushes—no one knows just where.

As I learned from Winston Lill, I was myself in error about the river's mouth, and with far less excuse than the mapless La Salle. There isn't any such thing as the river's mouth, Lill patiently informed me. There were instead mouths, plural, more properly termed "passes." I probably wanted to go down to the southernmost of these, called South Pass, and this could be arranged if we could get together a party to pay for a charter boat out of Venice. Two days later Lill had the party made up, and in his car five of us left the city on a bright morning that brought the first real feel of fall to this part of the Gulf. A cold front had passed through in the night, lowering temperatures twenty degrees, there was a snap to the air, and the skies looked harder.

We followed Route 23 along the river's west bank past Ironton and Myrtle Grove and on into a region that once so intensively cultivated oranges that it was known as Louisiana's Orange Belt. There were still some orange groves around Magnolia where the state's carpetbagger governor, Henry Clay Warmoth, once had a great sugar plantation, but below that you saw that the land was *just* holding its own. Inky mud was everywhere now, water stood in the fields, and the oaks were lower and flatter, as if Nature itself were here enforcing a strict building code. Roseau cane began to show up, the sure-enough signal that firm land was giving way to wetlands and brackish water. We passed Buras (altitude seven), where as shortly ago as the 1940s a form of voodoo was widely practiced, and then came to Venice, end of the line.

While we waited at the marina for final arrangements for our charter boat, I loitered in the dockside supply store, which was amply stocked with junk snacks and along with the usual varieties of beer, regional varieties of soda, especially Pop Rouge and Red Creme. These latter looked as if their manufacturers might not have heard the news about red dye number two. Among the lures on sale the most popular appeared to be those for marlin (long and glossy) and tuna (fluorescent).

Then we were out into the pass in our canopied, flat-bottomed boat and heading for the river. The craft was owned and operated by a brother-and-sister team from Pilottown, he at the controls and his sister providing a minimal but informative voice-over. Before we went down to South Pass and then over to the Delta National Wildlife Refuge they thought we might enjoy seeing where they lived.

This close to the Gulf in Louisiana there were a number of small hamlets perched atop pilings in a sea of grass and brackish water. But there were none more dramatically located than Pilottown. Not counting the lighthouse and fishing camp at Port Eads right at the mouth of South Pass, Pilottown was humankind's southernmost settlement on the great artery of North America, and while this huddle of wooden buildings and wharves was hardly as distinguished as the magnificent natural fact on whose sufferance it existed, still Pilottown did have this distinction. Nor was it one cheaply bought, for Pilottown was fearfully exposed and had, as our guide was now telling us, been "pretty much rolled up by Betsy and Camille." There was still a settlement here, she told us, but certain vital elements of the community—the school, for instance, and the general store—had retreated to Venice. For all essential goods and services Pilottowners now had to take the boat to Venice, but there remained a residue of year-round residents who stayed on "because they like it here, because they're from here." These people, she said, didn't mind the inconveniences of living out here but instead valued the peace that was the chief consequence of their isolation and precarious location.

At this season the cordgrass that provided a sort of buffer for the village looked brittle and rusty, and on our approach the buildings rising behind it seemed partly submerged, only the pitches of the roofs showing. Long lonesome wharves of warping gray wood led back through the grass. Main Street was a raised and reinforced sliver of concrete sufficient to allow perhaps four pedestrians to pass abreast—though walking its length without spying a living soul I had trouble imagining so festive an occasion. On either side were cottages, some with scraps of weedy lawns in front and chalk-white propane tanks for ornamentation. The school building was still there, but the swings and slides wore that deeply deserted look peculiar to artifacts abandoned by children. The general store was a battened and battered ruin. What life there was here seemed concentrated in the two large, rambling structures that housed the bar pilots and the river pilots. Bar pilots were those taking ships from this point out into the Gulf; river pilots were licensed to guide ships upriver to New Orleans and beyond. From the point of view of a "shitty landsman" (the mildly disparaging term habitually applied to me by a maritime friend) here again was the surprise of finding structures so neat, so thoroughly professional in appearance, so trig, so—*shipshape*— in such a beaten and silent outpost of progress. Here the lawns were grassier, the paint brighter, the eaves and spouts more serviceable than anywhere else in Pilottown. It occasioned in me that same sort of surprise I have felt in boarding the boat of someone I thought I knew on land—someone as disorderly as myself and as dependent on others for his transportational safety—to find a scrupulous order, a professional attention to detail that reminded you that you were, in truth, a landsman who knew nothing of the noble and perilous profession of piloting a craft, however humble.

On the way down to Port Eads I fell into conversation with one of our party, a semiretired lawyer who lived next to Winston and Dorothy Lill in New Orleans's Garden District. Joe Hero had very recently recovered from cataract surgery on both eyes, and this outing was one of his first into the wider world he had been resigned to losing until his successful surgery. He said he now had better than twenty-twenty in one eye and "only a little less in the other," and he was immensely grateful for having been "given back the world."

"The day after my operation," he said, "I was out in my backyard having a glass of iced coffee, and I went over to the border there between my yard and the Lills'. Dorothy is just a wonderful gardener, you know, and I bent down and looked at all her beautiful flowers—all yellow and purple—and I cried. I could *see* them. And at that moment I realized what I'd been losing."

Other things had changed, too. From his youth Joe Hero had been an avid fisherman and hunter, but now he said he had apparently lost interest in these sports. In part it might have been the slow onset of the cataracts, he guessed, but that couldn't be all of it because now with his sight restored he felt no inclination whatever to take up the rod or the gun. "And this is with the duck season almost here, you know." Instead, he had in recent years become a conservationist. "And you know what did it for me? It was that photograph of earth that was taken from space. It was so beautiful and small, and I thought, Is that where we live?"

But there was also the matter of his old sporting terrain and what was happening to it: the coastal marshes he had known intimately for decades had changed so much he hardly knew where he was anymore. "The places where I used to hunt are now all under water," he told me, waving his hand outward. "I don't have any of the old landmarks I used to go by down here. Just a year or so ago I had a case down here where we had to use a survey. We used to go by the old fort the Spanish built [Fort St. Philip, just upriver from Venice]. But we came to find it was all under water! Couldn't find it! So, the surveyors couldn't, you know, set up their markers. They had to go out and do like this [he made motions as if poking downward with a pole] until they could establish its outlines. And that thing has been here since early in the 1800s."

At the juncture of a pass with the river we waved as we passed a boatful of mullet fishermen who eyed us strangely from beneath the lowered visors of their faded and greasy caps. The sight provoked Joe to remark that mullet were bottom feeders and so picked up whatever "awful crap" was down there. He said he wouldn't eat them anymore. Ditto crawfish and for the same reason. Nor would he eat raw oysters at any New Orleans restaurant unless he knew from which beds they were drawing, "and even then I'm not sure they're really safe. But there are a few restaurants where I do eat 'em. Seems like my body at certain times gets an *appetite*, you know, for 'em. I understand they're all right if they're fried or cooked some kind of way."

Such talk led us to speak of New Orleans restaurants, those he liked and trusted and those he avoided. Among the former he mentioned Mosca's, a little roadhouse on the river's west bank beyond Westwego. I remembered it well: undistinguished in appearance both from the road and inside, but the food was superb. We both sang of Mosca's pan of fried oysters. Joe said that some years ago the Mafia don Carlos Marcello (believed by some to have been connected with the JFK assassination) was so taken with Mosca's that he made the owners an offer he thought they couldn't refuse. "He told them he'd give them the money to do whatever they wanted," Hero said, "travel, retirement, carte blanche, you might say. But they actually turned him down. They told him he could keep his money and go on doing the things he knew how to do, and they would go on doing what they knew best, which was running their restaurant."

I thought this must have taken some guts. "Where I come from," I told him, "when the Boys in the White Hats, as we used to refer to the Mafia in Chicago, came to pay you a friendly visit and tell you how much they admired what you were doing in your business, that was the first and last offer you were going to get."

He smiled into the wind. "I had an offer from Mr. Marcello once myself. Back years ago, a certain lady had a piece of property nicely situated in the city. She was a client of mine, and then I find out that Mr. Marcello is sending someone around sweethearting her, you know, to sell. Sweethearting? That's when you go around to someone all the time, buy 'em this and that—flowers, candy, dinner. But my client didn't really want to sell, and I couldn't advise her to do so if that was against her wishes. One day, I get this invitation to visit the office of Mr. Marcello, and I'm in there, and he's sitting at his desk, and he says to me, nodding at this envelope right on the corner of the desk, 'There's five thousand there for you if you'll get your client to sell me that piece of property.'

"I said, 'Well, wait a minute, Mr. Marcello. I'll have to think about this a minute.' What I had to think about was how I was going to tell this man no. So, I pretend to think a minute, and then I say, 'Mr. Marcello, I can't advise my client to do something she doesn't want to do and that there isn't a good reason for her to do.' And he just kinda lifts his hands, and that was that. But, you know, all that stuff you hear about the Mafia this and that: that isn't what's made the city so unsafe these days. Those fellows, you can stay out of their way. It's the casual street criminal now that you can't avoid. And a lot of it has to do with drugs. I got hit twice in one year. Once they took my wallet, and I was glad to let them have it. But the other time it was early in the morning, and I was on my way back from I won't say where. And here this fellow jumps out at me and wants my money. Well, only a fool won't give it up, and he's telling me to reach back real slow and give him my wallet, when all of a sudden I look up into this window right there at street level, and here's this little woman with this great big pistol. She's *waaaving* it back and forth like this, and just then the guy follows my eyes. I guess he was curious as to what else could get my attention in a situation like this. And he, too, sees this woman, and her eyes are getting bigger all the time. I guess he got just as frightened as I was that she was going to shoot the both of us because suddenly he took off, just running— There're two!" The old nimrod's arm shot out toward a stand of marsh grass which two ducks, frightened by our noisy entrance, were just clearing. We all sighted along Joe's arm at the birds slanting away in flight.

We were now right on the edge of the Delta NWR, and so I said as the ducks disappeared, "Joe, letting you into a wildlife refuge is like letting a fox into a hen coop."

"No, no," he demurred. "Not anymore. I'm safe now." The elegiac tone was unmistakable, and it was even more obvious moments later when he added, "But, you know, when I used to hunt, I got up *early* in the morning. And I felt better. I could see better. I could hear better. I could smell better. I was just more alive." The boat roared on toward Port Eads, but Joe Hero fell silent, staring grimly from beneath the brim of his khaki hat at the ever larger numbers of blue geese and ducks we now began to encounter.

And now, we too began to feel the tangy breath of the salt sea and saw the shores of the river begin to fall away from us, until at last there ahead was the end of this pass of the river and beyond it the "great Gulf" La Salle and his party had seen and of which Parkman had written. No one knows where that sliver of land was on which La Salle planted his possessionary—and presumptuous—column and cross and the lead plate bearing the arms of France. No doubt far under water now. But in Parkman's words is preserved his sense of triumph in that moment. This was not the end of anything for him, he thought, except the end of the river he called Colbert. It was instead the triumphant beginning of a grand enterprise: a string of forts founded here that was to extend all the way to the river's headwaters and that, when built, would forever establish French hegemony in this New World. He could not have known that this was in truth both the end of the river and of his scheme, as well.

No fort here, only a fishing camp once owned by the lord of Plaquemines Parish, Leander Perez, and a disused lighthouse whose rusty staircase wound its way up to turret windows that were smudged with dirt and salt air and against which hundreds of wasps buzzed and bumped in the last imprisoned heat of summer. From this hot, enclosed place you could look down into a perfect, dense sea of roseau cane waving in the wind and, beyond, the faint remains of the jetties placed here at the end of the 1870s by James B. Eads. Eads had proposed to Congress that he deepen the river's channel to make it navigable for large ships plying the Gulf, and that if he failed in the project, which had defeated previous engineers beginning with Adrien de Pauger in 1721, he should receive no compensation. By 1880 he had deepened the channel to thirty-two feet, and the river was open to deep-water commerce.

On this day no ships were visible, either in the pass or beyond in the Gulf. All I could see from the turret was cane, marsh grass, mud flats, and water that merged with the sky to form a slate-blue wall. La Salle had believed in Progress with a fervency exceeded only by his devotion to the Holy Mother. At this moment and place Progress seemed chimerical. There below me were the grasses, the wind, and the river finding the sea just as they had been on that spring day in 1682, just as they had been in 1721 when de Pauger proposed building a series of jetties to deepen the river's channel here. James Eads had built the jetties and deepened the channel, and Parkman had lived to witness this triumph of American ingenuity over an apparently intractable natural obstacle. That was why in describing this place, he had seen it as a void, primal chaos, on which a heroic human, godlike, had imposed a first and indelible order.

🌴 THESE days not all in lower Louisiana remain as taken as Parkman with the interpositions of humans on their land- and seascape. Certainly not those living along the lower reaches of the river. Nor those who for generations have taken their living from the Gulf waters. Nor those like Joe Hero who have grown up eating the seafood of the Gulf. Nor those living along the great marshes that cover the state's shoreline.

From Baton Rouge to New Orleans the river is now lined with poison-spewing petrochemical plants, over a hundred of them. From Barataria Bay all the way to Matagorda Bay in Texas shellfish beds are dangerously polluted at one season of the year or another, while from May through September there lies a huge biological "dead zone" in the same stretch of water. And from Little Falls, Minnesota, to Venice on the delta, Lord Mississippi has been controlled in his course by a sixteen-hundred-mile system of levees, locks, dams, and jetties that prevents the river from delivering the annual loads of fresh water and silt that Louisiana's marshes need to keep their heads above salt water.

The petrochemical plants located on the river were lured there after World War II by the state's oil and gas bonanza and by the ready availability of water, salt, and sulfur. They were attracted also by the deep-water shipping lanes Eads and his successors had created and by the state's historic disregard for even the most primitive of environmental safeguards. Louisiana, it had long been understood, was all for sale— its lands, its resources, its politicians—and the bids didn't have to be that high. So, following the lead of the petroleum industry, the petrochemical manufacturers came in force. They are now the state's largest employers in the manufacturing sector.

No one disputes the fact that they have greatly benefited both the state and the communities that are homes to the plants—Plaquemine, Seymourville, St. Gabriel, Geismar—but increasingly the hidden costs of the economic benefits are coming to the surface. How much, the question has now arisen, could the land, the air, and the waters of the lower river basin absorb of toxic chemicals? Could this relatively restricted region healthfully absorb the 400 million pounds of toxic pollutants annually released into its air? Could it safely handle the more than 500 million pounds of toxic chemicals dumped annually into its waters or driven into its soil? Could the Mississippi absorb the annual 75 million pounds of industrial waste poured into it in the ten-mile stretch from Plaquemine to Geismar? Many Americans sniggered some years ago when a portion of the Cuyahoga River that runs through Cleveland, Ohio, spontaneously combusted because of the heavy concentration of industrial wastes, but in a bayou fed by the Mississippi in the Baton Rouge area, Coast Guard divers reportedly suffered second-degree burns on their hands while gathering sediment samples. In fact, there may well be an even more dangerous kind of combustion brewing here than on the shores of Lake Erie. In what has been called America's Ruhr and Cancer Alley, cats and dogs have mysteriously lost their hair, Spanish moss has disappeared from the trees, lightning bugs, dragonflies, and river shrimp have vanished in places, and in some localities the rates of miscarriage and cancer (lung, stomach, gallbladder, colon, testicular) are suspiciously far above what is to be expected.

Until quite recently all this was pooh-poohed or, when it was not, was understood to be the price of progress and prosperity, as jet noise is said to be the "sound of freedom." This is in a state, it needs to be remembered, whose Department of Environmental Quality until recently wasn't even funded by the legislature and whose compliant politicians were given to boasting that they could be leased if not bought. But so serious have been the questions raised by the mutations in the natural and human order in the river basin that even Louisiana is beginning to pay some attention. Edwin Edwards, who once bragged that the only way he could lose a primary was to be found in bed with a dead woman or a live boy, did lose to reform-minded Buddy Roemer who went on to set some reasonably exacting environmental standards, including some governing the petrochemical industry. Speaking of the petrochemical companies, Roemer said that Louisiana welcomed them but that the state was no longer "making the highest bid for polluters." In September 1989 the legislature adopted regulations requiring alternative disposals of twenty-five toxic chemicals that routinely had been dumped into waters, and by 1994 toxic air emissions are supposed to be halved. But Roemer's start on cleaning up petrochemical pollution may have been costly. In the fall of 1991, he ran third behind Edwards and David Duke in the gubernatorial primary. Some of the most effective TV spots aired against him were paid for by Jack Kent, whose Marine Shale Processors had been harassed by the Roemer administration for numerous infractions in the recycling of petrochemical wastes. Edwards went on to defeat Duke, promising en route to be more reform-minded himself. Laws in fact have been passed and a schedule drawn up for environmental cleanup in the affected areas. Enforcement, though, is another matter, and this would be up to the new Edwards administration. Some environmental watch-dog groups are also claiming that the alleged cleanup is essentially phony and that the most dangerous materials continue to be released into the environment. In mid-1992, the EPA still gave the state the nation's worst rating for toxic emissions, and American Cyanamid at Westwego still led all American factories in number of pounds of pollutants released. But bad as this situation is and remains, it seems at least more amenable to solution than the matters of Gulf water pollution and marsh degradation.

In the pollution of the Gulf, one of the contributing factors is the geography of the Gulf itself. It is like a huge bowl—some 615,000 square miles of water—and except for some hugely deep holes near its center, it is also a shallow one, with an average depth of 5,000 feet. By comparison, the Atlantic, Pacific, and Indian oceans average well over twice that. And the exits for the Gulf's waters are relatively narrow: the Yucatán Channel and the Straits of Florida. Otherwise it is effectively surrounded by the United States, Mexico, and Cuba. What all this means is that what gets into the Gulf tends to stay there longer than in other large bodies of water, and because of the bowl's relative shallowness, the effects of the intruding elements tend to be more dramatically felt. A lot of deleterious stuff has been getting in, and the consequences are beginning to show, notably along the Louisiana coast where shellfish beds are now chronically polluted and where throughout the summer months there exists a "dead zone" of oxygen-depleted water. Septic systems—and the absence of them—have been identified as the major factor in polluted shellfish, with fecal coliform bacteria concentrating in the flesh of shellfish and rendering them unfit to eat, and each year more and more sewage is pumped into the Gulf with the buildup of residential areas immediately adjacent to it. Exacerbating the problem is the fact that the coastal marshes, which used to act as wonderfully efficient natural scrubbers, have been seriously degraded. Joe Hero, then, certainly had ample cause to be wary of Louisiana's oysters, and some health specialists will tell you that Louisiana's oysters have become unsafe no matter what beds they're drawn from or how they are prepared. Considering the prevalence of the oyster in Louisiana's cuisine and the prominence of that cuisine in the state's tourist image, this is a major problem and one that so far has not been effectively addressed.

As for the dead zone of oxygen-depleted water, Louisiana can hardly be solely blamed here, though surely it plays its part. The dead zone is presently a tadpole-shaped area of about four thousand square miles of bottom waters, its head snugged up against the delta and its tail trailing into Texas. The cause of the problem appears to be the Mississippi's daily discharge of nutrient-rich water into the Gulf, which would implicate all those who live and work in the river's vast watershed from Canada to Pilottown. Simply put, the water the river now sends into the Gulf is too rich in nitrogen and phosphorus due to modern agricultural practices, the effluent from sewage treatment plants, industrial operations, and a crowd of smaller but still significant practices of contemporary life, ranging from the overfertilization of lawns and gardens to the pervasive use of phosphorus-based laundry detergents. Nitrogen and phosphorus are, of course, essential building blocks of life, but in superabundance they deplete oxygen levels in bottom waters and in so doing kill off or drastically reduce the fauna upon which fish and shrimp feed. Some of the larger organisms dependent on bottom-water fauna apparently migrate away from this hypoxia, as the condition is called, returning when oxygen levels are once again sufficient. Others die. In either case, commercial as well as sport fishing in the dead zone is impractical during the warmest months, and with no feasible remedy currently in sight there are fears the zone will extend both in size and duration. The very fact that so extensive a portion of this divinely abundant body of water should be dead for a portion of the year's cycle is shocking when you think about the phenomenon itself. But when you think about it in the context of Louisiana's environmental history and politics and the currently "acceptable" trade-offs made everywhere in the world between environmental quality and short-term economic gains, the perception of the phenomenon tends to change from shocking to regrettable and at last to understandable.

But the condition of the state's coastal marshes is Louisiana's greatest environmental problem, and it is one that is in the process of becoming truly shocking even to those who have for years regarded it as understandable. It is the problem with the greatest number of long-range ramifications and also the one most difficult to solve.

From the Mississippi border to Port Arthur on the Texas line are some 6 million acres of the richest, most productive land in America, and it is disappearing beneath the Gulf at a rate something like fifty miles a year. Louisiana's wetlands produce one-fifth of the nation's fisheries products, one-third of its seafood, one-half of its fur harvest. A third of all species of North American birds are either resident here or seasonal visitors. The wetlands also serve the invaluable function of natural scrubbers, removing all manner of noxious substances. "Theoretically," a Terrebonne Parish wetlands expert told me, "in a healthy marsh you could pour raw garbage in at the top and it would come out clean at the bottom." And as if all this were not enough, the wetlands and their cheniers form the first vital line of defense against hurricanes. This last virtue was vividly demonstrated in the negative in 1985 when a welterweight storm named Juan inundated the town of Lafitte just below New Orleans and swamped communities on the west bank across from the city. There simply wasn't enough marsh left to form an effective defense, and those who saw what Juan did shudder at the prospect of what future heavyweight hurricanes will do to New Orleans, Houma, and Morgan City. This is not to more than mention the fates of those smaller and more exposed communities like Grand Isle, Golden Meadow, and Cameron.

You might think in view of these many and quite tangible benefits the wetlands deliver that Louisiana would do everything in its power to safeguard them and keep them healthy—and you would be wrong. Until very recently Louisiana has acted as if the wetlands could take any kind of treatment (rather like the lower Mississippi and the offshore Gulf) and still produce their multiple benefits. So, the marshes were hacked up for shipping channels, used as dumping grounds for all manner of human and industrial wastes, ravaged for the deep pockets of oil and natural gas they contained. And all the while the wetlands were being starved to death by that sixteen-hundred-mile system of levees, locks, dams, and jetties that was put together in the names of commerce and flood control.

Had the wetlands received as little as half of the Mississippi's annual overflow, they might have been able to go on building soil and plant communities sufficient to offset at least some of the man-made havoc. These springtime inundations were, in fact, what built the wetlands in the first place and maintained them against the natural tendency of these soggy lands to subside under their own tremendous weight. Now, though, human ingenuity has successfully deprived the coastal marshes of their vital annual infusions. So, when I'd told Winston Lill that I had always wanted to see the river sending its rich brown load out into the Gulf, I was really ignorantly saying that I wanted to witness the spectacle of the starvation of the wetlands. And then there is the problem of the present composition, so to say, of the river's water: even if the river was getting into the marshes, what would be the long-term effect of Mississippi water heavy in nitrogen and phosphorus on the marshes' ecosystem? Leaving that question aside, the unequivocal present fact is that the wetlands are being degraded both by land (freshwater starvation) and by sea (petroleum industry effects, shipping, Gulf water pollution, rising sea levels).

When you fly over any portion of them—as I did by plane and helicopter—you see this too plainly. This is now a terribly tattered, fragmented landscape in which even the most experienced native pilots have trouble locating old landmarks and for which maps become outdated with a surreal rapidity. Everywhere you see sunken cane fields, gray, dead stands of drowned cypress, roads that once went somewhere but now disappear into the encroaching Gulf. Lakes, ponds, and bayous have lost their separate identities and merged into the Gulf, sometimes leaving but a thin green rim to mark their former outlines. Canals once dredged to facilitate shipping and petroleum industry operations have spraddled out through age and erosion to three and four times their original widths, and the natural streams that once carried fresh water through the marshes like an arterial system have become weed-choked and stagnant. Great patches of marsh vegetation have been burned to death by the invasion of salt water. And everywhere are the deadly telltale tracks of the petroleum industry's marsh buggies that slice through and mat down the vegetation and so blaze trails for incoming salt water. Meanwhile, beneath these ravaged lands lies a rusting spaghetti bowl of petroleum industry pipelines.

Very belatedly the state and parish governments have been taking steps to try to save what's left. Their efforts, though, are hampered by the state's budgetary disarray; by a chronic lack of political courage; and by the apathy of that considerable portion of the population that lives north of Interstate 10. There is also the hovering issue of the nation's perceived energy needs, one made to seem even more urgent by the Gulf War and the consequent further unsettling of the Middle East. Dovetailing with this political crisis has been the development of new extractive technology in the petroleum industry and the discovery of what are thought to be "elephant fields" in the Gulf southeast of the delta.

In the 1980s, when petroleum seemed pretty much played out along the Louisiana coast and some companies were pulling up stakes, the industry showed signs of contrition for the large (but not sole) role it had played in wetlands degradation. In this climate legislative decisions were made to phase out oil and gas production pits in the wetlands, and some funds from petroleum revenues were earmarked for wetlands restoration. Now, however, all bets might be off, and some cynics are already saying that big oil will still have the wetlands to kick around pretty much as before. The war, they say, is one thing, generating yet again a national hue and cry for America to become much more petroleum self-sufficient—but not fossil-fuel conscious. When, asked Louisiana senator Bennett Johnston as the war became inevitable, is America "going to get the message?" When you hear this from Louisiana, you begin to feel along with the cynics that such terribly modest remedial actions as have been taken on behalf of the wetlands are now hostage to larger imperatives.

The new extractive technology is another thing, for it not only makes possible deep-water discoveries such as that in the Gulf's Mississippi Canyon; it also raises the real possibility of discovering new fields much closer to shore and of reviving old fields that had been thought exhausted. Much of this new technology has its most significant application at great depths, but the development of supercomputers that create startlingly accurate pictures of underwater geological formations has a general applicability, and it opens the possibility of further coastal prospecting. If this should prove true and a contest should take shape between oil and wetlands, the latter's chances would look bleak indeed. It should be noted here that the Bush administration is headed by an ex–oil man whose announced pledge of "no net loss" of national wetlands has so far resulted in nothing more than a proposal to redefine as much as 50 percent of them out of existence.

Having said all this, it needs to be added that the wetlands do have their staunch defenders who continue to hope that even in this climate something can be done to save this precious resource. There are a number of schemes for freshwater diversion into the marshes, some so small in scale as to be negligible, others very ambitious. Among the latter is one calling for the construction of a major navigational channel on the Mississippi delta's eastern side at Empire that would free up fresh water for diversion into the marshes. As it stands, said Sherwood Gagliano, a leading wetlands expert and long a proponent of freshwater diversion, by the time the needs of commerce are served along the lower Mississippi there is little water left over for conservation. The port of New Orleans is one of the world's busiest deep-water ports, and any scheme to deprive it of a significant portion of the river's flow would meet with gigantic opposition. Perhaps a less drastic scheme would be one calling for diversion of some of the river's water at peak flow into the Atchafalaya River that drains into the marshes in the western parishes.

But whatever combination of restorative measures taken, many residents of the coastal region agree that it can't wait. At Raceland, where I stopped for gas and a quick bite, a waitress I talked with said that "they've waited so long people are saying now it's already too late." She shrugged. "But what does that mean? If it is too late, like they say, does that mean we'll have to move up to Lafayette or Baton Rouge?" Cyrus Blanchard, standing on the back porch of his house in Lafitte and gazing at the apparently inexorable advance of the Gulf over the battered marshes, told author/conservationist Donald G. Schueler, "Man, I'm tellin' you, they better do something damn soon."

IT was the last week before Thanksgiving, and I had been in the Houma area for five days, mostly in the company of Bob Jones, the Terrebonne Parish engineer and a wetlands expert, and Donnie Lirette, president of the local chapter of Concerned Shrimpers of America. Now I was sitting with Lirette over a magnificent lunch of homemade gumbo at a café in his home village of Dulac. Lirette was one of those constant talkers who stun you into inattention, but just at the point where you've tuned out you find he's talking about something really interesting. At the moment he was telling me that he and his wife had cared for fifty-six foster children, and that this was "a cross to bear, don't you think it isn't." Also that he had a B.A. in mechanical engineering but that like so many of the Cajuns he had gone to work in the oil fields because that good money had been irresistible. "But then, after the oil field business turned sour, I went back to shrimping. I say 'went back' because really I had been doing it all my life. Now I just do it full time." He took a spoonful of his gumbo and called out to the man in the soiled apron who stood behind the counter. "Danny, whose gumbo is this?" Danny said it had to be May's, "because you know she ain't gonna let anybody mess with gumbo but her."

"How you like this?" Lirette asked as I scraped my bowl, and he smiled broadly when he asked because he knew how good it was. When we had finished he said he wanted to take me to his house to instruct me in the abundant absurdities of a National Marine Fisheries video promoting TEDs. On the way there he pointed out things he thought worthy of comment. In a short stretch of road there were a good many. "That's the fire truck we're gonna take Santa to the mall in tomorra." "That's a good friend of mine's boat. There he is now—dyin' of colon cancer and still working on his boat." "My cousin owns that hardware there. I put some money in it, and he's built up the business pretty good." "That house there, that belongs to the oldest shrimper on the bayou. That's his truck out front, the gray one." "That's a shrimp processing plant that's out of business. It's cheaper now to buy it processed from overseas than it is to do it here—and right here we have the major supply of shrimp." "That building is a warehouse owned by the Mardi Gras King, Blaine Kern."

I asked if he knew everybody along this road, and he said he did. "How many 'For Sale' signs you see along here?" I hadn't noticed any. "That's because the people here, they stay here. Not too many move away. This is the kind of community that doesn't look like much to an outsider. A tourist would zip right through here without looking, but he wouldn't see what's here to be seen. To us, this is just a real interesting place. This is home. I find it interesting because I know so much about it. I'm related some kind of way to most of the people here, somewheres along the line. That's why I don't like to come down this way unless I have a lot of time. It would take me an hour just to get to the end of this road because people would expect me to stop all along the way."

Standing in his driveway, he motioned me with his head to follow him across the road to where a bayou ran brown and solemn under a steely sky. We stood silently on the concrete embankment for a minute or so before Lirette pointed upstream and told me that as a kid he'd lived over there on the other side and in the early mornings had rowed across in a skiff to wake the priest for early mass. But what he really had in mind in bringing me over here emerged after he had made certain no one was looking. He wanted to point out a neighbor's sewer pipe that ran from the back of the house over fifteen feet of lawn to drape itself over the embankment. We had been talking earlier of the seasonal closings of oyster beds, and now Lirette nodded slightly in the direction of the pipe and said, "It's just raw. Yet you'd think they might at least put it underground, wouldn't you?" We walked back across the road and up the drive toward his neat split level.

"You were asking me about shoreline erosion, and land loss, and so forth. See back there beyond my shed? See those trees back there?" A clump of cypresses stood about four hundred yards distant. "When I bought this property it was twelve acres of solid land. Back there beyond those trees is now all broken swamp. You'll go a ways before you come across a more dramatic example of land loss than that."

By the time we had finished viewing the TED video, which Lirette had stopped numerous times to point out its inconsistencies and misrepresentations, it was late afternoon and a light, misting rain was falling.

There was a raw cut to the air I hadn't felt before. Tomorrow, as I had often been told, was the first day of the state's split duck season, and Lirette said the boys in the blinds would be "pretty cold by the time it gets light." And that was the problem, he said: some of those boys might fortify themselves against the weather and be in no condition to shoot safely come daylight. He himself wouldn't think of getting out in a blind on Lake Boudreaux on opening day. "You liable to get lead poisoning out there at a time like this."

He had a few calls to make in his car and invited me to accompany him; then he would run me out to my motel. On his second stop Lirette stood in the parking lot of Hi-Seas Seafood Company, talking with his longtime friend Raymond Authement. When they had concluded their business Authement walked Lirette back to his car, on the way passing a Toyota pickup. In its open bed lay two shotguns, their oily barrels and dark stocks beading in the mist. Authement gingerly turned one over. Its safety was off, and it was fully loaded. The same with the other. He shook his head slightly. "Look here, Donnie," he said to Lirette. "And with the safety off." Then they passed on to the car where they shook hands. On the way down the road Lirette said simply, "We been knowin' each other all our lives."

At Ray Boudwin's in Houma we had to wait a while until this wiry, compact boat builder transacted some business with a cousin. They spoke Cajun and so had no fear of being understood by this outsider. Lirette's presence apparently didn't concern them. When he had finished Boudwin turned to me and gave me a warm smile. "How you like this part of the country?" I said I loved it, and I did. "It is great," Boudwin said, still smiling, his weathered face a chart of the bayous, marshes, and coastline he had come to know so intimately. "It is great. Here the people have never had much money, and now since oil's gone way down, it's even less. But here a man can do just about anything he wants. Even without money, he can go huntin', fishin', eat his seafood." He paused, and a frown darkened his face. "But now the pollution is just so terrible. . . ." Lirette thought I would like to see a sample of the boats Ray Boudwin had built, and so we drove down to the bayou in central Houma where two of Boudwin's crafts rode quietly at anchor. He was especially proud of the *Equator*, more than half a century old and constructed, he told me, out of old-growth cypress that wears like iron. He gazed at the round-sterned craft, battered and paint-chipped, its windows showing black in the going light, and there was a professional fondness in his eyes. At last inspection, he said, "there wasn't an unsound timber anywhere." Then suddenly he leaped from the littered dock onto the deck of his ship and turned to face us, smiling, possessive. "Fastest shrimp boat in the whole parish!"

When Lirette and Boudwin deposited me at my motel, I invited them in on impulse, telling them I had a bottle of the new vintage Beaujolais and would be honored if they would have a glass with me. Neither man, as it turned out, was much of a drinker nor a connoisseur of wine. As we sat sipping in the ersatz elegance of the little room Boudwin said to Lirette that the wine might "go good with duck."

"It's pretty dry," Lirette said dubiously, holding his glass aloft to look at it and making a slightly wry face.

"No, no. I meant *over* the duck, to cook it in." Lirette seemed satisfied with that idea.

Despite the deficiencies of the Beaujolais the glass appeared to warm them a bit, and Boudwin quickly overhauled Donnie Lirette as monologuist. He told me of the many hazards of commercial fishing and concluded by saying, "If you work at this all these years, you're gonna get hurt. Period." His own father had once gotten snarled in a line and had been whipped overboard in Barataria Bay. He hadn't been recovered for an hour and forty-six minutes, Boudwin said, "and he lived. A fact. They got him to a hospital, and he lived. Course he was in very poor health for a long time after that, and his mind, seemed like it had suffered damage, too. For some time after we brought him home and he could kinda get around some, y'know, why, he'd just sit out there on the porch and do like this." He made knitting motions with his hands. "He was mending a net, you see. He thought he was. Didn't have nothin' in his hands, really, but he didn't know that. He'd just sit there and do the only thing he knew how to do." Later, Boudwin said, he had fully recovered and lived into his late eighties.

He asked me where I was bound for after Houma, and I told him up through Morgan City, Franklin, and Jeanerette to Lafayette. He said I shouldn't miss the famous oak tree in Jeanerette. "Years ago there was a white woman raped in that town, and they caught the nigger man said did it, and they hanged him from that oak. Then they put him in a box and just slung him up in that tree, and there he stayed, oh, for years and years. You can still see it. You ask anybody around Jeanerette, and they can tell you where the tree is. A fact." Later, he added, they found they'd lynched the wrong man.

Donnie Lirette said they must be going. We went out into full dark, Ray Boudwin still merrily talking away as if he wanted to cram in a last few anecdotes before letting this ignorant stranger hit the road. He wanted to tell me about the time he'd lived for fourteen days in Barataria

Bay on nothing but fried onions, about the motorist who tried to shoot the gap at the Chauvin Bridge after they'd swung the pontoon bridge aside to accommodate boat traffic. He wanted me to be sure to understand that with all the region's problems—the terrible pollution of the waters, the plethora of federal regulations on the fishing industry, the decline of the oil business—this was "still the greatest place to live in America. Here you can go into the home of the poorest man around, and what he's got, he'll give it to you. These are the friendliest, nicest people anywhere, the most generous. And now you know why the South lost the war!" He laughed.

WINTER

DECEMBER 30, A LEAD SKY, AND THE whole region from mid-Texas south to the Gulf and east to the Florida panhandle sealed beneath it; fields a matching gray or else a dead yellow, standing water in most of them, barren trees like still smoke. On the marquee of the Piggly Wiggly in Lafayette, Louisiana, the transparent brilliance of Christmas had departed, leaving behind only the homely and familiar specials: SALT MEAT, BLACK EYES, 3-LITER COKE.

I had some time to kill before my appointment with Barry Ancelet in Scott and filled it with mall shopping for inessential items and then with manic calisthenics in my motel room, pushing myself time and again up from the thin green carpeting, momentarily defying the clock and the gravity of sand that was running down on the year, the decade of the Eighties, and my own little allotment of mortality.

In the hamlet of Scott I had time, too, time to think about the impending appointment with Ancelet since I missed the turn for his dirt road both going and coming; time, that is, to reflect on the certainty that I was not wanted where I was going, that Ancelet's flat, inflectionless voice on the telephone had done everything this side of rudeness to warn me off. But in the subtly brutal way of a writer on the scent of material, I had ignored his signals, secretly trusting in my knowledge of the innate dignity of these Cajuns: if you didn't insult them, they couldn't ultimately bring themselves to refuse you their common courtesy. That maybe was the trump the Texans had held, then played, when they'd come into this country back in the Twenties with their oil rigs, their sweet technology, their talk, and convinced cooperation from the Cajuns, sucking out oil and money and wetlands soil, then leaving. I knew Ancelet was perhaps *the* essential Cajun of his time, a young man who had so fully mastered the culture and history of his place that an hour spent in his company would be worth months of random travel here, years in a library. What I didn't know was what—if anything—he was prepared to share with me.

When we'd talked by phone and I'd stumbled through a description of my mission, concluding with a request to spend a few hours with him, he'd said that he was very busy: when he wasn't teaching at the University of Southwestern Louisiana, or writing, or putting on festivals of Cajun culture, he was at home with his wife and kids. "And whatever time's left over these days, I spend in a duck blind. My wife's understandably jealous of what free time I do have, and so am I." He let these last four words hang out there on the line, then seemed to leave something of an opening when he volunteered that Saturday nights he hosted a live-audience radio show in Eunice. I barreled through that space like a runaway truck, all but inviting myself to accompany him to Eunice the following Saturday.

So here Saturday was, and here I was now at his house, a traditional wooden one with narrow dormer windows, raised high above the flat fields. On its wide, west-facing gallery my only greeter was a bowlegged hound with a chalky blind eye. Presently a little boy burst from the door carrying a toy musket, and behind him, sauntering, lean, handsome, with great brooding eyes and a mustache that looked out of the century before, Barry Ancelet. He stood above me on the gallery, unsmiling and guarded as I made my way across the muddy yard, then opened the door by way of invitation, and we went into the kitchen. His wife said hello with what I thought was a careful smile, then announced she had to run down to the store for a pie tin but wouldn't be gone long. I had to wonder if I wouldn't miss her company.

Ancelet seated himself in a rocker and asked me what kind of book I thought I was writing, and after I'd tried again to explain it, he interrupted with "Oh, kind of a *Blue Highways* type thing."

Trying to curry some sort of favor, I said, "Well, kind of, I guess."

"You know," he said, "that's a book I truly hated. All that sorry self-searching: it left me cold. And, you know, if you're going to work the underside of places, like that guy did, you're not going to get the average people in there. I'm not going to speak about the people in the rest of the book, but I can tell you he didn't come near getting the average people from here in there." All this without looking at his visitor, rocking in cadence with his words, his fingers, too, tapping out some code in accompaniment on the rocker's lowest rung, *tap, pop, tap.* . . .

"How long are you going to be in this part of the country?" he asked, glancing at me now. I told him just a couple more days, that I'd already spent almost two weeks in Louisiana and felt I had to move on into Texas. He shook his head, looking more and more like a Gallicized Christopher Walken. "Do you think you can get to know a country in a couple of days?" He shook his head again, mourning the evident folly of the enterprise, this man living on ground prepared and fertilized by the lives and deaths of generations of ancestors and now called to wedge himself ever deeper into its rich, fecund soil. And what, after all, could I say to the thrust of his question? What *were* a traveler's impressions worth, anyway, compared with the blood knowledge of one who had made his life the study of his native place? In the pleasant clutter of the kitchen, the little boy poking his musket under our chairs and into corners on a hunt, the quality of my own hunt seemed suddenly—though surely not for the first time—brought into an uncomfortably sharp relief.

I was saved from further such melancholy questions and musings by Mrs. Ancelet's reappearance, apologetically brandishing a small pie pan, the only size, she now explained, the store had in stock. "Well," she said at the sideboard and to no one in particular, "it'll just have to be a small pie."

Then we were out in Ancelet's spattered pickup, its front seat cluttered with hunting gear, and backing swiftly down the drive. "It's the second split of the duck and goose season," he said by way of explanation for the jackets, caps, boots, and cartridge box on the seat. He yanked the truck into first and spun out into the road's soft ruts. Rolling through the puddles toward the paved road, he told me that before we made the show in Eunice we'd be stopping at a friend's house where Ancelet was to pick up some tickets for tomorrow night's New Year's Eve dance. "I might have a bit of trouble finding him," he said. "He's my duck-hunting friend, and I've never seen his place in the daylight." But he found it well enough, a beige house trailer marooned in an inlet of muddy water.

Concrete block steps led up from the water to the trailer's door, but you still would have to find a way to get to them.

Ancelet had swung down from the cab and was about to slosh across when he jerked his head around. "Look there!" he exclaimed, dropping for an instant his reserve. "They're right over there!"

So they were: in the rice field across the road a great gathering of snow geese sat in the shallow water, and as we looked another long harrow came out of the north, braked over the field, then dropped quickly into it amid the cries and flutterings of those already settled. Ancelet stood there in the swimming light of the late afternoon, a man clearly torn between his present obligations and the sight of these beautiful creatures just a few hundred yards away. It wasn't, he explained when he'd come away with his tickets and turned the pickup north for Eunice, just the killing of them, the thrill of the hunt. Sometimes, he said, after he'd bagged his limit, he'd stay on in the blind, simply watching the great birds or taking photos of them.

It was forty-five minutes along the back roads to Eunice, and the plan I'd had in mind in inviting myself for this trip was to use the time to ask Ancelet about Cajun culture and his own intense involvement with it. Though our beginnings had not been promising, once I broached the subject, I found him a ready talker, personal in his approach to the culture and its preservation, impersonal in his delivery to this audience of one beside him: this, his manner said, is how it is, and I don't care especially who you are or what use you might eventually make of what I'm telling you.

At bottom, he saw himself and the Cajuns as an endangered species, endangered by the homogenizing forces of modernism, the economic erosion of traditional values and ways of living, endangered most particularly by the invasive presence of the English language. "To speak French today in Louisiana," he wanted me to understand, was a "daily decision. You go into a grocery store [motioning with a thumb at one that sat at a nameless crossroads], and you can say 'Give me some bread' or you can say '*Donnez-moi du pain*,' and the storekeeper will give it to you, because it doesn't make any difference to him, he can do it either way. That's the choice you're faced with every day here." He slapped the steering wheel lightly with the flat of his hand. The Cajuns, he said, had been facing this choice for more than a century and a half, but especially so in the past fifty years.

Soon after the Louisiana Purchase, he claimed, the Louisiana Creoles had gotten what he called "the message." "The message was that the key to the future was in becoming Americanized. But out here the Cajuns didn't get that message. They were much more isolated by geography and occupation. Most of them were subsistence farmers, or else they were hunters or trappers or fishermen. Their economy was basically barter and they were just much farther removed from the stream of history. So, where the Creoles saw what was going to happen, the Cajuns didn't. When the Civil War came along, what do you think the desertion rate was among them? Eighty-five percent or higher. It wasn't that they sympathized with the Union forces. It just wasn't their war. When they were conscripted and put into uniform, they just walked home. It didn't have anything to do with them.

"Well, after the war matters began to change. For one thing, after the turn of the century they discovered oil at Jennings. Then they passed the Education Act in—I think—1916, and this meant free public education. The Cajuns, like a lot of other traditional peoples, had been resistant to education simply because if kids went, they might learn things their parents didn't know. But now the kids had to go to school, and when they did the first thing they learned was that they were forbidden to speak French. They couldn't speak it anywhere, not even on the playground. If they did, they were punished. Some of those kids suffered real trauma in those first days because they couldn't say they had to go to the bathroom, and so they had to wet their pants." If Ancelet wasn't actually glaring at me now, he was certainly giving me a very direct stare. "This," he resumed, glancing back quickly at the road, then turning his glowing eyes on me again, "this is what America was up to then and what it's still up to: what I call homogenization and channeling. You try to take various ethnic groups and strip away their distinguishing differences, channel them into a narrower way of behavior and thinking so they'll fit in more easily with the national system." He quoted me some lines from that great bully-boy of early twentieth-century nationalism, Theodore Roosevelt, to the effect that America had room for but one language—English—because the goal of the culture was to turn out what T.R. was pleased to style "Americans" and not some nation that might be mistaken for a rooming house of various ethnic groups.

"Then, while this process was going on and the oil industry was siphoning off the Cajuns into that line of work, away from their traditional ways, there was the new system of roads built by Huey Long, and suddenly you had coming into the country a whole new set of outside influences. And not only that, but people found they could take these same roads out. And there came in, too, radio, which has the inevitable tendency to standardize. Instead of making your own music, your own entertainment, it's all done for you, it's all done by others who don't share anything of your background. Well, after three generations of all this, traditional Cajun culture was pretty well eroded around here.

"Me, I was a little bit different, maybe. Both my father and mother worked out, which meant that my grandmother, my father's mother, and one of the dearest people I've ever known—or ever will know—took care of me a lot, and all she spoke was French. So I grew up speaking it. My parents would come to pick me up at the end of a day, and they'd ask me something—in English—and I'd automatically answer back in French because I'd been talking with my grandmother all day. So they said, by the time I was getting ready to go to first grade (1957), 'Hey, we better teach this kid English.' They were a little worried, maybe. But I could speak both equally well, so they sort of gave up and spoke French with me. You have to understand that, because of the developments I've just mentioned, the French language here had become something parents spoke to each other at home and whenever they didn't want the kids to understand what was being said.

"When I went off to graduate school it was with the idea of coming back here and doing something, I didn't know what, but something that would in some way involve me with my roots. So, I ended up studying French, linguistic anthropology, and folklore at Indiana. Then I came back here and was lucky enough to land a job at USL. I teach in the French department, but we now have a much different emphasis than when I came here and was looked upon as something of a freak because I went around whistling or singing 'Jolie Blonde' [the Cajun cultural anthem]. We're now very involved with Francophone studies and French area studies, which means we study a number of cultures—Caribbean, African—where French is spoken."

He bristled when I asked him whether the French he'd grown up with was in fact a dialect. Did he, I wanted to know, teach his students in entry-level courses to speak French as he had learned it? "Many people," he said with asperity, had gone from here to France and to other French-speaking countries and had had "no trouble at all making themselves understood. They found they were perfectly able to order meals, sleep indoors, use public facilities. I teach French the same way I learned it, and there are now hundreds of students of mine going around pronouncing French the way they learned it in my classes."

Was it then an insult, I asked, to speak of Cajun French as a dialect? "No," he said shortly, "it's just wrong."

By now the muffled sun had sunk into the long prairies that stretched west into Texas, and the lights of the gas stations and convenience stores we passed were beginning to stand out. As we neared Eunice and the

Liberty Theatre where Ancelet hosted the show, I asked him to tell me something about how the show had gotten started. It had been, he said, the joint idea of the town of Eunice and the National Park Service. "But the Park Service wanted to do it in English. I told them, 'That's fine. But you've got the wrong guy here.' I wasn't interested in doing that. I wanted to do it in French, or I didn't want to do it at all. And this'll give you an idea of what I've been talking about: right up until the very last minute they were still trying to convince me to do it in English—and throw in a little French here and there, for the flavor. We had twenty minutes till air time, and they're *still* doing this! I said, 'Okay! Will you guys *just shut up*, and let me do what I'm going to do anyway, and then next Saturday night you can get someone else to do the show.'

"Well, I went on and started out in French, and the audience just went nuts! They hadn't heard anything like that in forty years or more. So, the show's in French—with a little English thrown in, for the flavor. We generally have a band or two, Cajun music or zydeco. We might have a storyteller. And generally we have a 'living recipe.' That's someone who'll give out a recipe and explain it.

"The effect of this kind of a thing is to encourage the truly local, and not only that, but also to create conversation and cultural dialogue. You see people in the audience who're from the outside, and they'll be leaning over to ask, 'What'd he say? What'd he say?' And suddenly you've got a totally new situation. Suddenly, the French-speaking people are in a new situation. *They* are the ones who have the knowledge. *They* are the ones who know what's going on, and the effect of this is to encourage pride and interest and enthusiasm and a desire to perpetuate traditions."

Whatever congeries of motives it was that brought them here, the folks at Eunice had filled the Liberty Theatre's seats by six-fifteen for the show at seven o'clock. In the alley in back two bands leaned against vans or the building's walls, talking and practicing a few licks. The fire exit lights on either side of the stage door were reflected in the puddles at the bottom of the steps Ancelet and I now went up. There was a sizable crowd back there as well, including the mayor who stood beaming at the general shape of matters, resplendent in shirtsleeves and broad red suspenders. I asked him if there was any place nearby where I might get a cup of coffee.

"There isn't any coffee right around here," he said with his big smile, "but across the street you could get lots of other things." I went where he directed, settled for a can of Bud, and brought it backstage.

Out in the glow of the stage lights Barry Ancelet was casually seated atop a high stool. In an almost conversational tone he warmed up the house with a few jokes, the punches of which were lost on me with my cast-iron, graduate school French. But I was too embarrassed by this deficiency to ask any of those standing about me, laughing in the shadows, "What'd he say? What's the joke?" Perhaps quite as he had intended, Ancelet's jokes were at least partly on those like myself who couldn't get them, those who were emissaries from that wider world that in its almost thoughtless way had crowded this little one toward effective extinction.

Primed by Ancelet's short course in Cajun cultural survival, I felt through the next two hours at the Liberty a certain sort of ardor, amounting almost to a kind of fierceness, in this joyful celebration of communal Cajunness. It was easy enough to see that these people—the performers and their friends and relatives, their audience—were having a good time. What might have been missed by the outsider, who also missed Ancelet's preliminary jokes, was the emotional intensity they had brought to this old brick building on a Saturday night in Louisiana's western parishes. Yet, once you looked and listened for it, it was there: there in the defiant metallic brashness of the old-style diatonic accordions that had all but disappeared from Cajun instrumentation by the early 1940s but now were absolutely *de rigueur* for any self-respecting Cajun band; there in the high, inspired madness of the fiddlers, descendants of those nameless folk artists who more than a century ago had made for the Ishmaelite Acadians the first esthetic accommodation to this new home, their heavy attack on their instruments wailing of exile, loss, the flat challenge of these unsung prairies and marshlands; there in the weathered faces of the audience, faces filled with surprise and joy and the remembered pain of having only yesterday been forbidden their native tongue and then disparaged as ignorant "coonasses."

After four bands performed, a pleasant-faced woman explained how to make a fruitcake, and Barry Ancelet took a solo turn on the accordion; then part of the crowd flowed backstage to congratulate the performers. An old man in a straw cowboy hat and bib overalls, holding a small boy's hand in his own rough paw, came up to the fiddler of the group Jambalaya and with a slight cock of the head patted the artist's arm. "We just so *proud* of you!" he said, and then simply stood there beaming.

I mentioned this episode to Ancelet as we whipped at what felt to me like dangerous speed back along the patched and bumpy roads from Eunice to Scott. To the south an oil field flare turned the night a cloudy carmine, and all about us lightning was hitting into the sodden fields. "That kind of thing," he rejoined, "is the kind of thing you see all the time." His postperformance adrenal rush, sustained perhaps in some measure by the six-pack of beer we'd stopped for, induced in him what might have been a friendliness. "What this show does is tell these folks over and over again that this music, this whole culture, is beautiful and valuable simply because *it is theirs.*" In the darkness of the lurching cab I heard the flat of his hand strike the steering wheel once again, and I could feel the glow of those eyes.

When I remarked on the uniform excellence of the four bands heard at the Liberty tonight, he told me that when they'd put on the first Cajun music festival in 1974, there had been no musicians in it who were under thirty, which, he said, "will give you another idea of what I meant about homogenizing and channeling. Cajun music—traditional Cajun music—was regarded then by young musicians as old-timey chankety-chank. Five years later at the same festival we had eight bands with musicians under thirty, and three of those bands had musicians in their early twenties." I said this reminded me of Allan Jaffe's experience with traditional jazz musicians at Preservation Hall: the more the old music was aired again, the more those who had known how to play it began to come out of the shadows, and eventually traditional New Orleans jazz made converts of younger musicians who had been playing in contemporary styles.

"Exactly. There were actually a lot more musicians out here than at first appeared. They had stopped playing, given it up, but when they heard it again, when there was a recognized outlet for it, when they saw it was honored, they began to come forward. And at the same time the kids were watching this development, and they began to say, 'Hey, I want to be up on the stage with that man! I want to play that music!'"

Now into his third beer, he suddenly turned back to a subject he'd dismissed earlier, my Gulf coast book, asking if I had a title for it yet. I said I'd thought about calling it *The Redneck Riviera*, but that the more I had gotten into the project, the more that seemed a smart-ass and inappropriate title.

"There was an anthropologist who used to be here," Ancelet said, "who claimed the Gulf coast was a world apart. He said it was 'south of the South.' One of the things that sets it apart from the rest of the South is that it really wants to be a part of the Caribbean instead of the North American continent. The Gulf coast *yearns* toward the Caribbean. Look at our crops: rice, yams, citrus, sugarcane. They're really Caribbean, not North American. And with virtually every one of them we've had to fiddle around to try to make them grow here. Rice wasn't a commercial product here until the Americans made it one. Sugarcane, they had to fiddle around with it to make it commercially profitable. We really don't have the proper climate for these things—as we found out again just the other day when that hard freeze ruined the citrus crops. When that hard a freeze hits, you can hear the trees just *popping*.

"But in spite of freezes and hurricanes and everything else, the Gulf coast seems to want to hang on, somehow. Of course, it gets harder every year, it seems. Every year there's less and less of the Gulf coast here. I don't know if you're aware of this, but we have a very serious shoreline erosion problem that is a direct result of the kind of channeling I've been talking about. They've channeled the Mississippi so much and built such a tremendous system of dikes and so on that the very thing that over the centuries made this such fertile farmland—the river—has been prevented from replenishing our lands. We're starving our shoreline to death."

He said other things, too, had been starved to death by the channeling of the Mississippi and the region's bayous and streams: traditions, communal ways. When I asked him for an example, he shot back that the tradition of hand fishing was a thing of the past because many of the region's watercourses had been so dredged and channeled that their flows were too swift either for the fish to make nests in their banks or for men to hope to catch them with their bare hands. And with the end of hand fishing, there had been an end to the community outings that had been an integral part of the practice.

We rolled presently into the lights from Ancelet's house. He looked into the sack that had recently contained our beer and said flatly, "Well, we did that proud." Then he alighted and stood there in the gloom with the gallery lights etching his tall, spare form. We shook hands quickly.

"The name of your book," he said, turning to go, "is *South of the South*."

A FEW miles below Abbeville on 82 heading for the Gulf the vegetation abruptly altered as the fields began to give way to swampland. There was more and more water, less and less land, and the plant life began to be dominated by those species like cypress and palmetto that can stand constant immersion. The oaks were lower, flatter than farther north, their limbs festooned with tillandsia (Spanish moss), and beneath them egrets poked jerkily through the thick-stemmed grasses. Looking directly south I could see a long scroll of angry air over those waters that stretched away unseen toward the bright islands of the true tropics.

It was the last day of the year. At the hamlet of Forked Island one of those plastic marquees on wheels announced there would be "Rooster Fights" today, and the parking lot at Cowboy's Hangout was brimming. So, too, were the roadsides for a hundred yards south. On the front of the building a hand-lettered sign advised ABSOLUTELY NO ROOSTERS ALLOWED IN THE BAR. ANYONE STARTING TROUBLE WILL BE "ASKED" TO LEAVE. Inside, the barroom was in fact quiet and barren of either roosters or troublemakers. A couple of men in denim jackets and ball caps sat apart from each other, hunched over cans of beer, but from behind the door across the room you could easily hear shouts, laughter, loud talk, and, cutting through these like blades, the high, strident challenges of the advertised roosters. I bought a Bud at the bar, then joined the action on the other side of the closed door.

The arena was hardly bigger than the barroom and jammed to the walls with men in hunting clothes: camouflage hats and jackets, bright neon orange caps, muddy boots, sleeveless quilted parkas. A few men evidently hadn't been hunting today and so wore wide-brimmed cowboy hats: Louisiana was shading, sartorially anyway, into Texas. Here and there I spied the telltale white rubber boots of shrimpers. In the room's center a pit had been raised waist-high and based and bounded with two-by-fours and chicken wire. Its floor was covered with hard-packed dirt in which the scorelines had been scratched out in lime, and as I entered, the afternoon's next two cockers were already in the pit with their feathered warriors cradled in their arms, waiting, evidently, for some signal to bill their birds and let them go at each other. I asked a cadaverous man next to me what the cause of the delay was. He drew on his cigarette so violently that his cheeks seemed almost to touch each other, then answered in a gray pall of smoke, "Waitin' for the bets to even." He explained that in order for a match to begin, an equal amount had to be wagered on each bird. At the moment, the blue rooster was short by more than twenty dollars. Slowly wagers on the blue reached those bet on the red, and when they did the referee, a tall man in a denim jumper, ordered the cockers to bill the birds and return them to their scorelines. Then the cry of *"Pit!"* at which the cockers released the birds.

Immediately it became evident why the red had attracted so much of the early action. It flew at the blue and knocked it sideways, then danced lightly back to assess the effect of this initial charge and went in again. The blue counterattacked and ran, and for the next few minutes it appeared its hit-and-run tactics might work: the red seemed perplexed, tentative, and the blue actually sent a few red feathers flying. Soon enough, though, all the fight went out of the runner. It ceased to counterattack and devoted its efforts to trying to find a hole through the wire fencing to escape its relentless adversary. The red now saw it had nothing to fear and chased the blue around the pit, sometimes riding its bent back, pecking its neck, raking its sides with flashing gaffs.

As the blue's efforts at escape grew weaker, they grew more frantic. At last, up against the wire again, it succeeded in getting its head and neck through a hole, but this only pinioned it for the red, like a boxer who gets entangled in the ropes. While the red savaged it from behind, the blue's eyes searched the faces of the pitside humans, and it looked to me in that moment as though the rooster had the better comprehension of what was happening. Seeing that it was no use there, that deliverance would not be forthcoming, the blue disentangled itself and again took up its tottering, weaving run, the red always at its side, cutting off the ring, forcing it into the boards. Finally, in a far corner, the match came to an end when the red flung the blue into the boards and drove home both gaffs. This was the match's first "handle," and when the birds had been disentangled the blue lay still, a mangled mass of feathers that didn't seem to add up to a bird, as if some vital parts might have somehow been flung out of the pit. Its handler, a burly, bearded man in a shrimper's white boots and wearing a Skoal cap, picked it up and brought it back to the corner where his rough ministrations—wetting the bird with water, smoothing its feathers, blowing on the shedded, dangling head—failed. When the referee announced that the birds must be returned to their scorelines, the blue lay motionless on its, dead or nearly so. The burly cocker scooped it up, shook hands with his opposing number, and ducked out of the pit. Already shouts attendant to the next match were rising out of the close, dense room.

The bookmaker was standing next to the meat scales that served here as the official instrument of measurement, his small spiral pad in hand. When a wager was called, he licked the end of his pencil and jotted it down in one of two leaning columns. Beneath the table holding the scales were the small wooden cases in which the cockers had transported their birds, and from these came the challenges I'd heard in the barroom.

A technique was employed in this contest I had seen nowhere else. Here both cockers, as they hovered over their fighting birds, uttered periodic loud cries, *"Brrrrrrr-eeeee-ahhhhhhh!"* I asked my cadaverous friend the meaning of these. "It gets their attention," he said above the din.

After the match I struck up a conversation with a father and son who were sipping beers near the door. Mike and Cal Fontenot had been duck hunting down on Grand Chenier a few miles to the southwest and had stopped here when they'd seen the marquee outside. They were from Baton Rouge and were not aficionados of cockfighting, "but, what the hell," Mike Fontenot said, and laughed. "Fight's a fight, I guess. What else you got on Sunday afternoon?" They wanted to tell me about a wonderful alligator farm they'd visited down near Grand Chenier. "Fella raises them from egg to four-foot long in a year!" Mike Fontenot said admiringly. "Think of it! It's all on account of a special high-protein diet he uses. That and a thermostatically controlled house he has the pens in. See, an alligator needs to have the temperature constant between eighty-eight and ninety degrees. Lower than that their digestive system will cut off, and they'll go into hibernation. Now, during that hard freeze we had a few days back the temperature went a lot lower'n that, and in order to keep the alligators from going into hibernation—which would stunt their growth for the year, you see—why, he cut off their food so their digestive systems wouldn't shut down. Then a couple of days later, when the freeze let up, why, he put 'em back on the diet." He said the French and the Japanese would buy all the hides the man could ship. I wondered whether he also sold the meat and was told he did, though there wasn't "near the market for it there is for the hides."

I said I'd had gator once and that the more I chewed a bite, the bigger it got. "Oh, gator's all right," Cal Fontenot said. "But you gotta know how to cook it. Best thing to do is soak it overnight in milk. That tenderizes it. Kinda."

A man at our elbow interrupted our talk by asking in a loud voice if anyone present had a knife. Instantly a grove of shiny toad-stabbers was in evidence, pulled from a dozen sheaths. The man, who proved to be the referee and presiding official, smiled and jerked his head back in mock terror. "Lord, Lord," he exclaimed, "where you fellas been with all them knives?"

"Cleanin' ducks," Cal Fontenot said with a smile, handing him his knife. The referee then went to work with it, whittling down the natural spur of a speckled red rooster so that the gaff could be taped on over it. While he worked, the bird's owner held it in his arms and clucked soothingly to it while the little pile of shavings grew on the tabletop next to the scales.

It is no more true that once you've seen one cockfight, you've seen them all than the same thing said about a horse race is true. It's true only if you don't know enough about either sport to really appreciate what you're seeing. I knew something about cockfighting, having attended mains in Arizona and New Mexico, but not enough to enjoy further feathers and carnage here, Sunday or no, and so I said good-bye to the Fontenots and went out into the dissolving light of this last day of the year and the decade.

ROSEAU cane is showing up now. Brahma cattle hock deep in puddles and reedy grasses; oil industry helicopters on their ways Gulf-ward; smashed fruit in the roads. Smashed creatures, too: nutria, coons, muskrats, skunks, cats, dogs. In lanes leading into marshes, hunters' pickups; on house porches lucky hunters cleaning birds; others empty-ing the cabs and beds of their trucks, carrying coolers indoors.

At Cameron there was a clutch of video movie shops, bars, a heliport, and—symbol of the flush past and also of the uncertain future—a giant drilling platform. Here a car ferry took me across Calcasieu Pass and into the Sabine National Wildlife Refuge. In the middle of the pass I saw a great flight of ducks zip in low over the marsh to my right, then wheel back on itself and settle out of sight. It brought to mind those travelers' tales out of the early years of the American story when men said the skies had been darkened by the passages of ducks, geese, pigeons. Those days were long gone, of course, and the passenger pigeon, once thought to be in inexhaustible supply, had been hunted into extinction. Even here at the Sabine NWR the numbers of birds had dwindled sharply in recent years.

Crossing into Texas, I saw the sun go down, setting in the oil industry haze of Port Arthur like a dirty headlamp, leaving the smokestacks, derricks, cranes, and refinery buildings etched in a purple relief that was beautiful if you didn't think about what had gone into it.

The Channel Inn at Sabine Pass was another of those terrific, utterly inconspicuous restaurants you stumble across from Everglades City to Brownsville, often shabby-looking on their exteriors, dimly lit and cheaply decorated within. Inside the Channel Inn everything was plas-tic: woodwork, tablecloths, dishware, glasses and pitchers. The waste-baskets parked next to the tables were plastic, too, and so were the liners within them. But the food was supposed to be wonderful, which was why on New Year's Eve I'd made the twenty-minute run down from Port Arthur.

The tableside wastebaskets, I quickly learned, were the thoughtful provision of the management because their most popular dishes were finger foods: shrimp and crab in half a dozen varieties. You were also provided with a large roll of paper towels so that when your deviled crab arrived you could plunge in, eat, wipe your hands and face, and discard, all in complete and handy comfort. No ceremony here and none tolerated, either: the festive crowd was casually dressed, boisterous, completely at ease.

In addition to its seafood the Channel Inn served as a side dish some of the best, most honest potato salad I had ever eaten. Hemingway used to tout the singular virtues of the potato salad at the Brasserie Lipp in Paris, and on a rainy fall afternoon I have amused and gratified myself by sitting on the terrace of that snooty establishment, eating the famous salad and watching the handsomely turned out *types* alighting from cabs and chauffeured cars to be fawningly greeted by the personnel who knew most of them by name. Lipp's salad was good, but it wouldn't pass muster at the Channel Inn, nor could it stand up to the brawny cuisine offered here.

Coming back into Port Arthur, I saw the city from atop a bridge and thought it must be the most brilliantly ornamented metropolis in the entire country this night. Times Square could have had nothing on this place I now beheld with astonishment, its thousands of refinery lights winking and glowing and the smoke from these plants standing out in the chilly darkness like great ornamental boas. In its peculiar, night-shrouded way it was truly beautiful, a sudden and unexpected gift made the random traveler who should come upon it from this concrete height.

On Gulfway Boulevard I saw another marquee, not for roosters now but JAZZ, SUNDAY NIGHT, 5–9. A sign inside the foyer of the Speakeasy Lounge advised of a "Strict Dress Code," then listed a number of sartorial items that wouldn't be tolerated on the premises, among them "Tennis Shoes." I looked down ruefully at my battered Reeboks, then motioned to them mutely as I stood before the throne of the big checker. He looked at them, too, then at me. "Oh, they're okay," he said with a small smile. "We consider those deck shoes. What we want to keep out are those things you play basketball in. Those we discourage." A five-dollar cover and I was in, and once I was and my eyes had made their adjustment, I discovered that I was the only white who was. After the merest struggle, vanity triumphed over fear, and I moved to the bar where perhaps courage might be obtained. Fortified with a glass, I turned back to face the busy room, its spotlights and revelers.

No jazz here, I quickly learned. Instead, a DJ in a glassed-in booth spun heavy soul for the dancers on a raised platform bounded by shiny brass railings. Some of the men wore white cardboard fedoras, and I noticed the barmaids did, too. When I asked one of the latter where these items came from, she said they were party favors of the management and shortly produced one for me. It contrasted somewhat with the rest of my drab and none-too-clean traveling attire and might have made me stand out even more from the rest of the patrons, something I didn't feel I needed. Still, how could I refuse to wear the gift, the barmaid looking straight at me as I pretended to admire the thing? Oh, well, I thought, jammed it on my head, and took a long swallow. But no one seemed to notice me, white hat, white skin, dirty white Reeboks and all, and I was free to admire the styles of the women in here, many of them beautifully turned out in clinging dresses and with grand bows in their hair. One statuesque woman wore a dress that was black below the waist with a leopard skin–patterned top and pillbox hat to match. She had the leopard's dangerous grace at the same time she had the trainer's unchallengeable air of command.

Next to me was a man whose name, I subsequently learned, was Paul Braught, a broad-shouldered fellow with brilliant gold-capped teeth, glittering rings on the huge fingers of both hands, and marcelled hair that hung beneath his party-favor fedora almost to his dark suit coat. He wore a starched white shirt with a white tie and a gold collar pin. A large tie pin in the form of an anchor dangled just below his collar, and he completed this stunning ensemble with a great flourish of crisp white handkerchief in his breast pocket. I felt just as underdressed as I was, seated next to Braught, and so I asked him if, in view of our evident contrasts, he wanted me to move over a seat or two. "Oh, no, man." He smiled broadly, spreading wide his hands in tolerant welcome. "It's fine. Fine with you? Then fine with me. See the white hat [pointing to his head]? That's so you can tell I'm a good guy." I said I appreciated the signal but that in South Chicago the guys who wore white hats and ties were the ones you had to fear. Braught smiled again. "Yeah, Capone. He wore a white hat. But I'm talkin' about Hopalong Cassidy, Tom Mix, and like that, you know?" But he acknowledged there had been the Port Arthur equivalent of the boys in the white hats, too. "Used to be, back thirty years ago, whatever they had in Chicago or New York, we had it here: gambling, women, and so forth." Now it was mostly shut down. He didn't say why, but I guessed it must be related to the oil industry blight.

Like most others here, Braught had been involved in oil, "but no more now." Apparently he was too old for whatever oil-related work he'd once done, though he appeared to me a very vigorous fifty or so. I forbore asking what work he now did, for he looked too prosperous to be either unemployed or wholly retired. Whatever work it was, he was well known: people kept stopping by his stool to speak with him, and one of them, a handsome woman in her thirties, lingered and finally led him up to the dance floor. "I'm going to learn the Harlem Shuffle," he explained to me over his shoulder, then shrugged and smiled.

While Paul Braught was being taught a new move a woman sat down at the stool on my other side and ordered a drink. She said her name was T.C., that she was from nearby Belmont, where she managed a dress shop. We chatted about music, dances, and what had brought me into the Speakeasy, looking all the while out at the dancers. It had been the sign advertising jazz, I told her. She laughed lightly. "Well, we call all this jazz, but it really isn't." I said it had been a happy mistake, that I was glad to have blundered into the Speakeasy where I had been made to feel welcome. She chuckled, this large young woman, her beautiful, carefully made up face as impassive even in laughter as the Sphinx.

"People figure you're a cop," she said.

Did she know the Harlem Shuffle that Paul Braught was just now learning?

"Oh, we call all this style 'Swing Out.' It's pretty easy to learn."

It looked tough enough to me, and I said so, adding that back in the Sixties Eldridge Cleaver had claimed that even the simplest dances were beyond the physical and emotional range of what he called the "stiff-assed honkies." I wasn't at all sure T.C. would know who Eldridge Cleaver had been, but she must have because she came back with, "Well, he was right about that, anyway." While we chatted and sipped and watched the dancers, a large TV screen right above us silently showed a Vanna White film, *Goddess of Love*, her vapid, utterly predictable features and wooden gestures flickering out, unattended, over the dark and vibrant crowd. T.C. never so much as glanced up at the screen that was less than five feet over her shoulder.

When Paul Braught came back from the dance floor with his new step, he and T.C. smiled and spoke, and then he said that he'd have to be going. "See, my people taught me long ago to be with your family to see the year out and see the new one in. My wife is home, not feeling too well, so I've got to go home to her, to be with her tonight, to see the year out. And I'll have my shotgun, my handguns, everything—" He made a gesture as if firing guns off into the air. Then he flashed that broad, glittering smile again and blew on his noisemaker, another favor from the management. Turning its tasseled bell toward a barmaid, he rolled his eyes and blew it again. She looked at him with what might have been a mild disdain.

"You're too early," she said shortly, and went on with her work.

"I was tooting at you, Tootie," Braught said with his undiminished smile, then stood and straightened his tie and suit coat. "I'll be home when you get off," he said to Tootie. "Have a window open." Tootie didn't even look up. He nodded at T.C., shook hands with me, and strode out into the night. It was hard to read Tootie's attitude, and T.C. beside me acted as if she hadn't heard any of this. When I myself said good night to her a few minutes later, I wished her a happy new year and a good decade.

"It's got to be better," she said with what I was coming to recognize as characteristic acerbity. "The 1980s kicked my ass."

BACK at the Ramada Inn the celebration was well under way in a banquet room so dimly lit it was hard to see the white faces of the dark forms who sat here and there at round tables covered with white cloths. Above the tables balloons had been suspended by paper ribbons tied to light fixtures, and they bobbed just above the tabletops the management had strewn with confetti. Little horns and crank-handled noisemakers had been provided each table, though none was yet in use. Instead, two DJs at the front of the barnlike room spun country-western that boomed out of a pair of six-foot speakers on either side of a long table stacked with record albums, recording equipment, and bottles. But here, in startling contrast to the scene I'd just left at the Speakeasy, the dance floor was almost deserted. Only a few large couples groped slowly in the gloom, shuffling to the lachrymose sound and lyrics.

Once I had adjusted to the virtual absence of light, I could see that the couples at the tables were oddly subdued as they went at the jugs of whiskey they'd toted in for the occasion. Most were festively dressed, and there were even two men in tuxedos, as well as numerous women in gowns of the sort I hadn't seen since the days when I had nervously attended proms. But the character of the talk and the drinking seemed to me tremendously ponderous. Maybe it was because the Houston Oilers had lost to the underdog Steelers in the NFL playoffs this afternoon? I knew how seriously Texans took their football. Or was it the music: in what mood could you go to the dance floor with this stuff? In what mood return? Were these inevitable lyrics of love lost, of love to be regained, of betrayal, heartbreak, and despair, conducive to revelry? At what level were they accepted, as existential anthems or merely as culturally comfortable background Muzak? If none of these, still at some level, in some way I was debarred from appreciating, these songs were loved, even if they were not conducive to lightness of foot or perhaps even of heart, and when the DJs put on that most self-sorry of all country ballads, the one that begins "Put your sweet lips a little closer to the phone," then the tables emptied onto the dance floor and the dark shapes coalesced there into a slowly drifting sea. The balloons on their curly tethers swayed sadly in the currents of the air-conditioning, and at a table near me a lone man, perhaps a trucker stranded by the circumstances of his trade on this strangest of all the year's nights, cranked his noisemaker over and over. Plainly, T.C. hadn't been the only one whose ass the Eighties had kicked.

GALVESTON Bay is shaped like a butterfly with its wings spread. From Port Bolivar, where the ferry takes you across to Galveston Island, to La Porte on its northern shore, it is about thirty miles long, the largest estuary in Texas and one of the largest in the U.S. It is also very shallow and except for the dredged shipping channels is nowhere over ten feet deep. Outside the bay the waters of the Gulf are very shallow here, too, and when the tide is out Galvestonians sometimes say that you could walk to Cuba. Because the bay is so shallow and is heavily used by the petroleum industry, big-time shippers, commercial and sport fishermen, and recreational boaters, and because the human population continues to cluster on its shores, it is under enormous environmental stress. Around its shoreline fecal coliform bacteria is now showing up in high concentrations, so much so that more than half the bay's oyster beds are closed to harvesting. Since the bay has historically provided over 70 percent of the state's oyster harvest, this is a significant loss. When he and his miserable shipmates were cast up on the shore of the island they called Doom in 1528, Cabeza de Vaca found that oysters were the major staple of the island's natives as well as a building material. The same was true, he reported, of the tribes that lived around the inland shores of the bay. Back in the last century a Galveston visitor complained that there was nowhere you could go to get away from the smell of oysters. It was that sort of place, but no more. You could still get a plate of oysters in Galveston, and you still saw the shells used as the local substitute for gravel, but bay oystering is in definite decline.

What remains of traditional bay maritime life here is further threatened by a proposal to greatly widen the Houston Ship Channel and the channels in Galveston Harbor, Bolivar Roads, and Texas City. Naturally, the proposal has the support of the U.S. Army Corps of Engineers, which over the years has become mindlessly enthusiastic about almost *any* dredging project. In the case of Galveston Bay, marine biologists have warned that the project, if enacted, would precipitate an environmental catastrophe by drastically increasing the salinity of the bay's water. This would, they say, adversely affect the shrimp and oyster populations as well as upset the remarkable mixture of marine life the bay continues to support. "That would be a disaster," Jack Rudloe said, when I called him in Florida to discuss the matter. "The remarkable things about Galveston Bay are, one, the wonderful mix of life there is in it; and, two, the fact that it's so resilient. It looks terrible. It's all trashed around the shores, and when the shrimpers bring up their nets there's all sorts of crap in there—oil drums, tires, bottles, sludge. But along with the drums, the nets are full of shrimp. It's amazing, but it's not *infinitely* amazing. Shrimp populations, especially white shrimp, are very sensitive to salinity levels. And when the water gets too salty, you get predators and diseases attacking the oysters. You can't just go in there and dredge away and expect the life to remain the same as ever."

The bay did look pretty bad coming across it on the ferry, its horizon dominated by the refinery works at Texas City, the water a dull brown, and the shoreline wearing that beaten, frowzy look peculiar to bodies of water in heavy commercial use. In fact, Galveston Bay on this New Year's Day looked uncomfortably like Lake Calumet, which lies between Whiting, Indiana, and Chicago and which I had always regarded as about the unhealthiest-looking stew imaginable. Under a sheet metal sky the bay waters were riffled by an onshore breeze and were almost devoid of other boats. Maybe the recreational boaters were still sleeping off the night before.

I had long wanted to see the city of Galveston. When I was much younger and living in Rhode Island, I occasionally played tennis with a man who had been born here. In his youth Dick Martin had been a champion singles player, and though that youth was well behind him and in our matches he hobbled about the court on swollen, phlebitic legs, he still handily beat me with a cunning assortment of lobs, drop shots, and the like. Galveston was then only a name to me until one afternoon after giving me my customary drubbing he invited me to his house for some lemonade. Then he had brought out a book of black-and-white photographs, and I saw the elegant, often ornate buildings of his hometown. These, he told me, were only the structures that had survived the great hurricane of 1900. Before that, much of the town had looked like this.

After the hurricane Galveston looked like the Powers had spilled the cosmic box of matches on this narrow stretch of beach. But, of course, it wasn't only the physical town that had suffered so grievously: somewhere between six and seven thousand of its human inhabitants were also destroyed. Capriciously—as the Powers characteristically act—many of the victims were found in trees, festooned from bridges, trestles, or telegraph poles, or mashed within the mountains of wreckage that choked the downtown area. As the magnitude of this loss of life gradually became evident, conscripted black burial details were made up to take the bodies into the Gulf, weight them, and bury them out there. Alas, the dazed survivors had failed to reckon with the shallowness of the Gulf at that place, and so, two days later, a man who had thought the tragedy might have a small silver lining for him found that his dead mother-in-law was back—washed onto the beach with other corpses that had returned home along the shallow bottom. They burned those bodies there on the beach. Others had to be burned wherever found since in hauling them to the beach, the burial details found the corpses were beginning to go to pieces. In Houston, long disparaged by the haughty Galvestonians as "Mudville," the black, smudgy fires could plainly be seen, night and day, for over a month. When the ghastly business was at last over, Galvestonians could begin to think about what future—if any—their town might have.

The Hotel Galvez, where I put up, was built by the town's leading citizens as a public expression of their faith in Galveston's ability to rebound. If you were born before World War II and lived near a large metropolitan area, you probably saw a relative of the Galvez—in New York, Miami, Chicago, St. Louis, or Los Angeles. Huge, winged, and stuccoed, these palatial structures contained vast public rooms on their lower floors with French doors and balloon curtains that shut out the mundane world and created a dim and regal coolness within. Their woodwork was darkly burnished, and here and there Remington bronzes and Delacroix-derivative paintings gave a sense of established taste. The carpets were thick, the staff professional, and your parents, you noticed, tended to speak to each other with unaccustomed politeness. There you have the Galvez, which has survived subsequent hurricanes and equally destructive shifts in public taste to remain a monument both to civic faith and to the cultural style of the late nineteenth century.

The stolid splendor of the Galvez this day, however, was somewhat vitiated by the crowds of college kids who had spent New Year's Eve there. At midday a sufficient number of them had recovered to be milling about in the brass- and plant-decked lobby and at the bar, the boys red-faced, swollen, ready to become boisterous all over again as they downed their first Bloody Marys. The girls looked less worn by the night's revels and most of them less certain, too, that they wanted to extend them into the new day. I paused down there only long enough to admire the moldings of the lobby and the main dining room, the woodwork in the bar, and, most of all, the amplitude of the idea.

My high room looked out onto the Gulf, which from up here wore more of a gray cast than the brown of the bay as I'd seen it from the ferry. Normally, on arrival at a new destination I'd have set off to explore it as soon as I'd dropped my bags, and especially in a place like this that I had been looking forward to seeing. Yet now, sitting by the window and looking out on the Gulf, I began to find a perverse pleasure in the prospect of spending New Year's Day holed up in my room alone, writing up my notes. I recalled without the slightest nostalgic fondness, so I thought, the New Year's Days of my adolescence and young manhood when, badly hung over, I had spent the day with my brother in front of the TV, watching mesomorphs bounce off each other in the bowl games we took so seriously. Thus I had had no trouble recognizing my avatars in the lobby; nor, for that matter, the vaguely bored looks of the girls who faced the prospect of a stupefying afternoon such as those my brother and I had once subjected our girlfriends to. Considering my night at the Speakeasy and the Ramada in Port Arthur, I was shockingly clearheaded for a January 1, and the dead gray of my turned-off TV never looked better.

And yet . . . Here it was, after all, New Year's Day. Surely *some* self-indulgence was required. With a quick glance at the hotel menu I rang Room Service, ordered up a shrimp-and-rice dish, broke out a bottle of wine from my baggage—and flipped on the TV. An hour later, stunned by food, drink, and first downs, I was unfit for work and ready to experience the ambience of the first-floor bar and the dregs of the day and the crowd.

Wally and Lee were seated next to me, a comely couple from nearby Rice University. Both looked as if they had stepped out of the pages of a 1959 edition of *Life*: "On campus, American kids claim they worry more about calculus exams than about Khrushchev. Here Wally Johnson and his steady girl stroll beneath Rice University's oaks, their thoughts on the future." Wally and Lee had Bloody Marys before them, and Wally had evidently been dodging back and forth between the game on the tube and his girl at the bar. But now with a middle-aged stranger next to him he gave him the full sun of his attentions, bringing him up to date on the progress of the game and lamenting the sorry state of Rice's football program and of Texas college football in general. "The other states just *raid* us," he said with what I read as a proud smile. "There isn't a boy anywhere in this state with any size and speed to him that some recruiter in Louisiana or Oklahoma or California doesn't have his eye on by the time that boy's a damn sophomore in high school! Used to be, the football players would all stay in state. Not anymore. Plus, of course, Rice isn't like [Texas] A & M or UT, Austin." I could hear the hoofbeats of his next remark, and presently it arrived. "You know why they had to close down the library at A & M? *Somebody stole the book!*" Lee had surely heard that one before, but she politely giggled and said though she'd never dated anyone from A & M, "my roommate went out once with one of the cadets, and he was a pretty weird guy. She didn't say he was stupid, understand, just real *limited*, you know?"

On my left was Mac, B.O.I., as he soon informed me (the locally recognized initials for "Born on the Island"). He was fully as middle-aged and gray as I and with a face whose color nicely picked up the fire-engine red of his plaid vest. Since he was a native and certainly old enough to have family attachments, I had to wonder what his excuse might be for being in here by himself on such a day, and I was going to ask when he, too, got into a lengthy rap about Texas college football. He wanted me to be sure to understand that things hadn't always been this way. Why, he said, just think of all the terrific running backs Texas had produced in his own lifetime, from the incomparable Doak Walker to Jim Swink to Earl Campbell to Eric Dickerson. "And those are just the great names everybody knows. Some of the greatest you never even heard of out of state, like Sid Blanks and Pistol Pete Pedro." Somehow, whatever it was I might have had in mind in wandering down here, this was not it, and shortly I excused myself to walk around Galveston's historic district in the fading light.

Out on the streets, though I sniffed for it, I couldn't detect the scent of oysters, but there was a briny quality to the air, and high up in my nose I was reminded that I walked after all on a narrow spit of land surrounded by salt water. Visually, however, everything in the historic downtown almost shouted "New Orleans." There were, in fact, so many echoes of that place that I began to doubt where I was, wondering if I had like that nameless mother-in-law of the 1900 hurricane been somehow blown back along the coast to the Crescent City. When I turned onto Broadway, I might have been on New Orleans's Esplanade, except this broad boulevard with its grassy median, oaks, and palms was much better cared for, and its homes bore the sure signs of historic preservation. And there was something else here, too, that was distinctive and radically local: the houses gave me the feeling that they had sailed ashore here in the long ago and then disdained ever afterward to weigh anchor.

So here they sat in a kind of elegant dry dock—galleried, furbeloweded, gingerbreaded ships with wonderfully suggestive crannies and angles.

Nowhere on Broadway were the signs of preservation more grandly on display than at the houses once owned by two of the Island's (always the capital "I," we are told) old elite: Open Gates and Ashton Villa.

The former was built between 1887 and 1889 for the prominent merchant/banker George Sealy, who in an ostentatious effort to outdo his neighbors hired Stanford White of the famed New York firm of McKim, Meade & White to design his palace. His snub of Nicholas Clayton, the locally favored architect of conspicuous consumption, was one-upmanship on a grand scale, and especially so when he allowed Clayton to design the carriage house. Open Gates, however, struck me as a colossal failure, like some of the grotesque palaces I'd seen at Newport, Rhode Island, and it looked anything but open. It looked in fact like a cross between the rectory of a prosperous diocese and the administration building of an old-style correctional institution. Later I was told it served now as a conference center for the University of Texas Medical Branch.

Warmer by a good measure and with endearing Italianate idio-syncrasies was Ashton Villa, a brick structure adorned with lots of cast iron and the un-Italianate double galleries that are the distinguishing feature of classic Galveston style. James M. Brown, like George Sealy, had wanted to make an imposing, lasting statement with his home, and so he had—though had it not been for the efforts of the Galveston Historical Foundation, his statement would have been razed years ago. Brown's daughter, Miss Bettie, wished to make her own sort of statement with her life. Out of this home she led the life of the town eccentric, never marrying, smoking cigarettes in a day when this was emphatically not done, and racing her matched team of black stallions down Broadway.

Warmer still and far more human in scale and feel was the Samuel May Williams home on Avenue P. Williams was one of those resourceful freebooters who came to the Island in the wake of the old buccaneer Jean Lafitte and who laid the foundations of the town. And like Lafitte, whom he had previously known and done business with, Williams had come to the Island in 1822 as a fugitive from Louisiana. In his first years here Williams lived under a pseudonym, something the pirate refused to do. Lafitte set up operations on the Island's eastern end and built there a fortified house called Maison Rouge; legend says the Devil built it in one night, having gotten the worse of a wager with Jean. Williams hadn't the money to build anything right away, but he was an energetic, imaginative soul, and by the time of Sam Houston's Texas Revolution, Williams had prospered sufficiently to send Houston's provisional government vitally needed matériel. Then, in 1836, when the rebels' war with Mexico ended in the swift slaughter at San Jacinto, Williams received his reward for that timely gift: the Island became his and his associates' to divide up pretty much as they pleased. Despite that, Williams had not built grandly, certainly not on the scale of Sealy or Brown or Colonel William L. Moody. Instead, he seemed to have remembered something of his Louisiana days, for his house looked like one you might run across along the corridor of Bayou Teche that takes you from Franklin to Lafayette. There was an attractive, modest graciousness to the old place. It looked to me as if humans might have lived in it.

As far as I was able to ascertain there wasn't a building here commemorating the life of the young surveyor Samuel Williams and his associates hired to lay out the townsite. That was too bad because Gail Borden must rank right up there among Galveston's authentic characters. Like so many Americans of the mid-nineteenth century, Borden was obsessed by the urge to invent things that would make life easier, if not better. After another of yellow jack's seasonal scourges gathered up hundreds of Galveston's citizens in 1844, Borden's wife among them, Gail Borden turned his considerable imagination to devising a solution. Since the disease was clearly a warm-weather phenomenon, Borden imagined a gigantic icebox in which to enclose the city's populace and so protect it from the invisible enemy. The idea proved impractical. His subsequent invention of a "meat biscuit" that could be mass-produced and preserved for delivery to troops, ship crews, and other sequestered groups also failed to catch on. But when he turned to the idea of mass-producing condensed milk, he hit. I recall that as a child I felt vaguely comforted by the Borden Company's maternally sexy image of Elsie the Borden Cow. And her milk certainly was sweet.

After Broadway, the Strand, and the rest of the historic district, Seawall Boulevard might have struck me as a crude descent into contemporary commercial reality. Except I knew just enough of Galveston's history to see it as an organic part of the place Lafitte had founded. Seawall was tack, to be sure, but it was tack the way it should be, which is to say it was straightforward and self-aware and showed what I thought was a certain regard for its historical and geographical context. Along it were long, narrow souvenir shops built on piers that extended into the Gulf. These offered the usual awful items, interspersed with local variations such as huge seashells inset with starfish painted a shocking roadcrew red. A sign in front of one shop warned against selfishness: DON'T FORGET THE FOLKS AT HOME. Along here you could rent bicycles, as you could at many another Gulfside spot, except that here they had been providentially provided with red plastic cup holders mounted on the handlebars so that tourists could drink and drive. I wished I had known of this earlier. Now it was too late to cycle, a murky dusk having fallen, making the lights of the buildings look fuzzy and unattached. But it was not at all too late for a drink at the Galvez bar. Inside it I was now able to examine its handsome appointments in leisure, the crowd gone, the last of the bowl games over. Mac was still there, Boiled on the Island, but he wasn't talking.

TEXANS, as the foregoing might suggest, take their sports very seriously, and not just big-time college football. Football is, to be sure, a passion here, and Texas is the first place, I think, where a grade school player has been "red-shirted" (i.e., held back a year in school) so that the year following he would be bigger than any players on opposing teams. But hunting is an equal passion, and the annual opening of the dove season is a major event, complete with the sort of media coverage that the opening of the basketball season gets in Indiana. Fishing, amateur boxing, alligator wrestling—these are all dear to Texan hearts. Jacques Barzun is often quoted to the effect that if you wanted to understand America, you had better get next to baseball. Similarly, if you wanted to understand what makes Texas tick, you had better understand something about its love of sports and its veneration of the men who have excelled in them.

So, from Galveston I swung north over the bay thirty miles inland to the town of Conroe to talk with one of the state's favorite sons, Roy Harris, who came out of the Big Thicket in the late 1950s to challenge for the world's heavyweight title. And then I angled back along the coast to Sinton, a rifle shot from Corpus Christi, where I met with the Paul Bunyan of Texas baseball, Clint Hartung, once known as the "Hondo Hurricane."

For the past quarter century Roy Harris had been the clerk of Montgomery County. When he wasn't attending to his official duties, he practiced law in Conroe and Houston and sold real estate. Considering the sorry ends so many prizefighters have come to, Harris's settled prosperity struck me as surprising: Joe Louis ended up as a shill for a Las Vegas casino; Sonny Liston was found dead in the same town, possibly as a result of a failed drug deal; and the great lightweight champion of the 1940s, Beau Jack, ended up as a shoeshine boy. Considering, too, the mass media's image of Harris when he burst upon the national scene in 1958, it was surprising to find him in so civilized a setting. Back then reporters had been delighted to find this handsome, black-haired heavy-weight living in a raw cabin in the wonderfully named hamlet of Cut & Shoot. Here was a white boy from the wild and woolly Big Thicket who had relatives named Coon, Roe, Blue Jay, and Armadillo. This last named, a cousin the same age as Harris, had no teeth; they had all been knocked out, reporters were informed, in sparring matches with Harris and his older brother, Tobe. Henry Harris, Roy's father, had been the bare-knuckles champ of the Big Thicket and had raised his boys to scrap from the time they could stand. This was all almost too good to be true—but almost all of it was. Roy Harris appeared on the cover of *Sports Illustrated* in August 1958, posed casually on the gallery of his family cabin, barefoot, holding an antique musket, and flanked by two lean hound dogs. He was undefeated then and about to challenge Floyd Patterson for the world title. By the time he entered the ring in Los Angeles later that month, he was an American folk hero, a kind of cross between L'il Abner and then-current movie heart throb Rock Hudson.

Now here he was at ease in his spacious, well-lit office in the county seat of Conroe: a big-shouldered man whose thick, jet-black hair was only flecked here and there with strands of gray. His eyebrows were thick and black, too, unlike those of so many ex-fighters whose brows are a seamed mass of scar tissue. He was wearing a snowy white shirt, bright-red tie, and well-cut charcoal-gray suit. Cowboy boots peeked from beneath his pants' cuffs. When we shook hands I noted that his wasn't especially big. In fact, about the only aspect of his appearance that suggested a prizefighting past was his flattened nose, and I thought that up here in the Big Thicket there must have been a fair number of men walking around with that same sort of mild disfigurement. Later, when I remarked on his lack of scars, he smiled in his shy sort of way and pushed his nose to one side with his index finger. "I got that in Baytown," he said, "fighting Fred Buckles. Nobody remembers him, but anybody who ever fought him will never forget him." Then he pushed aside the fringe of his left eyebrow, exposing a long, faint scar that trailed away into the brow's thicket at the bridge of his nose. "That's from the Patterson fight. They stitched it up—I don't recollect just how many they put in there, but it was a good many. But I knew that stitches leave scars, so the next day I just tore 'em out, and a few days after that it just scabbed off."

Behind Harris's desk was a large, framed photo showing two lithe teenaged boys stripped to the waist, two adults, and another kid on a horse. One of the adults wore a coonskin cap as did the horseman, who was positively dripping with huge knives. Machine parts lay in the foreground. Ropes covered here and there with some sort of sacking were stretched around a grassy enclosure in which a few pigs rooted and a hound dog stood watching them. I asked Harris about the picture, and he turned to it.

"This here's my dad," he said, pointing to the adult figure with the coonskin cap. "William Henry Harris. He was named for William Henry Harrison, but everybody called him Henry, including me. This here is my older brother, Tobe. This is the high school principal. He had a car, and so he could drive us around to fight. This is me. I was about seventeen then. The fellow on the horse is a cousin. We called him Armadillo. He had to go to the penitentiary for murder. Then he got out, but he had to go back in for carrying a weapon. He's still there." He waved his hand over the photo's surface. "This here was our gym in Cut & Shoot. See this gas flare?"—pointing to a thin pipe sticking out of the ground—"This was so we could work out at night." I asked about the machine parts lying about in the foreground, and Harris said they were disassembled motor parts that had served as the boys' barbells. "We used to lift the cylinder heads when we were about that age," he said.

As we stood talking about the photo, Harris's younger brother Henry came in. He, too, had boxed and looked it. His hooded eyes had old nicks around them, and his nose was even flatter than Roy's. Like Roy, he was handsome, though in a more menacing sort of way than his famous brother, and I thought that I wouldn't want to meet up with Henry Harris in an alley if I was on the wrong side of the situation. Henry joined in the discussion of the photo, concluding simply, "We were just raised out in the woods and the oil fields. Nothin' to do but scrap." He said he currently trained and managed fighters, including a heavyweight for whom he had good hopes. Mike Williams, he claimed, might be a champion soon if he got the breaks. He was certainly better than Evander Holyfield (the current champ) and better than Mike Tyson, too, whom both brothers thought was the best of the current crop. "Holyfield doesn't have the legs to be a great heavyweight," Roy Harris said. "He's not really a heavyweight. He's really a light-heavy, or what they call now a cruiserweight. He won't be able to keep Tyson off him if they ever fight." Henry Harris said his boy, Williams, had sparred with Tyson "and had him in so much trouble they made the reporters leave the gym."

On another wall was a plaque reading FOR SERVICE TO THE MEMORY OF JACK JOHNSON, FIRST BLACK HEAVYWEIGHT CHAMPION OF THE WORLD. APRIL 2, 1985, GALVESTON, TEXAS. What was the significance of this? I wondered. "Oh, that," Roy Harris said, glancing at the plaque. "Johnson was from Galveston. There's a monument or statue or something down there to him. He learned to fight on the docks. I think I gave them money for it. Anyway, they had a ceremony down there, and Muhammad Ali was there. You know, his mind is still real quick; it's only his speech is slurred, and his movements are real, real slow. And it's kinda pitiful when you think how quick he used to be. But he stood up at the banquet and said a few things. He said, 'Jack Johnson was a guy that would drive fast right down the main street of your town with the top down in his convertible and a blond woman next to him in the seat. There was *one bad nigger!*' " Harris shook his head. "Now, you know," he said, "if it had been anybody else said that, there'd be hell to pay. But it's all right for him."

Henry Harris couldn't join us for lunch, saying he had some contractual details to attend to involving one of his fighters, and so just the two of us drove over to the China Delight in the Conroe shopping center. Once we were inside and seated at a corner table, Roy Harris glanced about the room and shrugged his shoulders. "Used to be," he said, still looking about the large room, "you'd walk into a restaurant here and know everybody in it. Nowadays I don't know anybody here. My dad and Tobe and their wives said it has got so polluted with people they were going to move up to Arkansas where it wasn't so civilized. They did, and they're still up there." He said Conroe had grown so that Cut & Shoot was "what we call the suburbs. And Conroe itself is really a suburb of Houston now. Used to be, when I was a boy, this was what you'd call the Sticks."

I asked him how his hometown had gotten its colorful name.

"Well," he said slowly with another of his shy, measured smiles, "that would depend on who you asked. There's lots of different stories. I think the one closest to the truth, whatever that is, is that it came about through a fight between two different kinds of Babdiss [Baptists], the Hardshell Babdiss and what we call the Stolic—Apostolic—Babdiss. The Hardshells had control of the local church, but the Stolics got a new preacher in town and said he was going to preach that Sunday at the church. Hardshells said no, he wasn't. Well, they met down there under the tree in front of the church, and the Hardshells had their guns and knives, and when the preacher saw that, why, he took off down the road and then cut through the brush, trying to get away. So, they named the place after that: he cut down the road, and he went shooting through the brush. That's one story, anyway."

When we had placed our orders I asked Harris to talk about his background, and he was politely willing. His father's people, he said, had come from Arkansas by way of Oklahoma, where John Wesley

Harris, his grandfather, had been a marshal. When they had come into this country, it had been barely tamed, and the people spent their time hunting wild razorback hogs, making whiskey, and dynamiting the streams for fish. They also hunted alligators, and some, like his brother Tobe, would wrestle them for the pure hell of it. "My mother, Gladys, would have been the valedictorian of her class in school only she didn't go to the first grade there, so they gave it to someone else. Nowadays they only count the last four years anyway. My dad never had much schooling, but he wanted us to get our lessons. He was in timber first, and then, after they discovered the Conroe oil field, he got into that. There were some pretty rough scrapes here when the boomers—the oil field people—came in. My dad would cut timber and haul it to the railroad. Then, later, he loaded ties. He'd balance one of those things on his shoulder, then run up the embankment and heave it into the boxcar. Don't you think that wasn't hard work. Henry [Senior] was the strongest, fastest man I ever knew. He would've made the best fighter of any of us. He ran a nine point seven hundred [yards] once. And another time, he whipped nine men in a kangaroo court. That's a kind of free-for-all they had in jail." I asked what Henry Senior had been in jail for. "Oh," his son said casually, "he whipped some folks, and they put him in jail, in a cell with nine others, and then he whipped them, too."

The ring behind the house had been Tobe's idea, but the scrapping had been a family trait. Harris said that when he was a small boy a relative had told him that he might favor his mother's side of the family more than his father's, but that all the Harrises were fighters, and Roy would have to learn to be one, too, "or else get out of the woods." He said he guessed his nature was perhaps a bit more gentle than that of his male kin. He had enjoyed looking for Indian arrowheads more than fistfighting. "But Tobe just loved to fight. He'd rather fight than eat. Still would. He was redheaded and freckle-faced, and you know what they say about fellows like that. It was his Irish nature, I guess. Anyway, he traded some mallards to a neighbor for some boxing gloves they'd gotten tired of or wore out, and then we set up the ring and went at it out there. I either had to learn it or get whipped all the time by Tobe. So, I started when I was around ten.

"Tobe would beat most of the good heavies now, I believe, though he wasn't but a middleweight himself. He was quick, and he was tough. He fought a lot down there on the waterfront at Houston and Galveston. He fought all over the world on waterfronts as a longshoreman. One time I remember was at Sam Houston College. There was this big football player who was giving him a rough time. So Tobe says to him, 'Let's you and me go outside,' and the fellow just laughed. 'You won't be laughing when I get finished with you,' Tobe says. So, they go outside, and Tobe hits him quick a couple of times, busts his teeth out, knocks him down the hill. That was the end of that. Afterwards, they became friends.

"Tobe was more a chip off my father's block than I was, I guess. My dad and his relatives, they were all raised rough, and they protected their rights pretty good. John Wesley Harris knew how to handle himself. So did my Uncle Bob. One time some fellows came up on him and hit him with a tire iron. Then this fellow got him down and stabbed him thirteen times before my Uncle Bob could get his knife out. Then he had to cut that man's head off." As for himself, he had never had any sort of a scrap after hanging up his gloves—except to "spar some" with his brothers. "If a man is determined to fight me," he said, "I'll try to kinda joke him out of it, and most of the time I'm successful at that."

But these were the words of a man in middle age with a sterling ring career behind him and no need now to protect his rights with his fists. Before this there were the hard lessons of that ring behind the cabin in Cut & Shoot, lessons Harris had to learn from Tobe, and then from his father who wanted him to know the tactics that might well be used on him in the gritty world of Texas Gulf coast amateur boxing: how to thumb, how to lace a man, how to "open a man's leg from his knee right down his shin to his shoe" by using your own shoe, how to smother a man with your glove in a clinch.

From age sixteen until he turned twenty-one, Harris fought in Golden Gloves tournaments, beginning as a welterweight. Four times he was Texas Golden Gloves champion in various weight classes; six times he was a regional champion. Meanwhile, he was continuing his academic lessons, first at Tarleton State College in Stephenville, where he majored in petroleum engineering, and then at Sam Houston State College where he studied vocational agriculture. He got married, too, and started a family. "I needed money then," he said, "so I decided to turn pro. I fought around Texas, usually for seventy-five dollars a fight. I fought in Houston at this club. I fought in Tyler. I became Heavyweight Champion of Texas. Then—I think this was 1956—I defeated Oscar Pharo and became Heavyweight Champion of the South."

It was while he was training for the Pharo fight that Harris met the legendary Jack Dempsey, the Manassa Mauler, who like Harris had learned his trade in the rough and tumble of small western towns on Saturday nights when the crowd would be satisfied with nothing less than blood and a body on the canvas. Later Dempsey would assist in Harris's training for the Patterson challenge, but then he was training one Buddy Turman. "Turman was from Noonday," Harris said. "That's up near Tyler. One day we were in the gym in Houston, working out, and Dempsey talked real ugly to Turman, called him a coward, and so on. Then, after Turman had gone to the shower, Dempsey turned to Tobe, who was there with me, helping out, and he said, 'What would you have done if I'd talked to you the way I just did to Turman?' And Tobe said, 'I'd have knocked you on your ass!' And so Dempsey turns to Turman's manager and says, 'See, I been telling you you've been managing the wrong boy.'"

After the win over Oscar Pharo, Harris stepped up in class and began taking on nationally ranked heavyweights and beating them handily. He was never, he said, noted as a big hitter, "but I think I had one of the best jabs in the game. I could box. And I could take a punch." He beat the tough trial horse, Charlie Norkus, and highly ranked Bob Baker, and then the former Light Heavyweight Champion, Willie Pastrano, the "Dancing Master" from New Orleans. That positioned him for his challenge to Floyd Patterson, then himself undefeated. I asked Harris if he could recall much about that big night more than thirty years ago.

"Sure," he said, "a lot of it." By this time he had polished off the pepper steak he'd ordered and its accompanying mound of fried rice, and now pushed his empty plate away from him with a small sigh. "It was August 18, 1958, in Wrigley Field in Los Angeles, where the ball club [the old Los Angeles Angels of the Pacific Coast League] used to play." He looked up from his plate and stared at me, not glaring, really, but with a steady, level look. "I should have beaten him. I still think about it once in a while. I wish I had a film of it so I could study it. I was undefeated at the time, but really I didn't know anything about training. I got on this high-protein diet for that bout, and by the time my manager got a look at me, I was down to one seventy-eight. I was actually losing weight. He wanted to call it off, but we didn't. I gained most of that weight back, but it wasn't real weight, you know, not solid. I was actually whipped three weeks before that fight.

"But I felt strong at the bell. I was a seven-to-one underdog, but I felt I had a chance. I had my jab, and I went out there after him with it. In the second round I knocked him down. I slipped under his jab like this"—he half rose from the table and made a weaving motion, his hands held high, his jaw tucked in behind the padded shoulder of his suit coat—"and then I hit him with an uppercut. I actually lifted his feet off the canvas. Then I hit him with a hook, and he went down. But that hook, it wasn't really a good one. I hit him as much with my forearm as with my fist, and I didn't think it was enough to knock him down. I thought he might be possuming, you know. So I didn't follow it up. Looking back, I see this was a mistake. I should have pressed him more then.

"The third round might have been even. I think at that point I was ahead. But the tide started to turn in the sixth. I wasn't in any condition to fight. He started hitting me pretty good, and I was feeling weaker and weaker. We went on to the twelfth, and that's when they stopped it." He smiled, shrugged, and raised his hands outward in a what-can-you-do-but-your-best? gesture.

"I wanted to fight him again, and we were negotiating for a rematch when he fought Johansson." In that bout the underdog Swede with the photogenic smile surprised the boxing world by knocking out the champion. And so then there had to be a rematch between the new champion, now the darling of the media, and the dethroned Patterson. Harris was forgotten, but he had to keep busy.

"I was offered a fight with either Eddie Machen or Zora Folley [both good, highly regarded heavies]. But those guys, they'd dance, weave, clinch, and so on, and they never seemed to settle anything. So, we took a bout with Sonny Liston because we thought it would make a better fight." The first time Harris had seen the menacing ex-convict who would eventually become the champion himself was in 1953 in the Golden Gloves. "He could hit. He knocked out our heavyweight, Ed Sanders," Harris remembered. "Later, Sanders won a gold medal in the Olympics. Then, after he turned pro, he got killed. Well, like I said, Liston could hit. He had a fast jab. He had a good left hook. I think his left hook was probably his best punch. He was a real good fighter, maybe a great fighter.

"In the first round I went out and hit him three good rights. He was sort of slow, and my thinking was that if I hit him a couple of times right off, maybe I could keep him from rushing me." He paused, took a sip of his soft drink, and looked down at his empty plate. "He stopped me in the first round. See, the thing was they had this three-knockdown rule: if you got knocked down three times in a round, they stopped it. That's what happened to me. But I believe if they'd have let us go on, I'd have outboxed him. He had long arms. His arms were six inches longer than they should have been for his height. I guess I didn't account for that. I didn't give him enough slack." He chuckled, then turned serious quickly.

"I've often wondered if I wasn't set up for that bout." I asked him what he meant. "Set up. See, you always warm up before a fight. You want to get warm, get yourself slightly sweaty, get limber. But here we were in Houston, waiting to go on, and I was just sitting there in the dressing room. I kept asking my manager if I shouldn't warm up. But he kept saying we had plenty of time. Then all of a sudden he looks at his watch and says, 'Something must be wrong with my watch. We got to go up.' So, I arrived in the ring stone cold, and then I hear him asking if the three-knockdown rule was in effect." I said he wouldn't have been the only person who crossed paths with Liston and wound up feeling that something shady had gone on.

Our fortune cookies arrived. Harris snapped his open, stared at its message a long moment, then read it to me: " 'The loss which is unknown is no loss at all.' " He shrugged, still looking at the tiny, unfurled banner. "I guess that means if you never knew you had it, you don't miss it." I asked him then to speak of the rest of his career, and he said there really wasn't much to it, that after the loss to Liston and another to British heavyweight champion Henry Cooper, he had known he would never get another title shot, and so his heart had gone out of the whole thing. The Cooper fight had been over there, in Wembley Stadium. "I busted him up pretty bad, and at the end of the fight I said to my corner that we'd won this one for sure. But my trainer said, 'Don't be too sure. I wouldn't be surprised if they didn't give it to you. He's still breathin'.' And that's the way it turned out: they gave it to him on a decision. It was pretty hard to believe, but it was in England. . . ." He had fought four or five more times—he couldn't remember these last bouts very well, or didn't wish to—and then had hung up his gloves. He was tired, he told me, of the travel, of the constant disruption of his family life, and of all those years of training, of keeping his body honed to its combative edge.

At age twenty-eight, when most American men are deeply into what will be their life's work, Harris's career in lights was ending, and he had come back to Cut & Shoot to figure out what he would do with the rest of his years. He had taught math in junior high for a while, and then pursued his studies, as his mother had wished, getting his undergraduate degree in history from Sam Houston. He got another undergraduate degree in elementary education and did graduate work in this area as well. But by this time he had developed an interest in the law, and in the old-time rural way where a young man was said to have "read law" with the local barrister, Harris read law with a lawyer friend in Conroe. "He gave me the books to read," he said simply, "and I read 'em. And he showed me how law was practiced. He showed me how to proceed on a case. I helped him some at the office." Thus, without having attended law school, Harris took and passed the Texas bar exam. Since then, he said, he had been about equally in law, real estate, and politics. He paused in the gentle, unassuming flow of his narrative, almost as if he were embarrassed by having talked so much about himself, and looked down at his hands spread out on the table, as if they held the key to his life's story.

"I've made a pretty fair amount of money along the way," he said slowly, with just a trace of wonder in his tone. "That's not a brag. It's just that it's sort of funny the way things have worked out. I made a hundred thousand for the Patterson fight, and maybe at the time I thought that would be the most money I'd ever make in my life. But it hasn't turned out that way. It's kinda funny. And to tell the truth, boxing's a pretty tough way to make a dollar. I have two sons that box, but neither one is going to really follow it. I can't say I'm sorry about that. Robert was light heavyweight champion at Texas A & M. Kevin was the same at Sam Houston." There was a silence now, and in it Harris looked at his watch. It was time to get back to the courthouse.

He wanted me to have a couple of items that were upstairs in his office, and so up we went. One was a book about Cut & Shoot and its famous son written by a local author. The other was Harris's business card. He gave me a few of the latter, saying as he fished them out of a desk drawer, "Whenever I have to make a call somewhere and send in my card, it's surprising to me how they'll always come right out." When I looked at the cards, though, I thought it wasn't so surprising after all. On its back side the card carried the usual vital information: the carrier's name, occupation, address, and phone numbers. But its front—its business end, as I saw it—was a miniature reproduction of that *Sports Illustrated* cover of August 18, 1958, its caption reading THE CHALLENGER FROM CUT AND SHOOT.

He seemed not quite ready for me to go. He pulled from a bookshelf a copy of Nat Fleischer's *Ring* record book and began leafing through it, looking, I supposed, for his own entry in it. But he stopped at that of Cleveland Williams, a heavyweight from Houston who had once himself challenged for the title. "Cleveland could hit," Harris said, looking at the book's photo of an incredibly muscular man, every definition in his massive torso showing. "And he could move. That's why they called him 'The Big Cat.' But if you hit him, he'd kinda freeze up like this"—he held himself still with his hands raised in a defensive position—"and kind of wait for you to do it again. He was a beautifully built fighter from the waist up. But he was like this Holyfield, didn't have any legs. These boys don't have legs. If Cleveland had had my legs, he'd have weighed four hundred pounds." He snapped the book shut and returned it to its place in the shelf and then from next to it pulled out an enlarged photo, blurry in focus and grainy in texture. It showed a young man running through the woods in tattered cut-off shorts and sneakers and about to leap over a barbed-wire fence. It was Harris. "This was training," he said.

On the courthouse steps he said with a fine smile that he'd surely look me up when he came through New Mexico, as he did every summer. Then he nodded at the Cut & Shoot book he'd given me. "I never read that," he said. "Let me know how it comes out."

SINTON at eight in the evening and the sky so black and without stars it made me slightly dizzy and disoriented. The new year's cycle had hardly had time to start cranking over into gradually lengthier days, and there seemed a dead stillness to everything, as if this portion of the earth was stuck in a featureless chaos between phases. At the Texaco station on Sinton's business loop I was the only customer, and it felt to me as if I were the *only* customer who had ever wandered in there to trifle with the few magazines in the racks and try on the dusty sunglasses that were unaccountably for sale. The young attendant recommended with what I thought a weary realism that I not stay in Sinton but "go right on to Corpus Christi." At the town's only motel, named simply "Motel," the young Pakistani behind the counter recommended that I not eat at any of the town's few local restaurants. "When I go out to eat, I only eat at Pizza Hut," he said with a smile. But I said I thought I'd try Freddie's, a local spot I'd noticed. He raised his eyebrows, still smiling, and handed me my key.

Directly in front of Freddie's main entrance a large pool of vomit lay wetly reflecting the thin strip of neon that ran just under the building's roofline. Inside there were but five diners, two men in white beards, a young couple (Anglo with black cowboy hat, Hispanic girl), and Freddie, who was sitting off by himself, morosely picking through his chicken-fried steak. I thought of telling him about the bad advertising he was getting at his front door, but when I heard his sepulchral smoker's cough I figured he had more serious matters on his mind. And then I thought of the fortune cookie's message: If you didn't know you had it, maybe you never knew you lost it.

Under the bleak overheads a TV was perched on top of a cigarette machine, its screen filled with snowy images of some sitcom no one in the place was watching. Some tired, hand-lettered signs said YOU ARE THE WAITER—NO TIPPING! (true: you called at the kitchen counter for your order when your number came up); STEAK NOT DONE ENOUGH?

BRING IT BACK, WE'LL ADD MORE FIRE; JUST LEAVE THE DISHES, WE'LL DO 'EM LATER. A pitcher of Lone Star was $1.15, and, as I discovered, the round steak submerged in onion gravy with beans, rice, and salsa was a good deal better than I had eaten in tonier establishments.

Back at the motel it became evident to me that the management was homesick for summers in Pakistan, for even though the night air was balmy, the room temperature was ferociously pitched, and the thermostat was controlled from some central location. So, at various hours during that night I arose from my sweat-soaked pallet and opened the sliding glass door for relief, usually when freights of the Texas Mexican Railroad had announced their presence with far-off rumbles and premonitory shakes and then chugged past, fifty yards away, hooting the blues out into the coastal night. At dawn Freddie's lay heavily on me, and when the next train came past I simply left the door open and trusted in the protection of the wan light.

How much of a memory Clint Hartung was in Texas I didn't know, but once he was a hero here. Once, too, his name was on the lips of the nation's baseball fans as another spring and its hopes came into bloom.

His state herohood had been in the years just before World War II when he was still in high school and making his name known with his pitching and his slugging for the Hondo Owls high school team. Then in the long, hot summers he'd starred in the Highway 90 League, a fast, semipro circuit that had teams in the little towns that stretched west from San Antonio to the Mexican border: D'Hanis, Castroville, Hondo, Sabinal. Some of the towns, a man who'd umpired in the league once told me, "was just wide places in the road, but they all could get up teams in those days." It had been through that umpire, Rusty Lyons, that I'd heard the legend of the kid from Hondo, of the speed of his fastball, the length of his home runs. One spring Lyons had taken me out on a little tour of some of those towns, the bluebonnets just coming out on the gentle rolls of the hills, the skies bright and fleecy, and the country not yet under the anvil of its summer heat. I think it was in Castroville that Lyons stood in a weed-grown and disused ball field and pointed out a row of stores across the road. Atop the hardware store, he claimed, a Clint Hartung homer had once landed. It was talk like this that had eventually brought Hartung to the attention of major league scouts who in those primitive days still beat the country bushes for kids who might have the talent if not the particular ambition to play professional baseball. The New York Giants had signed Hartung, who told me later this day that until then he hadn't thought much about playing except on weekends along Highway 90.

I called on him at his neat bungalow on a quiet back street of Sinton. You could see the high school football field from his front lawn, and on fall afternoons the cheers of the crowd could serve as echoing reminders of his own time in the sun. Walking up to his front door, I was slightly apprehensive. On the telephone he'd been a man of very few words and had been reluctant to grant me an interview. Only when I'd mentioned that I'd heard of him through Rusty Lyons did he loosen up a bit. I did not say that I also knew that in the spring of 1947 he had been one of the most highly touted baseball rookies of all time, a player the New York papers were talking about as if he were the next Babe Ruth: a superman who was as fabulous a pitcher as he was a hitter, who had hit way over .500 in wartime service ball against some seasoned professionals, many of them major leaguers doing their duty by providing athletic entertainment for the troops. Speaking of this phase of Hartung's career, Rusty Lyons had said he thought Hartung's pitching record during the war was something like thirty-three wins against only two losses. And as Rusty had so pungently phrased it, "I don't care if you're pitching against the Little Sisters of the Poor, that's good pitching." A contemporary photograph shows Hartung in that spring arriving at the Giants' Phoenix training camp. It is obviously a posed shot, which tells you something about the fanfare for a player who had yet to swing a bat or throw a pitch in major league competition. Yet there he was wearing a tie and sport coat, striding in to destiny with a suitcase in his right hand and his glove held in his left. A reporter who was there for the Hondo Hurricane's arrival recalled that with a group of his colleagues he had rushed over to the motel where the team was staying "to see this Paul Bunyan character," only to be told he was sleeping. "You'd have thought," he said, "they were talking about the president or somebody. Pretty soon we were tiptoeing around and whispering, too."

No one, of course, could possibly have lived up to this sort of hype, and there will *never* be another Babe Ruth. So, inevitably, as it would now seem, Hartung had failed. He had been a pitcher in the Giants' regular starting rotation for a few seasons but was never better than average. After that, he'd played a little in the outfield and at first base with only rare appearances as a pitcher. In the famous playoff game between the Giants and Brooklyn Dodgers that had ended the 1951 regular season, Hartung had been a pinch runner on third base when Bobby Thomson hit his "Home Run Heard Round the World" to give the Giants the pennant. But no one remembered who scored ahead of the hero, and you have to know what you're looking for in the photo of Thomson engulfed by a mob of delirious teammates to pick out the big guy up the third base line clapping his hands. He was a very marginal player on that team, and in the World Series that followed went hitless in four at bats. He also made an error in the outfield. Two seasons later he was gone, to be recalled if at all only in those perverse conversations where writers and fans recall colossal flops.

How could that not have hurt? It had not been, after all, his doing that he had been so sensationally portrayed, nor that he had turned out to be only an average major leaguer. But it was that huge gap between the rather foolish expectations and Hartung's average abilities that had haunted him through his career, that had even followed him to this back street in Sinton, where he was occasionally sought out by the curious, his life permanently warped by the easy words of long-dead sportswriters of a city a thousand miles away, one of whom had actually wondered whether Hartung ought to bother playing baseball with his mortal contemporaries and ought instead to go straight to the Hall of Fame in Cooperstown.

He was so big that when he came to answer my ring at his door I could see only his lower half through the door's glass, and when he swung the door open and I could see the rest of him, he seemed to just keep going and going up like a tree. He must have been six and a half feet tall and over two hundred fifty pounds, with massive thighs, hands, shoulders, and head. His hair was full, still ungrayed, and he wore it slicked back, just as he had in the photograph of spring 1947. This morning he was dressed in Sears-type blue work pants and matching shirt, and without anything more than an inquiring glance into my eyes and a quick hello, he led the way up the steps into his living room where his small, white-haired wife offered some coffee. Hartung settled his bulk into a reclining lounger and without looking at me waited for what questions I would put. I decided to start with oil.

For twenty-nine years he'd worked for Marathon Oil as what he called a "gang pusher." "Basically, it's oil field maintenance. Had two gangs of five men each. We put in lines, put in plumbing, replaced lines—anything out there needed fixing." I asked if this was dangerous work, and he shrugged. "Anything in the oil fields, it's hazardous." I asked his view of the current situation of the American petroleum companies along the Gulf, saying that in my travels westward from New Orleans people had spoken of what had happened to big oil in awed tones, as if talking of some great natural disaster that had leveled the whole country and so changed it forever.

"The oil's playing out around here," he said. "You have to go down deeper and deeper to get it, and when you bring it up, it's mostly water.

Takes about three thousand barrels of that stuff to make about eight barrels of oil. Now, when the price of oil was thirty-five dollars a barrel, why, you could do it. But not at the prices you can get now. Don't pay to bring it up." Another problem was how to dispose of the discharge. "Used to be you could throw it in the channel and so forth, down to the bay. Now with the regulations, you got to put it back into the ground, and that's expensive and dangerous. It was takin' us about three hundred and fifty pounds of pressure to drive that stuff back into the ground and down into a cavity there. We heard people say Texaco was using eleven hundred pounds of pressure to drive it down. Now that cavity's filling up, so where you gonna put it?" He looked out the window a moment, rubbing his hand musingly over his chin. "Cheaper nowadays to buy oil overseas than it is to produce it here." I told him I'd heard the same thing said about shrimp in Louisiana.

"It makes you wonder," I went on, "what is worth producing in our country as opposed to buying it abroad." He looked at me without speaking, as if to say it was my question, not his, and so I had to go on from this small, dead point to ask him how he'd gotten into oil in the first place. Was it, I asked, something his father had done before him?

"No. My daddy was a carpenter. He encouraged me to play ball, said it would be a whole lot easier swatting balls than nails. But that was after I'd been playing awhile and got noticed. I probably would've been a carpenter like him. But before I came down here all I ever did was play ball." So now we were into it fairly, and I asked him about the old Highway 90 League that had played on weekends in good weather. Had he been intimidated as a kid just out of high school playing with mature men? "Naw." He gave the first—and last—hint of a smile, as if he were now glancing briefly back at these dusty days and the long afternoons on the hardpan diamonds where sometimes the ground was so hot under your spikes your feet felt singed. "That was just good ol' country ball. We had a good time. But some of those fellas were pretty good. Many of 'em played into their forties—as long as they could until some younger fella came along to shove 'em out."

In 1941, when he was nineteen, the Giants had signed him and sent him to Minneapolis in the American Association, just one rung below the Show. Had there been much money involved? I asked. He laughed shortly and without humor, and answered, "My daddy got five hundred dollars." He had finished that season at Eau Claire in the Wisconsin State League. That winter came Pearl Harbor, and the next year he was in the service where his cruel fame awaited him.

Hartung arose from his lounger and excused himself, nodding at his empty mug as he left the room. His wife took it and mine, too, into the kitchen and brought back steaming black refills. She had been sitting silently in the corner of the living room while we'd talked, not knitting or reading but simply listening, her hands folded in her lap. "I came along later," she explained now. "He met me in Corpus Christi where I was waitressing. By then all this business was over. He's had a rather unusual life, but he doesn't talk about the earlier parts of it, so I like to listen and hear how it was."

How it was was that Hartung had been sent by the air force back to his hometown of Hondo where he spent the next three and a half years in maintenance—and playing baseball against other base teams. When the war was over and his hitch was up, there wasn't enough of the baseball season left to make it worthwhile to get out and try to play, and he had reenlisted for the year of 1946. Then came the spring of '47.

I wanted to tread carefully here, but even attempting to do so, it was clear from the brevity of Hartung's responses and the ever longer silences between them that this was troubled ground. Whether he knew—or sensed—that I was aware of what had happened to him when he joined the Giants, I can't say. Maybe after all these years he simply assumed everybody who asked to speak with him knew about the ballyhoo and its aftermath. Why else would they seek him out?

The team's manager, he said, had been Mel Ott, the great Giants slugger of the 1920s and '30s. Originally Ott had been attracted to Hartung's raw talents as a hitter, but before the team broke camp and headed north, Hartung was taking a regular turn on the mound. It was, I suggested, a very unusual situation, since almost every player specializes in one skill or the other. Hartung shrugged and said, "You play where they tell you." The fact seemed to be that even he didn't know then what he really was, either a hitter or a pitcher, or some Ruth-like combination of the two. "I didn't know what I could do," he said, looking now down into the mug balanced on one of his trunklike thighs.

What sort of pitcher were you? I asked.

"Chunker," came back the reply.

"What's a 'chunker'?"

"Thrower. Fastball. Curve. Change-up. Mainly fastball. Never had good control."

He did, so the record shows, manage to win more games than he lost that season, and as a hitter had batted a very respectable .309. Not, you would have to say, a bad first season, especially considering that Hartung then had less than a full season behind him in professional baseball.

The next season the Giants team of slow-footed sluggers that had won through sheer power began to fall apart, and Hartung with them. The year after that he went 9-11 as a pitcher and hit .190, and that was the year the great manager Leo Durocher took over the team and began to recast it in his own image. Hartung was not to be an integral part of the Durocher Giants, though Leo kept him around. He was on the team that made the astonishing late-season stretch run to overtake the Dodgers, but not really a part of that achievement. It seemed safe enough, though, to ask him about that famous season, and I did. But his response was spare. No one at the All-Star break, he said, thought "we had a chance. But Durocher kept tellin' us we did. And we kept playing goin' and goin', and then, there we were at the last game."

His last season in the major leagues was 1952. "Hurt my arm" was all he said of that year. He'd played then for Minneapolis, then Havana, and finally Nashville. He was thirty-three and finished. "When it's over, it's over." I said I'd read somewhere that Charlie Gehringer, the great second baseman of Detroit, had observed that baseball players did things backward: they played every day when they were young, then retired and went to work. Hartung said nothing to this, only looked at me out of his great, red, weathered face. "So," I trudged on, "you had to start over," and tried to get him to talk about getting into the oil business.

All the bigger petroleum companies had baseball teams, he said finally, and he'd been recruited by Plymouth Oil (eventually bought by Marathon) to play for them. "Came down here in 1956. We'd work half a day, then practice. We'd play maybe fifty, sixty games a year against other company teams." This had lasted two seasons, and then "we had a guy who was a cheapskate working for the company. Didn't want to pay for uniforms, equipment, and so on. So, we quit. Lots of others on the other teams dropped out, too. You couldn't get a schedule together. Anyway, I'd had it." In the silence of the room I knew I couldn't budge him another inch in any direction. He'd had it with me, as well. I glanced at Mrs. Hartung sitting in the corner, so still and poised, looking at her husband, waiting for some sign. Next to the couch on which she sat was a small color photograph of the young Clint Hartung in his Giants uniform.

"Well," I said at last, rising from my chair and heading for the door, "you've done something that George Bush never did, and something he wanted to do, too: you pitched in a big-league game and won it." Hartung remained seated, looking into his empty mug, and for a moment I thought he wasn't going to utter another word and that I'd have to slink out of the house in a guilty silence. But then he sighed and said, "Yeah, but he went on to be president."

THE landscape from Sinton to Brownsville along Route 77 looked as if it couldn't make up its mind what it was. Was it south Texas rangeland and cotton-farming country—miles of hardpan dirt and mesquite and oak? Or was it semitropical coastland with palms, opuntia cactus, and that heavy openness of sky that announces the presence of a large body of water? The closer I got to Brownsville, the more it looked like the latter. But the range and farmland wouldn't give up, and right on the outskirts of Brownsville there were cattle and cotton fields. Also on the outskirts were a large number of billboards advertising bail-bond services, these the characteristic vegetation of towns all along the American-Mexican border.

If you are trying to crack a strange town, often you can do worse than to make your first stop the Chamber of Commerce. Sometimes these people turn out to be very helpful, especially if you can get the secretaries to talk with you off the record and tell you what truly happens around town. And sometimes a visit to the Chamber of Commerce turns out to be a wallow in mindless PR crap that sticks to you for days after. In Brownsville the official with whom I talked had been in the game so long he couldn't speak English anymore, couldn't, in fact, communicate in any language known to me. Later, when I looked at such notes as I had taken in his office, I couldn't translate them, except for a few sentences. These ran: "Everybody over there [across the border, in Matamoros] speaks good English. You don't have any problem making yourself understood anywhere in Matamoros." And: "You don't need to go to any exchange. The dollar over there is *cheerfully* accepted" (this with a broad wink). And: "The river, you need to understand, doesn't divide us. It unites two great cultures."

But all my questions about Matamoros—wasn't I interested in Brownsville, which was, after all, "an American city with a great many attractions your readers should know about"? Yes, yes, I was sure of this, but clearly one of the American city's major attractions was the geopolitical fact that it was right across the Rio Grande from Mexico. No question, he agreed. And this being so, what had the impact been of the grisly ritual murder of the American college kid, Mark Kilroy, a year or so ago? Must be considerable.

"Oh, no, no, no. You're quite wrong there. The media coverage of that hasn't affected tourism here one bit. And that's because people understand that could have happened anywhere else. It could have happened in the towns they themselves come from. You look: they've had cult slayings in California; they're finding bodies under houses in Illinois; fifty unsolved murders in Oregon. People aren't stupid. They're not about to be scared off by an isolated incident. We were talking about accessible attractions in Matamoros, right? Well, don't tell your readers they'll need a rental car, because they won't. You can walk right over the bridge to the central market area. I do it all the time myself. And you can walk to a number of excellent restaurants." He excused himself to get a large-scale tourist map of Matamoros to prove his contentions. While he was out I scanned his office library and found it intriguing: *Keeping Livestock Healthy*, *The World's Best Jokes*, *Farmers in a Changing World* (1940), *After-Dinner Speeches and How to Give Them*, *The Magic of Thinking Big*, *Water* (1955).

He recommended I stay at the immediately adjacent Fort Brown Motel, which, he said, "doesn't have to take a back seat to any of your major chains." As it happened, when I'd checked in and had occasion to pull the chain of my room's toilet, I discovered that no water discharged beneath my own back seat. The motel's water, I soon learned, had been turned off for the day while repairs were in process. Nothing to do then but take a stroll across the unifying river into the other great culture and hope for positive developments with the plumbing.

The Gateway International Bridge was only two blocks distant, and I had just arrived at it when action erupted: three border police, one with his nickel-plated pistol drawn, were in furious pursuit of a young man in a dirty T-shirt and sneakers. The crowd parted for the race, but within a block the young man had sped around a corner at a slant that would have done full credit to one of those great running backs I'd heard about at the Galvez bar and left his pursuers far behind. They came back through the wondering, milling crowd, and the one with his pistol out now dropped it into the street in returning it to his holster. It lay there a minute, shiny, lethal, out of place as if it had been an object from outer space, the crowd standing back from it as if it had been alive. Then someone picked it up and handed it to the red-faced officer, and life went on. Up on the bridge other officers were talking about the incident but not, I thought, with any special excitement. I asked one of them what the trouble had been about, and he turned his face to me, grinning a fat, foolish grin. "No trovel," he said. "We don't have no trovel."

The central marketplace was a good half-hour walk from the bridge, and on the way there I passed several of the restaurants that had been so enthusiastically recommended to me, resolving to return to the Drive-Inn, "A Gourmet Restaurant," for dinner. In the central market there was a remarkable plethora of leather goods for sale. I'd seen Juarez and

Nogales, border towns that specialized in cheap leather goods, but Matamoros was easily king: here you could buy boots, shoes, vests, chaps, belts, sandals, hats, saddles, bridles, bullwhips, purses, and wallets, all of these items looking like they had just been flayed from beasts that now wandered bloody and skinless in pastures just beyond the city. Beggars almost outnumbered vendors and shoppers. One beggar, blind and apparently crazed by a life of unimaginable deprivation, sat legless in front of a leather goods stall, his stumps covered in thick, deeply scarred leather casings that incongruously reminded me of a baseball catcher's shin guards. Here and there were herb carts filled with trays in which were the ranked and sovereign remedies for all that could ail you, from warts to impotence. At intersections vendors with rubber-tired carts sold roasted ears of corn and corn soup, the cinders from the shucks fluttering about their heads like flocks of tiny crows that never rested.

In the evening flow of pedestrians bound to or from the bridge a teenager shot from a side street into the auto traffic on a skateboard, which he rode sitting down, his legs stretched out, feet crossed at the ankles. He whizzed between blue-belching cars, propelling himself with his hands, then shoved his board up onto the narrow, beaten grass of the median and scanned the traffic coming from the opposite direction, looking for his break. The dirty light of day was going swiftly now, but as I watched the kid I could see that here was no sport but instead a sport of Nature, for his legs were wasted and his feet tied to the board with one of those bungie cords motorists will use on luggage racks. Nor was the board on which he so bravely rode even a skateboard as an American kid would understand it, but a homemade job that clearly was this rider's only means of locomotion. While I watched, I saw him lean forward in anticipation, tilt his board down the little slope, then give himself a mighty shove, and off he went, shooting through a hole in the traffic, across to the other side of the street, on through a parking lot, then up onto the cinders of a railroad embankment where he came to a halt. He deftly undid the cord at his ankles, rolled off, then dragged himself farther up the embankment where he produced a sack from somewhere on his person, opened it, and began to eat.

At sunset there were thousands of great-tailed grackles that flaunted the border so sedulously guarded here against the free flow of human beings. Without hindrance or letup they swung back and forth over the river and its trashed and denuded banks, settling into trees, stalking sidewalks and lawns, then flying out again for other roosts. Along Elizabeth Avenue leading back to my motel the palms were clamorous with them, their bodies clashing against the dry, metallic fronds and their cries forming a piercing kind of vespers. The air of dusk was oddly exciting and menacing with their cries and with the mingled odors of auto exhaust and burning corn husks.

OFTEN where Mexico abuts on the U.S. what you get on the Mexican side of things is a simulation of what the Mexicans think Americanos expect in restaurants, hotels, and shops. Sometimes the simulation is tired, impoverished, as thin as tissue paper. Other times it amounts to a wonderful sort of parody of both cultures. When it achieves this level it can be diverting, even hilarious. The Drive-Inn was not, but it certainly answered perfectly the American-held stereotype of what a stylish Mexican restaurant ought to be. Doubtless the Brownsville Chamber of Commerce had contributed to this scene, and I was glad its man had suggested I come here.

Its single cavernous dining room was dimly lit by an enormous chandelier that gave you just about enough light to see your hand in front of your face—but not enough to show up the threadbare plushiness of the room's appointments. The waiters whisked about in black tie, and the maître d' wore a cutaway. On the large bandstand a five-piece orchestra played tangos, sambas, and Latinized versions of American popular songs of forty years ago, the pianist picking out his solos on such numbers as "I'll Be Loving You Eternally" and "Moonglow" in that single-note style you associated with *all* piano south of the border. The two violinists, though, were never quite in concert, and one appeared to be having trouble reading the charts. Probably it was the light.

I was not surprised to find the Drive-Inn pushed margaritas, the drink Americans popularly associate with Mexico. And they were good, too, properly astringent, full-flavored, but light. Here they came with a double olive garnish (as they did elsewhere along Mexico's Gulf coast) in glasses that matched the scale of the dining room. Of like amplitude was the menu, which oddly echoed both in its size and the number of announced entrees those of some of the flashy and hopeless resort restaurants of southern Florida. I went for the *cabrito*, kid goat: when this is done the right way, it is one of the New World's unique gustatory experiences. When it isn't, it's like sawing through a Mexican saddle. I feared the latter, but in the meantime, I could sit back, sip my margarita, listen to the music, and watch the spectacle.

Near my table a group of young Americans waited submissively for their waiter to do the tableside preparation of the house's shrimp specialty. With appropriate flourish he rolled up to their table with his large cart, its chafing dish lit from beneath with what looked to me like a two-alarm conflagration. After dumping the shrimp into the dish along with other ingredients, the man fell into an animated conversation with two colleagues, and presently they drifted off toward the kitchen together, the door swinging shut after their gesticulations. Behind them the table of Americans waited dumbly for what would happen, their talk stilled by the uncertainty of the situation: were they being taken? poisoned? or simply abandoned? Ten minutes later the man reappeared, still in conversation with his fellows, and then with an evident reluctance took up his cudgels. In went generous dollops of Heinz 57 and Hunt's ketchup, both out of their plastic, commercial-size squeeze containers. In also went some alcohol-based solution that caused the dish to burst into a great fireball that threatened the ceiling. When this had subsided the waiter disappeared again into the kitchen, reappearing after a lengthy interval when the steam from the dish had settled low over it and the diners' shoulders suggested they had given up all hope of dinner and now hoped merely for simple survival. When the waiter served up the shrimp the orchestra was playing "Strangers in the Night." My fears about the *cabrito* were not assuaged by this spectacle, and in due course were fully justified.

Later, back in my motel room at the Fort Brown and with the water system mercifully functional once more, I was to encounter other strangers in the night. Shortly after midnight I was awakened by the angry buzzing of motorbikes that seemed aimed directly at my ground-level glass door. But they pulled up just short of it, and I could hear the two riders dismount and walk away into the distance. An hour or so later, the unseen riders remounted, revved, and rode away. At three-thirty they were back. On this visit they hadn't been gone long enough for me to drift off again, and so when I heard them at their bikes I foolishly flung open the curtain and the glass door and walked out into the cool, breezy night. Two lithe young Hispanics sat astride their white Hondas, talking in conversational tones. Would they, I asked, think about parking somewhere else in the spacious lot if they were going to be in and out all night? They listened attentively, looking at me with curiosity out of a mist of booze and I didn't know what else. Then one asked me if I spoke Spanish. Only a very little, I said. "Well," he said, "we don't speak much English, either," and with that they started their engines and wheeled away, leaving the rumpled Anglo behind under the glare of the outdoor lights feeling savage in a dull way.

Half an hour later they were back, same spot, and now I felt certain I wouldn't be getting any more sleep this night. I wobbled down the corridor in my undershorts in search of a Coke machine, certain I would not be embarrassed by other guests. At the corridor's end I came upon the scene of the repairmen's efforts of the afternoon before: a section of the wall was open and the pipes and wires within it exposed. Two sawhorses blocked off the area and within was the Coke machine, its red glow beckoning someone in need of cheer just at that moment. I stepped around the sawhorses, got my Coke, and was in the act of returning to my room when my eye lit upon a tray of screws left behind by those workers who would be returning in a very few hours. They would not, I suddenly felt sure, miss a couple of the two-inch screws I took from their supply, and with these I now went down to the front desk where I explained to the groggy clerk that I needed a hammer for some light repairs on a piece of luggage. He said he would try to find me one, and a few minutes later did so. Back in my room my previously dull savagery had sharpened, and out in the parking lot with just the faintest hint of dawn showing above the indistinct outlines of the palm trees I drove the screws into the back tires of both bikes. And then I slept.

IT was a very bright day with that refracted sort of sun coming through clouds and humid haze that mounts to a glare. Even behind my sunglasses my eyes wanted to retreat into my skull. The air was heavy, and at nine in the morning it was hot. "We get northers now and then," said Melvin Maxwell, "and then it'll get pretty cool. But really we don't have winter. This is winter." We were standing in the parking lot behind the offices of the Laguna Atascosa National Wildlife Refuge outside Brownsville. As we waited for Steve Thompson, the refuge manager, two green jays flitted about in the thorny trees, and when the sun caught their spread wings and blue heads just right they looked like emeralds on fire. I had never seen a green jay before, and they were so beautiful I had trouble holding up my end of the conversation with Maxwell, one of the rangers here. He understood and smiled. The birds, he said, were one of the principal reasons people came down here to winter. "Folks follow the same flyways as the birds do. They come from the Dakotas, Minnesota, Iowa. People down here call them 'Winter Texans' or 'Cottonheads'— that's because so many of 'em have gray or white hair." I said I'd seen one estimate that a quarter of a million people came to the refuge each year to see the birds. Maxwell judged that about right for the refuge, but he thought the number much greater for birders in the valley as a whole.

The "valley" is the Lower Rio Grande Valley. Biologically speaking it is one of the most unique areas in North America. Known to biologists as the Tamaulipan Biotic Province, it lies three degrees north of the Tropic of Cancer, a marvelous—and bewildering—mixture of the tropical, temperate, desert, and coastland. Here tropical flora and fauna reach their northernmost limits to mingle with temperate-zone species reaching their southern boundaries to form a biological crossroads of some 700 vertebrates and 1,200 plants. Simply to confine yourself to an investigation of the bird population is to be overwhelmed by its complexity and abundance: waterfowl, shorebirds, songbirds, raptors—370 species, including such endangered ones as the aplomado falcon, the southern bald eagle, the whooping crane, and the brown pelican. Eighty percent of North America's redhead duck population winters here. Here also commuters from the Mississippi and Central flyways converge, and Melvin Maxwell said there were even a few species over here from the Pacific flyway. "It's like Nature was trying to force everything through a small-necked bottle," he said with a smile. Nor, of course, were the birds the only notable creatures at the refuge, only the most conspicuous. In addition to such common wildlife as the white-tailed deer, the javelina, and the bobcat, there were also the American alligator (now making a comeback), the ocelot, and the last few jaguarundi left in America.

Laguna Atascosa, the Santa Ana NWR, the Sabal Palm Grove Sanctuary, and the embryonic Lower Rio Grande Valley NWR are the only remnants of that fantastically tangled and teeming landscape the Spaniards encountered in their coastal probings of 1519: a 4,000-square-mile region of tidal mud flats, palm jungle, inland ponds, thorn forest, and upland chaparral. Here were Sabal palms, lime prickly ash, wild olives, Montezuma bald cypress, elms, sugar hackberry, Texas ebony, sotol. . . . But it wasn't the Spaniards or their Hispanic descendants who so reduced this wilderness to the few islands of it that remain. That was the work of twentieth-century Anglo-Americans, beginning in 1904 when rail lines reached Brownsville and land speculators realized that the valley had an almost year-round growing season. Speedily then, the Sabal palms came down, the thorn forest was bulldozed and burned, the ponds and wetlands drained, the river entrained. It was a reprise of what had happened (and was then still happening) in south Florida, which shares the 26th latitude and has a similarly generous climate. Much later the Mexican government joined in on its side of the border so that now a scant 5 percent of the aboriginal biotic province remains. Of an estimated 40,000 acres of Sabal palms that so impressed the exploring Spaniards that they named the great river that ended here el Rio de las

Palmas, less than 100 acres remain—and these doubtless wouldn't be here, either, had they not come under protection. Of the once-abundant cat population, there are currently only about 80 to 100 ocelots left and possibly as few as 15 jaguarundi. The great jaguar is gone.

The Laguna Atascosa NWR is by far the largest of the remnants—45,187 acres that to an unversed traveler looked wonderfully exotic. Riding around in it with Steve Thompson and Melvin Maxwell, I was continually interrupting them to ask a very basic question: What kind of landscape is this that I'm in now? And the answer was always different as we moved through desertlike terrain, coastal prairie, seasonal wetlands, and seashore. At one point as we crawled along a narrow road bracketed with snarled, thorny vegetation, Steve Thompson observed that this was "prime ocelot territory." "If you can throw a pencil at it and it bounces back," he said, "that's ocelot heaven." Not far away we crossed a bridge over a green pond and Thompson pointed out a very large American alligator half submerged at its edge, its ridged back covered with drying algae; as we watched, it slumped downward toward the bottom, the water sliding up toward its tail until there was only a small ripple to mark the presence of its great bulk and then not even that. On our way to Laguna Atascosa (Muddy Lake) we passed through a stretch of field management was allowing to return to native vegetation, and through Thompson's informing eye I could see the historical clock cranking slowly backward as the Johnson grass and buffle grass gradually crowded out other exotic flora and a few slender shoots of Texas ebony and lime prickly ash snaked up toward the sky. Thompson said more and more farmers in the greater valley area—and throughout the state—were letting their fields revert "because they're finding that they can make more money leasing their land for hunting deer and quail than they can dry-land farming." Texans, he observed, "spend a good deal of time and money chasing animals around." (Indeed, and though Thompson didn't bring it up, I knew that some Texans in recent years had converted their farms and ranches into mini–game preserves on which they allowed well-heeled sportsmen to kill exotic big game species such as black leopards, tigers, and jaguars in the equivalent of shooting fish in a barrel.)

At Laguna Madre a warm stiff breeze blew in our faces as we stood in the sand, waving grasses, and cacti, watching a long string of redhead ducks feeding on the laguna's beds of shoal grass. Thompson estimated the flock to number between five and six thousand. The laguna, he explained, had been formed by Padre Island, which now defends it from the Gulf. It was yet another of the area's unique natural phenomena, the only hypersaline lagoon in the United States and one of only three such bodies of water in the world. Much saltier than the sea and without any significant freshwater inflow for the last four thousand years, Laguna Madre is a hundred shallow, narrow miles of some of the most productive water anywhere, filled with fish, specially adapted mollusks, and the sea grasses certain migratory birds love, like the redheads we were looking at now, and the reddish egret. Thompson obviously admired these redheads for their hardiness and versatility, remarking as we watched them feeding that when they first came down for the winter they had to make repeated trips to freshwater Laguna Atascosa until their salt glands were built up once again. "Usually," he said, "this takes a month or so. Then they won't need fresh water anymore." As he talked and the three of us took turns with the field glasses the ducks kept flurrying up from the grass beds to light on other stands farther south, so that slowly the whole great flock moved along the shining surface with a rhythm that became more and more evident the longer you looked at it. For me there was something hypnotic about the spectacle—a part of the globe's natural process, its breathing, so to say, that I was privileged to witness. And it may have been so for these veteran observers, too, for they seemed in no hurry to move on.

But finally we did. On our way back to headquarters we passed a parked school bus. "We get a lot of school groups coming out here to experience a bit of the natural habitat," Thompson said, "to see it, to touch it, to get poked by it. And many of them are just scared to death by this wilderness. Yet this was the way this part of the world—their world—used to look." He paused. "We have a hard time convincing them of that."

LOS FRESNOS was equidistant from Laguna Atascosa NWR and Brownsville, a dusty little crossroads with a few stores on the main drag, a bank, and a couple of farm implement outlets that looked as if they had recently gone out of business or were just about to. A couple of big, old-style garages of the kind that used to do heavy-duty service were definitely out of business, their bays empty, windows boarded up. All around the town lay broad, flat fields. A cotton gin sat off to the east, its corrugated sides glinting dully. In the steady wind signs flapped and hammered at the buildings, and a couple of rusty palms bent westward outside the bank. Inside Lila's Diner there was only one other customer, and he was on his way out. At the cash register Lila engaged him in talk, pointing to his T-shirt. RATTLESNAKE JAKE'S, it read in a gaudy design. "Ooooh," exclaimed Lila, raising her pudgy hands to her cheeks, "I don't like no rattlesnakes!" Her customer smiled behind his shades and said he'd never seen one hereabouts, though, he added, he wasn't native but was instead a "California wetback."

"Well," said Lila, her eyes still wide, "you go out in the woods or the fields, you'll see one, all right! Big, too! Ooooh, I don't like those snakes!"

The shelves behind Lila's counter were filled with softball championship trophies and photographs of the teams she'd sponsored. "Yes," she told me, "they do very well in the tournaments. Very well. I have a couple of second-place trophies, too, but I don't show those. Only the first place. I sponsor them every year, and then at the end of the season I throw them a big party." She smiled broadly. "They like to drink that beer and eat my fajitas, let me tell you! Oh, yes!" When I went outside onto the raised sidewalk Lila followed me, and we stood there a minute watching a big tractor roll slowly past with the wind rolling a paper plate along behind it like an odd extra wheel. Across the street the man with the Rattlesnake Jake T-shirt was rummaging about in the bed of his pickup. Lila pointed at him and gave a small laugh. "Oooh, I don't even like to think about those snakes," she said again.

Here was farm country, for sure, except now I knew that this wasn't all it was, however much Los Fresnos looked as if it belonged in west Texas or even Oklahoma. Twenty miles east on Farm Road 100 was the Gulf, and driving toward it I kept looking for signs that I was approaching a coast and was in fact moving through a landscape tinged by the tropics. But until arriving at Port Isabel just about the only sign were the clouds: big, billowy, and ill defined, they didn't look like inland clouds, and at Port Isabel it was clear they weren't. For here was a jumble of boat shops, beachwear outlets, and snack bars with names like "The Outrigger." And on the other side of the long causeway lay the utterly improbable spectacle of South Padre Island—five miles of high-rises, souvenir shops, and lounges that would have done credit to Ft. Lauderdale's route A1A. But as I rolled in slow astonishment onto the island I could see a vast difference between Ft. Lauderdale and this place: there was nobody here. South Padre Island on this winter day looked like a scene out of the Fifties anti-nuke film *On the Beach*, where the city stands silent and abandoned, and the only thing moving is something swinging in the wind. There were, to be sure, a few cars in the lots, and the traffic light just ahead was operating, but for a moment the only thing I could see that moved was the heavy mist coiling in off the Gulf, wrapping itself around the lower stories of the high-rises and enveloping the shops. The whole thing was so chimerical that it wasn't until the cop had given me a couple of blips with his siren that I shot a glance into the rearview mirror and saw his lights flashing. He had, he said, been signaling me to pull over since back at the traffic light.

He proved to be one of those petty officials who takes a certain delight in the leverage their position gives them, and from behind his mirror glasses he impassively requested that I get out of my car and surrender my license and registration, his manner vaguely suggesting that here was a big bust. Nor was he going to tell me right away just what it was I had done. Still, in a sense I was glad to see him as I stood there in the wind and mist and occasional flashes of sunlight while he scanned my documents. He at least was alive and proved that I hadn't wandered into some terrible valley of death. On the other hand, maybe he was the sole occupant of this place, and I had wandered into his well-laid trap where we would be keeper and kept forever.

"You crossed a double yellow when you came off the bridge," he said at last. I said I'd been distracted by the emptiness of the place but couldn't have been going more than two or three miles an hour. Was there to be a fine for this? He cocked his head in an attitude that plainly said that he hadn't asked for any chin music and that, yes, there just might be a fine if that was what I was aching for. So we stood there a long moment, he with my papers in hand, his legs spread in the stance of a fighting man at the ready. He wanted to know my business here and how long it would take me. I was working on a book, I said, and in these matters it was hard to say how long it might take. Then I got my papers handed to me, and he said he would let me off this time, but "many people come out to the island and think they don't have to respect our laws. This might be vacationland for you, but it's home to us. Please remember that—and enjoy your stay." And so as I drove north along the boulevard I had a new friend for close company. Clearly it was a slow day in a slow season.

There was, though, life here, and as I began to see that I was reassured. There were a great many CLOSED signs to be seen and vacant-eyed windows that announced even more plainly their situation. The high-rise hotels had distress signals out—WELCOME WINTER TEXANS—WE LOVE YA! SEASONAL SPECIALS FROM $45—but here and there I could see some humans in the shops, and an occasional car passed me on an errand to somewhere. At a travel agency there looked to be a little flurry of activity; maybe the natives of this derelict vactionland were planning to flee. On impulse I pulled into the parking lot at the Bahia

Mar Resort and Conference Center, and as I did so my official escort continued on up the boulevard. Inside the cavernous lobby there didn't appear to be another soul besides Randy, a young man at the front desk. Behind him every one of the niches I could see had its plastic-tagged room key in it. Indeed, Randy admitted with what I thought was a trace of shame that "things are pretty slow." I wondered when they picked up. "Should be any time now. We start getting people who fish and so on about now, and it goes on picking up until the end of February. That's when this place really starts to jump." His eyes lit up a bit at this. "From there on to the end of April you can't get in here with a shoehorn." In spring the island became in truth Ft. Lauderdale–on-the-Gulf, the place jammed with thousands of college students from all over the South and the Southwest. "We even get some from California," Randy volunteered. And would I like to see one of the rooms? For the fact was that even the seasonal bargain specials could be improved upon: I could have a Gulf-side double on an upper level for forty dollars.

On the twelfth floor my room was big, blue, and barren-feeling. A full-length mirror reflected the blue carpeting, the blue bedspreads, and the solitary traveler who looked back into the glass. What was he doing up here, anyway? He was, he guessed, testing how it might feel to stay here overlooking the Gulf in a ghost town where you couldn't beat the rates. Maybe I could go even higher in price, a "junior suite," say? Down at the desk Randy informed me the junior could be mine for fifty bucks. Hell, I was paying a good deal more than that at the Fort Brown where my room by no stretch could be called a suite. What about the junior suite with kitchen? That would be—checking here—$56.25. "In season it's one-fifty," Randy said. He raised his eyebrows. Would I like to see 307? I would.

But 307 was if anything more barren in feel than the twelfth-floor room, and standing for a while on its narrow balcony, looking out at the Gulf through the mist, a fear came over me: this cut-rate splendor wasn't worth it at any price. If I died here, nobody would find me until some fresh-faced collegians tried the door in spring and found it jammed against them by my body, by that time become so bloated as to completely fill the room, one grossly bulbous leg jutting out onto the balcony like a special-effects monster. I would much rather, I thought as I descended to the lobby, take the Fort Brown—higher rates, plumbing inconveniences, motorcycle bravos, and all—where in the worst case my next of kin might at least be notified.

Before taking leave of the ghost town I drove out past the last of the developed area, the high-rises giving way to bars and then convenience stores until at last there was nothing but road and high dunes on either side and the sand blowing and piling up on the pavement in windrows. Surprisingly, there was more human activity out here than in town. A few families clambered about on the Gulf-side dunes, surf-casters stood knee-deep in the mild surge, and there were some beachcombers strolling meditatively along, heads down, hands in pockets. Where the road ended and Nature took over, a pickup was parked slantways in the road and in it two young men were drinking beer and listening to rock with the windows down, so to share the joy. Out on the beach a bus the size of a Greyhound was parked with the doors of its cargo space open. In there I could see a jumble of tools, cans of oil, and a bicycle. The rig had two solar panels on its roof and a kayak lashed up there, too, and looked thoroughly professional in its setting, as if the owners really had this style of life down and knew precisely what they were doing here. As I came around to the passenger door a cur shot out from underneath, its lips pulled back, yellow teeth bared. I swatted at it with my notebook as it went for my trouser cuff, and a big voice from within the bus said, "*Aaah! Aaah* there!" The cur retreated under the bus, reluctantly, I thought, and presently the man behind the voice materialized into the misty sunlight, huge, deeply tanned, and wearing only bathing trunks. "You scared of dogs?" he asked, looking past me to the water.

"No, I love 'em." I was wondering whether I needed to make an apology for the swipe I'd taken at the pet I could see glaring at me from its greasy haven behind the right front wheel. But the owner didn't make an issue of it and proved friendly enough in an offhanded way. He told me he came down here each October from Ontario, Canada, where he worked as a sandblaster, and parked on the island until April when he went back to work.

"Try to get a little sun. Kayak. Fish. Ride my bike. It's peaceful. Kinda gives my ears a rest." He smiled slightly, his blue eyes still on the water. I asked if the spring migration of the collegians disturbed his routine, and he said that was when he began packing up.

"Mostly, though, they don't bother to come this far up the island. All the action's down there"—waving southward. He turned now to fully face the Gulf and stretched. "Just another beautiful day," he said, and then looked at me as if seeing me for the first time. "You'll have to excuse me now," he said, "I got my dinner cooking," and he turned to mount the bus's steps, the tawny hair on his back waving in the wind like a stand of sea oats.

JOHN CREWES had been in Brownsville four years as an Assistant U.S. Attorney. Before that he'd been a cop. He was raised in the Middle Atlantic States, and it wasn't difficult to see that he wasn't thrilled with the locale of his current assignment, serving, as he put it, in the "buffer zone between the First and Third worlds." He had kindly consented to talk with me about law enforcement problems here on the border and in particular about what parallels there might be between southmost Texas and southmost Florida.

"We have as many problems as they do, any day," he said somewhat contentiously. "In 1988–89 our district was the busiest in the whole country." He emphasized that point by rapping the tabletop between us with the cast on his right hand, a souvenir, he explained, of his frustration "at the way a case was turning out." He acknowledged the problems of the law enforcement people in the Keys and the Tampa area but quickly added that "we have as many drugs coming through here as they do, plus, because we're on a border, our problems are compounded. In the summer of 1990—just to cite you one example—we had a coke seizure here of over nine tons, second largest in U.S. history [to the twenty tons seized in Los Angeles]. More cash leaves the U.S. at Brownsville than anywhere else in the country. You can draw your own conclusions about that. We don't do the maritime surveillance that they do because we can't: we simply don't have the resources. Up above Corpus Christi they do more. We have one cutter. One. I don't know of any major country that's so lightly protected on one of its borders against maritime smuggling as we are."

But though drugs were a major problem here, Crewes wanted me to understand that they were by no means the only problem. There was also the business of smuggling illegal aliens. "We prosecute more illegal aliens," he claimed, "than anywhere else in the U.S." (The next day with his help I would visit the government's illegal alien detention center at Bayview, as grim a "nonprison" as could well be imagined with its razor-wire fencing, armed guards, and dark-faced, fluorescent-clad inmates.) The Brownsville area, Crewes said, was the American port of entry in the long corridor of migrating aliens that began down in Central America and ended in Houston. Then there was the smuggling of exotic bird and animal species: Amazonian parrots and scarlet macaws were popular contraband items these days. Even the TED matter was heating up, and Crewes made it clear that his office was vigorously enforcing the law with ten to twelve convictions in the past year. Eight other cases were pending. It all seemed, I observed, to add up to a rather alarming snarl of problems.

Crewes didn't bite at this except to remark that the Brownsville area was certainly unique. The United States, he said, "really stops at Corpus Christi. This is another country. The whole valley—if it is part of America—is a forgotten part. Brownsville isn't like other border cities you may have been to. It isn't anything like San Diego, which is a real American city. There's a military presence there that means that thousands of people from the rest of the country are moving in and out at all times. The same for El Paso: a military presence, but more, it's on an interstate, there's manufacturing there—it's part of America. On any street in San Diego or El Paso you know basically where you are. In Brownsville sometimes, you're not sure."

As for what lay across the bridge, he said he knew all he needed to know about it from his position over here. He hadn't, he said with what I thought was a certain pride, been to Matamoros in about two years. "Custer," he added in a punchy gloss, "doesn't vacation in the Black Hills." And as for the rest of Mexico, he knew it held nothing for him.

"My house," he said, "is fairly near an H.E.B. [a chain department store], and if I need something there, some household item, I know I've got to get down there early in the morning. If I get there too late, the place is just packed with Mexicans. And what are they buying?" He waited for me to come up with an answer, but I shook my head. "They're buying Pampers, they're buying lard, they're buying generic toilet paper. Now, if they have to come over here to buy such basic stuff as that, what could there possibly be over there that would interest me?" And again I had to shake my head and shrug.

ON the night of March 13, 1989, Mark Kilroy and three friends joined hundreds of other vacationing college kids in the drive down from South Padre Island to Matamoros. What drew Kilroy and all the others were some of the very things that kept John Crewes away: Mexico's endemic poverty and hence its often frantic efforts to lure tourists with cheap prices; its accessible exoticism; even the faint whisper of danger there was to the place. After a day of surf, sun, and girls, what better way to cap it off than to drive down to the bridge, park, and then stroll across to hit the string of bars along Avenida Alvaro Obregon? And that was what Kilroy and his friends did on this night, just as they had on the night before and as they might yet again the night following. Except that on

March 14 as the four made their way back to America in the morning's small hours, they separated briefly at the tiny triangular park that lies at the Mexican end of the bridge, Kilroy lurching off behind it to empty his bladder. His friends never saw him again.

A little less than a month later, with the police on both sides of the border still searching for Kilroy, Serafin Hernandez, a Mexican national, ran a drug interdiction roadblock south of Matamoros and was tailed to a ranch that proved on inspection to be a staging area for drug smugglers. But when on April 11 Hernandez was taken by police back to the ranch, what was discovered there was something no one had bargained for. On the ranch was a hut that had been used by the smugglers for ritual practices that included human sacrifice. Subsequently fifteen bodies were discovered in shallow graves, and among them was that of Mark Kilroy. In an iron cauldron found in the hut, along with a variety of ritual objects (magic sticks, railroad spikes, horseshoes), was Kilroy's decomposing brain.

The case was made for sensational treatment by the mass media, particularly when it was learned that the cult leader was still at large and that with him was his *bruja* (witch), a tall, attractive woman who until the Kilroy murder had been an exemplary student at Texas Southmost College in Brownsville. Two weeks later Adolfo de Jesus Constanzo, the leader, and Sara Maria Aldrete Villareal, the alleged *bruja*, were cornered with other cult members in a Mexico City apartment. Constanzo escaped mortal judgment by ordering one of his followers to shoot him. Sara Aldrete was captured alive and subsequently claimed she'd been nothing more than a captive accomplice, à la Patty Hearst/Tanya. Law enforcement officials immediately discounted this plea, and she was jailed along with other cult members.

Aside from its sensational aspects (and leaving aside, too, my mischievous remark about it to the man at the Brownsville Chamber of Commerce), I was interested in the case because certain of its cultic aspects suggested the influence of the Caribbean islands. Then, too, it appeared to me to be another example, bizarre to be sure, of that massive cultural syncretism that has been at work in Mexico almost since the moment of the Conquest, combining contradictory elements of the indigenous and the imported to form a third entity that is Mexico. Here, for instance, in the bloody rites of Constanzo's personal cult was a combination of African-Caribbean religions, traditional Mexican witchcraft, and European Christianity. True, Constanzo hadn't himself been Mexican but Cuban. But he had been in Mexico long enough to see what could work in that country, what might possibly draw converts to him. John Crewes had dismissed any wider significance of the case because he felt Constanzo's deadly combination of the African-Caribbean religions, Santería and Palo Mayombe, with Mexican witchcraft had been entirely singular. "We hadn't seen anything like that before," he said, "and nothing like it since. In that sense, the case isn't symptomatic of anything more than smugglers' attempts—which you see quite a bit of here—to provide themselves with some kind of magical protection. I've been in houses we've raided where there've been all sorts of candles and so forth, little signs that say 'Law Begone.' You might consider the killings simply as an extreme form of that same effort to get magical protection." But instead of animal sacrifice, common to both Santería and Palo Mayombe, Constanzo had ordered kidnappings and killings, both here and in Mexico City where another eight victims were discovered.

Bob Kahn, city editor of the *Brownsville Herald*, took a kindred view, saying that once you understood that the urban entity of Brownsville/Matamoros had historically been devoted to smuggling, it made a sort of sense that those engaged in that line of work would be trying to get an edge, however they could, whether by planting moles in the police departments or by resorting to traditional Mexican white magic. "They've always been running something here," he told me with a small, sardonic smile, "booze, automobiles, electronics, aliens, and now it's drugs." Killings in the drug trade were on the increase, he said, because the stakes had gotten so high. "These days," he went on, "when bodies are found in the river, they rate an inch of type, and that's all." Still, he granted a certain grim uniqueness to the Constanzo case because of the methods the gang had used to gain magical protection. When Serafin Hernandez had run that roadblock, Kahn told me, he had done so because he believed the rituals had rendered him invisible to the law.

I had learned that Constanzo once bought ritual materials from a Brownsville store specializing in such items, and one afternoon I went in search of it through the hard-bitten streets closest to the river and its bridge. John Crewes was right about these streets, anyway, for in walking them you might well have been in Mexico. The stores specialized in those everyday items like shoes and clothing that were much more expensive on the other side; the cafés were thoroughly Mexican in their offerings; the signs were in Spanish; and everyone I saw looked Mexican. When I came upon a policeman filling out a ticket and asked him where La Esmeralda was he started out in rapid Spanish, then saw the blank look of incomprehension slide over my face and finished in English.

The store was just a half block ahead, a narrow front with its shingle projecting into the street, its window jammed with religious items from all over the world—candles, votive glassware, playing cards, incense bundles, santos, necklaces, beads, bulbs of garlic. Within, I found the shopkeeper distant and watchful, though he wasn't hostile, and he offered no comment when I asked him the significance of the many African items on display, except to say they were popular. I decided some sort of purchase might be helpful, settled on a cheap pair of sunglasses, and was rewarded by his immediately brighter interest. He obligingly brought down African wood carvings for my inspection and volunteered that he'd bought them in New York on lower Broadway. Also cans of spray bearing such labels as "Nine Indian Fruit Oil," which was advertised as a "Money House Blessing Offering Spray." I recognized the once-popular black folk remedy High John the Conqueror in its Hispanic guise but was surprised to find it had been manufactured in Piscataway, New Jersey. "Caution," its fine print read, "Contents Under Pressure Keep Out of Reach of Children." Neighboring cans read "Seventeen African Powers Incense," "Chango Macho Incense," and "Jinx Removing Incense." Next to this last, a can bore the label "Eleggua Incense." I knew that Eleggua was one of Constanzo's high gods and asked to inspect the verse I could see printed on the can. It read:

> To you Lord of the Roads, glorious warrior immortal Prince
> I raise this humble supplication
> Keep evil away from my home
> Keep my home safe from evil
> In my absence and when I am present
> When I am awake and when I am sleeping.

Many of the store's items, I ventured now, seemed to have a connection to the Caribbean as well as to Africa. Yes, he smiled, that was true. These masks, for instance, had come from Kenya. We weren't getting any closer to the Caribbean there, but I dutifully inspected the masks he had laid out on the counter. Then I took a further step and asked whether he had any *palo azul* (one of the twenty-eight ritual sticks used in Palo Mayombe ceremonies). He raised his eyes up from the masks, his brow furrowing, and gave me a long stare from behind his thick, smudgy spectacles. I smiled back, fingering the new sunglasses that were my only entree. Then without a word he turned and disappeared into the jumbled recesses of the store, returning shortly with a bundle of dead gray sticks encased in heavy plastic. They were each about eighteen inches long and numbered in white chalk. A handwritten list of the names with the corresponding numbers was visible within the wrinkles of the wrapper, and the shopkeeper made a show of consulting it as he fumbled the sticks, but if he had a *palo azul*, it was pretty clear I wasn't going to see it. He mumbled the arcane names in his simulated search, then gave a stagey sigh.

"No *palo azul*. *Palo chango?*" He fingered a stick, his brown forefinger poised along its length. I shook my head and then asked what the sticks were used for. He shrugged. *"No sé."* (I don't know.)

Then, "No good. Santería. Palo Mayombe. No good. For the country people, you know?" He flattened his hands, palms down, and made pushing motions toward the floor. "Low." The people, he continued, "come from all over for this. Very popular. Mexico, Miami [where, in fact, Constanzo had come from]. All *brujería* [witchcraft]. No good. All like this," handing me a booklet with the title "La Brujería: Biblioteca Practica" (roughly, "Witchcraft: A Book of Methods"). And with that he gathered up the bundle of sticks and returned them to their unseen place.

When he came back into the light he was smiling his careful, commercial smile once more. He wanted evidently to return to safer subjects and pulled down some love and good luck sprays, which he said he'd also bought in New York. "These," he told me, "they are made by Jews. No believe. Just sell."

AT first Armando Ramirez appeared to dismiss the magical aspects of the Constanzo/Kilroy case as the "salt and pepper" the cult leader had added to draw in his adherents and then get them to follow his every order. Maybe the metaphor was associative since at the moment Ramirez was making liberal use of the condiments at a huevos chorizo breakfast he was treating me to on Brownsville's north side. Ramirez was the DEA's Special Agent in Charge and had been intimately involved in the case. He went on to say that brujería, Santería, "and all that bullshit" was simply a part of the effort the "dopers will make to get any kind of edge they can." And as for Constanzo's personal adaptation of Palo Mayombe, "we haven't seen that shit before or since, and if we were beginning to see more of it now, we'd be in worse trouble than we already are." Yet, as I was to notice over the next several hours I spent in his company, Ramirez kept circling back to the magical aspects of the case, as if he didn't feel entirely comfortable with his profane dismissal of them. But for now, he wanted me to understand that however terribly it had turned out, the fundamental nature of the case was drug smuggling, and that I was in a place where smuggling was a traditional and accepted part of life.

Over on the Mexican side, he said, "it's just a thing you do. Nobody questions its legitimacy. The kids there start early, hustling. You go over there, they want to shine your shoes. They want to watch your car. They want a quarter. My own kids are kind of sheltered over here: we have 'em in Catholic school, and they don't see that aspect of the local life. So, once in a while I'll take 'em over there just to see what's going on. I'll point out, 'See that kid? He's a hustler.' He's maybe nine. By the time they're twenty-one, twenty-two, they've picked up a lot, and they're ready for *big* things." He smiled bleakly. He said he looked for little help from his Mexican law enforcement colleagues on any of the problems commonly faced on the border. The whole Mexican system, he said, from the cop on the beat to the highest echelon of the judiciary, was "fundamentally corrupt, always has been, always will be." The Mexican police, he wanted me to know, were so poorly paid they almost had to be on the take in order to make ends meet. Soon, he said, representatives of the Mexican Federal Judicial Police would be stationed at several points in the United States in an act of reciprocity for the presence of DEA personnel on the Mexican side. He did not look forward to this development.

Out in the restaurant's parking lot Ramirez deftly executed an involved sequence of maneuvers to unlock his car and turn on its ignition, explaining casually that these were necessary to prevent its being hotwired. "We have 'em rigged up different ways," he chuckled. "In one you have to hit the window switch and the interior lights in a certain sequence, and so on, before you can start it. They take 'em over across the river, and once they do that, they're very hard to trace." Inside his car and rolling toward his office, the landscape of Brownsville began to look different to me as he pointed out phenomena I'd been taking for granted but that were for him integral, significant parts of his workplace. He reminded me, oddly, of Steve Thompson and Melvin Maxwell and that tangled, wonderfully complex landscape whose features they had come to know so well. Here was another tangled, complex landscape, and Ramirez was alive to all of it.

The many used car lots, for instance. "What the hell are they all doing here, so many of 'em? Ask yourself that. Where's the big market for used cars here? Who in the valley has the money for these cars?" Where, he rhetorically asked, had the cars come from in the first place? "Some of 'em, you drive by, and you notice these same cars have been here for months and months, some of 'em for years." The same sort of question arose about the dozens of *cambios* (money exchanges) clustered near the bridge. The peso wasn't fluctuating that much, he claimed, and so where was the need for all of them? Some, he said, were probably legitimate, but the others were laundries. "To me," he said in summation, "the whole economy of the valley can be related in one way or another to its status as a drug corridor."

Up in his office behind a Church's Fried Chicken outlet Ramirez called in his assistant, George Gavito, who had been out at Rancho Santa Elena for the exhumation of the bodies and the subsequent ritual puri-fication by fire of the hut and its contents. Together Ramirez and Gavito took up almost all of the space in the room: both were huge men, well over six feet and two hundred pounds. But whereas there was a steely professional reserve always peeking out from behind Ramirez's affability, Gavito in this setting at least was almost boyishly enthusiastic. Had I seen him on "A Current Affair"? Well, then I knew he'd been in on the case right from the start and had seen the worst aspects of it. I was interested in the case's magical aspects, right? "Well, the fundamental thing here is that there's a big difference between the *brujo*, or the *curandero*, and this Constanzo stuff. The *brujo* is trying to ward off evil for his clients. He's using white magic, which is different from black magic where you're trying to gain power to hurt others. That black magic stuff really comes from the Caribbean and Miami. We don't see that here." As he gave me this short course he lunged about the room, bouncing off filing cabinets and walls and gesturing to make his points. Sitting quietly at his desk, Ramirez followed him with his eyes, a slightly amused glint in them.

"The use of *brujos*," Gavito went on, "that's been going on a long time, and the druggers have been using these guys a long time, too, to try to find out what the signs are for a particular activity. Now, this business, this was more of an 'import,' like I say. These guys weren't going to traditional *brujos. Palo Mayombe*—that's from the [Caribbean] islands. The gang members got into that through their *padrino* [leader or godfather], and he was tellin' 'em, 'Hey, we got power by sacrificing animals, why not do humans? That would really give us power!' That's how the thing began, and that's how it began to spiral. Once they got that far into it, they had no way to get out, y'know." A secretary poked her head in through the doorway to tell Gavito he was wanted on the phone, and he backed out of the room, still talking, his big, square hands framing concepts and explanations in the air. There was so much he needed to have me understand. . . . When at last he had disappeared and the door had closed behind him, Armando Ramirez glanced at me and smiled a little. "He's a piece of work, isn't he? But don't be fooled. He's a hell of a good cop and he's been invaluable to me."

Ramirez had videotapes of the confessions of Serafin Hernandez and his brother Ovidio that he thought might be of interest to me, but since all of the office VCRs were currently in use, we'd have to go out to his home to watch these. On the way there he spoke again of the drug runners' resort to magical assistance in their work, saying that he, like John Crewes, had seen numerous altars and ritual paraphernalia dedicated to warding off the evil of law enforcement. "One guy we raided," he said, "we had him there in his house, and then suddenly he runs down the hall to his bedroom and comes out firing. He thought he was invulnerable to our bullets because of all this protection he had." He paused as he wheeled into a secluded suburban area, its winding streets lined with shade trees and lawns and large, quiet-looking ranch homes. "He wasn't. But neither were two of our guys. He had candles lit up all over the place and jars with the names of the agents written on slips of paper underneath them—all kinds of shit." Still, he said, after another pause, he thought it wasn't a great idea to go around destroying other people's religious items, whatever view you might take of these, because you could never be entirely certain what you were dealing with in those situations. It was far better, he thought, "just to leave all that stuff alone." In the matter of the ritual burning of the hut out at Rancho Santa Elena, he said that had been the work of the Mexican police who had hired a *curandero* specifically for that purpose.

Ramirez's home was like the others here with a neat lawn and flower beds near the front door. Since he'd told me he'd grown up poor in Laredo, I thought he must take a certain pride in being able to live in such a place, and maybe he did. But now he heaved a sigh as he fitted the key into the lock and glanced down at the flower beds. "I think we must be gettin' old," he said, looking at the flowers, then nodding in the direction of the cat and dog who stood waiting just inside the opened door. "We have a dog for me, and this one for her [his wife], and all these flowers. She never used to be interested in these things. Now . . ." His voice implied some sort of question he didn't feel like articulating, and I followed him into the living room and its TV. He squatted next to it and slotted the first cassette into the VCR. Placing a forefinger on the "Play" button, suddenly he was all business, the casual reflections and personal ruminations now vanished.

"The context you need here is that these guys were into drugs before they ever heard of Adolfo Constanzo, but what happened was their organization had been hit with two murders, and they were leaderless.

That's where Constanzo came in. He was able to exploit that vacuum. Then what I think you should notice is the casual, the *remorseless* nature of their comments: 'Yeah, we killed fifteen people. Yeah, one of them, after we got him out to the ranch, we found out he was a relative of ours. But, so we killed him anyway.' No regrets, no nothing. Watch this."

And I watched as Serafin and Ovidio talked, the former small, quiet, and handsome in a delicate way; his brother larger, more expressive and assured, even at times arrogant. Ovidio spoke in Spanish with Ramirez providing a running gloss for me. At various points Ramirez would stop the tape and reverse it, either because he thought the admission being made was especially worthy of note or because he wanted to give me a more precise translation. And he himself, though clearly he'd seen the tapes numerous times, still evinced a fascination with them, as if they had really been a compelling kind of melodrama we were watching, the two of us taking a truant time-out from a weekday afternoon to sit around the box in his darkened living room, his back lawn with dog visible through the partly closed drapes, birds calling—everything as it should be. All that was missing to complete the scene were beers and snacks, and in fact Ramirez apologized for not being able to offer these.

Probably it was this setting as well as the framing, distancing nature of the medium itself, but whatever the cause, I found it hard to truly take in what I was hearing as Serafin calmly described how he had been re-cruited by his brother into the gang. "He said that there was a new religion where we wouldn't have a problem with women or money, but we have to kill people, and did I want to get in?" Then to follow that with the remark that the gang routinely took the hearts out of their victims, "but not to eat." Sara Aldrete, he went on, was not party to these sacrifices, though she had witnessed one murder and he was "pretty sure" she knew about the others and had in fact lured an ex-boyfriend into capture and death. In the same even tone he came to telling how his *padrino* had ordered them to get a young white male. His brain was needed for the ritual pot, Serafin said, "so we could think better." He described Kilroy's abduction at the little park by the river, how they'd brought him to the ranch to await the *padrino*'s further instructions, and then the arrival of Constanzo. While the rest of them waited outside the hut, Constanzo had gone in alone to where his victim waited helplessly, bound head and foot. After a while they'd heard a sound "like a coconut splitting. At first, we thought it was a coconut. Then the *padrino* came out and said to go in and get him. His [Kilroy's] head was split like this [demonstrating a vertical line], and his back was split open." Shortly, a wire would be attached to the backbone so that after the corpse had sufficiently decomposed the backbone could be ripped out and used as a necklace. Serafin claimed Kilroy had not been tortured, though subsequent examination indicated Constanzo had both tortured and sodomized him. Neither Serafin nor his brother had more than incidental remarks to make about the practices of that "new religion" they had been so captivated by, though it was possible that in Serafin's case at least belief had begun to fade under the pressures of incarceration and interrogation by the Mexican police—who are not known for a rigorous respect for the rights of suspects.

Armando Ramirez was obviously doing me a favor in showing me these tapes, and I tried to be attentive, taking notes, asking questions. But the longer the tapes rolled out their monochromatic horrors, the heavier the demand they made on me, and now it was the very reassurance of that frame that added to the burden. What was the reality, anyway? I was glad when they were over and Ramirez said he'd have to be getting back to the office. I had found out much more than I'd wanted about the case's sickening specifics and much less about its ritual and magical dimensions. Maybe these latter had been after all only a kind of seasoning.

As we exited the house, then rolled back down the street, I had once again the odd sensation of the two of us as having taken time off to watch something fictional, as two buddies might spend a lunch hour together watching a soap. But it had been real, even the composure of the Hernandez brothers, which I found so hard to comprehend. I had no doubt that to Armando Ramirez that had meant something entirely different; he not only had seen these tapes before but lived daily in a world where the unthinkable was routine and murder was a necessary action. In these quiet streets—a woman was bent over her flowers with a hose and another walked her dog and waved at us—I was in the company of a man whose reality was that I'd glimpsed within the TV's frame, not this scene.

Did he, I now asked, ever fear for his own life? He did. Couldn't be helped, he supposed. "I always carry this," he said, swinging aside his jacket and patting the butt of the big pistol in his belt. "We're pretty visible—on TV and so forth. But, I'll tell you what: I'm not going to lose any sleep over it. No hours lost there. The bad guys are smart enough to know that if they go after a cop, there are twenty more who'll take his place. They are just now beginning to find this out now in the Camarena case. There are developments there I can't discuss, but I can tell you we have the doctor who kept Camarena alive so they could torture him to get more information. The doctor claims he was kidnapped and forced to do it. Anyway, we've never quit on that case. Never. They get one of ours, we'll drop a lot of stuff to get them."

🌴 BACK in the verbally inventive American Sixties your customary line of work, the thing you did that was your signature, was said to be your "bag." Anthony Zavaleta was into so many bags it was a bit bewildering, though evidently to him they all made sense. He was by turns anthropologist, author, professor, health-care professional, and Brownsville politician. (When we met he was serving as mayor pro tem.) This morning he was a politician, but while we talked he was an anthropologist. Later that day he would be a professor at the ceremonies celebrating the incorporation of Texas Southmost College into the state university system. In his spare time he was currently at work on two books, one a social and political history of Brownsville, the other an explanation of *curandismo* and related folk beliefs along the border and their role in mental health. American health care professionals down here, he claimed, were as a rule shockingly ignorant of their Hispanic patients' beliefs and were therefore often baffled and frustrated in their dealings with them. He said that sometimes in their efforts to disabuse their patients of folk beliefs they unintentionally provided more harm than health. In the Oasis Café next to the bus station he talked about his study of folklore over coffee, tortillas, and eggs. "This," he said without glancing around, "is basically a café for illegal aliens. The bus you get next door goes to Houston, which is where you get off if you're lucky and have the right papers."

He was native to the area and had come by his interest in folk beliefs natively, too: his grandparents had once owned a cotton farm employing Mexican laborers, "and that was where I began to pick up all sorts of things, what you would call 'folklore.' At night, the workers would sit around the campfire and talk and sing, and I'd be right in there among them, listening. Later, I was a student of Américo Paredes [the preeminent student of border lore] at Austin, and he encouraged me to go on with this." This was a rich area for study, he said, with a plethora of medico/magical beliefs, many of them all but unknown in the Anglo world. He mentioned the adherents of the twentieth-century icon Doctor Boy Jesus, and the followers of El Niño Fidencio, a faith healer who had appeared near Monclova, Mexico, at the end of the 1920s and whose spirit was still strong among those now known as *Fidencistas*.

I wasn't long in his company before it became evident that Zavaleta took a fundamentally different view of border culture from the law enforcement people I'd been talking with. The more he spoke of the border, the more I was once again reminded of the rangers up at Laguna Atascosa, for to him also this was a rare place, uniquely itself and requiring a patiently acquired appreciation. "People either love it or they hate it," he said. "Me, I love it." I said I'd been talking with some people here who rarely or never went across the bridge, and he shook his head at that. "Such ignorance," he said softly. "With that kind of attitude, it's no wonder there's so much misunderstanding, miscommunication, misinformation. I can't get enough of this life. Every chance I get, I'll go over there. A lot of what happens here is what you might call the 'Dance of the Border,' and if you don't understand that it is a dance, then you don't get what's happening right in front of you. A dance implies a kind of regular movement and a balance. Here the dance has been going on a long time. Part of it has to do with competing and sometimes conflicting systems of belief, as in modern medicine and folk medicine. Part of it has to do with wearing two identities as you move back and forth across the river. Part of it has to do with smuggling. Today it's drugs. Back in the Twenties it was bootlegging. But in the Mexican world smuggling is seen as just another business. By the same token, you can't live in Brownsville without knowing lots and lots of people who are involved at one level or another with illegal activities. That's the nature of the border generally and of Brownsville specifically. Matamoros has always been a smuggling town, and so has Brownsville. That's why Brownsville exists, and if law enforcement was ever successful in completely shutting off drug trafficking here, Brownsville would just disappear. Understand, I'm not taking a stand when I talk to you like this. In my role as an anthropologist I meet all sorts of people on both sides of the border, on both sides of the law. My role is not to judge what kind of work they do. My role is to observe and try to understand."

For three or four years before what he called the "problem" in Matamoros Zavaleta had been predicting the rise of Santería and kindred African-Caribbean religions. "People say these things are on the wane. On the contrary. They're on the rise. The stakes are higher than ever, the contrasts between wealth and poverty are greater than ever, and consequently the resort to magical aids—both black and white—is greater, too. Drug runners are going to have recourse to both white and black magic practitioners. They're going to go to anybody they think can help them.

"Now, I didn't predict human sacrifice. In that sense Constanzo *was* an aberration. But the practices on which he based his 'cult'—if that's what you want to call it—were not aberrant. They are widespread. *Palo Mayombe* is indeed gaining adherents here, and if law enforcement tells you that Santería is an aberration or that there are no other *palos* in Brownsville, that's like the people at South Padre telling you we don't have shark attacks. Brownsville is unique in its position as a corridor for all the beliefs and practices of Latin America, and also, to some extent, as a port of entry for the beliefs of the islands. People come through here by the thousands, and they bring their beliefs with them."

I asked him if he would speak about Sara Aldrete, for I knew she'd been a student of his at Texas Southmost. He looked into his cup just a moment, as though he were going to choose his words here with more than ordinary care.

"I don't think anybody but Sara knows the full truth," he said at last. "Yes, she was a student of mine, and I remember her well because she stood out. She was tall, attractive, and she was an A student. I could use more like her. And, yes, I've talked with her numerous times since the problem, and I don't know the full story. I can tell you that right now it isn't good for my politics to be dealing with her. You get branded pretty quickly and easily as someone who has dealings with witches. But when I'm through with politics I'm going to do a book with her. I have her promise on that. I'll go down there [to Mexico City] and spend several weeks with her. Maybe then we'll know more of what really went on. I can tell you that at this point I don't believe she was a participant in any of the killings. I don't think she was present at even one of them. I do think she got into something *way* over her head.

"Serafin Hernandez was also a student of mine. You didn't know that? Sat in the back of the class, was absent a lot." He stopped and smiled at his own grim little jest. "Here I was, up there in front of the class, talking about cults, deviant behavior, and so forth, and he's back there taking notes." He stopped again and shook his head once in silent acknowledgment that here indeed was an ironic commentary on the old axiom that a teacher can never know where his influence ends.

But as for the conclusion of the case, Zavaleta was definite, telling me he was "categorically certain" he had been responsible for the breakup of the gang and for Constanzo's mental crack-up as well. "Until I went down to the ranch," he said, "neither the Mexican nor the American police knew what they were looking at. When I got down there and had a chance to assess the evidence, I could tell them right away. It was all perfectly clear to me. Then I filmed the burning of the temple, and that film was shown on TV all over Mexico and south Texas. When Constanzo saw my tape, he saw all his power going up in smoke, and he knew the thing was over. That was when he lost it." With this claim on the table there between us we both sat in silence a few moments, the noise of plastic dishware being rinsed and stacked filling in. Zavaleta glanced at his watch and then at me as if to say he'd given me as much time today as he could well spare.

Today was a busy day for him (weren't they all? I wondered), and he had a number of calls to make before the college ceremonies that afternoon. On our way out of the café he shook a few hands and exchanged a confidence with the owner, and then we were out in the dusty street with litter blowing about in the wind off the unseen Gulf. He asked me where I was going next, and I said my immediate goal was the city of Veracruz and beyond that the Yucatán Peninsula.

"Very interesting place, Veracruz. Both the city and the state. We were talking about African-Caribbean cultural influences, right? Well, you won't find any place along the whole of the Gulf coast where they're more pronounced than there. The whole state is the magic capital of Mexico. Every year they have a convention of *brujos* in Catemaco."

ON my last night in Brownsville/Matamoros I walked again over the bridge to have dinner at the Mocambo Restaurant, which had been recommended to me by Bob Kahn of the *Brownsville Herald*. "It's convenient," he'd said, "right by the bridge. The sauces are out of a can, but the seafood's fresh." The seafood was indeed so, and in traditional Mexican fashion the waiter brought out my snapper to exhibit it before cooking. I should have eaten it right then; the next time I saw it, it looked like a crude wooden effigy of the real thing and tasted like it, too. Still, it was pleasant in that little room under the unforgiving fluorescents. The only other customers were two couples who had come to watch Mexican melodrama on the TV and sip cans of beer wrapped in toilet tissue. There was something cozy about that, even to a foreign observer who didn't get much of the programs they watched.

Out the front door of the restaurant lay the little park into which Mark Kilroy had disappeared. Beyond its rear entrance was the dark street where Serafin Hernandez had nabbed him. Some truckers were parked there now, a few asleep in their cabs, a couple of others standing around a tiny hovel of a snack bar illuminated by a single naked bulb. A kid was fooling around on the sidewalk with two bent aluminum cans tied to the soles of his sneakers. His feet went *klackety-klack* on the pavement, and his friend behind the counter waiting on the truckers giggled.

Out on the bridge the mercury vapor lights reflected off pavement that looked slick enough to skate on, a patina, so it seemed to me now, of sweat and tears. At both ends of the span fat men in stretched uniform shirts and wearing pistols stood in the whine and poisonous breeze of the big trucks and passenger cars. In the bridge's middle young girls sold roses wrapped in cellophane, and a little farther along toward the American side there was a man selling them, too, and singing to keep himself company. At the turnstile that let you back into America they asked you if you were bringing anything back. You knew, of course, what the correct response was, but was it also the true one?

SPRING AGAIN

WHEN I WAS A KID BACK IN THE YEARS surrounding World War II the nation had a brief and shallow fling with Latin American culture. Adults drank Cuba libres and sombreros. There were songs like "The Carioca," "Flying Down to Rio," "Babalu," and "Managua, Nicaragua." Xavier Cugat was so popular he was simply known as Cugie, and Carmen Caballero's limpid piano stylings sold right along in the company of Jan Garber ("The Idol of the Airwaves") and Frankie Carle. One of the more famous magazine articles of this period proclaimed that "Latins Are Lousy Lovers." Argentina was, of course, verboten because of its alleged Nazi sentiments, but the rest of the Latin countries of the hemisphere were, as we might now say, "hot."

For most, the accessible Latin American country was Mexico, except for the high rollers who preferred Fulgencio Batista's Cuba. When people went down to Mexico they came back with straw handbags and sombreros and serapes. My parents, who had never been out of the country before, made this excursion into exoticism, and for years thereafter big, colorful straw baskets sagged in our attic, filled with curling

Brownie snaps of Mom and Dad astride tiny burros, the white heat beating down on them and lots of spiky-looking plants in the background. For years Dad carried a dark-red wallet with the eagle and serpent incised on one of its folds, and we kids wonderingly fingered the leftover cartwheels that were pesos.

All of this faded away quickly enough, and Mexico was returned to its former status as a messy, inconvenient place. It wasn't until the development of coastal resorts like Cozumel and Cancún in the 1970s that Mexico once again became a favored American tourist destination. The rest of Latin America still awaits another quick embrace from the north. We are not likely to hear soon, I think, an updated version of "Managua, Nicaragua."

I was thinking of these things as I entered the outskirts of Tampico, and the reason for this was that back in that same period there had been a sappy song whose refrain went

> Tampico, Tampico,
> On the Gulf of Mexico,
> Tampico, Tampico,
> Down in Mexico.

Once that kind of thing gets into your head it sets off a kind of brain disorder, and I needed all my wits to get across the Río Pánuco. Trying to rid myself of that refrain so that I could get out of this place of blackened skies, glow-in-the-dark marshlands, and bumper-to-bumper truck traffic, I tried to remember as much as I could of B. Traven's descriptions of Tampico in *The Treasure of the Sierra Madre*. Whereas the art of "Tampico, Tampico" with its easy end rhyme and innocuous lilt did nothing but confuse me as I looked for my signs, Traven's descriptions of the city's oily skies and air like needles in your lungs somehow gave me a better purchase on the place. Or so I thought as I approached an intersection in heavy company. We all went through it on an amber-turning-red light, and I was looking for my signs on the other side when I noted a battered VW bug next to me, its driver motioning me to pull over. He was hatless, but through his open window I could plainly see the epaulets of his uniform shirt.

When at last we had nestled next to one another around the corner on a less-trafficked side street and I had approached his car, he already had his citation book open on his lap, though he had not yet begun to inscribe the nature of my offense. My Spanish was very rudimentary, sufficient for me to make my primitive requests known (if not understood), and the officer's English only a little worse, but quickly it became clear that he was stopping me for having run the light. He wanted my license. Up close he looked like Charles Bronson with big, rippling muscles along his forearms, and in his thick, grimy hand my license looked as insubstantial as a bubblegum card. He scanned it with a show of vigilance, though I doubted he could make much of it, and while he did so I had occasion to recall the disparaging remarks made about Mexican police by John Crewes and Armando Ramirez. A sudden sweat stood out on me as I waited there in the street.

Experienced Mexico hands will tell you it isn't quite accurate to say all Mexican police are on the take. They remind you that most police there have to buy their own equipment and uniforms and that they are so poorly paid they expect supplementary compensation from citizens, whether these be simply people who live on a cop's regular beat or those arrested for infractions or crimes. This form of compensation is popularly known as *La Mordida,* or The Bite. Most bites are routine, very modest in size, and therefore painless: in Mexico where almost no one has much money a cop didn't expect people to hand him significant sums. Once, when I was going through Customs at Nogales, Arizona, with my wife and children, I was treated to a classic illustration of *La Mordida.* When he had finished the paperwork attendant to auto travel in the country, a Mexican Customs officer pulled the document from his typewriter with one hand and opened a desk drawer with the other. "Give what you can," he said, nodding casually at the drawer within which I could see randomly piled American dollars. Here, though, the case was plainly different: I was in a strange city far from the border, the man held my license, and I had the mark of a sucker graven on my flushed forehead.

Now we limped into the negotiations. The light had turned red, yes? Well, I would then have to surrender my license as my bond to appear in court *miércoles entrante* (next Wednesday), at which time I might get it back. Five days waiting in Tampico to pay a fine: this was the sentence that now stared at me. I looked around wildly—maybe the American consul was loitering on this corner? But there was only a shoeshine man and a news vendor there, watching the scene with knowing eyes. So now we had arrived at the critical stage where the parties were obliged to work together to find some way out of my difficulty, my guilt and his probity having been firmly established. Perhaps I could give him the money, and he could pay my fine for me? That would be a great help, one I signified I was willing to pay for. A sham look of dubiety crossed his features, and presently he pretended to consult a table of fines in his book, reading down a fine-printed list with his forefinger and mumbling some sort of computation. Then, unclipping a ballpoint pen from his shirt pocket, he wrote the figure "150" on his black-creased palm and held it up for me to see. "Dollars," he said in serviceable English, then spit a gob into the palm and vigorously erased the evidence.

Later, on the other side of the river and heading for Veracruz, everything from the crown of my head down through my thorax was blazing with indignation and fright (I now had almost no American cash in reserve). And I thought about what else I might have done back on that side street. I might have refused to pay anything and demanded to be taken to the nearest police station. No, too risky. I might have pretended to agree to appear in court as scheduled and simply let the man keep my license, trusting in the laxness of Mexican justice and in my own ability to replace the license back in the States. Still too risky: what if I were stopped again between here and Mérida in the Yucatán or involved in an accident? Or I might have begun to haggle, starting, say, at fifty dollars, to see where we might end up. Yes, yes, that was surely it! Christ! Where were my native wits, my South Chicago street smarts? How could I have been so dumb, so meek, that such an obvious stratagem hadn't occurred instantly? Indignation suddenly was transformed to self-loathing, and I tried to strangle the steering wheel. I was glad no one else was with me, that the shameful business had been witnessed only by strangers, and I had occasion to recall a remark my mother used to make to me when I was a boy. "You," she would say with a withering contempt, "are the only one who never knows what time the parade starts." This was not the first occasion I had suspected she was right.

SOMEWHERE above Tampico I had crossed the Tropic of Cancer. Years ago my wife and I had taken a train into the Barranca del Cobre region, which is the heart of the Sierra Madre and about as inaccessible and Mexican as you can get. But now, south of the line, I felt for the first time that I was in the heart of the heart of the country. The feeling was exciting, yet I had to admit to myself that there was a true tinge of anxiety to it as well. When I had checked into a hotel on the plaza of Veracruz's old center, the first thing I did was to get out my large-scale map to see where I was—which was really to see how I might escape from where I was if I needed to. The evidence spread out before me produced the same mingled sensation of excitement and fear I'd felt on arriving in the city. I was certainly way down there. Yes, sir, way, *way* down. I was in fact a lot closer to Guatemala than to anywhere in the U.S. I was somewhat reassured to see a drawing of a tiny ship on the map and a dotted line indicating there was boat service between here and Key West. But shortly I was a lot more reassured by the spectacle of Veracruz itself. Walking out into the plaza was like walking into a movie set, with the vital difference that this was real, intensely so.

On three of its sides the plaza was bordered by heavy, confectionary buildings whose fronts formed an arcade, the arches lined with strips of red and green neon tubing. At one corner sat the weathered pile of the cathedral, its bell sounding as if a child were striking a tinny toy with a stick. Balancing it was City Hall. In between, strings of small light bulbs had been swung across the marble-flagged square, attached here and there to palms and acacias. Clusters of globed lights like slightly tarnished moons stood atop white painted poles. In the very center a fountain flung its waters up through the lights toward the evening sky. There must have been at least four marimba bands at work when I entered. They were serenading the tables under the arcade, and at 6:30 on a weekday evening those tables were full, some of them already showing a serious collection of empty beer bottles and piles of shrimp peelings. There were crowds of strollers here, too: white-suited sailors from the naval base; young girls linked arm in arm; and a long succession of portly business types in short-sleeved shirts with briefcases in hand who frankly gave the girls the thrice-over.

I settled myself at a table outside the Hotel Prendes, ordered a beer and some ceviche, and turned to face the music, in this instance entirely a pleasurable choice since I found myself between two of the marimba bands, both playing furiously. And if you thought—as I did—of a "marimba band" as producing a soft, pellucid sound, you have the wrong idea of what was to be heard in Veracruz. Both bands had two marimba players, plus tenor sax and drums, and they produced one hell of a sound and beat. Here in the complex cross-rhythms over which danced the hollow sound of the marimba was in truth the African-Caribbean voice. Listening to it was like taking a bath in salsa picante. Some of the tables did appear to be listening to this phenomenon, but most took it for granted (as Americans do Muzak), even when they were seated right under the bell of the sax or touching the rims of the drums. Soon the lead band moved on, its percussionist passing his gourd scraper among the tables, and a trio of singers came on, backed by a mandolin, guitar, and harp. Looking farther down the arcade on my side, I saw a strolling guitarist with a colleague rolling along his big bass. It was like knowing what your next course was going to be.

White-jacketed waiters, vendors, beggars, and streetwalkers vied for what little space there was between the tables, the waiters balancing full trays on flattened palms while executing balletic avoidance maneuvers. Men and children sold necklaces, souvenir cane spears, nuts, dolls, candy, seashells, wallets and assorted leather goods, cigars, cigarettes, Chiclets, sunglasses, shawls, tablecloths, and bouquets of flowers. The streetwalkers were selling themselves, of course, but they seemed pretty good-natured about that, and when two of them came past my table and saw me scribbling in my notebook, they paused and asked, "¿Que haces?" ("What are you doing?") "Uno hombre de letras," I replied, giving myself airs. They thought it was funny, too, giggled, and passed on. Even if this had been ridicule, I felt it conferred a sort of status on me, that I had been taken as a potential customer and so was a functional part of this scene. By the time I had followed my beer and ceviche with two margaritas and the famous local dish, huachinango veracruzano (red snapper in a spicy tomato sauce), I was feeling even more at ease here—if a little less functional.

By this time, too, the plaza was getting into full swing, the tables under the arcade now jammed, the spaces between clogged, and the benches in the square filled with spectators. Balloon men were out in force, and when they passed directly under the globed lights their high, floating wares were illuminated as from within. Up on the bandstand in front of City Hall a twenty-piece naval band in starched whites was hoisting its glinting instruments in preparation for entering the musical lists. When at last it crashed into heavy play the cacophony was magnificent. I asked my waiter in delight and astonishment whether all this went on every night, and he smiled, shrugged, and said, "Oh, yes." I had to wonder how long it would take before I, too, like those veterans of the ringside tables, simply took it for granted.

My hotel room unfortunately didn't overlook the plaza, otherwise I might have tried to stay awake to see how the whole set was at last dismantled as dawn came up. But when I opened my window I could distinctly hear the festivities coming up at me, and as I drifted into a happy sleep there was the naval band, charging with spirit high above the strings, percussion, and mallets of the musical competition.

VERACRUZ, I thought, wore the burden of its long history with admirable nonchalance. It seemed sure of itself. Yes, it was something of a resort town, and it was also host to sailors and ships' crews. But it wasn't going to turn itself inside out for any of these ephemeral visitors—as New Orleans seems bent on doing and my hometown of Santa Fe as well. Veracruz had seen too much change to want to alter its basic character. It was here, after all, that the history of modern Mexico began with Cortés's establishment of a garrison town in 1519. It was here that the royal stooge Maximilian disembarked to begin a doomed reign ending in the fusillade of a firing squad. From here Benito Juárez fled to exile in Cuba and the U.S., and a few blocks from the old plaza stood a heroic statue of him that was the centerpiece of the Plaza de la Reforma. Here, too, in the Mexican War U.S. Marines landed to begin a latter-day march on the "halls of Montezuma." "Yes, yes," the city seemed to say with an easy smile, "all this is true, and who can say what will come in the future? Meanwhile, we will go on being Veracruzanos, *ahora y siempre.*" That kind of assurance is certainly easier on the traveler than the often-frantic hustle of Mexican places that lie farther north in the giant shadow cast by the U.S.; easier, too, than the air of tragicomic resignation met with elsewhere in the country.

Maybe Veracruz got up late and leisurely because it was so self-assured. Or maybe it was this and the fact that it played late. Whatever the case, at six in the morning the streets were empty of all but a few navy personnel walking toward the base and an occasional bicyclist, dim, dusty, hunched over the handlebars of a rusty gate of a machine. At strategic corners there were a few cabbies, but they looked as if they'd been there all night and would any minute now give it up and go home. I wanted a cup of coffee from the Gran Café de la Parroquia, but it wasn't open yet. Inside I could see waiters moving slowly about, placing sugar and napkins on the tables, conversing in low voices, but not even a stray whiff of the coffee so touted by the guidebooks wafted out into the dark street where I stood under the arcade. Above me a young man on a ladder did a high-wire act, cleaning seven-foot sections of fluorescent lights. Only the hundreds of birds in the trees of the plaza seemed fully alive to the promise of another day in this town that had looked on so much.

I thought of simply going back to bed and waiting there until the rest of Veracruz decided it was a new day, but my room was Spartan, and the thought of lying alone in it, tangled in morning's gray sheets, was awfully unappealing. I decided instead on a walk along the Boulevard M. Ávila Camacho, which ran along the curve of the waterfront. You could, if you wanted, walk that way (with a few detours) all the way out of town to Boca del Río where the Río Jamapa empties into the Gulf. As it happened, I didn't get nearly that far, but I got far enough so that coming back with the sun on my right shoulder and well up out of the Gulf, Veracruz was alive in its distinctive, languorous, daytime way.

To be sure, not everything was awake. The *palapas*, thatched-roofed, open affairs that sheltered bands and bathers, were empty. The string of waterfront restaurants was shuttered, and here and there I saw a man asleep on the seawall. But right next to some of the sleepers were fishermen mending green plastic nets suspended between lampposts. And now, too, those harbingers of sure-enough day, the *jaiba* (crab) men, were out, though who their customers were at this hour was a mystery: there was almost no one on the dark-brown beach or along the boulevard. Maybe it was passing motorists, of which there were now a fair number. Whoever it was they were hoping to sell to, I found there was something admirable about these men rolling their umbrellaed carts along the streets: they reminded a displaced American traveler of that ready resourcefulness of the chuck-wagon cooks of the American range who had to make do with what supplies were available and had to be all things to their cowpuncher customers. The *jaiba* men were not nearly in so exposed a position, of course: the fish market stalls were, after all, only a few blocks away. But they went out into their urban range wonderfully stocked, their carts like miniature chuck wagons, to service their waterfront clientele. They had their crabs on ice, salsa and lemon to go with the crabs, beer for the thirsty, and tightly scrolled copies of the morning newspapers. Thus in theory a customer might summon the *jaiba* man, get fresh seafood, garnish, an appropriate accompanying beverage, and the day's latest news without having to stir from the contemplation of the Gulf's placid roll and the low, vague hump of the Isla de los Sacrificios where the coasting conquistadors first blundered into the aboriginal realities of this world they were about to change forever.

By the time I had returned to the area of the plaza, Veracruz had yawned, stretched, and begun the business of the new day. The food markets were open, and right next to them the proprietors of the shellfish stalls had their rows of tall glasses filled with shrimp and racked up on the splintered wooden counters. On the plaza itself there was water standing on the marble flagging and the cleaning men were pushing puddles of it around with their long-strawed brooms. Others were at work with small wire brushes, cleaning the intricate scrolling of the iron benches lining three sides of the square. Four workers painted the portable bandstand on which the navy band had so handsomely performed hours earlier, but two of them gave only occasional strokes, most of their attention being openly focused on the tightly sheathed women office workers who clicked across the plaza on high heels. Outside the shabby old Hotel Imperial a crew shoveled a large pile of rubble into a truck bed. Since I had seen the rooms of that establishment the night before when hunting a room, it occurred to me that this might simply be the daily maid service. The men didn't bother to look over their shoulders at the effects of their labor, and a fair amount of the rubble was now beginning to slide off the pile and back onto the plaza where it sent up an exhausted plume of dust. On the corner, the friendly vendor of the newsstand was using the empty tables of the Hotel Prendes to assemble the sections of the morning newspapers; the *"periodico inglés,"* he explained, would be delivered sometime very soon. Out in front of the Gran Café de la Parroquia the first of the morning's marimba bands was setting up and the marimba player was limbering up his hands and wrists and essaying a few preliminary strokes. By the time I'd found a seat inside the white-tiled, high-ceilinged room the band had launched into "Perfidia," and so my attention was torn between that wonderful sound and my efforts to attract the attention of a waiter.

Almost everywhere I touched along Mexico's Gulf coast the coffee was a disappointment, usually being either powdered or "flavor crystals" and served with a pot of warm water. The milk wasn't in powdered form when you got it, but experience suggested that recently it had been and had probably also been cut with water. Not at the Parroquia; here both the coffee and the milk were wonderfully genuine. After I'd been there a few minutes I learned how to summon a waiter. You banged your spoon on your glass, and soon enough he would approach, threading his way between the crowded tables, strolling photographers, shoeshine men, and boys with long strings of lottery tickets. When you placed your order he would pour two fingers of thick, inky coffee into a soda glass and then bang on it himself to summon his colleague, the milkman. The milkman carried a large tin pitcher in either hand, steam from them evident as he approached, and then right abov⸴ you and with a pitcher held head-high, he would triumphantly deposit a stream of hot milk into your glass, topping the coffee and producing a frothy, light-colored beverage that was a species of earthly salvation: as good as the best of New Orleans but with a deeper coffee flavor because it was not cut with chicory. When you wanted a refill, you banged your glass, and the process was repeated, so that at all times the room was filled with the insistent tinkling sounds of metal on glass while through the opened windows came the sounds of the band. I had to wonder as I sat there how much better the mood of America might become if we could have such coffee in the morning and mambos with it.

LESS than an hour's drive north of Veracruz lay two sites of critical importance in the history of the New World: La Antigua and Cempoala. The first was associated with Cortés's landfall, the second with his march to Tenochtitlán.

The accounts of the first Spanish settlement on the mainland of North America are understandably vague as to place, for in fact nobody knew where they were—and after the sack of Tenochtitlán they didn't care where they'd been. Neither Cortés himself, nor Bernal Díaz who was with him, nor Cortés's secretary, Gómara, who wasn't, are specific about the place of the landfall or the first settlement. Clearly, the present city of Veracruz was successor to a settlement made a bit farther up the coast, but just where is a question. About the only thing the old accounts agree on is that the landfall was made on Good Friday, 1519. Also that there were high dunes, heat, and mosquitoes. That takes in a fair stretch of the coastline of what is now the state of Veracruz. Some authorities believe La Mancha was the place, and in a perverse way it would be nice to think so since La Mancha is about as humble a settlement as may be imagined. In America, of course, or probably anywhere else in the well-developed world, a hamlet with even the most spurious connection to so signal an event would do its damnedest to merchandize the claim. Here there wasn't even a sign for the existence of the village, and I went up and down a stretch of 180 several times before I asked a parked trucker where exactly La Mancha was. You had to know what you were looking for: only a lumpy sand road led off the highway toward the Gulf through high marsh grass and bushes. At the road's end was a huddle of cinderblock buildings, some with thatched roofs and others with tin ones, mud puddles, a few rusting cars, and a cantina. As I got out of my car my only companions in the street were some chickens and a sow I wanted to steer clear of, but from beneath the overhangs of the roofs I glimpsed some shadowed faces and brown arms and hands. Evidently here the arrival of a car was an event.

In the cantina I ordered a beer, more in this instance at least for the flavor of the setting than out of any thirst. The place was dark and barren, and I had the impression I was in the cabin of a sunken ship where things had slid into unnatural positions. The proprietress was friendly enough, though, a thin, hawkish woman whose smile revealed blackened teeth and holes where others once had been. She wondered whether I wanted fish with my beer, and again I was tempted, simply for the experience. But I said no, finished off my beer, and decided I'd take a walk down to the beach. Surely the villagers did this every day, but the ignorant stranger never found the path, being balked at every attempted penetration by thorny bushes and cacti. Only in retreat and climbing the road back to the highway did I glimpse the Gulf—through the rearview mirror.

Maybe La Mancha was the site; more likely it was La Antigua. The weight of tradition says so, and Cortés, in his first letter to King Carlos V, mentions leaving men behind at a fort as he commenced his march on Moctezuma. In La Antigua there were the ruins of a fort long identified with Cortés, though it bore no marker. Its roofless walls were under siege by giant banyan trees that had gained an entrance at the doors. Inside there was nothing but spots of sun glancing down through the branches, earth, the customary casual refuse, and the reptilian infiltration of the banyan roots, gliding along atop the ground. I felt certain that here at least natural history would eventually triumph completely over the human variant, and the banyans would constrict like boas and crush these ruins into indistinguishable rubble. Standing there in the shadows and the mottles of sun, I became aware of a thin shawl of smoke drifting past me and shafting upward where the sun struck it: somebody's backyard abutted on the fort, and this afternoon they were burning the garbage out there.

Outside in the benign spring sun there was a single cannon mounted on a concrete cradle, the barrel badly pitted under its coat of black paint. In the little plaza lined with concrete benches Benito Juárez presided on a pedestal. Just behind the bust stood the village church, a thick-walled, irregularly shaped structure with pigeon-stained bells and a frayed rope hanging from the belfry down over the front doors. Inside it were examples of that realist religious art that is so striking to lapsed American Protestants when they chance to meet it. Blood-and-guts realism in the religious art of Europe was, of course, a tradition for centuries, and even in the nineteenth century at folk levels the most straightforward representations of the crucified Christ were still being produced. Van Gogh was working in this vein early in his career, though it was by then somewhat passé to do so. In America this tradition continues to have a sort of half-life in that mass-produced art that turns out photo-realist images of a Jesus who resembles an Anglo-Saxon athlete. But in Mexico the old tradition continues with undiminished vigor: here there were life-sized statues of the participants in the Nativity scene, heroic archangels, and in a glass coffin a wooden statue of a very dead-looking Jesus. On the lavishly decorated altar a bank of votive candles flickered, and looking at them I was reminded of the title of Anita Brenner's once-famous study of the Mexican spirit, *Idols Behind Altars*. That, I thought, was about as neat a summation of the fundamental dynamic of Mexican religious syncretism as will ever be made. Here was the altar, decked with its profuse Christian symbols, but you felt that just behind it there might repose some ancient Tontonac idols; and that indeed it was the hidden presence of these idols that gave the Christian symbols the strange, garish vitality they possessed; as if the native religious impulse the conquistadors and priests had tried to destroy had survived everything and continued to give its blood to Christianity.

Across the street and around a corner was another church, one of the first built in the New World, a tiny, stuccoed building surrounded on three sides by a low wall into which in more recent years tiles had been set demarcating the Stations of the Cross. The ruined interior was exposed to the weather in several places, and the roof was peppered with holes the size of 5,000-peso pieces. Within the walled enclosure a small flock of red chickens pecked at the grass. Here as at the fort down the street there was no sign of any sort; this unassuming monument to the Conquest was just there, and nobody seemed to give it much mind.

La Antigua was so innocent of motorized traffic that in walking its cobbled streets I noticed spears of grass thrusting up between the stones. Only one car passed me there, a cab with its tail pipe belching badly. In another place a boy leading three horses clopped past. The bus stop was down under the trees on the Avenida Emiliano Zapata. In the lengthening shafts of the sun, grackles sailed and settled in the thick boughs and in the arbor of the Carmona Restaurant. It was now that dead slack period between the end of lunch and the beginning of dinner, but everything was already in place for evening, each of the restaurant's tables fully set and decorated with an artificial rose. The marimba band was seated on the little bandstand, reading comics and magazines and nibbling snacks. The waitresses were eating dinner, one of them praying long and fervently over her plate of *huevos*. Behind the bar the resident mixologist stood at the ready, a towel on his shoulder, his hands flat on the polished counter. Mexican rock music poured from speakers set up in the arbor, but it didn't bother either the grackles or the chickens that were probing beneath the tables for anything that might have been left over from lunch. It looked like slim pickings to me as the concrete floor gave off a dull sheen of industry. I almost hated to intrude on this tranquilly set scene, but when I bit into my shrimp cocktail with its sea of tomatoes, onions, and cilantro what hesitation I had instantly vanished: it was superb and in itself worth an excursion to La Antigua. I was thinking of having another when the management signaled the commencement of the dinner hour by turning off the canned rock. Up on the bandstand the men began to stir. There wasn't that much good light left in this day, and I wanted to see Cempoala.

Cempoala was on a west-running spur of 180, a dusty town of mostly dirt streets surrounded by fields of sugarcane. There were fires of stalks in the fields, and the sky was marked with drifting patches of smudgy smoke. In the village itself there was but one small sign for "Las Ruinas," and yet it was here that Cortés had understood for the first time the lay of this new land and had then formulated his audacious plan to march on the Aztec capital. Here he had a glimpse of the wealth of the natives, for Cempoala was a city much larger than most of the conquistadors had known in the Old World, green, shady, its markets bustling, some of its buildings sparkling so with whitewash and gypsum that one of the Spanish scouts rode back to tell Cortés the houses were made of silver. This was soon proved to be a mistake, but there was no mistaking that these Tontonacs were a substantial people, far more advanced (by European standards) than those naked islanders the Spaniards had so quickly enslaved and exterminated in the Caribbean. And then to learn through his suddenly invaluable native interpreter, Doña Marina, that these people were the unwilling subjects of the great Moctezuma! When he understood that, Cortés knew he would go to see this distant prince whose wealth must be fabulous. And as he listened to the grievances of the ruler of Cempoala, a man so obese he had to be carried everywhere, Cortés knew something else as well, and this was that the Cempoalans and the peoples of the twenty Tontonac towns around were potential allies. With Doña Marina translating, Cortés heard how Moctezuma had ruthlessly extended his rule all the way to this coast, had levied heavy taxes on the Tontonacs, and annually carried off locals to become sacrificial victims. In short order Cortés promised the Cempoalans and their "fat cacique" (as Bernal Díaz persistently called him) protection from the Aztecs in return for their help in overthrowing the tyrant. When he imprisoned five of Moctezuma's tax-gatherers, the Tontonacs felt they had no choice other than Cortés, for they knew Moctezuma would now blame them, and punishment would be severe. Thus a treaty was made. "Then," as Bernal Díaz remembered it, "messengers were sent to relate all that had happened to the other towns in that province. And as they no longer paid any tribute and no more tax-gatherers appeared there was no end of rejoicing at being rid of that tyranny."

At the end of the short side street leading to the ruins of that shining city, the houses abruptly gave way to an avenue of palms, and beyond in a great clearing sat five temples, stair-stepped toward grand, flat tops. A tiny museum stood at the entrance to the clearing, and the bored caretaker collected an equally tiny fee. A wind was up off the Gulf, waving the palm fronds into feathery shadow rhythms on the beaten expanse of grass and dirt and kicking up funnels of dust beyond the palms where schoolboys held soccer practice while other children clambered over the gray, rounded stones of the temples.

After crossing the expanse, I climbed the crumbling steps of the largest temple to survey what was surely the central plaza when the fat cacique ruled this place. On all sides I could see the smoke from the cane fields rising above the tangled canopy of trees, and there was a heavy, sweet smell on the wind. I could see, too, the green humps of other large Tontonac buildings that still awaited exhumation. Sitting down on the steps I felt the warmth they retained from the day now fading. A few small lizards darted over the stones. High above a hawk sailed, the light catching the fringes of its wings. Below, soccer practice had ended, and the coach had gathered his boys in the shade of the palms far across the now emptying plaza. The clambering children had left their playground, and only a solitary mother and child were visible, the woman walking slowly across toward the houses of the village, her bright print dress blown against her body, her child scampering from side to side. When the coach had finished his talk and the boys had gone off down the side street, I had the ruins to myself. The only sounds now were the muffled buzz of battered car mufflers from the town and the dry clacking of the palm fronds, but these seemed suddenly inconsequential in a vast silence. Octavio Paz has called that silence "prehistoric," and said that it is the ultimate ruler of Mexico. It is a silence, he says, that wells up out of Mexicans' profoundly felt understanding that everything that has happened in their country—the Conquest, the Revolution, even the ancient kingdoms like this one—is evanescent, chimerical. What is real is only the land itself, which broods over all.

But that was Paz's perception, not mine, and though I, too, could now feel that silence and feel the ravaged land brooding on human folly, the silence here seemed to me not so much prehistoric as it was a commentary on the history that had begun right here. Perhaps it had been on this very temple that Cortés had reached his wily accord with the fat cacique and the other headmen, an accord that, says Bernal Díaz, was witnessed and recorded by "Diego de Godoy, the scribe." But what was really inscribed here were the first characters that would eventually spell out the fate of the Aztecs and of every single native tribe of the New World. For no sooner had the parties become allies than Cortés commenced the work of tearing apart the Tontonacs' culture, telling them that they must now destroy their abominable idols, cease their equally abominable practices of human sacrifice, cannibalism, and sodomy, and instantly embrace Christianity. If they would not agree, he said, he would have to abandon them to the justice of Moctezuma, whose messengers even now were probably in Tenochtitlán with the news of the Tontonacs' defection. So now the Tontonacs understood they had two tyrants to fear. Still fearing the old one more, they told Cortés he could do as he would with their idols, but they would not dare to approach them. Speedily a group of soldiers climbed these steps and sent the idols crashing down while the caciques and priests "wept and covered their eyes, and in the Tontonac tongue . . . prayed their gods to pardon them, saying that the matter was no longer in their hands . . . and that they did not attack us on account of the fear of the Mexicans." So Bernal Díaz.

Nor was it just the tribes whose fate had been inscribed here with the iron point of history. It was also the fate of all of the New World—of an astounding number of species of animals and plants, of rivers and river systems, of whole bodies of water like the Gulf, and of the very contents and conformations of the earth. And all this undertaken and accomplished by the successors and heirs of the hairy, helmeted men who rode in here on a spring day in 1519 and saw in these temples the symbol of a huge material opportunity.

It is now a commonplace to observe that the white men who toppled the Tontonac idols into the dust worshipped an equally false god—gold. Soon enough after the sack of the Aztec empire the tribes of Central and South America began making this charge themselves. And even Cortés, whose Christian piety cannot be doubted, may have suspected as much. His secretary Gómara records that in a message Cortés sent Moctezuma from here he asked for gold "because I and my companions suffer from a disease of the heart which can be cured only with gold."

ONCE you cleared the city of Veracruz at Boca del Río, Route 180 angled along the coast toward Alvarado. To begin with, the terrain was ranchland, the rugged, broken country on either side of the road dotted with grazing cattle whose bony backs and flanks reflected the sun like armor. At rail crossings sellers of beans, nuts, crabs, shrimp, and sunglasses awaited drivers who had to slow to negotiate the tracks. Laguna was only a wide place in the road, but it broke up the starkness of the range with a stretch of pineapple farms. The fields bristled with the deep-green plants, and there were a half-dozen thatch-roofed stands advertising their wares by large pyramidal piles of the fruit placed on the shoulder of the road. I stopped for a glass of juice, which was drawn for me out of a plastic drum by a small girl. Keeping her company at the shed were a black rabbit, two large turkeys, and several dogs. Whatever it is that Dole has been doing to pineapple juice over the years, it hadn't at all prepared me for the taste of the real thing. It was so good—and so cold—that in gulping it down I sprang a headache it took me a few moments to get over. And then I had a second and more leisurely glass of this nectar.

Between Laguna and Alvarado I kept catching tantalizing glimpses of the Gulf, but there were few available spaces where I might have pulled off and gone to investigate the shoreline. I did stop a couple of times, leaving my car perilously exposed to traffic, and struggled up through the high, burned-looking dunes dotted with prickly pear. In both instances I found the same scene on the dunes' other side: a thatch-roofed hut or two with wearily dependent sheds and pens, some chickens in the scant shade, splintery dogs with their tongues hanging out in the heat. And beyond this was the astonishing blue of the Gulf. At my second investigation I saw a woman herding her goats through the thorny brush, a long stick in hand and accompanied by a toddler and the inevitable dogs.

But I was determined to have a longer and closer look at the Gulf along here before the road swung away from the coast at Alvarado, and when I saw a truck parked on a narrow shoulder, I pulled in behind it and went up through the sand. Whatever the truckers had been doing down at the water it hadn't been swimming, for I now met them on my way down through the deep, scorching sand, and they were dry and dusty looking. We eyed each other, nodded, and proceeded on our divergent missions.

At the bottom of the dunes was a steep, narrow beach of coarse-grained sand strewn with logs, flotsam, and clumps of cacti. No huts here, however, and so I had the place to myself. I could see the shoreline's northward curve toward Veracruz, while hidden from me was that deep southward curve that ended in the Yucatán Peninsula. And there right before me was the Gulf in its brilliant and placid folds. I was determined to bathe in it and so complete a private ritual I'd begun back in Florida. There I'd made a vow to dip into the Gulf everywhere along it my travels would take me—Florida, to begin with, and then Alabama, Mississippi, Louisiana, Texas, and now here in Mexico. Such private rituals may be utterly meaningless to outsiders, but since the literature of travel reveals how often they have been practiced, there may be something creaturely about them, like bears rubbing up against tree trunks to mark passage and possession. In my case, of course, it could only be the former, and musing as I had been these last few days on matters of discovery and the natural rights of native tribes and other living things, nobody could have been more keenly aware of his transience than I was on this afternoon. Gingerly I entered the water, aware that undertows are often strong in places such as this and that sharks were natives here, as well.

Afterward, I sat on a wave-enameled log, drying my feet with my socks, and feeling the Gulf waft me into a meditative mood I knew was inappropriate: I had a good many miles to make before twilight intensified the dangers of the Mexican road. But helplessly I felt myself going into a kind of nod and recalling dreamily the opening to *Moby Dick* where Melville says that all footpaths inevitably lead down to whatever water is available, and that there at the water's edge—even if it was only a humble pond—you would find people staring off into the depths. Water and meditation, he claimed, are forever wedded. I had followed no footpath to this shore, but I had surely felt the lure of the Gulf and had followed the two truckers down here. Maybe they, too, had been lured by the simple, grand presence of the Gulf and had sat wordless on the sand, thinking of time and transience.

But if I believed myself alone with these thoughts, I now realized that I was about to have company, for along the slant of the beach there came a lone horseman. It was futile to think of running for my clothes: they were well out of reach of the wavelets, and when I spied him at last the horseman was much too close. There was nothing to do then but sit there and wonder what this bearded man would make of the person he saw sitting on a log wearing nothing but a 1929 St. Louis Browns cap. He came on, his eyes wide but his bearing completely graceful. When he was abreast of me, he glanced casually, his eyes died down, and a small smile came across his lips. He pointed up at the high sun and said simply, "*Caliente*," and then he was past, his bright chestnut horse nimbly picking its way along the strand just out of reach of the lapping tide.

DESPITE my intention of taking the quickest, most expeditious route from Veracruz to the Yucatán, I found I had great difficulty just getting out of the state. First it had been that dip in the Gulf that had lengthened into a minireverie. That sort of thing has a tendency to blunt your purpose every time, and so it was here: when at last I got back on the highway I found I wasn't hell-bent for Campeche or Uxmal or Mérida. I was just there where I was, an attitude probably conducive to peace of mind but inimical to travel. Then there was Alvarado, which I found so sturdily pleasant that I wound up spending the rest of the day there. And finally there was the unexpected gem of a town, Tlacotalpan.

Alvarado was a fishing town at the mouth of the Río Papaloapan and with a sizable lagoon behind it. Gómara, in his life of Cortés, says the place was named for Pedro de Alvarado, that rash and daring man who provoked the great battle at Tenochtitlán in which Moctezuma was killed and the Spaniards driven out on the Noche Triste. The river here was "deep and clear," Gómara reported, and "full of good fish." So was the lagoon. He wrote, too, of the phenomenon of the iguana, found in great numbers here, and said to be a creature harmful to syphilitics. I didn't know about that, but as for the waters, it was evident that what had been true in the time of the Conqueror was true today. Alvarado wore a prosperous, bustling air, at midday its docks alive with trucks, mule-drawn ice wagons, fishermen in hip boots, and children carrying empty plastic gasoline drums up from the boats. Housewives had already been along the dockside fish stalls and were now going homeward with plastic sacks filled with bloody cuts of fish; also with mangoes, oranges, and bananas. At the dockside bars men who had been at work before dawn relaxed in animated conversation over bottles of the local beer, Victoria. The bars hung out over the water and at the tables you could see the water glinting under the sun and the breeze through their opened rearward doors.

Along the curving quay in the afternoon the bustle of the arrival of the daily catch gradually faded. But in the shady stalls men still cleaned, weighed, sorted, and butchered. I stopped at one where two men were cleaning and cutting up five-foot eels and tossing the offal into the gutter. A pride of cats, tellingly sleek of coat, waited for these prizes, then went to work on them in leisurely fashion. Aboard the local fleet snugged up to the dock, crews rested in the shade of cabins, their T-shirts heavily stained, faces dark and unshaven, and their legs splayed out on the decks in attitudes that spoke plainly of fatigue. A few talked and smoked; most simply sat silent. A few vendors ambled along—men selling gum and candy, boys balancing trays of cakes and cookies atop their heads, shoe-shine men. Farther along and on the landward side sat a string of small cafés. Under their faded awnings radios blared news and music and middle-aged men played checkers, cards, and Parcheesi. I stopped at one, a triangular sliver of a place, and had a cup of coffee, which made me miss the Parroquia. Next to my table a portly man in a Batman T-shirt and a cap saying CANCÚN opened clams on a block of yellow-painted concrete that had seen long, hard service. The sign on the café's wall advertised *barbacoa* (barbeque), and already a man was laying billets of wood in the bed of the grill. The place had such a clean and industrious feel to it that I made a mental note to visit it for dinner. What could possibly go wrong, I asked myself, between the stalls where the fish were unloaded and this place where they were prepared? Not a thing, as it turned out.

The day following, there was Tlacotalpan, which required a short detour I hadn't planned. But here as at Alvarado I was handsomely rewarded by a small, brilliant place on the same river. Approaching it, I went past banana groves that sang to me of the true tropics, and then there was the town, a perfect postcard with colonial-style buildings in several shades of pink, aqua, daffodil, and carnation. But the dominant color was white—so much was newly applied that I had to turn away from time to time just to give my eyes a rest. In the square in front of two white-painted churches there was a wonder-ful, vaguely Moorish gazebo, also painted white. You entered it from a little stairway beneath and emerged, grateful for the shade, under the metal roof. There you looked out on the white-painted cast iron benches, the white curbing, the white of the marble flagging, and the tall, swaying palms whose trunks were also painted white. Here only the sky was blue.

The river was a sparkling blue as well, and along it were three small, open-air seafood stands. I chose the one that had a hand-lettered sign on one side that read:

ESTIMADO CLIENT:	VALUED CLIENT:
Trabajar es mi Destino,	To work is my destiny,
Atender es mi Alegria,	To serve is my joy,
Hoy se trata con Dinero,	Today we deal in cash,
Y Hasta Mañana se Fiá.	Maybe tomorrow there'll be credit.

Hopelessly addicted to the shrimp cocktails of this state, I foolishly ordered the "Grande" and was abashed when presently the waitress brought on a brimming glass that would nicely have fit a Waring blender. In the shade of the roof four middle-aged men in straw cowboy hats watched with what I suspected was a mild amusement. The waitress gestured invitingly toward a counter that was completely covered on the side nearest the tables with large bottles of dark-hued sauces in which I could dimly discern peppers submerged like submarines in ambush. There was enough firepower right there, I thought, to blow up half of our mothball fleet.

I didn't come near finishing this phenomenon I'd ordered and cursed myself for trying, since in doing so I'd spoiled my enjoyment of what I did eat. The men in the hats continued as before, talking softly and drinking from cans of soda. Maybe gluttonous gringos came through here often enough that this little show wasn't that extraordinary. Then, sluggishly, I got behind the wheel again, making weak resolves to get out of Veracruz this very afternoon. On my way out of town I saw a man asleep under his hat in a cart parked next to the riverbank. The warm sun played across his peaceful trunk. Maybe it was the shrimp cocktail, or the fierce brightness of Tlacotalpan, or the prospect of all those Mexican miles that twisted between where I was and Mérida, but I had a sudden urge to join him.

MEXICO, as everyone knows who has driven in it, is emphatically not a country in which you should be determined to "make time" on the roads. By the same token, there is a fair amount that may be learned about the country while crawling along a road system that is by the standards of the developed world primitive. If you choose to travel along Mexico's Gulf coast road, there is plenty of time for that kind of learning with the numerous delays where car ferries take you across bays and lagoons. Inland from the coast the roads are more heavily used, in rougher shape, and your opportunities for learning severely circumscribed by dangers. On these roads if you see an "Aviso" (Warning) to slow down, you had better heed it: the sign is likely telling you that the pavement utterly disappears around the next curva peligrosa (dangerous curve).

It isn't just the road system that is in bad repair, of course. Because of the pervasive poverty many of the vehicles you meet with are in alarmingly poor condition, but because of the ethos of the road they are driven as if they were prime. By far the best-maintained vehicles you meet are the company trucks. The petrol tankers and beer company rigs I saw were huge and spotlessly shiny, many of them bearing nicknames or slogans emblazoned on their front bumpers, and their drivers were true paladins of the highway. Inevitably, I traveled in company with these men and found myself awed by their nerve and élan. To be chased into one of those *curvas peligrosas* by a trucker and then to try to force yourself to accelerate through it while all your instincts screamed (like your tires) at you to brake—this was the daily duel of the Mexican road. And when your nerve failed and you did brake, you saw every glowing inch of your taillight reflected in the chromium grille behind you. Yet, to be sure, the trucker wasn't trying to kill you; he was merely trying to make time under difficult conditions. You either had to run with him and his fellows, or cede the road, and to run with them hour after hour took a stamina and a steadiness of will I found hard to maintain.

There were other hazards, as well, almost all of them symbols of a culture that exists in some apparently perpetual limbo between ancient ways and the modern industrial state. In agricultural areas at all hours but especially toward sundown you routinely encountered herders moving stock along the highway or its margins. Slow-moving horse- or ox-drawn carts, perhaps heaped in this season with stacked cane, lumbered along two-lane stretches, backing up motorized traffic for miles, but nobody honked in exasperation. At least, I thought as I waited out one of these processions, I wasn't in danger here of being shot by a motorist crazed by delays on roads where he assumed a right to travel full throttle. Always there were the pedestrians, either in the road itself or just off it. In the long, sobering reaches of Tabasco and Campeche there were solitary *campesinos* walking the roads with machetes slung at their hips, their faces like carved wood under battered straw hats. Outside Escárcega in Campeche I saw a peasant woman walking the sizzling asphalt barefoot. When cars blew past her with inches to spare the wind flattened the folds of her bright dress against her, but her expression never changed, and her eyes seemed set on some long horizon.

Dead dogs were everywhere—tossed up on medians where they withered to the consistency of wood; flung aside by impact to lie for who knew how long, stiff-legged and belly-up; newly smashed and right in the flow, their innards smeared wider with each successive hit, tails grotesquely wagging again and again, as if they hoped still for some token of human friendship.

At dusk dangers clustered. In broad daylight the burning of the fields, the pollution from oil refineries and sulfur plants, and diesel emissions combined to create a mist over the land. At dusk, though, the air thickened, and you felt you were driving through an endless veil of dark gauze. Even so, few drivers did so much as turn on their parking lights, and when I cravenly turned on my headlights, approaching truckers would flash theirs at me to ask what the hell was the matter. Even at the very edge of full dark many drove lightless. And at that hour, too, we were all hurrying toward our destinations and taking the kinds of risks we thought were worth it. So we hurtled, braked, stopped, waited, started, and hurtled on again in the not-light, a herd of vehicles thundering toward Villahermosa or Champotón or Campeche, hazed by the truckers who, perhaps alone, truly knew what they were doing.

My arrival at Villahermosa was representative of how I ended those days on the road to the Yucatán. I'd been driving in heavy traffic through a pestilential landscape of diseased marshlands bestrode by giant utility towers, sulfur plants, and oil refineries, the sky plumed yellow, black, and gunpowder gray. In the marshes were huts surrounded by head-high grass that looked tough enough to thrive at Chernobyl. Small children played about the huts in the company of chickens and starveling dogs. Dusk rained down on us in sooty particles. The closer we got to the city's outskirts, the heavier the pedestrian traffic became: *campesinos*; children bent under great loads or shooing along strings of goats and pigs; women carrying bundles atop their heads. At the city limits I was horrified to see three children lying so close to the road that one of them actually had his or her head on the patched, pocked pavement itself. When the truck ahead of me roared past, the child's dark hair flattened about its little skull like feathers. Was this a game of some sort, a rehearsal of life's existential hazards—either you were hit now or else later? Then, coming into the lights of the city and at last its *centro*, I found Villahermosa's shops and sidewalks densely crowded at eight in the evening and an open-air cantina I passed filled to the curb with couples, but I was too dazed and frazzled to more than merely note all this as I circled in search of a hotel.

Once up in my large room with acres of bare red tile to stroll and what proved to be a balky toilet enthroned in an outsized bathroom, I realized I was as bent out of shape as I had been in a very long time. I had a dandy tension headache, my back and neck were a Gordian knot of muscle, and my hands were curled like claws from gripping the steering wheel. Clunking about in the room, I wondered dully whether this was the way Mexican truckers felt at the ends of their days and decided that a lot of what I was feeling just then was nothing more than an amateur's stress.

Some relief might be right at hand in the bedside telephone. I rang up Room Service and ordered three margaritas, then drew a bath of hot water and waited. When the waiter arrived with the three tall cocktail glasses rimmed with heavy crystals of salt, I lined them up on the tub's edge and eased myself in. Alas, somewhere along the line the hot water had quit, and so what I eased myself into was a tubful just this side of tepid. It was more like easing into a swimming pool than what I had been anticipating. Still, I had the margaritas, and I tried to be grateful for the bath, too, remembering as I sat in it the advice I'd been given some years ago, before my first trip into Mexico. It came from a friend, an experienced, resourceful Mexico hand who had learned most of the country and its culture through trading there in Indian artifacts. Most Americans, he told me, ended up being disappointed with Mexico because they were unwilling to notice how the country really worked. They appreciated the picturesque, all right, but were annoyed with contemporary realities because nothing worked the way it did back home (like the road system and the plumbing, for instance). So when they got back to the States they had souvenirs of Mexico and photographs of ruins, but they always felt there were better places to go, easier ones: the Bahamas, maybe. In order to truly enjoy your travels in Mexico, he said, you had to begin to pay attention to how the people made do with what was available, rather than whining about what was unavailable to tourists. Octavio Paz had also said something like this when he'd observed that even for the best-intentioned tourists from the developed world Latin America was "ruins and scenery, with here and there a dim, bungling human being—the waiter and manager at the hotel." The shift in perspective my trader friend encouraged was probably crucial, I thought, sitting in the tub and working through the second of the margaritas. Maybe part of that terrible fatigue I felt in checking in here had been because I'd been gritting my teeth against the realities of the Mexican roads instead of assenting to the deeper realities of Mexican road culture.

And in truth, if you could make this mental shift, there was much to admire about the way things were lashed together in this country where minimum and maximum wages were perilously close together and both were considerably below what could be earned, say, in Costa Rica or the

Dominican Republic. If you could in fact get over your privileged American irritation at the seemingly causeless delays, the dozens of things daily encountered that didn't work as you thought they should—or didn't work at all—then you might begin to notice how things were made to work, sort of, in the absence of the money that would be necessary to their smooth and efficient functioning. And the absence of the money to do things American style had endured here for so long that by now it had become a part of the national spirit. It was reflected in a kind of sardonicism like that exhibited toward death and an amused improvisationalism.

If, for example, you were on a road crew doing repairs but lacked signs to advise drivers of lane closings, you took some items you were working with—rocks, say, or plants, or pieces of asphalt curbing—and placed these at intervals in the affected lane. They would nicely serve as a generic sort of notice. In my hotel room in Villahermosa I noticed the woodwork was newly varnished, and as I did calisthenics one morning I found myself in position to note that one corner of the bed was propped up by the last can of varnish and the brush of the now-departed worker. I imagined the manager telling his man, "And, say, when you finish four-oh-eight, take the varnish can and prop up the leg of the bed that fell off the other day. The maids have been slamming those legs with their vacuums for so many years it's a wonder any are still standing." But the worker had found the can wouldn't quite do and so had added his brush. It wouldn't be needed—in 408, anyway—for a good long time. At that Laguna pineapple stand, if you wanted your *jugo* to go, they filled a glass to give you the full measure, then poured that into a plastic Baggie, tied it up (with room for your straw), and off you went. In Mérida, I came across two men on the patio of my hotel. They were old friends, they told me, and had grown up together; tonight they were out on the town. Juan had brought his guitar, and they were singing duets. Then, on a samba number, Pedro slipped the cellophane wrapper off his pack of Raleigh cigarettes, held it in both hands, and by deft movements of his thumbs and forefingers transformed it into a percussive instrument.

What the improvisational remedy was here for the lack of hot bathwater, I couldn't guess, unless it was the margaritas. And, in fact, by the time I'd finished that third one the matter really did seem inconsequential. That must have been why, emerging from the tub, I felt relaxed and able to turn my thoughts to further pleasures, like dinner. There were said to be several good restaurants in the central area, and I hadn't had anything more than a roadside Popsicle since morning. I recalled, too, that things had certainly looked lively down on the street when I'd checked in. Villahermosa must be like wonderful Veracruz, a city that stayed up late.

Not so at all. When I hit the street again it was half-past nine, but it might as well have been three in the morning: hardly a soul was to be seen, the iron shutters had been pulled down on the shops, and the folding metal gates closed. The cantina I'd seen was dark, its chairs and tables stacked and chained. I stood there dumbly a few minutes, wondering whether my earlier travel-induced derangement had been deeper than I'd suspected. Surely I had not imagined all of that lively scene I'd driven through? Probably I had not, but it was clear as I walked the darkened, silent streets that Villahermosa had gone to bed, not a bar or restaurant open anywhere in the four-block area I scouted. At any moment I expected to hear a rumble and a grinding noise and turning a corner find yellow-suited municipal crews coming along on their big, blinking machine that rolled up the sidewalks.

Back at the hotel, I found the bar open. The restaurant was said to be open, as well, but it was dark and empty, and the two waiters I saw in the shadows didn't encourage me to come in. Arriving at any new place, no matter what the hour, I am characteristically eager to at least sample its flavor before going to bed, reluctant even under the most discouraging circumstances to call it a day. But this was a night on which I had to do just that.

NOWADAYS American travelers know Mérida as the staging area for trips to the Maya ruins at Chichén Itzá and Uxmal or the island resorts of Cozumel and Cancún. It is slightly less well-known as a rest stop for superannuated American hippies, but it serves this function, too. But it has been quite recently—given the time scale here where written history goes back more than a thousand years—that the peninsula has become generally accessible. A friend of mine told me that back in 1932, "the only way you could get to Chichén Itzá and Uxmal was through Mérida, and the only way to do that was to take a boat across." With his high school class my friend had come across from New Orleans on a spring vacation excursion.

"We left from the bottom of Canal Street," he recalled, "and as soon as we cleared the three-mile limit, the bar opened. These were students, you have to understand, who had absolutely no experience whatever with alcohol. Repeal was a couple of years off. Some of them got very enthusiastic.

"That was too bad, because we had head winds most of the way over, and the ship was pitching around a good deal. But finally we got there, outside the port of Progreso, but we had to wait part of one day and the next to go in because it was too choppy. Then in the morning the port officials sent a lighter out. You had to go down a long ladder to the lighter platform that was bobbing up and down, and then you had to wait until it came right and make your jump.

"The Customs officials made quite a show on shore in their starchy whites with rows of brass buttons. We were met there by a man named Fernando Barbachano. He was the fellow who founded Mayaland Tours, but back then tourism had hardly opened its eyes. Now I suppose there are four-lane highways everywhere. Well, that wasn't the case then. But Barbachano had three phaetons there to meet us—that's a five-passenger car, what used to be called a 'touring car'—and off we went. The road was pretty rough and ran between jungle on either side or else fields of henequen. When we got to Mérida, we were amazed because we couldn't see any other cars. Oh, there may have been three or four others, some buses, but the rest of the traffic was horse-drawn cabs pulled by perfectly proportioned little horses. They'd been bred by the Spaniards, we were told, because a sixteen-hand horse isn't going to fit very well between decks. They looked like deer. Wonderful little beasts. The cabs were covered, and the driver would talk to you through a hole in the roof.

"That was a very nineteenth-century-feeling town then. Very Spanish-feeling, too. I remember the streets being very narrow with lots of pastel-colored plaster houses with wrought-iron balconies and high, shuttered windows. We stayed at a place called the Gran Hotel. Very nice. In fact, I liked it better there at the hotel, drinking beer and listening to the mariachi band, which was very good. So did some of the others, I think. There was one fellow who was always coming up with funny stuff, and at that time there was a song, 'This Is the Missus and She's Mine.' He'd go around singing, 'This Is the Missus and She's Mayan.' Anyway, we were there to study and sketch the ruins, so one day we got up at four in the morning and went down to the train station where we had huge omelettes and Mexican cocoa flavored with cinnamon—pretty wonderful stuff. And off we went on this narrow-gauge railroad. The engine was the old wood-burning kind with a great flowerpot for a chimney with a screen on top so we wouldn't set the jungle on fire. We went chugging along through the jungle at about five miles an hour—we went that slow because there were frequent derailments. The cars were mostly made of wood and about the size of small trolley cars, and when one of them would go off the tracks, the crew would get down and hoist it back on with crowbars.

"We stopped everywhere, and those stops were like celebrations: the whole village would turn out. There were people selling everything from parrots to tortillas. Finally, we got to a town I remember as Dzitas, where we got off for the drive to Chichén Itzá over a road that was naked limestone. I was on top of the car with an Indian kid and the baggage, and I can tell you it wasn't a very pleasant trip. Then at the nineteen-kilometer mark the Indian pointed ahead through the jungle, and I caught my first glimpse of Maya ruins. It was El Castillo."

Mérida is not like that now, nor are the sites of the ruins, either. Both in the city and out at the sites the tourist industry had definitely opened its eyes, and if it was not as wide awake to the main chance as, say, southern Florida, it was certainly aware of commercial possibilities. In Mérida in the area around the Plaza de la Independencia where the tourist hotels and restaurants are clustered, images of the Mayas and their works were everywhere. Less conspicuous were advertisements of the allures of Cozumel and Cancún, and I found something attractive about the primacy given the aboriginal kings and temple builders over sun and sand, as if the successors of the pioneering tour guide, Barbachano, had a certain respect for the past. It made walking around what was, after all, a tourist ghetto quite bearable: the Maya images you saw everywhere encouraged you to feel that you were the guest of a people with a long, honored, and imperfectly understood history. It was a little like the feeling you got anywhere in Greece where images of the past kept all but the most benighted tourist in his place.

There was nothing of the deep, sonorous sound of history in the Sunday morning bells from the cathedral in the Plaza de la Independencia, however: only that same, shallow sound I'd noticed in Veracruz. By the time I entered the park the sun was well up in a hot and cloudless blue. At the Restaurant Express on Calle 59 opposite the cathedral two waiters served the entire large room in leisurely fashion, stopping to chat with acquaintances and regulars, slowly working their ways from the dim counter outward toward the street-side tables where the tourists sat in the sun. If you had your coffee and *papadzules* (tortillas filled with eggs, onions, and various other vegetables) out there, you got double your money's worth, for the heat from the coffee and the food augmented that of the atmosphere, and halfway through your breakfast your face was as wet, shiny, and happy as everyone else's.

Across the street the vendors of fried potatoes, fried plantains, peeled oranges, and ice cream had set up and were doing a good business. A steady stream of brightly dressed women and children flowed past, coming from mass or going to it. Mixed in were a fair number of fellow Americans, especially women; I noticed there were a number of these who appeared to be traveling together, thirtyish, serious-seeming and carrying guidebooks, their exposed legs bright pink from the sun. While I sat there enjoying a second cup of coffee a marimba sextet began to play, but with their first notes I knew this wasn't going to be Veracruz again: the music lacked that African-Caribbean lilt and complexity. It was straight-ahead and probably aimed more at the tourists than the mass-goers.

That was emphatically not the case a few blocks away at the Parque Independencia where a dynamite twenty-three-piece band with five percussionists and piano poured out tropical music—mambos, sambas, and the lambada—into a green square bounded on two sides by the arcade of municipal buildings. They played from a raised wooden plat-form, the apron of which served as a dance floor on which a dozen middle-aged couples executed the intricate steps with a superbly con-trolled sexuality, the women pulsating and turning with completely impassive faces behind sunglasses. My immediate favorite was a stocky woman who might have been sixty and who so evidently enjoyed herself, wiping her streaming face between numbers and smiling to her hus-band, then going back into the dance again, her features set, her feet in their high, black heels making the mincing mambo steps while her wide hips spoke to him under her beige knit dress. Equally arresting were the faces of some of the players. They looked as if the profiles from the Maya stelae had magically freed themselves of the stone surfaces and had come to life, and the juxtaposition of those classic features with European wind instruments made me gape.

And then, of course, there was the sound of the music. It seemed to me as I stood surrounded by it an informal, concise history of all that had gone into the making of this culture: the Spanish tinge, the African influence, and that greater influence of the tropics themselves—all that sun, for which so much in this land had been given; the hot blue of the skies; the sea; and the tough, heavy vegetation. So that the sound was playful and joyful, yes, but with a *heat* to it that sang of sadness and of danger. And beneath the melodies lay the rattling, chopping cross-rhythms of the percussionists, which I imagined now as the orchestration of that feverishly busy insect world that irrigated and fertilized the soil and so made possible the rain forests of the peninsula. Meanwhile, under the arcade the busts of history's famous men—Pepe Dominguez, Cuty Cárdenas, Ricardo Lopez Mendez—looked on. True, their faces were implacable, but their presence made them seem participants in this joy.

Beyond the band and the dancers a large audience sat in rows of folding chairs placed in the shade of the trees, and beyond this were the vendors of Panama hats adorned with bright rainbow sashes. Others sold T-shirts that said UXMAL, and THE YUCATÁN, and MÉRIDA—HEART AND SOUL OF THE YUCATÁN. Also available were cassette tapes of Mexican popular music; illustrated guidebooks to the region; fruits; herbs; nuts; ice cream; even a set of encyclopedias, if that was what you had strolled down here for. Some Maya women sold traditional dresses and blouses, and high above all these wares were those of the balloon men. When the band finished up and began packing its instruments, there was a small flurry of activity for the vendors as some of the audience and the dancers came out toward the street. Most of the people stayed put, however, for already the two actors of a mime show had pranced on stage dressed as a parrot and a rabbit.

In the steadily mounting heat of midday, traffic thinned, though in the baking yellow streets you still heard the swinging *clip-clop* of the hackies' horses, full-sized successors to the deerlike creatures of a half century ago. The hackies carried tourists, of course. Other tourists who weren't riding the hacks were peddling bicycle rickshaws that rolled almost without sound over the cobbles. As for the Meridanos, they stayed well out of the sun and clear of strenuous activities. Long lines of them stood in the shade near the two movie houses adjacent to the Plaza de la Independencia, eating ice cream and waiting for the early show to let out. When it did and its throngs had quickly melted into the afternoon, those in wait shuffled forward, pausing to pay at the wickets, then entering the air-conditioned dimness.

Now the café tables were the exclusive province of the Americans— the pairs of women I'd noticed earlier, couples, and the aging hippies. The young couples looked as if the heat, the beggars, and the language barrier had taken a lot out of the romance of the place. They no longer held hands but sat silent at the tables, grateful for the shade of the umbrella awnings, the women sipping soft drinks, the men beers. Guidebooks and maps lay closed and folded between them. "What next?" their attitude seemed to say. "What else is there here to look forward to?" For ordinary tourist purposes Mérida could, after all, easily be "done" in a day, and if they had already seen the ruins at Chichén Itzá and Uxmal, they were sort of stuck here, a realization that can seem particularly heavy on a Sunday.

As for the middle-aged couples, I watched them come flopping across the park toward the cafés, portly, slump-shouldered, their faces blazing with the heat, the men in the lead, the women in sundresses and carrying cameras and handbags. And whereas the natives seemed able to negotiate the heat and the traffic with a certain minimalistic grace, the Americans looked positively awash in the heavy swell of this Yucatán spring. Middle-aged myself and feeling the heat, I cringed to think that I, too, must appear so graceless and out of place. When these couples reached the shade of the umbrella awnings, they fell into the café chairs with such finality that I had an image of them being swept up at the end of the day with the rest of the refuse.

Mérida must be one of the favored places in the country where American hippies come to roost, or maybe to hide out and make further deals. Or maybe they liked to hang out here on the fringes of university life. Whatever the attraction, I saw quite a number of them sitting in the cafés and wondered whether they were not unlike the old hidalgos of post-Conquest days who found themselves unaccountably stranded here in the jungle, far from the place of their birth and left to muse on the strange tides of history. The hip types were almost all lone men, their long, sun-bleached hair worn thin at the crown, faces bearded, sunglasses, patched jeans, sandals, backpacks—the whole bit, as they might themselves once have said. They nursed beers through the afternoon and pored over the English-language newspaper out of Mexico City. In the evenings I saw them around the cafés of the University of Yucatán where they smoked, nursed beers or coffee, and read the newspaper some more. Theirs did not appear to be an inspirited existence, but they did seem to have made an accommodation to the climate and pace of life here, which was more than could be said of other foreign visitors.

Including myself: I was now feeling lethargic and also a touch of that Sunday strandedness I'd recognized on the faces of others. I'd seen the market, heard the band, stepped briefly inside the cool vault of the cathedral, and now what? The sun was throwing long shadows over the square, and I was beginning to think of a nap before dinner when my attention was captured by an American couple who sat down next to me and ordered piña coladas, which here were served inside the very pineapple itself. The waiter was at this hour obviously more interested in clearing his tables and leaving things to the evening shift, but eventually he brought their drinks and requested immediate payment. The man paid, but they hardly noticed the drinks. He was a heavyset, muscular fellow in his mid-thirties, unshaven, and wearing an old Panama hat. He suffered with a nonchalant goodwill the precoital embraces of his younger consort, a comely blonde only mildly disfigured by the violent shade of eye shadow she wore. She continued to plague him while the drinks sat unattended by any but the flies who now began to make more and more brazen visits.

At length something more was plainly called for, the woman's embraces having reached a frontier beyond which lay another and more private terrain. She fished out of her handbag a slip of paper on which she wrote something, then slid it over to her man who read it with that same casual air he had maintained throughout. It was only a very brief note, but when he had finished reading it, he folded it over once and stared down at it a long, dramatic moment. Then he lifted his flat, gunner's eyes to her and without a word rose from the table. They moved off across the square and soon were lost from view. Behind them on the table with the untouched drinks lay the folded slip of paper that had been the occasion of the sudden departure.

I couldn't resist. In a round, careful schoolgirl's hand that clearly had been coached by some patient proctor of twenty years ago, the woman had written, "*Eat Me*, I love you very much, Starla."

MÉRIDA was, when all was said, a city that was kind to the traveler, even if that traveler was feeling as tired or displaced as some I had seen there the last few days. There were certainly enough of the familiar amenities in the cool inner gardens of the tourist hotels with their plashing fountains and quiet rooms; in the shaded plazas with their souvenir vendors and charming *confidencias* (S-shaped seats for couples); and in the many good restaurants within walking distance of the hotels. All of which would make you feel reasonably at home, unless you'd reached that obstinate point at which *nothing* would do but Shaker Heights or Poughkeepsie itself. And yet, to the extent that you wanted to be alive to it, there was here plenty of the radically foreign. The city sat, after all, in the heart of the peninsula that had for so long been inaccessible and that had become a functioning part of modern Mexico comparatively recently. In the city you noticed that behind the rainbow ribbons of the souvenir straw hats and the façades of the handsome Spanish buildings there were a good number of Maya place names. The same was true and even more evident out in the countryside, as though the true directions and mental grid of the place were aboriginal. Long after the Aztecs had fallen, the Spaniards continued to have a tough time here. The great force and energy that had erected the Yucatecan Maya kingdoms and those in Guatemala had died out before the Spaniards had so much as punched a few miles inland on the peninsula, but the descendants of the kingdoms continued to hold out, silently determined to remain unassimilated. In 1846 they rose up in the bloody and protracted War of the Castes, and it wasn't until 1902 that all of the peninsula came again under government control. Some think that control is still superficial and that the Mayas retain a sense of themselves as a people apart, pursuing a destiny that does not look forward to some utopian future, but back, back to the great past. In Maya antiquity their historiography, graven in the glyphs of their temples, palaces, and stelae, told of the endless return of the eternal. And the actions of their *ahauob* (shaman kings) confirmed that human history was not processional but the reenactment of cosmic symmetry. Perhaps then current conditions were for the modern Maya simply that—current—and in no way immutable. Walking one afternoon out of Mérida's tourist area, I got that feeling in the dusty back streets where the familiar amenities didn't exist and the faces of the people looked untouched by forces I and my world took so blithely for granted.

The same sensation came over me out in the countryside and going to Uxmal. Out here it was Mexico, not the United States, that seemed chimerical. To be sure, the exterior signs at the ruins confirmed the triumph of modernity: a cafeteria, vending machines, and native women selling T-shirts to customers in shorts and sundresses. But I had the persistent sense that all this was thin, that if somehow it could all be turned sideways, there would be no profile to any of it, that it would look as flat as a sandwich board. I remember having felt this way only once before, and that was back in what I thought of as my "native land." Late one night some years ago I found myself on a moon-washed winter road of the Pine Ridge Reservation in South Dakota. There wasn't an electric light visible anywhere, and Lakota music from station KILI near Wounded Knee was pouring into the cockpit of my car. At that moment and for the first time I felt like a ghostly intruder into the timeless realities of what was not the New World but the old, the ancient.

And here at Uxmal was that feeling again. Maybe those giant pyramids and palaces were superficially foreign to the Mayas I was looking at, but in a deeper sense the spirit that had gone into all this must live on somehow in these people who looked back at you out of an impenetrable reserve even while holding up a bright aqua T-shirt with pyramid design and insisting it would fit you fine even when you knew it wouldn't. The impression was inescapable when just behind them towered the works heaped up by their ancestors.

To be sure, Uxmal had come near the very end of the great story. Current scholarship places it in the Late Classic Period (c. A.D. 600–909), later even than Chichén Itzá. By the time of the date on the ballcourt marker here (901) the Maya kingdoms that had grown and gorgeously flowered had begun to fall apart, the blocks of their intricate masonry falling unheeded to the forest floor like heavy petals. At Chichén Itzá and Uxmal the institution of kingship—the defining cultural institution of the classic periods—had undergone the kind of rationalization that is the sign of the waning of belief and cohesion. Still, there had obviously been sufficient energy to build this city and to erect that ballcourt that symbolically replicated the archetypal one on which the heroic twins of myth had played and defeated the Xibalban Lords of Death. Here, too, as in the great kingdoms of Guatemala the public buildings towered heavenward from the Middleworld, symbolic mountains reflecting the people's aspirations and their understanding of the interrelatedness of earth, sky, and Underworld. Here the *wacah chan*, the sacred World Tree, had flowered. And here also that tree had withered. By the middle of the fifteenth century Uxmal was abandoned, the symbolic contest with the Lords of Death no longer played out on the ballcourt. Since the very beginnings of their history the Mayas had built and then rebuilt on the same sites because such places were understood to be those where access to both the Underworld and the heavens was most available. Successive rebuildings on the same site made the membranes between the spheres more and more permeable. But when power was felt to have been used up at a given place, it was abandoned. When the American lawyer and professional traveler John L. Stephens first saw Uxmal in 1839 and subsequently made it famous in his writings, it was like all the other Maya cities, overgrown, silent, empty, its resident spirituality departed. "A strong and vigorous nature," Stephens wrote, "was struggling for mastery over art, wrapping the city in its suffocating embraces, and burying it from sight." And so it remained until restoration work was begun during World War II.

But if its native spiritual power had departed in the long ago, Uxmal still had plenty of power for the visitor. Too much so for me as I came into it past the shops, cafeteria, and rest rooms—the amenities that condition our every experience. Beyond these, it loomed and glared at me, a huge and bristling challenge I felt suddenly unequipped to take up. For the moment I couldn't even resort to framing it in my camera viewfinder and in that way reducing it. I looked for diversions while trying to regain some equipoise and found one in the play of two large dogs at the base of the Great Pyramid. They were chasing an iguana toward the steps when the white dog darted in front of the lizard, cut off its retreat, and turned it back into the path of the black-and-white pursuer who pounced and made the kill. The dog came on toward me through the dry, short grass with its great, fat prize dripping from its jaws, then set it down at my feet and regarded it carefully. I wondered whether it might be an offering. The iguana lay in the sun and the grass, its small eyes open on nothing. I could detect no wound on it, so probably the dog had snapped its spine. The white dog stood off at a distance, and it didn't look to me as if it were going to get a share of the spoils. Above us the Great Pyramid regarded the sacrifice of the lizard with a massive indifference.

A chain had been run up the pyramid's vertiginous steps—ninety-nine feet to the top, my guidebook advised, and by the time I had hauled myself up there I believed it. On my way up I wasn't quite sure why I was climbing but supposed the sheer physical exertion to be another diversion, even as it brought me face to face with that Maya world I was finding so overwhelming. A temple sat atop the pile, its façade decorated with carved macaws, and I was beginning to inspect these when a bright something caught my eye and turned me away again from the ancient stones.

At first I thought it must have been the flash of a bird's plumage against the dry green of the spring foliage, but as I stood out there in front of the temple I could see it wasn't a bird, though it was certainly tropically brilliant: a thousand yards distant at the edge of the city's cleared space a tiny figure in chartreuse was jumping in place and waving its arms. And the longer I stood there in amazement, the more violent the gesticulations became. Here was a diversion, sure enough, and twenty minutes later when I had reached the ground again I was determined to inspect this phenomenon at closer range. It proved to be a woman with a big, professional-looking camera mounted on a tripod, and as I approached I could see her hot eyes still trained on the temple. I, too, turned to look up there where two figures moved slowly about over the stones, one in a red shirt, the other in a yellow dress.

Up close Chartreuse Woman was a striking American in her mid-thirties, deeply tanned to the color of good cordovan leather. Her forehead and the exposed upper portion of her chest had peeled many times already, and the deepest layer was a dangerous red. *"Get off! Move! God-damn you!!"* She was yelling toward the figures on the pyramid's summit and still hadn't so much as glanced at me, though it was clear she was aware of my presence because she now addressed remarks in my direction. "All day long I've been trying to shoot this site, and I still haven't been able to get even half my work done because of fools like *that!*" She flung a hand contemptuously out in the direction of the little climbers. I stole a quick glance at my own attire to see if it was conspicuous enough for her to recognize another of the fools, then decided to come clean and told her I was sorry to have been one of those who was making her life so difficult this day. What, I asked, was the nature of this work?

"*Architectural Digest!*" she spat out. "I'm on *assignment!* Now, at Chichén Itzá, they closed off the whole place for me for four hours after I told 'em I was Indian." Her hair was certainly black enough to allow the possibility, and I asked what her tribal affiliation was and where she was from.

"Oh," she replied offhandedly, "I'm from Indiana, but my people are all from Oklahoma." But the past wasn't her problem here, it was the present. "I had a guy here today who stood on top of the ballcourt wall for forty-five fucking minutes while I was trying to get a shot—just posing, like this." She stepped out from behind the tripod and stood, hands on hips, feet spread, one knee slightly cocked. "Can you believe it?!" I said meekly that a camera could sometimes make people do funny things and was surprised to hear her agree.

"Ohhh, boy, *yeah!*" She shot a glance at the camera I had slung around my neck and asked what I was doing here. Just traveling a bit of the peninsula, I said. Did she have any recommendations for Mérida?

"Stay out of downtown," she said, her eyes once more focused on her subject, her problem. "It's filled with gringos and putas. Stay in the suburbs." I thanked her and moved off. "Have a good shoot," she called after me.

IN ancient days spring was the time for ritual raiding between the Maya kingdoms. In this dry season before the summer rains it was possible for the noble war parties to move more easily over the land in their search for captives. In recent years when quantum leaps in Maya epigraphy have made it possible to read some of the history preserved in the glyphs, it seems clear enough that this ritualized raiding did not have as its object the actual subjugation of neighboring peoples so much as it did the taking of kings and the highborn. For the victorious king the conspicuous display of the captives demonstrated to his people his continuing power and ability to subdue his neighbors, all the way to actual conquest, if that was ever needed. But for a long time it wasn't. It was enough to make the captures, to parade the bound kings and nobles, and eventually to sacrifice them to the gods. Oftentimes the sacrifice took the form of the sacred ballgame at the end of which the captives were decapitated. Or they might be trussed up like the latex balls themselves and hurled down the long flights of the temple steps. At Chichén Itzá the ballcourt was adorned with a rack on which were displayed the skulls of the decapitated. Sometimes captives were sacrificed en masse on the sacrificial stone, their beating hearts hacked from their breasts and their blood offered as divine nourishment. And sometimes, too, it happened that a great prince was too valuable a captive to be sacrificed quickly, in which instance he would be kept around by his captor for years and ritually displayed on high occasions, until at last all his potential had been exhausted save that final one of offering.

In its large outlines Maya ritual warfare reminded me of that of other peoples, including the Plains Indians of North America, who fought for honor and trophy horses but not for territorial conquest; and the recently encountered tribes of New Guinea who would periodically meet at a boundary river to hurl spears at one another and then go back home. There was in these instances something peculiarly attractive, as though these "savages" had understood and assented to the reality of the male aggressive drive and had at the same time understood that unchecked it was too dangerous and threatened the proper functioning of those sacred worlds in which they lived. So they had channeled it into something like a dangerous game in which the only stake worth playing for was honor, not territorial conquest, nor political hegemony, nor genocide—all practices of more advanced peoples. Standing in the ruins of the ballcourt at Uxmal with its masoned banks brokenly rising on either side of the playing area, I was reminded of the ritual uses of aggression and of the central significance of the Maya ballgame as it was revealed in the *Popul Vuh*, one of the very few written Maya texts to have survived the purging hand of Bishop Landa and other Spanish clerics. The text told how the heroic twins tricked the Lords of Death and so escaped with the win. The point apparently was that existence itself was a dangerous game with the odds favoring Death and that only through the exercise of ingenuity and ritual observance might Death be overcome.

It is possible, though, that the Mayas may have overestimated the uses of ingenuity. Inheritors of the cultural innovations of the Olmecs, whom they acknowledged as ancestral benefactors, the Mayas had brought their own culture to a high plane by the beginning of the seventh century A.D. From that summit they could look around them at their marvelous system of agriculture that coaxed the maximum yield from the forest; at the gorgeous and elaborate institution of kingship that sanctified all social inequities; at their magnificent cities; and at the artistry of their glyphs and reliefs that told their history. Perhaps, then, it was no more than human that they be profoundly impressed by their ingenuity and that out of that they might be tempted to overreach. Why not even greater kingdoms, larger in extent, more magnificent of aspect, and drawing tribute in labor, agricultural products, and sacrificial victims from neighboring states? What if, instead of ritual warfare—which, after all, resulted in negligible practical returns—a king decided to play for "real" stakes, to play for keeps? Mayanists based in Guatemala are beginning to speculate along this line and to ask whether such a development might be the key to the gradual decline and fall of the Maya kingdoms. A Maya ruler called Flint-Sky-God K of the city of Dos Pilas in the Lake Petexbatun region is now thought to have taken warfare to a new and more lethal level in a twenty-year campaign (A.D. 664–684) against neighboring states that fundamentally upset the balance of power and changed all the rules. A consequence of his conquests and those of his successors was that Dos Pilas became the center of a swollen and ultimately vulnerable empire of some two thousand square miles before the tide turned and it had to go on the defensive. Anthropologist Arthur Demarest of Vanderbilt University, who has been heading a research team at Dos Pilas, has suggested that what happened there may have established a disastrous pattern that went rippling through the rain forest all the way north to Chichén Itzá and Uxmal. In this pattern vital attention and energy were diverted from agriculture, internal affairs, and religious observances to the necessities of a new sort of warfare. This was particularly evident and calamitous in agriculture, where farmers no longer had the opportunity to devote themselves to traditional practices but had instead to think about attack and defense. They began, therefore, to pull back from militarily exposed areas toward the city and to abandon their successful symphony of farming techniques in favor of more radically extractive ones that took less time and used less land more intensively. Eventually, Demarest's team thinks, the city-state had contracted to the fortified city itself set in an immediate landscape that was badly overworked. Perhaps even more significantly, Dos Pilas had adopted a siege mentality in which everything was forfeit to the simple urge to survive. In the terminal stage the people of the city had run a defensive wall right through the sanctum sanctorum of the royal palace and had partially dismantled the palace façade to build it. By 700 it was over, and the empire had disintegrated into petty chieftainships quarreling over the bones.

Much more investigation will be necessary before a convincing case can be made that what happened at Dos Pilas accounts for what happened throughout the Maya lands, and standing atop the high buildings at Uxmal, I could literally see how much more, just here alone, remained unexamined, for in every direction there were the shrouded remains of the once-magnificent city. Who would be bold enough to say now that their buried secrets will confirm the Dos Pilas hypothesis? But if argument from historical analogy is ever of use (and if it isn't, what of history's lessons?), then maybe the record of the high civilizations of the ancient Near East can help us to read correctly the emerging story of this one. For there, too, were master builders, historiographers, stargazers, whose mighty kings caused their names and deeds to be graven on stelae. And then, as we know, all these civilizations fell—the Sumerians, Egyptians, Babylonians, Assyrians—leaving behind their blurring stelae and broken ziggurats for poets to muse on and archeologists to puzzle over:

"My name is Ozymandias, king of kings:
Look on my works, ye Mighty, and despair!"
Nothing beside remains. Round the decay
Of that colossal wreck, boundless and bare
The lone and level sands stretch far away.

This was Shelley on the ruins of Ramses II's tomb at Thebes. For these, too, were overreachers whose designs of empire proved grander than reality could bear, who first marshaled men into fighting phalanxes and sent them on missions of conquest, and who savaged their fragile lands until the once productive Near East had become a marginal desert. Only the great Nile continued to flow and bring forth, but not for Egyptians: when Alexander the Great conquered Egypt, its days of glory were long in the past, and the country was a granary for others, not an empire for itself. But there and northward in the Near East the palaces and pyramids had towered toward the sun and the stars, monuments to the deathless human desire for transcendence, a desire that like the Tower of Babel eventually became an arrogance that toppled them.

For those living in the Americas, wrote a prominent Mayanist, the Mayas and their kingdoms are our antiquity, our dynasties, our Egypt. Back in my cool, quiet hotel room in Mérida the silence of Uxmal still rang in my ears. I pulled from my sheaf of notes and guides a map of the Yucatán and looked again at its outlines. I could not understand why, at the beginning of my long and broken journey, I had seen the peninsula's shape as a dog's head. It was so clearly a Sphinx.

SECONDARY SOURCES

SPRING

Baker, Carlos. *Ernest Hemingway: A Life Story.* 1968. Reprint. New York: Avon Books, 1980.

Carr, Archie. *The Sea Turtle: So Excellent a Fishe.* 1967. Reprint. Austin, TX: University of Texas Press, 1986.

Derr, Mark. *Some Kind of Paradise: A Chronicle of Man and the Land in Florida.* New York: William Morrow and Company, 1989.

Douglas, Marjory Stoneman. *The Everglades: River of Grass.* 1947. Reprint. St. Simon's Island, GA: Mockingbird Books, 1988.

Fishburne, Charles G., Jr. *The Cedar Keys: Prelude to the 20th Century.* Cedar Key, FL: Seahawk Publications, 1982.

_____. *End of the Line at the Cedar Keys, 1843–1861.* Cedar Key, FL: Seahawk Publications, 1982.

_____. *Of Chiefs and Generals: A History of the Cedar Keys to the End of the Second Seminole War.* Cedar Key, FL: Seahawk Publications, 1982.

Hemingway, Ernest. *To Have and Have Not.* 1937. Reprint. New York: Collier Books, 1987.

Hotchner, A. E. *Papa Hemingway: The Ecstasy and the Sorrow.* 1955. Reprint. New York: Quill, 1983.

Jahoda, Gloria. *The Other Florida.* 1967. Reprint. New York: Charles Scribner's Sons, 1978.

Josephson, Matthew. *The Robber Barons: The Great American Capitalists, 1861–1901.* 1934. Reprint. New York: Harcourt Brace Jovanovich, 1962.

Ludington, Townsend. *John Dos Passos: A Twentieth Century Odyssey.* New York: E.P. Dutton, 1980.

Mitchell, John G. "The Perils of the Everglades." *Wilderness* (Winter 1986).

Mormino, Gary R., and Anthony P. Pizzo. *The Treasure City, Tampa.* Tulsa, OK: Continental Heritage Press, 1983.

Rudloe, Jack. *Time of the Turtle.* 1979. Reprint. New York: E.P. Dutton, 1989.

————. *The Wilderness Coast: Adventures of a Gulf Coast Naturalist.* New York: E.P. Dutton, 1988.

Schueler, Donald G. *Adventuring Along the Gulf of Mexico.* San Francisco: Sierra Club Books, 1986.

Swanton, John R. *The Indian Tribes of North America.* Smithsonian Institution, Bureau of American Ethnology, Bulletin 145. Washington, D.C.: United States Government Printing Office, 1953.

Wallace, David Rains. "Of Buccaneers and Biodiversity." *Wilderness* (Winter 1989).

Wertkin, Gerard C. Telephone interview regarding Dr. Cyrus B. Teed, February 1992.

Williams, Joy. *The Florida Keys: A History and a Guide.* New York: Random House, 1987.

Williams, Ted. "The Exclusion of Sea Turtles." *Audubon* (January 1990).

SUMMER

Anderson, Agnes Grinstead. *Approaching the Magic Hour: Memories of Walter Anderson.* Jackson: University Press of Mississippi, 1989.

Anderson, Walter Inglis. *The Horn Island Logs of Walter Inglis Anderson.* 1973. Reprint. Edited by Redding S. Sugg, Jr. Jackson: University Press of Mississippi, 1985.

Cabeza de Vaca. *Adventures in the Unknown Interior of America.* 1542. Translated and edited by Cyclone Covey. Albuquerque: University of New Mexico Press, 1984.

Clark, Garth, Robert A. Ellison, Jr., and Eugene Hecht. *The Mad Potter of Biloxi: The Art & Life of George E. Ohr.* New York: Abbeville Press, 1989.

Ohr, George E. "The Potter and the Pot," *New Orleans Times-Democrat* (November 29, [1902?]). Courtesy, Biloxi Public Library.

Pickard, Mary Anderson. "Introduction." In *Birds*, by Walter Anderson. Jackson: University Press of Mississippi, 1990.

Schueler, Donald G. *Adventuring Along the Gulf of Mexico*. San Francisco: Sierra Club Books, 1986.

Sullivan, Charles L., Murella Hebert Powell, and Nedra A. Harvey. *The Mississippi Gulf Coast: Portrait of a People*. Northridge, CA: Windsor Publications, 1985.

FALL

Asbury, Herbert. *The French Quarter*. 1936. Reprint. New York: Ballantine Books, 1974.

Hersh, Seymour. "My Lai: Breaking the Story." *Memories* (October/November 1989).

Lomax, Alan. *Mister Jelly Roll*. New York: Grove Press, 1950.

Maraniss, David, and Michael Weisskopf. "Life in the 'National Sacrifice Zone,'" *Washington Post National Weekly Edition*, January 25–31, 1988.

McLain, James J. "Economic Impact of Mardi Gras on New Orleans." *Louisiana Business Survey* (Spring 1987).

Moffett, Matt. "Even Mr. Mardi Gras Has Trouble Keeping Everybody Happy." *Wall Street Journal*, March 3, 1987.

Parkman, Francis. *The Discovery of the Great West: La Salle*. 1869. Reprint. New York: Holt, Rinehart and Winston, 1963.

Rabalais, Nancy N. "The Dead Zone." *Gulfwatch* (April 1990).

Schueler, Donald. "Losing Louisiana." *Audubon* (July 1990).

Turner, Frederick. "Losing It in Louisiana." *Wilderness* (Winter 1985).

———. *Remembering Song: Encounters with the New Orleans Jazz Tradition*. New York: Viking Press, 1982.

Watsky, Steven. "Wasting Louisiana." *In These Times*, October 5–11, 1988.

Weber, Michael, Richard T. Townsend, and Rose Bierce. *Environmental Quality in the Gulf of Mexico*. Washington, D.C.: Center for Marine Conservation, 1990.

Wilson, William. "I Had Prayed to God That This Thing Was Fiction." *American Heritage* (February 1990).

WINTER

Cabeza de Vaca, Álvar N. *Adventures in the Unknown Interior of America*. 1542. Translated and edited by Cyclone Covey. Albuquerque: University of New Mexico Press, 1984.

Cartwright, Gary. *Galveston: A History of the Island.* New York: Atheneum, 1991.

Dobie, J. Frank. *Coronado's Children: Tales of Lost Mines and Buried Treasures of the Southwest.* 1930. Reprint. Austin, TX: University of Texas Press, 1979.

Douglas, Carole. "Corridor in Peril." *Wilderness* (Winter 1989).

Garcia, Guy. "The Believers." *Rolling Stone,* June 29, 1989.

Humes, Edward. *Buried Secrets: A True Story of Serial Murder, Black Magic, and Drug-Running on the U.S. Border.* New York: E.P. Dutton, 1991.

Lively, John. "Island City Woodworks." *Fine Homebuilding* (April/May 1987).

Montgomery, Robin Navarro. *Cut 'n Shoot, Texas.* Austin, TX: Eakin Press, 1984.

Morris, Jim. "Lovely Lagoon." *Houston Chronicle,* February 3, 1991.

Parvin, Bob. "The Disappearing Wild Lands of the Rio Grande Valley." *Texas Parks & Wildlife* (January 1988).

Payne, Richard, and Geoffrey Leavenworth. *Historic Galveston.* Houston: Herring Press, 1985.

Turner, Tom. "Playa del Ruin?" *Defenders* (January/February 1988).

SPRING AGAIN

Blacker, Irwin, and Harry M. Rosen, eds. *Conquest: Dispatches of Cortez from the New World.* New York: Grosset & Dunlap, 1962.

Brenner, Anita. *Idols Behind Altars: The Story of the Mexican Spirit.* 1929. Reprint. Boston: Beacon Press, 1970.

Coe, Michael D. *The Maya,* 4th ed. London: Thames and Hudson, 1987.

Díaz del Castillo, Bernal. *The Discovery and Conquest of Mexico.* 1632. Translated and edited by A. P. Maudslay. London: George Routledge & Sons, 1929.

López de Gómara, Francisco. *Cortés: The Life of the Conqueror by His Secretary.* 1552. Translated and edited by Leslie Byrd Simpson. Berkeley: University of California Press, 1966.

Paz, Octavio. *The Labyrinth of Solitude; The Other Mexico; Return to the Labyrinth of Solitude; Mexico and the United States; The Philanthropic Ogre.* Translated by Lysander Kemp, Yara Milos, and Rachel Phillips. New York: Grove Press, 1985.

Reavis, Dick J. *Conversations with Moctezuma: Ancient Shadows Over Modern Life in Mexico.* New York: William Morrow, 1990.

Recinos, Adrián, trans. *Popul Vuh: The Sacred Book of the Quiché Maya.* 1950. Translated by Delia Goetz and Sylvanus G. Morley. Norman, OK: University of Oklahoma Press, 1975.

Schele, Linda, and David Freidel. *A Forest of Kings: The Untold Story of the Ancient Maya.* New York: William Morrow, 1990.

Schueler, Donald G. *Adventuring Along the Gulf of Mexico.* San Francisco: Sierra Club Books, 1986.

Simon, Kate. *Mexico: Places and Pleasures.* 1962. Reprint. New York: Harper & Row, 1988.

Stephens, John L. *Incidents of Travel in Yucatan,* 2 vols. 1843. Reprint. New York: Dover Publications, 1963.

INDEX

2/93

mcib